GEOMETRY, PROPORTION
AND THE
ART OF LUTHERIE

GEOMETRY, PROPORTION AND THE ART OF LUTHERIE

A study of the use and aesthetic significance of geometry and numerical proportion in the design of European bowed and plucked string instruments in the sixteenth, seventeenth, and eighteenth centuries

KEVIN COATES

CLARENDON PRESS · OXFORD

Oxford University Press, Walton Street, Oxford OX2 6DP
Oxford New York Toronto
Delhi Bombay Calcutta Madras Karachi
Petaling Jaya Singapore Hong Kong Tokyo
Nairobi Dar es Salaam Cape Town
Melbourne Auckland
and associated companies in
Berlin Ibadan

Oxford is a trade mark of Oxford University Press

Published in the United States by
Oxford University Press, New York

© *Kevin Coates, 1985*

First published 1985
Reprinted 1986
First printed in paperback 1991

All rights reserved. No part of this publication may be reproduced,
stored in a retrieval system, or transmitted, in any form or by any means,
electronic, mechanical, photocopying, recording, or otherwise, without
the prior permission of Oxford University Press

This book is sold subject to the condition that it shall not, by way
of trade or otherwise, be lent, re-sold, hired out or otherwise circulated
without the publisher's prior consent in any form of binding or cover
other than that in which it is published and without a similar condition
including this condition being imposed on the subsequent purchaser

The Author and Publishers gratefully acknowledge the generous
assistance of the Calouste Gulbenkian Foundation, London, towards
the production costs of this volume

British Library Cataloguing in Publication Data
Coates, Kevin
Geometry, proportion, and the art of lutherie.
1. Stringed instruments—construction
I. Title
787'.012 ML755
ISBN 0-19-816139-5
ISBN 0-19-816246-4 (p/bk)

Library of Congress Cataloging in Publication Data
Coates, Kevin
Geometry, proportion, and the art of lutherie.
Bibliography: p.
1. Stringed instruments—construction.
2. Geometry. 3. Ratio and proportion. I. Title.
ML755.C6 1983 787'.672 83—23611
ISBN 0-19-816139-5
ISBN 0-19-816246-4 (p/bk)

Printed in Great Britain by
Butler and Tanner Ltd
Frome, Somerset

Acknowledgements

My sincere gratitude is extended to those many people who, in diverse ways, have given of their talents, time, and patience to make my task easier and more enjoyable.

Without the aid of the Gulbenkian Foundation, who so generously endorsed their broad-minded enthusiasm for my project with the financial support both for my necessarily extensive travels, and, indeed, for the subsequent production of this book, it is true to say that the work would probably have had to remain unrealized.

To Charles Beare, Robert Graham, and the staff of J. and A. Beare, my warmest regard and thanks for the benefit of their knowledge, and for welcoming my intrusions upon their time with so friendly an interest—an interest which for me has given the work a real sense of practical worth.

I should also like to show my appreciation to the museum staffs who have offered their help and co-operation in my researches, at the Victoria and Albert Museum; Ashmolean Museum; Donaldson Collection; Warwick County Museum; Paris Conservatoire; Brussels Conservatoire; Gemeentemuseum; Comunale di Milano, Castello Sforzesco; Stradivari Archives, Museo Civico, Cremona.

In particular, my most cordial thanks are presented to Mme Josiane Bran-Ricci, Mme Florence Abondance, Mme Mia van Vaerenbergh-Awouters, Miss J. Morris, Peter Thornton, Dr Clemens von Gleich, Gerald Taylor, John Thomson, Peter Brinson, and the private owner-players who have so kindly entrusted their treasures to my scrutiny.

My sweetest thanks, saved until last, are for my wife, Nel, who has organized, driven, translated, read, and helped copy, but, above all, has been herself; to her, this is dedicated.

Contents

1	**Introduction**	1
2	**A mathematical background**	3
3	**Geometry, a short history**	5
4	**Proportion**	15
	Types of Proportion	15
	Rational and Irrational Numbers	16
	Golden Section, and the Fibonacci Numbers	16
	The Root Proportionals	18
	The Vesica Piscis	18
	The Ionic Volute in the Geometry of the Head	19
	Systems of Measurement	22
5	**The instruments**	23
	The Drawings (Plates I–XXXI)	23
	The Analyses	25
	Categorization	26
	Selection of Examples	27
6	**Analysis of instrument examples**	29
	VIOLS	31
	Ex. I. Bass viol, Pelegrino di Zanetto (c.1550)	31
	Ex. II. Treble viol, Giovanni Maria da Brescia (c.1575)	35
	Ex. III. Bass viol, Battista Ciciliano (c.1590)	39
	Ex. IV. Tenor viol, Henry Jaye (1667)	44
	Ex. V. Bass viol, Joachim Tielke (c.1700)	48
	Ex. VI. Pardessus de viole, Louis Guersan (1759)	52
	LIRAS DA BRACCIO	55
	Ex. VII. Lira da braccio, Giovanni Maria da Brescia (c.1575)	55
	Ex. VIII. Lira da braccio, Gasparo da Salò (c.1585)	59
	Ex. IX. Lira da braccio (maker unknown) (c.1570)	62
	VIOLINS (VIOLA, VIOLONCELLO)	65
	Ex. X. Violin (small model), Andrea Amati (1564)	66
	Ex. XI. Violin, Nicola Amati (c.1670)	71
	Ex. XII. Violin, Antonio Stradivari (1666)	75
	Ex. XIII. Violin, Antonio Stradivari (1703)	79

	Ex. XIV. Viola, Giovanni Paolo Maggini (*c*.1610)	82
	Ex. XV. Violoncello, Barak Norman (1718)	86
VIOLAS D'AMORE		90
	Ex. XVI. Viola d'amore (maker unknown) (*c*.1750)	91
	Ex. XVII. English Violet, Paulus Alletsee (1724)	95
KITS OR POCHETTES		100
	Ex. XVIII. Pochette, Gaspar Borbon (1686)	100
	Ex. XIX. Pochette d'amour, Battista Genova (*c*.1760)	103
LUTES		106
	Ex. XX. Lute (drawing), Henricus Arnault (*c*.1460)	107
	Ex. XXI. Tenor lute, Hans Frei (*c*.1550)	110
	Ex. XXII. Alto lute, Giovanni Hieber (*c*.1580)	114
	Ex. XXIII. Chitarrone, Matteo Buechenberg (1614)	118
	Ex. XXIV. Theorbo, Jacobus Henricus Goldt (1734)	122
	Ex. XXV. Theorbo, Michael Rauche (1762)	122
MANDORE AND MANDOLINES		127
	Ex. XXVI. Mandore (maker unknown) (*c*.1640)	128
	Ex. XXVII. Milanese mandoline, attr. Antonio Stradivari (*c*.1710)	132
	Ex. XXVIII. Neapolitan mandoline, Johannes Vinaccia (1753)	136
CITTERNS		141
	Ex. XXIX. Cittern (maker unknown) (*c*.1650?)	141
	Ex. XXX. Bell cittern, Joachim Tielke (1676)	144
GUITARS		147
	Ex. XXXI. Guitar, Belchior Diaz (1582)	148
	Ex. XXXII. Guitar, Christopho Cocho (1602)	150
	Ex. XXXIII. Chitarra battente/Guitar, Mango Longo (1624)	153

7	**Summary of analyses**	157
8	**Observations**	164
9	**Conclusions**	167

Appendix A — 171
Some early sources of geometrical and proportional information

Appendix B — 172
The violin moulds of Antonio Stradivari with reference to Exx. XII and XIII

Appendix C — 174
Body-outline chart of summary for development of four Cremonese violins

Bibliography — 175

Index — 177

1 Introduction

Beauty will result from the form and correspondence of the whole, with respect to the several parts, of the parts with regard to each other, and of these again to the whole; that the structure may appear an entire and complete body, wherein each member agrees with the other, and all necessary to compose what you intend to form.

This is one of 'the several particulars that ought to be considered' with which Andrea Palladio, with 'Vitruvius for master and guide', begins the first chapter of his *First Book of Architecture* (Venice, 1570). In fact, this particular 'particular' provides us with a good working idea of what artists mean when they talk of 'proportion', for although he himself does not here use the word, Palladio is really saying that where there is design-interrelatedness—where there is *proportion*—there, also, will be Beauty.

Such is Palladio's view, an opinion shared by countless practitioners and theorists of all epochs, but one also hotly contended by many others, drawn mainly from more recent ages. In writing the study which follows, I am, of course, declaring my allegiance to the former group of 'believers'; certainly I could never have undertaken the rigours of the work which follows without the fundamental conviction of my belief that the luthiers of the sixteenth, seventeenth, and eighteenth centuries, like so many of their contemporary confederates, the architects and painters, did indeed make conscious use of numerical proportion in their designs. I imagine that this has long been suspected by many 'instrumentophiles' who, like myself, have found just such a 'beauty' as Palladio's in the myriad forms of stringed musical instruments, and wondered at the strength and integrity of their shapes.

These are designs which I, for one, have found difficult to reconcile with the widely held chain of ideas that the luthier was an early Craftsman, and the Craftsman was a mortal born half-way between the Artist and the Workman, by the wisdom of providence lacking the undisciplined imagination of the one, but compensated by the humble diligence of the other, enabling him to develop Special Understanding as he became a Master Craftsman. This, clearly, is a wearisome, lazy-minded, apriorist view, which, whilst well-meaningly acknowledging the craftsman as a medium of intuitive forces, simultaneously castrates him of any objective, directive intellect, as though it were plainly impossible that two such diverse processes could work together, and least of all through the mind and products of a 'manual' worker.

In the case of musical instruments, which, since the Lute or Lyre of Orpheus, have often been regarded as possessors of a particular sympathetic magic of their own, there is a further reluctance, seen especially in the conservative nature of the player, who has an active, rather than a contemplative, relationship with an instrument—a reluctance to accept the idea that an object as warm and 'feeling' as a musical instrument may be the result, if only in part, of an agency as cold and mechanical, as positively INHUMAN, as mathematics. Ironically, in view of the supportive evidence to follow, the power of this subjective rejection is a measure of exactly how successful the creators of these artefacts were, in reconciling what are commonly held to be two opposing design polarities: the calculated, numerically structured approach, and the personal intuitive vision. And it is, of course, not through the agency of *craft*, but of *art*, that this alchemical fusion is consummated.

In recent years, some excellent works have been written which have sought to establish historical precedence for the principle of numerical proportion in art and design, most particularly in architecture, where perhaps its use can be more easily apprehended. Even the best of these studies, such as the significant *Architectural Principles* of Rudolf Wittkower,[1] the fruit of considerable research and a profound scholarly insight, although widely acclaimed, have also not been without their critics, while lesser, weaker offerings become weighty missiles hurled back against the very movement of thought their authors had felt they were supporting. It is therefore with more than a little diffidence that I make my own small contribution to the field on the behalf of stringed musical instruments and their makers.

Although my aims are not dissimilar to Wittkower's, that is, the establishment of the principle of governing proportion within a given discipline, the problems encountered in a like study of musical instruments are of a very different nature, engendering a different approach. Not least of these problems, as we have already had cause to examine, is the popular image of the instrument-maker as 'mere' craftsman.

The architectural theorist is also more fortunate in his researches in being able to consult, besides the existing buildings themselves, a considerable body of historical documents, often written by architects themselves, about architects and the use of numerical proportion in the formulation of their work. To my knowledge, no equivalent archival material has ever come to light concerning the use of such design processes by the luthiers of the same period, and yet the evidence that their designs were conceived with a high degree of dependence on formalized geometry and proportional knowledge is overwhelming, as we shall come to see. Why no such 'written' records have emerged, despite some exhaustive localized researches, is a mystery which we will need to consider later in our discussions.

Given this situation, then, this study will concern itself with historical documents of a different, but no less valid, kind. It will be an examination, by careful measurement and design analysis, of a relevant cross-section of historical stringed musical instruments, by which means I hope to establish finally the 'proportional design approach' of early luthiers, and perhaps to reveal a few design principles which I should like to think will be of use to modern luthiers seeking to re-create such instruments today. Above all, it is essential to understand that it will be a study of the *aesthetics of proportion* in musical instrument design, and, as such, *acoustical considerations will not arise*. It would be true to say that the acoustic success of an instrument relies far more on the correct thicknessing (and, where applicable, arching) of the most suitable wood, which will contain the proper resonant volume of air, than it does on an aesthetically satisfying planar disposition of two of the three dimensions of that volume. Where the two combine, however, we have the art of the luthier.

---

[1] Rudolf Wittkower, *Architectural Principles in the Age of Humanism* (first published 1949).

2 A mathematical background

Musical instruments have, for me, always been objects of a very special eloquence, either as a player and listener to whom their mystic voices have sometimes been entrusted, or simply as a beholder to whom something of the unique richness of their personalities has been unfolded. As historical documents, they are objects, too, of particular significance, revealing the technological resources of the art of the innovative designer in service to the art of music, expressed through a decorative art influenced by social convention. In this way, they are a living reflection of the Muses, of art and society, their makers, and the generations of players who preserved and cherished them as intimates, leaving with them something of their presence and their communicated thoughts and feelings. Throughout this study, the instruments themselves have been a never-fading source of inspiration, wonder, and curiosity, and in a relationship of trust, have disclosed to me some of the more secret aspects of their design make-up. In a very real sense I have thus been privileged to share some of the previously lost thoughts and considerations of their makers.

These thoughts, like the language of a past age, were shaped by previous custom and contemporary attitude; they will therefore be appreciated and understood better if, before examining the evidence of geometric and proportional thinking in the instrument examples, we consider the mathematical outlook of the age which created them. To do this, however, we must first understand our own present-day relationship with mathematics, which is of a very different nature from that of our early luthier and his contemporaries. Indeed, so removed are the two polarities of mathematical approach, that perhaps the greatest obstacle to proving my thesis, that geometry and proportional planning were used by the early luthier, lies not in demonstrating that such *was* the case, but in finding acceptance from twentieth-century readers that such *could be* the case.

To be fair, it is not a failing peculiar to our own age alone that, when viewing the achievements of a previous time, one should do so through the wrong end of a metaphorical telescope; and with our own opinion of ourselves as unsurpassed technocrats and with our comprehension of mathematics as a tool of technology, it is understandable that we should be a little unwilling to credit the artisans of the technologically less enlightened past with a familiarity with, and knowledge of, mathematics, seemingly superior to our own. It is an understandable viewpoint, but one betraying a little anxiety and much prejudice. Here we have a problem of belief, but one whose solution is only a short way beyond the prejudices of our twentieth-century education. If we can dispel our own school-engendered concept of mathematics as a lifeless bag of tools and tricks, of use to engineers and accountants, but an unheeded mystery to refined people of culture, then we shall have come at least as far as having an open mind before the problem of understanding the mathematical beliefs of an earlier age.

For the Renaissance, mathematics was a universal language in which was expressed the sum total of its ideas. The abstract expression of these ideas exists still in our modern culture in the form of structures of thought and behaviour, whilst we have inherited their concrete expression in the form of artefacts, such as some of the musical instruments which we shall here discuss. All were united by the language of mathematics, and in order to comprehend any of these parts, or the whole itself, it is essential to understand that language as did the culture which engendered it.

As society has altered over half a millennium, so too have the role and function of mathematics changed to serve mankind's needs. Those needs are now overwhelming, with the very future of our existence threatened by increasing demands on ever-diminishing physical resources. Caught up in this giddy race, man sees his only hope as hypertechnology. For this technology (perhaps as often master as saviour), the chameleon mathematics is once again the language—but it is a *language of quantity*: a terrifying measure of the finite, and not just of how much, but of how little there remains.

Renaissance man, however, although eagerly setting off upon the trail towards a higher technology, was, of course, blessedly free and unaware of its dire responsibilities. The soul of mathematics had not as yet been offered up to technology, but worked in harmony with, and *qualified*, the works of man. Just as the universe for Pythagoras and Plato was tuned to a heavenly harmony that could be 'heard' with the divine sense of mathematics, so for the Neoplatonists of the sixteenth century the world and its phenomena were infused with, and united by, the mystic thread of number. The ancient quadrivium itself was a doctrine of this faith; its articles—arithmetic, geometry, astronomy, and music—were gospels to the eternal order of number in its different modes, that is, as pure, stationary, moving, and applied number. Thus, the study and knowledge of mathematics inspired the devotion due to a universal truth, and its application was an act of faith that qualified the work with the grace of universality. In short, it was a *language of quality*.

This much has our relationship with the immutable reality of number changed from its role as a profound *means of expression* in the art and life of the Renaissance to its prime use in present-day technology as an *expression of means*.

It may be helpful at this stage to consider how this climate of thought was brought about, by examining, albeit briefly, the influence wielded by mathematics in the history of our culture. In this respect, I have been guided by the stimulating work of Professor Morris Kline, whose lucid study *Mathematics in Western Culture*[2] I would recommend to anyone wishing to pursue this exciting subject.

---

[2] Morris Kline, *Mathematics in Western Culture* (Pelican Books, 1972, first published in USA, 1953). For Professor Kline, 'mathematics is more than a method, an art, and a language. It is a body of knowledge with content that serves the physical and social scientist, the philosopher, the logician, and the artist; content that influences the doctrines of statesmen and theologians; content that satisfies the curiosity of the man who surveys the heavens and the man who muses on the sweetness of musical sounds; and content that has undeniably, if sometimes imperceptibly, shaped the course of modern history.'

3 Geometry, a short history

Herodotus, that ancient 'father of history', relates a story which accounts for the birth of geometry through the seasonal invasions of the Nile. Following the division of land amongst the people by King Sesostris (fourteenth century BC), a method of calculating the amount of land taken by the Nile's overflow had to be contrived in order that the owner's land-tax could be adjusted proportionately. This led to a formularized system of land measurement—'geo' meaning earth, and 'metron' meaning measure—and thus, geometry was a 'gift of the Nile'.

Although this is a somewhat fable-like explanation of the origins of our subject, much truth lies in the spirit of Herodotus' tale, for it is generally believed that the civilizations of the Near East, those of Egypt and Babylonia, were the first fully to develop numeracy, and it is fairly easy to imagine that the next step toward arithmetic and geometry should have been made by them, in order to satisfy just such a practical need as the one described by Herodotus.

The Nile and its cultures, however, do not provide the source of our own particular study; its fountain-head lies in Classical Greece with Pythagoras and his followers, who, by their philosophical approach, transformed the elements of the mathematics which they had inherited from the Egyptians and Babylonians. Aristotle tells us that the Pythagoreans 'applied themselves to the study of mathematics and were the first to advance that science'; accordingly, they are credited with giving the subject a special and independent status. Pythagoras did much to determine the nature and philosophy of Greek mathematics, raising arithmetic and geometry to their liberal-art rank, as pursuits of the intellect, freed of any material or commercial utility.

For our purpose, perhaps Pythagoras' most important revelation was not his traditionally attributed theorem of the square on the hypotenuse of a right-angled triangle, or the consequent, deeply disturbing discovery of the irrationality of the square root of two, but that of the analogy between music and arithmetic. Pythagoras discovered that the musical consonances—the prime musical intervals of an octave, a fifth, and a fourth—were produced by strings of the same thickness and tension but of lengths in simple arithmetical proportion. Thus, strings in 2 : 1 ratio give an octave, or *diapason*; in 3 : 2 ratio, a fifth, or *sesquialtera*; whilst those in 4 : 3 ratio give a fourth, or *sesquitertia*. This was also found to apply to strings of similar length, but of tensions in 'harmonic' proportion, and to the mass of the vibrating membrane, whether it be of strings, anvils, bells, glasses of water, or the speaking length of pipes. Such diversity of examples is illustrated in the charming woodcut from Gafurio's *Theorica Musice* of 1492, and shown here in Fig. 1. This discovery is primarily important to us because it marks the emergence of a 'philosophy of numbers', which was to be a corner-stone of Greek belief and an inspiration to Renaissance thinkers.

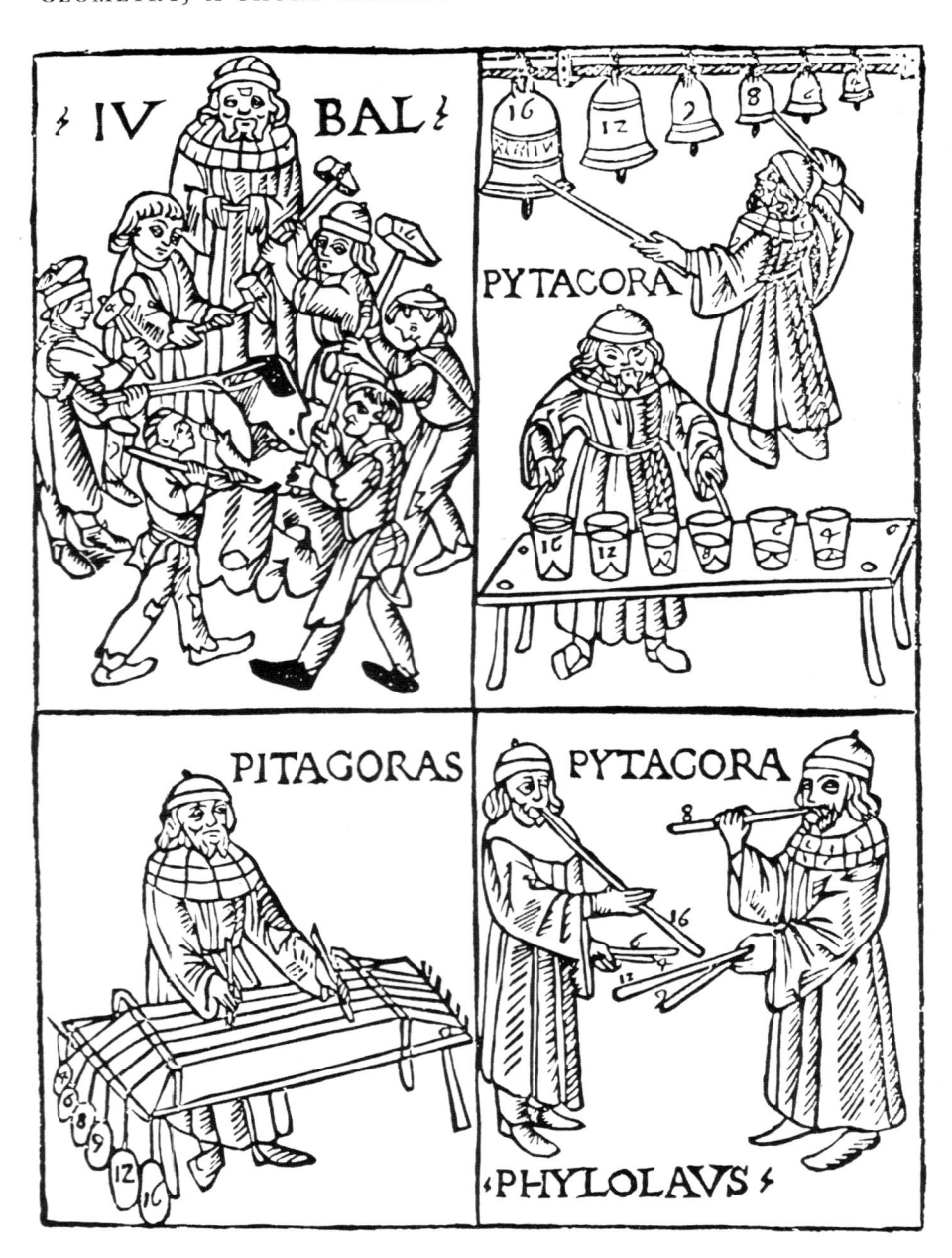

FIG. 1. Mathematics and musical harmony, Franchino Gafurio, *Theorica Musice*, 1492

To the Pythagoreans, numbers were the elements of nature and the essence of all things; the whole of heaven was a musical scale in which the planets glided in divine harmony, making 'music of the spheres'. Fig. 2 shows a later graphic realization of this vision, from Robert Fludd's (1574–1637) *Utriusque Cosmi Historia*. A famous follower of Pythagoras, Philolaos, shown with his master in Fig. 1 demonstrating flutes of different ratio, distilled their belief in the universality of number in the lines:

> Were it not for number and its nature, nothing that exists would be clear to anybody either in itself, or in its relation to other things.... You can observe the power of number exercising itself not only in the affairs of demons and gods, but in all the acts and the thoughts of men in all handicrafts and music.

Another Pythagorean 'discovery' which concerns us is that of the theory of proportion—the three means: arithmetic, geometric, and harmonic. These are fully explained in Chapter 4 under 'Types of Proportion', but for the present can be understood as 'modes' of proportion. The Pythagorean theory of proportion, however, did not

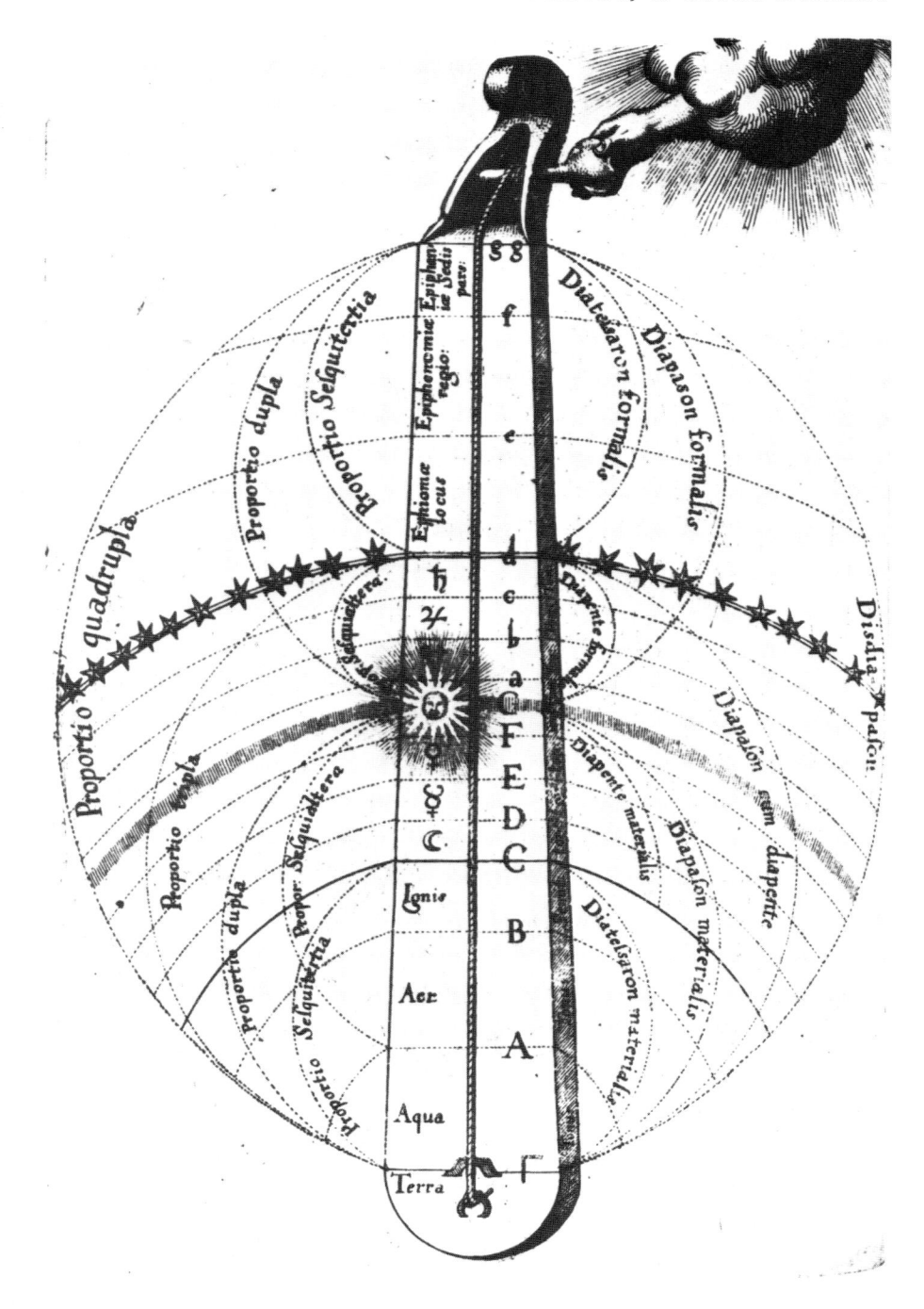

FIG. 2. The Cosmic Monochord, Robert Fludd, *Utriusque Cosmi Historia*, 1617

account for, or apply to, incommensurable magnitudes (amounts which could not be rationalized by whole numbers), and yet, as we have seen, the Pythagoreans did recognize their existence; one supposes, therefore, that they regarded such phenomena as 'anti-number', belonging to a primitive and incomprehensible chaos, and mathematically 'beyond the pale', involving, as they do, the terrifying concept of the infinite.

The natural heir to Pythagorean mathematics was Plato, who, although naturally more important to us for his philosophical writings, was also the founder (?387 BC) of the renowned Academy, the recognized authority in mathematics, and a connecting link between Pythagoras and the later geometers of the University of Alexandria, and thence eventually to the scientists of the Renaissance, as can be seen by the Academy's famous motto, which reads 'Let no one ignorant of mathematics enter here'—a principle later adopted and disseminated in stern prefaces by both Copernicus (*On the Revolutions of the Heavenly Spheres*, 1543) and Leonardo (*Trattato della Pittura*).

It could be said that in his mathematical beliefs Plato was more Pythagorean than Pythagoras, for the conviction that nature is precisely ordered to a mathematical rationale was given greater significance by the Platonic belief in the supreme power of human intelligence; this led Plato to seek beyond observable nature, to ideal nature—the true reality, 'the most real existence'. Whereas Pythagoras was concerned with the number found in the harmony of music, Plato, believing knowledge to be removed from sensation, sought, through a 'chain of causation', the harmonies of numbers themselves, harmonies heard only by the mind. For Plato,

... the things of this world are all imperfect copies of Forms which exist externally somewhere; which are the true and only objects of knowledge, but can only be apprehended by direct contemplation of the mind, freed as far as possible from the confusing imperfections of the physical world.[3]

Without question, the greatest contribution made by Plato to the mainstream of our subject was his study the *Timaeus*, for us one of the two most important literary works of ancient times, a book that was available, in Latin, to European thought even through the Dark and early Middle Ages, when its 'God', as creator, was seen by Christians as analogous with the Creator in Genesis.

The *Timaeus* is a formal embodiment of much of the Pythagorean/Platonic number-cosmology, the spirit of which we have already glimpsed above. In describing the material and structure of the World-Soul, Plato explains its constituent divisions according to the harmony of the numbers 1, 2, 3, 4, 9, 8, and 27, which is the combination of the squares and cubes of the double and triple proportion, starting from unity, that is, the two geometrical progressions 1, 2, 4, 8, and 1, 3, 9, 27. These numbers, often drawn in the *Lambda* arrangement (Fig. 3), contain in their ratios all the actual musical consonances as well as the divine harmony of proportion. The square, 4 and 9, and cube, 8 and 27, are numbers of two-dimensional planes, and three-dimensional solids. Plato further demonstrates how 'God eternally geometrizes' by assigning, in a mystical atomic theory, to each of the four elements one of the four regular solids, in which form take the particles of that element. The fifth 'Platonic' solid is the dodecahedron—which, incidentally, cannot be constructed from Plato's 'two basic types of triangle'—this 'God used for arranging the constellations on the whole heaven'. These familiar, truly elemental, figures are given here in Fig. 4.

The other important book from Classical Greece relevant to our study, and one having a most profound influence in the shaping of our culture, is the renowned *Elements* of Euclid (*c*.325 BC). This master-work—the standard textbook of geometry for over two thousand years—was a unification of Greek mathematical knowledge, collected and presented in an arrangement so coherent and logical that its great and enduring influence on civilization has been as much for its rational systematization as for its content. In fact, it contained thirteen books, the first six and last three of which were devoted to geometry (plane and solid), the seventh, eighth, and ninth to arithmetic, and the tenth to irrationals. The title *Elements*, according to one ancient commentator,[4] means 'beginning at

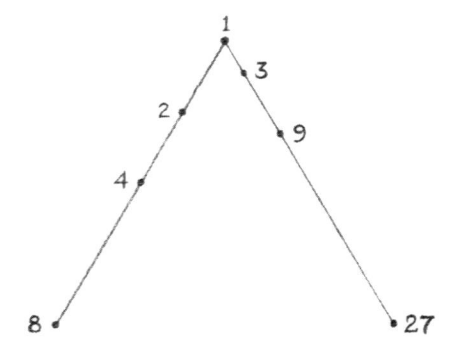

FIG. 3. The Lambda

[3] Hugh Tredennick, introduction to *The Last Days of Socrates* (a collection of Plato's Dialogues) (Penguin, 1967).
[4] Proclus.

the beginning'; Euclid does so by giving a number of definitions or Axioms. These set out properties of points, lines, surfaces, and figures, and are carefully formulated to be accepted as unarguable truths—the *materia* from which the succeeding Propositions are logically built to form the entire system of geometry. This included, in book five, the theory of proportion, both commensurable *and* incommensurable, attributed to Eudoxus of Cnidus (408-355 BC), a master mathematician/astronomer who had also originated several theorems of the golden section of a line.

The achievement of the *Elements* was threefold: firstly, it presented in concise and accessible form the corporate Greek understanding of geometry, a body of knowledge which—philosophy and 'liberal' education aside—was also to prove of inestimable practical value to many of its students. Secondly, it demonstrated, with all the irrefutability of its own proofs, the supreme power of human reason, and its ability to deduce and formulate according to systematic laws of thought. Thirdly, by its universal acclaim as a model of pure and elegant logic, the *Elements* finally elevated the study of mathematics from the merely useful to the definitively aesthetic.

Euclid himself was educated in Athens, it is thought by the pupils of Plato, but with the conquering of Egypt by Alexander, and the consequent endowment of the city of Alexandria, Euclid was to become one of the founders of the great 'museum' and library established there under the culturally enlightened rule of Ptolemy I (306-283 BC). With the magnetism of an early Diaghilev (further aided by some financial inducement) Ptolemy assembled the greatest minds and talents of the ancient world around a new intellectual hub, its spokes radiating out through Arabia, Greece, Asia, Europe, and Africa.

Culturally the true *nombril du monde*, Alexandria achieved one of the first cosmopolitan societies, a centre not only of Hellenism, but also of Semitism. Its singularly diverse peoples mixed and freely exchanged both culture and commerce—the great explosion of trade making the practical demands of geography, navigation, and engineering on the previously aloof and abstract art of mathematics. In this way, Hellenistic mathematics became a very different study from the removed idealistic philosophy of the Classical scholars; instead, it embraced practical application by measurement, surveying, and construction.

The science of mechanics, particularly, burgeoned in an atmosphere hungry for the wondrous and the astonishing. Water-clocks, water-organs, pumps, and all manner of pneumatically and hydrostatically powered automata appeared, to advance knowledge, expand the economy, and dazzle the populace. For the Alexandrians, mathematics was a powerful but obedient servant, and one of its greatest masters was a man whose intellect and whose fate symbolize those of his age—Archimedes (*c.*287-212 BC). He was born in, and returned to, Syracuse in Sicily, but studied at Alexandria. Although his most important work was in the field of geometry—extending the work of Eudoxus and Euclid, determining a value for π, discovering the proportional relationship between a cylinder and its inscribed sphere, working on conoids and spheroids, on spirals and parabolas—his contemporary fame was founded neither on mathematics nor on the celebrated hydrostatic principle that bears his name, but on the ingenious mechanical devices that so fired the popular imagination, contrivances which, incidentally, his lofty Greek mind disdainfully dismissed as so many gewgaws and beneath the dignity of true

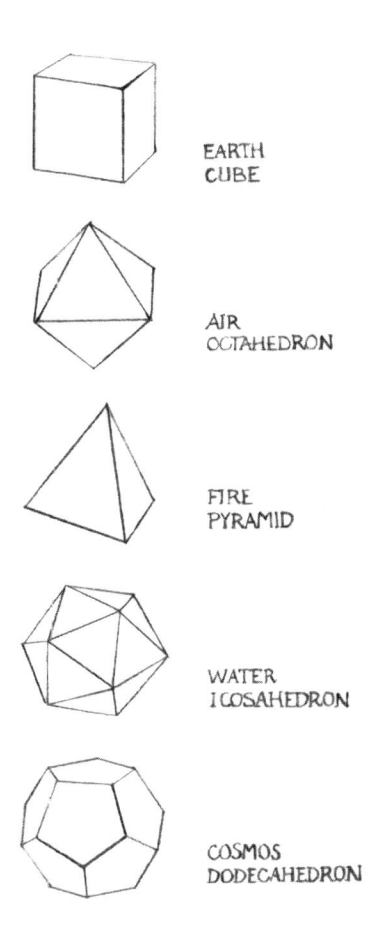

FIG. 4. The elemental polyhedra. Plato, *Timaeus*

intellectual pursuit. Amongst these inventions were engines of war, built to defend Syracuse against the Roman advance; one such was a giant concave mirror used to burn the Roman ships as they came within bow-shot. Archimedes, it is well known, died beneath the sword of a Roman soldier while in rapt contemplation of a mathematical figure—a grievous incident, and one which sadly symbolizes the fate which was to befall the Greek spirit of learning before the brutal indifference of Roman ignorance.

Other Roman conquests in the Mediterranean included that of Alexandria itself. Here, fire was used by Caesar to destroy the Egyptian fleet as it lay at anchor in the harbour; disastrously, the flames sweeping inward from the sea engulfed the Great Library, annihilating the most precious archives the world had ever known. Roman suppression followed Roman persecution, and the stifled people inevitably turned to the hope offered by the new Christian ethic, an appeal lodged in simple faith, and one renouncing the amassed abstract knowledge of the Greek culture as pagan. The scholars of the Museum of Alexandria had to flee the city, scattering with them the dormant seeds of their bright Greek culture. What remained of the Museum was callously put to the torch by the Muslim invasion of 640, the remaining books and manuscipts, according to legend, supplying the furnaces of the public baths with six months of hot water and steam.

Before following our summarized mathematical history into the bleak wastelands of the Dark Ages, there is perhaps one exceptional Roman to whom we should be introduced, and he is Marcus Vitruvius Pollio, an architect working for the Emperor Augustus. Vitruvius' *De Architectura Libri Decem* (The Ten Books of Architecture), are a rare and wonderful marriage of Greek theory, which he profoundly respected, and his own Roman practical application, containing all the Emperor of Rome should desire to know concerning engineering and architecture. In fact, Vitruvius' greatest readership was probably not in his own Imperial Rome, but in the Italy of the Renaissance, when his work was to become the bible, the *locus classicus*, of architects and architectural theorists. He lists some basic requirements that the architect should fulfil, such as having a knowledge of history, of philosophy, of medicine, and of astronomy; he should also be instructed in geometry and have an understanding of music. This last is explained away to any puzzled Roman reader in suitably prosaic terms concerning not only the acoustics of a theatre but, perhaps more acceptably, the correct 'tuning' of the stretched strings of the ballista, or war-catapult—Roman music indeed.

Nevertheless, Vitruvius did introduce, if to the more receptive ears of a later audience, some concepts of profound and far-reaching influence. Not least of these was the idea, of Greek origin, that the human body itself was the repository of the most important canon of proportion to be found. These proportions, which are straightforward commensurable ratios symmetrically deployed, he records, before explaining in a highly significant passage how a man with limbs outstretched describes both a circle and a square. (Effectively, man is born of these two prime figures of perfection, by the juxtaposition of their centres at his umbilicus, the point of his birth.) Many drawings, and indeed design philosophies, arose out of this passage from the hands and minds of Renaissance artists; two of the most beautiful drawings are included here, the now quite familiar image from Leonardo (Fig. 5), and a second, by the important architectural theorist Francesco di Giorgio (Fig. 6).

Only one incommensurable proportion is used or mentioned by Vitruvius—and that only in passing—the diagonal of the square (Fig. 7), whose irrationality had so disturbed earlier Greek authors. Vitruvius' didactic approach embraces the fundamental principles of architecture which he sees in terms whose exact meaning we have a little difficulty in fully comprehending, or accurately translating: *ordinatio, dispositio, eurythmia, symmetria, decor, distributio*; that is, order, arrangement, harmony, symmetry, propriety, and economy. Many of these are, however, founded axiomatically, on the proportional basis of beauty in design, and therefore were also of great relevance to arts and disciplines other than architecture. Vitruvius' 'order' is one giving due measure to the members of a work considered separately, whilst his symmetry gives balance to the proportions of the whole, by using ratios based on the size of those members—the modulus, or unit of measurement. This, as we shall see, is an important design process, evident in many of the instrument outlines to be discussed later in this study. Eurythmy, incidentally, is a beauty of disposition; according to one sixteenth-century Vitruvian commentator, Daniele Barbaro: 'This beautiful manner in music as well

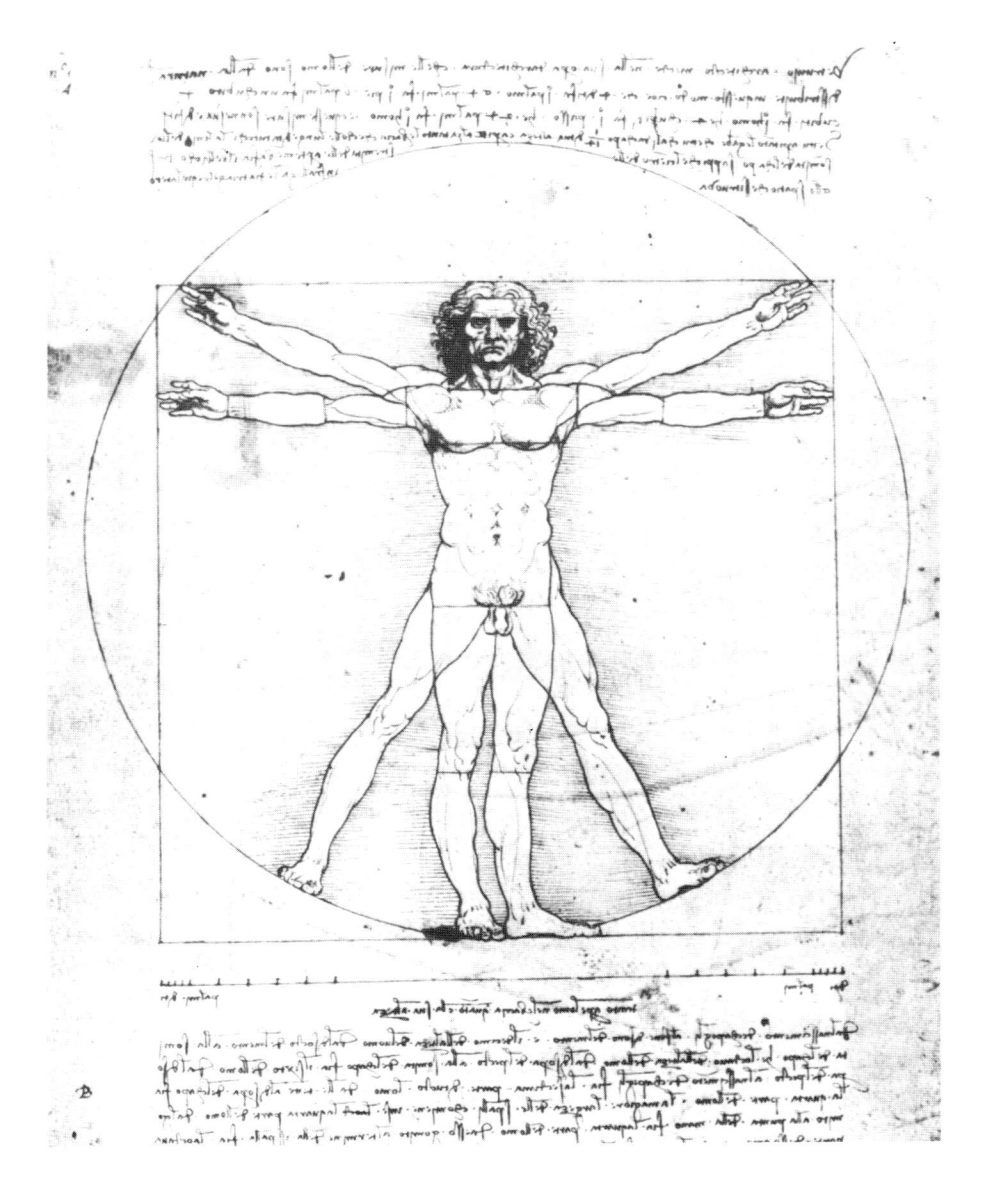

FIG. 5. Vitruvian figure, Leonardo da Vinci. (By courtesy of the Accademia, Venice)

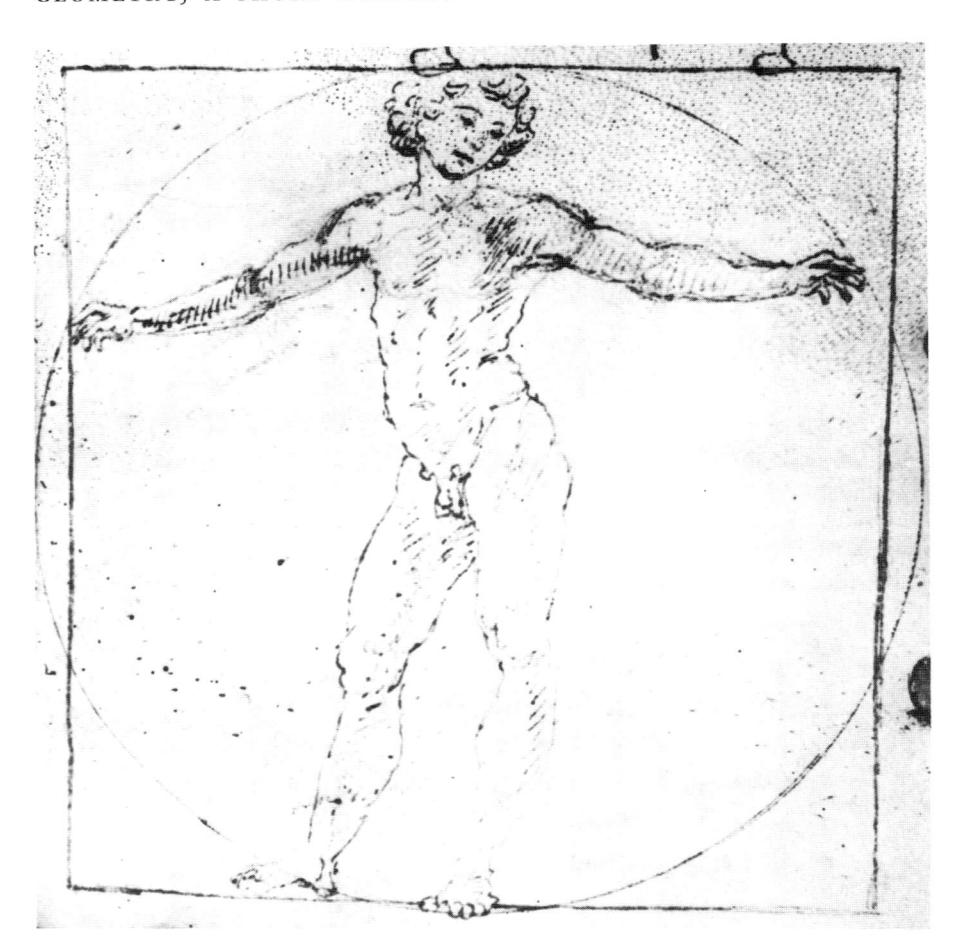

FIG. 6. Vitruvian figure, Francesco di Giorgio. (Biblioteca Laurenziana, Florence)

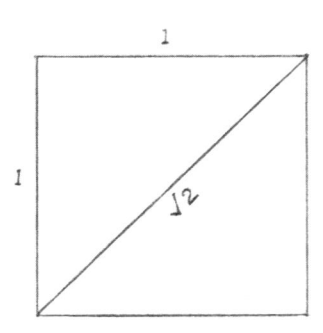

FIG. 7

as in architecture is called Eurythmia (harmony), mother of grace and delight.' Before their rediscovery in the fifteenth century at St Gall, the *Ten Books* had been lost for a long time, a barren period in our cultural history in which Eurythmia herself withdrew unseen into the darkness.

The eclipse of Greek culture and the collapse of Rome left a vacuum of mathematical thought in the West. The fragments of Greek knowlege were scattered in the Eastern world, but would eventually be driven to Europe to re-emerge and re-form into a structure of powerful influence. Until then, many such fragments were preserved and explicated on by a highly organized Arab culture. Indeed, the science of mathematics owes a great deal to Arabic scholarship, as do our systems of economics, finance, commerce, and industry, not only for the invention of the algebraic approach, but also for our very number system and notation, which itself is Hindu–Arabian in origin.

The bright torch of Greek learning was passed on to medieval Europe by the Arabs, both directly and indirectly. The *Elements* of Euclid were first translated into Latin (*c.*1120) from an Arabic version obtained in Spain by that brave scholar Athelhard, or Adelard, of Bath, amongst whose other Arabic translations was the *Liber Algorismi de numero Indorum*, a study of the Hindu numerals written in about 825 by al-Khowarizmi. A more oblique path for Neoplatonic thought came through the many works of Al Kindi (?*c.*873). Sometimes called 'the Philosopher of the Arabs', his full, glorious, name was Abu Yusuf Ya Qub Ibn Ishaq ul-Kindi. He was one of the earliest translators and commentators of Aristotle, and was in turn translated into Latin by Gherard of Cremona[5] (1114–87). Al Kindi wrote on a wide range of topics in which mathematics can be seen as the connecting theme; his *Libellum sex quantitatum* was apparently[6] referred to by Ghiberti, and was probably used by Leonardo, as well as by Daniele Barbaro.

Never in our cultural history has the study of mathematics been held in lower esteem than it was during the Dark and Middle Ages. At first it seemed that practically its sole function was to make astrological forecasts, and, as an understanding of astrology was an essential part of medieval 'medicine', it was largely the physicians who received the most complete mathematical education of their day. One of the earliest universities offering this teaching was the twelfth-century University of Bologna. Such mathematics was comparatively elementary, and no doubt the basic geometry which was taught in this atmosphere of dry scholasticism achieved a metaphysical significance which was perhaps rather nearer a superstitious number-mythology than a truly Neoplatonic philosophy. Neoplatonism did endure, however, and was tolerated, and even embraced, by the Church, although naturally with certain theological reservations.[7] At the time of the miraculous twelfth-century surge of building, Neoplatonic mathematical ideas were circulated, and were to provide mystic food for the hungry imaginations of the great Gothic builders; Chartres was an early centre of Neoplatonist learning, and her most marvellous treasure, the Cathedral, the subject of many interesting proportional analyses,[8] shelters beneath her exquisite stone portals, in the company of earthly kings and queens and heavenly saints, prophets, and angels, the images of the Greek philosophers, including Pythagoras himself, complete with the bells of mathematical harmony. Europe was awakening, and awakening to a distant Greek call. Following the first contacts with Classical works through the Arab world came further exchange, now directly from Greek sources, in the manuscripts brought to Italy by scholars migrating from Constantinople, and from Turkish tyranny.

Exactly how the mighty explosion of intellectual and creative energy that we call the Renaissance came about is too broad a subject for any but the most sketchy and economic of annotations in our short history of mathematics. We can at least say that the igniting spark for this explosion was the rebirth of the power of human reason, and that much of the tinder was provided by the influx of 'new' knowledge and the new possibilities that it suggested. Commerce and industry, and the new class of free labour which gave power to them, liberated the artisan imagination and engendered the independent incentive to improve working processes. These included an invention of previously unimaginable power—that of printing, a process which amplified and spread the turbulent intellectual forces which had led to its birth.[9]

Much of the renewed belief in man's reason was 'borrowed faith' transferred from the increasingly disputed tenets of Christian theology. Divided, and falling, the Church was robbed by the Catholic–Protestant schism of much of the unquestioned confidence it had previously enjoyed, forcing the new intellectual energy to make a new approach towards man's position in the universe. And logically, like a child, it placed man at its centre. The Vitruvian figures (Figs. 5 and 6) examined earlier are thus not only academic commentaries on an ancient text, but contemporary philosophical declarations of an unmatched eloquence and economy. Mathematics was again hailed as a universal truth, and a universal language, in which all was written and through which all might be

---

[5] Also one of the earliest translators of Euclid.

[6] R. Wittkower, *Architectural Principles*, p. 138 n. 1.

[7] 'The doctrines of the incarnation, the resurrection of the flesh and the creation of the world in time marked the boundary line between the church's dogmatic and Neoplatonism; in every other respect, theologians and Neoplatonists drew so closely together that many of them are completely at one.' (Essay on 'Neoplatonism' by Adolf Harnack and John Malcolm Mitchell, *Encylopaedia Britannica*, 14th edn.)

[8] See L. Charpentier, *The Mysteries of Chartres Cathedral* (1972).

[9] The first book traditionally accepted as having been printed from movable type was the Gutenberg Bible, issued at Mainz in Germany in about 1454.

understood and—such was the new confidence—be *controlled*. This regard for the certitude of number is reflected in the words of Leonardo:

> The utmost joyance to the body is bestowed upon it by the light of the sun; the utmost joyance to the spirit is bestowed upon it by the clarity of mathematical verity.

Mathematical verity was even reconcilable with Mother Church, providing its application was restricted to the nature of God's earth and did not seek to reorder His heavens as Copernicus, Kepler, and Galileo did. God created the world according to rational mathematical principles (the Creator is often depicted with dividers in hand) and He created man so that he might understand and, as 'love is the daughter of understanding', might love His creation. Thus could a scientific study of nature's mathematically defined processes be sanctified as an act of worship, as Galileo confirms:

> Nor does God less admirably discover Himself to us in Nature's actions, than in the Scriptures' sacred dictions.

We have established, then, that the climate of the Renaissance was mathematical. It was mathematical, though, not only in its beliefs, but in the utilitarian aspects of its everyday affairs. Within this community, the artist, if not a geometrical thaumaturgist, was at the very least a highly accomplished practitioner of mathematics. He had to be: frequently he was not only painter and sculptor, but also architect, engineer, ballisticist, and general designer. Indeed, for Alberti,[10] the first requirement of the painter was knowledge of geometry.

The impact on this society of the newly translated Greek works was not only one of content, but also one of form. As we mentioned earlier, a work like Euclid's *Elements*—it was first printed in Latin in Venice in 1482—had a profound influence on its readers, in part because of its elegant and lucid methodology. The rebirth of the spirit of Greek learning cleared the way for a flood of pedagogy; the desire to communicate research and expound philosophies of work was given further stimulation by the societies, academies, and guilds which grouped themselves around their subjects, and further opportunity for dissemination by the new wonders of publication. As a result, 'instructional' treatises abounded, and with them came a comparatively easy access to proportional knowledge. Appendix A (page 171) gives a general list of early works dealing either directly with geometry and proportion, or with specific applications, such as architecture, painting and sculpture, or music itself. At least some of these were sources of information available to the early instrument-maker or to any guild society to which he may have belonged. Most of the treatises quoted are Italian, but the belief in the importance of number as a universal harmonic instrument of creativity, which is their common link, was one held in other parts of Europe, including France, England, and Spain.[11] Indeed, we may leave this account of the mathematical climate in which the art of the luthier established itself with a voice not from Italy, but from the north—Albrecht Dürer writing to his friend Wilibald Pirkheimer about the wider applications of his work on human proportions:

> ... as this book deals with nothing but proportion, I desired to keep all references to painting for the book which I intend to write upon that subject. For this doctrine of proportions, if rightly understood, will not be of use to painters alone, but also to sculptors in wood and stone, goldsmiths, metal-founders, and potters who fashion things out of clay, as well as to all those who desire to make figures.

---

[10] *della Pittura* (1435).
[11] R. Wittkower, *Architectural Principles*, pp. 119, 121, 143, 144 ff.

4 Proportion

Palladio's remarks on Beauty, which opened this study, give, as we have said, a sound idea of what proportion in art implies; they suggest a quest for a 'natural', reposeful beauty through the virtues of unity and simplicity. Sanctified by the faith of the artist, this quest becomes the fulfilment of a sacred, timeless pledge between *forma* and *materia*, a homage to the original creation of Order out of Chaos, and of Harmony maintained by the divine economy of Nature.

But if the consequences of proportion may be seen as profound, its application is usually simple. Simplicity is one of the prime directives of *proportionalità*, and for all their significance and effectiveness, the geometries and proportional schemes used in the following instrument-designs are, on the whole, accordingly easy to follow, the mathematics involved being of an elementary nature.

Before embarking on our own quest of proportion, however, it would be as well at this stage to acquaint ourselves with the *principia* of our subject, the rudimentary laws and processes of proportion which we shall meet during the course of our specific analyses.

Types of Proportion

In mathematics, proportion is order in relationship; it is constant ratio between three or more terms. This constancy can operate in three distinct modes of proportion, which are called 'means'. These are the arithmetic, the geometric, and the harmonic means, and their origins are traditionally held to be Pythagorean.

Mean, of course, denotes the intermediate term in a series, or progression, of three terms, and the above types of proportion describe the different relationships, each of them constant, which the two outer, or extreme, terms have with their 'means'. To explain how each of them works, I shall need to employ some simple algebra.

The arithmetic proportion applies when the second term exceeds the first by the same amount as the third exceeds the second (that is, $b-a = c-b$). This is an additive progression, where the terms are increased by the addition of a constant factor, so that the arithmetic mean, b, is quite simply an 'average' of the two extremes, a and c, or

$$b = \frac{a+c}{2}.$$

The geometric proportion applies when the first term is to the second as the second is to the third (that is, $a:b = b:c$). This is a multiplicative progression, where the terms are increased by multiplication by a constant factor, so that the geometric mean will be the square root of the product of the two extremes, or

$$b = \sqrt{(ac)}.$$

PROPORTION

Both these types of progression arise in the designs analysed later in this study.

The third type of progression, the harmonic proportion, was not found. It is a good deal more complex than the other two; Plato thought it

a gift from the blessed choir of the Muses to which mankind owes the boon of the play of consonance and measure, with all they contribute to rhythm and melody.[12]

It can be said to apply when the first term is to the third term as the difference between the first and second terms is to the difference between the second and third terms. Algebraically that is

$$\frac{a}{c} = \frac{b-a}{c-b}$$

which is to say the harmonic mean

$$b = \frac{2ac}{a+c}.$$

Expressed in numbers, with a constant mean b of 4, the respective arithmetic, geometric, and harmonic series would then be

$$3:4:5$$
$$2:4:8$$
$$3:4:6.$$

Rational and Irrational Numbers

A progression, or series, then, is a succession of three or more numbers related by a constant ratio. Ratio itself is the relationship between two comparable magnitudes, such as 3:4. We shall be encountering many ratios which can sometimes be expressed commensurably, that is, in whole numbers, or, according to the scheme or individual ratio, may alternatively be expressed as a decimal ratio—a single amount, obtained by dividing the larger term by the smaller. In decimal-ratio terms 3:4 would be, to the customary three places, $1.33\dot{3}$.

To be able thus to express a relationship by one term is extremely convenient, and in this way the proportions of rectangles may be perfectly described by one figure—a $1.33\dot{3}$ rectangle, for example, would be one whose sides were in 3:4 proportion. Here, however, the decimal system has introduced us to another puzzling aspect of numbers. Whereas we 'know' that $1.33\dot{3}$ is really the straightforward fraction of $\frac{4}{3}$ or $1\frac{1}{3}$, in decimal terms it is irresolvable or *incommensurable*, the repeating or recurring figure stretching into an infinity of decimal places, coming nearer and nearer to the 'true' value of $1\frac{1}{3}$, but never being able to achieve it—a sort of mathematical tantalism. Where a decimal amount not only cannot be resolved, but also exhibits no repeating sequence of numbers, it is called an *irrational* number, and is in effect a special case of incommensurability. A familiar example of the infinite irrationality of what has to be a finite quantity is π, the formula which haunts the geometry of the circle, the sphere, and their relatives.

Golden Section, and the Fibonacci Numbers

Another well-known and inexhaustibly intriguing irrational quantity which we shall be meeting is the *Divina Proportione* of Fra Pacioli's treatise,

[12] Plato, *Epinomis*.

the irrational ϕ, our so-called golden section, which measures 1.618 to three places of decimal. As can be seen from its formula

$$\phi = \frac{1+\sqrt{5}}{2}$$

the irrational ingredient in ϕ is $\sqrt{5}$, a proportional factor (2.236) which we shall also encounter separately.

The golden section, according to Kepler one of geometry's 'two great treasures', has been the subject of endless research and study, an object both of passion amounting almost to deification, and of derision of the fiercest anti-proportionist kind. Witness the lyrical waxing of Pacioli's descriptions of its effects—*essentiale, singolare, ineffabile, mirabile, innominabile, inextimabile, supremo, excellentissimo, incomprehensibile, dignissimo*. Despite the fascination felt by writers such as Pacioli and Piero della Francesca for the remarkable properties of ϕ, the golden section, it appears to have been rather neglected by Renaissance architects,[13] although according to the analysis of some paintings[14] and a few of the instrument-designs which follow, it was utilized elsewhere.

For Pacioli, there was 'insufficient ink and paper in existence' to describe all the properties of his *Divina Proportione*; here, however, we must be less ambitious and list only a few of its essential peculiarities. The alternative name, golden 'cut', most probably derives from one unique characteristic which accounts for the particular richness of resonance of the ϕ proportion, and this is the section, or 'cut', at the golden mean point, b, of a line of any length, ac (Fig. 8), so that $ab : bc$ as $bc : ac$. If distance ab is quantified as 1, then bc will be 1.618 and ac will be 2.618 (which incidentally also equals ϕ^2). The reciprocal of ϕ, that is $1/\phi$, is 0.618, which with the equations

$$\phi = 1 + 1/\phi$$
$$\phi^2 = 1 + \phi = 1 + 1 + 1/\phi$$
$$\phi^3 = \phi^2 + \phi = 1 + 2\phi = 2 + \phi + 1/\phi = \sqrt{5} + 2$$

etc., etc.,

demonstrates something of the endless proportional consonance encapsulated in the value of ϕ, and also its fundamental affinity with both unity and $\sqrt{5}$. If, for example, a square or unity is removed from a ϕ rectangle, it leaves a rectangle measuring 0.618×1, which in its turn therefore has a ratio of ϕ, 1.618. This relationship is exploited in a grid complex in the planning of the Alletsee viola d'amore (English Violet) which is Ex. XVII below.

Another important property of the golden ratio seen in a progression, e.g. 0.618, 1, 1.618, 2.618, 4.236, is that it constitutes a summation series, which is to say that each vector is the sum of the previous two terms; this, of course, is perfectly illustrated by Fig. 8, where ac is plainly the sum of ab and bc.

In this way, the golden-section progression parallels the well-known summation series commonly known as the Fibonacci numbers, a whole-number progression which starts 1, 1, 2, 3, 5, 8, 13, 21, 34, 55, 89, 144, and so forth. This was first propounded by the mathematician Leonardo of Pisa, called Fibonacci, in connection with the breeding output of rabbits, and set down by him in 1202 in his *Liber Abaci*, which has survived in its second version of 1228. (It was also through this book that the spread of Hindu-Arabic numerals was encouraged.)

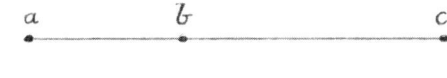

FIG. 8

[13] R. Wittkower, *Architects' Year Book*, v (London, 1953).
[14] See C. Bouleau, *The Painter's Secret Geometry*; also M. Holt, *Mathematics in Art*.

PROPORTION

It may seem strange that a breeding pattern should follow a Fibonacci, or whole-number, golden-section series, but in fact very many natural phenomena clearly follow geometric progressions in their growth or activity patterns. The number of 'nodes' in the contra-spirals of a pineapple or a fir-cone, or the seeds in sunflower heads or artichoke hearts, all coincide with the above series, as does the distribution of leaves around the stems of plants; this is the 'law' of phyllotaxis. Similarly, the exquisite geometries found in many sea shells reflect the natural economy of form engendered by this and other 'pleasing' geometric progressions.

The Root Proportionals

In the geometrical discussions to follow, irrational proportional systems other than ϕ will be encountered, as well as straightforward ratios of whole numbers found in the commensurable schemes. Specifically, these are $\sqrt{5}$ (to which we have previously been introduced by its golden-section cousin), and also the $\sqrt{3}$ ratio, which appears but once as a major proportional element.

The root proportions, which each possess their own individual characteristics, are best explained first in diagrammatic form. Fig. 9 shows the simple geometric generation of the root rectangles ($\sqrt{2}, \sqrt{3}, \sqrt{4}$, and $\sqrt{5}$) from the original unity of the square. We have already met the value of $\sqrt{2}$, as produced by the diagonal of a square, as Vitruvius' only irrational proportion (Fig. 7); by dropping this diagonal down and retaining a short side of 1, our new rectangle will have a ratio of $\sqrt{2}$ (1.4142). The diagonal of this rectangle will promote a $\sqrt{3}$ (1.732) rectangle, which in turn promotes a $\sqrt{4}$ (2) rectangle (the double square), whose diagonal will give us a $\sqrt{5}$ (2.236) rectangle in the same way, and so on.

In Fig. 9 these ratios are expressed as rectangles, and as such, $\sqrt{3}$, $\sqrt{4}$, and $\sqrt{5}$ appear in some of the grid schemes which occur in the instruments, while $\sqrt{5}$ is also occasionally utilized in governing series, or progressions.

A simple rule-and-compasses method of generating both the ϕ and $\sqrt{5}$ rectangles directly from a square is given in Lesson 2 of Hambidge's *Elements of Dynamic Symmetry*.[15] Hambidge explores the structure and characteristics of various fundamental rectangles in a way which, although not totally relevant to the particular applications which here follow, may give the reader a fuller understanding of rectilinear proportion than I have room to give.

The Vesica Piscis

Another important geometrical device, one which has consistently appeared in the analysed designs, is the figure commonly called the Vesica Piscis, the vessel or bladder of a fish. It is formed (Fig. 10) by drawing, with compasses of a fixed radius, first one circle, centre A, then a second of the same radius, centre B, on the circumference of circle one, whose centre, A, it will intersect. The two circles cross at points V and P, and it is this described shape which has earned the figure its name. The eye of the fish is situated at point C, the eye of the $\sqrt{3}$ rectangle *DEFG* which contains the vesica. The whole-number and $\sqrt{3}$ resonances of this figure are discussed further in the design of Ex. XXX. *VBPA* is a rhombus of two

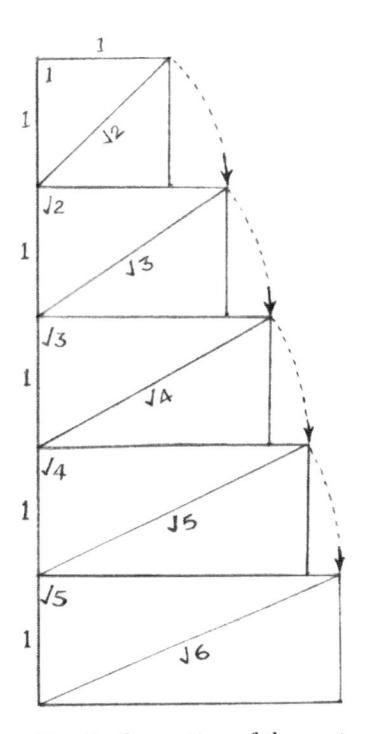

FIG. 9. Generation of the root proportions, by rule and compass

[15] Jay Hambidge, *The Elements of Dynamic Symmetry* (Yale University Press, 1948 edn.).

FIG. 10. Construction of the vesica piscis

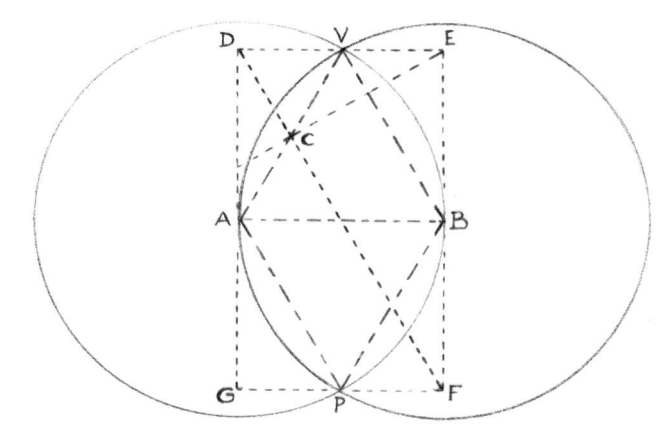

equilateral triangles; from these can be derived a hexagon, and, following a method published by Dürer in his *Course in the Art of Measurement with Compasses and Ruler*,[16] by the addition of a further circle, a pentagon (see Fig. 11). This was a quick method for drawing a pentagon, which was also included in the *Geometria deutsch* (c.1484); it is, however, not totally accurate, in that the two base angles of the pentagon come out at about one-third of a degree too obtuse. For many practical purposes, of course, this would be quite adequate, as would the myriad other constructions which can be generated from the vesica mother-figure. In fact, from this initial molecular collision of two equal circles, the equilateral triangle, the square, pentagon, hexagon, octagon, decagon, dodecagon, as well as the $\sqrt{3}$ and golden-section rectangles, can all be extracted.

It is hardly surprising, then, that a device so simple to draw, but having such profound potentiality, should have been adopted as a sacred womb of geometrical generation by the ancient builders of both Eastern and Western (particularly Gothic) religious architecture.[17] In fact, '. . . it constituted the great and enduring secret of our ancient brethren'.[18] The vesica is also to be found as the geometrical basis of the *mandala*, which is so much a part of the iconography of Christian Art (Fig. 12 shows the vesica throne of *Christ in Majesty* from the Psalter of Westminster Abbey, c.1200). In his *City of Revelation* John Michell gives the meaning of its Greek name, ὁ ἅγιος τῶν ἁγίων, as 'The Holiest of Holies', and writes:

> Although the vesica was particularly influential at the beginning of Christianity, as it is at all such periods in history, it has been respected from the earlist times as a symbol of the sacred marriage, with the spiritual world of essences as the circle on the right penetrating the world of material phenomena on the left.

When used in the design of musical instruments, however, it is more usually *not* the mandala form of the vesica itself which is significant, but the 'vesica relationship', as it were, of the parent circles. Most commonly these will coincide with the anchoring lower-bout corner arcs of an outline whose relationship, left and right sides, is thus geometrically defined and secured in its symmetry, while in other schemes the vesica arrangement of circles is used only as an 'invisible' planning agent. In practically all cases, however, the vesica radius proves to be proportionally significant to the scheme in which it features.

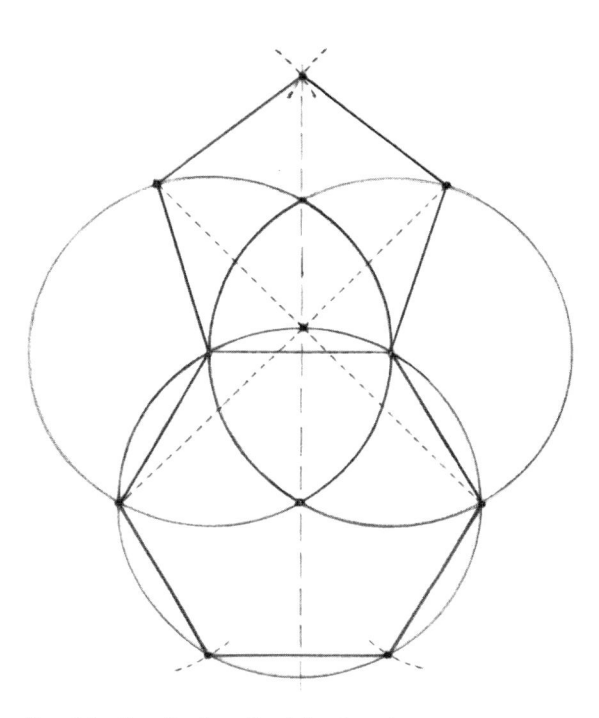

FIG. 11. Practical method for drawing a pentagon

The Ionic Volute in the Geometry of the Head

The heads of the instruments which follow, although all serving the same practical, mechanical, function, display an enormous variation in form—a diversity which echoes the multiformity of the body outlines.

[16] *Underweysung der Messung mit dem Zirckel und Richtscheyt, in Linien, Ebnen und ganzen Corporen* (Nuremberg, 1525, 1533, 1538; Latin translation: Paris, 1532 and Arnheim, 1605).
[17] Keith Critchlow, *Glastonbury. A Study in Patterns* (RILKO, 1970); John Michell, *The View Over Atlantis* (Abacus, 1975); T. C. Stewart, *The City as an Image of Man*.
[18] Dr Oliver in *The Canon*, ed. W. Stirling (1974).

Fig. 12. Illumination: *Christ in Majesty*, from *Psalter of Westminster Abbey*, c.1200. (British Library)

They may be straightforward, like the simple, straight-sided, trapezoidal, open frame for pegs, found on many lutes; the leaf-shaped, rear-mounted peg-box of the lira; the flat, fanned-out peg-board of the guitars; or they may be the more sculptured affairs found on the viols, the violins, and the few other instruments which have lateral pegs mounted in a peg-box of flowing curves, terminating in either a carved head or a volute.

This latter type of head, whether it terminates in a carved head (human or animal) or a scroll, affords the luthier more opportunities for aesthetic expression freed of acoustic strictures than almost any other part of the instrument. It is in the conception and execution of the 'head' that we not only observe the continuation of the maker's skills seen elsewhere in the instrument, but, more particularly, gain a greater insight into his personality and aesthetic vision. The same can be said of the design and cutting of the sound-holes. Even in the case of scroll-heads, where a particular volute form is the established model, as in the case of all but one[19] of the scroll-heads covered by this study, there is a seemingly infinite capacity for its aesthetic interpretation.

The geometric archetype, which forms the standard model for the scroll spirals found in the heads of the majority[20] of members of the violin family, is the volute of the Ionic order of classical architecture. In practice, only the centre two turns of the two and three-quarter turns of the classic volute are most usually adopted by the luthier, who could have originally acquired the necessary drawing knowledge either from architects, masons, or carpenters, or directly from the editions of Vitruvius, or writers and commentators after Vitruvius.

For those wishing to follow its geometry, I reproduce here the text (below) and diagram (Fig. 13) given by Joseph Gwilt, *Encyclopedia of Architecture* (London, 1894), describing the construction of the Ionic volute according to Vitruvius:

> ... the volute, the centre of whose eye, as it is called, is found by the intersection of an horizontal line from E, the bottom of the echinus, with a vertical from D, the extremity of the cyma reversa. On the point of intersection, with a radius equal to one part, describe a circle. Its vertical diameter is called the cathetus, and forms the diagonal of a square, whose sides are to be bisected, and through the points of bisection the axes 1, 3 and 2, 4 are to be drawn, each being divided into 6 equal parts. The points thus found will serve for drawing the exterior part of the volute. Thus, placing the point of the compasses in the point 1, with the radius 1D, the quadrant DA is described. With the radius 2A another quadrant may be described, and so on. Similarly, the subdivisions below the points used for the outer lines of the volute serve for the inner lines. The total height of the volute is 16 parts of a module, whereof 9 are above the horizontal from E, and 7 below it.

[19] Ex. IV, tenor viol by Henry Jaye (1667).
[20] Certain makers of the Brescian school, notably Maggini, the Venetian, Sanctus Seraphim, and some later Saxon copyists occasionally made scrolls bearing half-turns more or less than the accepted 'standard' pattern.

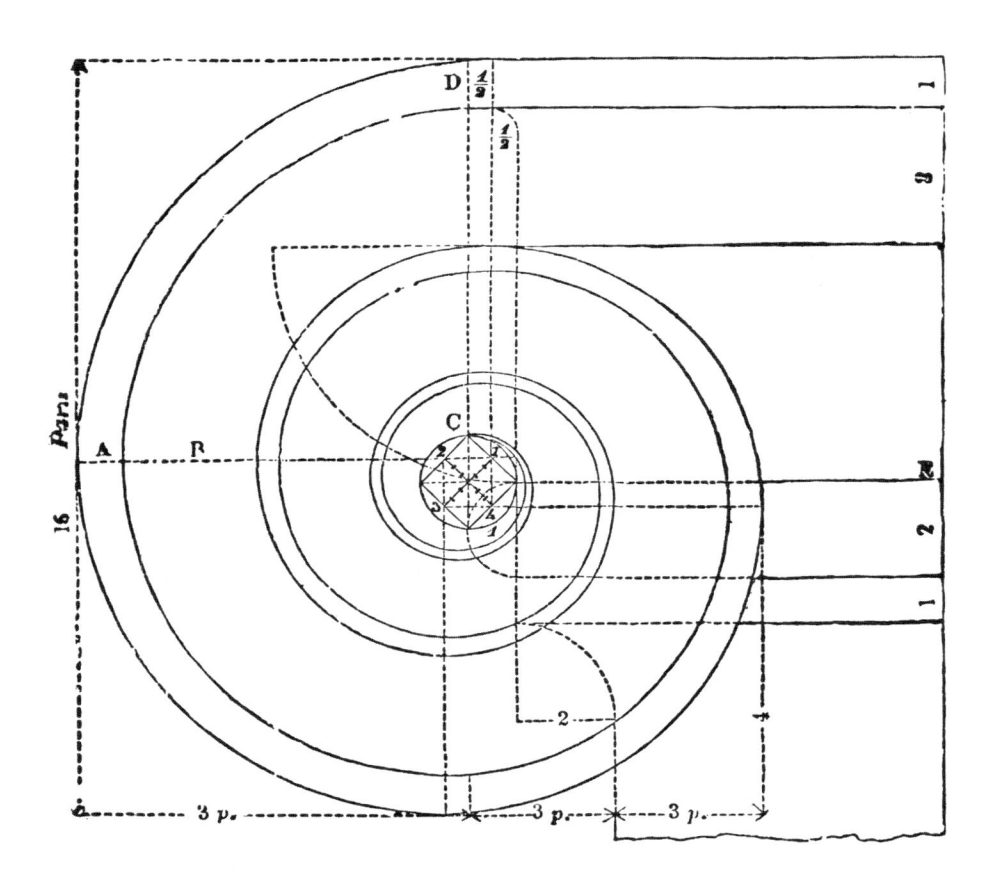

FIG. 13. The Ionic volute according to Vitruvius, after Gwilt

Systems of Measurement

In discussing the mathematics of instrument-designs spanning a period of over three centuries, and seven or eight European countries, we are fortunate in being able to unite our findings by one system of measurement served by one method of proportional calculation—the metric system and the decimal ratio. Neither of these, however, was employed by the early designers whose work we are examining. For them the whole number was an important concept and one which was retained, in dealing with quantities less than unity, by the use of fractions, which are themselves the expressions of whole-number ratios of unity—this made calculation a rather complex affair. But when we come to consider the units of measurements which were used, we are faced with even further complications.

In Italy alone, practically each major town had its own system of measurements, set out in a public place for the consultation of the different trades and occupations, which, often in the same town, would be using individual specialized units which differed according to their work, so that a cloth merchant could be cutting to a different *braccio* from his neighbour, a mason or carpenter. Moreover, many of these craftsmen were not necessarily native to their town, or even country, of work, and with the possible existence of specific guild traditions of measurement now lost to us, a known origin of an instrument is no guarantee of the application of a particular standard of measurement in its manufacture—a state of affairs confirmed by more than one analysis.

The whole question of units of measurement is a field which is particularly poorly served by written study. Such little knowledge as can be gleaned is often confusing and contradictory, while even the direct measurement of the surviving public 'standards' has proven an unsatisfactory source of information. Therefore, as above all we are seeking by this study to establish the conscious use of geometrical and proportional systems by early luthiers, and as, by definition, these considerations are independent of specific units of measurement, particular systems are only referred to when their use has seemed obvious, directly relevant to a proportional unit, or sufficiently unexpected to have significance. This was thought to be the safest course, particularly as in most cases only a certain proportion of vectors appear to correspond to a suggested unit. (It would appear, however, that the Brunswick system, the Brunswick inch, which can be transcribed as 23.78 mm, was used by very many makers, not only those working in the north. It can be found directly governing overall measurements in units of commensurability, as in Ex. III, a Venetian instrument, or merely as an intangible resonance occurring in an instrument's proportional scheme.)

This is perhaps too contentious a question about which to make definite statements, even in Ex. III, where Brunswick inches seem clearly present—their apparent domination could be accounted for simply by their coincidence with a pervading unit of commensurability. As levels of proof vary so considerably between individuals, it is probably best left to the reader to make his own decisions on the matter of original units of measurement and, if he so wishes, to ignore any conclusions suggested in the text regarding such systems.

5 The instruments

The next chapter comprises the instrument examples themselves, which are discussed individually with main drawing or plate, text, and supportive figures. They are preceded here, however, by a few paragraphs in explanation of drawing and analysis procedure, categorization, and criteria governing their selection.

The Drawings (Plates I–XXXI)

Faced with the problem of recording information from three-dimensional objects for two-dimensional geometrical analysis, the initial choice of medium lay between the use of photographic or drawing techniques. It was an easy choice, made easier by long familiarity with the drawing process, and an almost equally long personal record of photographic incompetence. But the real reason, apart from this quite valid practical one of controlled and relaxed examination, is the element of distortion which is introduced by a camera recording an image from a single viewpoint at varying distance from the different parts of the instrument. Added to this, there are very special problems to be overcome in photographing the rounded edges and modelled plates of instruments often covered by shiny varnish, as well as the practically insurmountable difficulty of controlling conditions of light and environment 'in the field', in such places as museum workrooms. By using drawing, however, I have been able to maintain a constant relationship of viewpoint to each *part* of the instrument, whether it be large or small, and have been able to control aspects of light and reflection to express the form and modelling of three dimensions within a rigidly accurate two-dimensional outline. In this way, too, the diversity of the conditions of light (and comfort!) under which these drawings were made has been minimized by adopting fairly standard light sources and the white void of the paper as background.

Drawing was necessarily restricted to parts of the instrument that were analysable and likely to yield information, which meant primarily body outlines and head-plan and/or elevation. Where, for instance, a peg-box was of extremely shallow curve, which would probably not be proportionally planned by radius, and exceptionally difficult to analyse if it were, its elevation has been omitted from the main drawing. In the case of instruments having a wall of ribs separating table from back, rib depth (a measurement constantly varying within each example, in a violin usually presenting the slightest of tapers toward the top block) would be recorded for later reference, but was never found to have any proportional significance. The measurement of the vault type of sound-box, found in members and relatives of the lute family, is discussed in the introduction to the lute family section.

The method of measurement finally adopted was an established one, consisting of making card-patterns covering the outlines (cut away in the centre, in the case of modelled or arched plates, to avoid distortion) on to which the contours were carefully drawn, symmetrical accuracy being maintained by linking the patterns. A 'tracing' method, linked with the main pattern, was used to record the sound-holes in an arched plate, their correct orientation being confirmed, as were all body and head outlines, by exhaustive multi-directional, perpendicular calliper checks. Accuracy was of the essence, there being no point in proceeding with analysis of a faulty drawing.

Musical instruments are another reflection, among human artefacts, of the deep-seated craving of man to create symmetries analogous to his own. Symmetry brings with it its own balance and harmony which, probably, we subconsciously recognize as being present in our own image, and therefore posing no visual disturbance or threat. Not all instruments, for practical reasons, *can* be symmetrical, but, wherever possible, symmetry dominates, even to the adoption, in many viols, violins, and like instruments, of the two-piece back, where a piece of timber with strong horizontal grain configuration, or 'flames', is split, turned inside out, and joined to present a perfect (or near-perfect) symmetry of pattern flaring outwards from the central seam.

The axial demarcation of a symmetrical design becomes in this way a powerful yet invisible agent, a line of duality as inscrutable as a mirror, a line denoting a plane, in which is seated the very spirit of the instrument, just as for Leonardo the human soul was situated within the axial plane of symmetry of the brain.

This particular design idiosyncracy proved to be extremely convenient in the compilation of the drawings, the vertical axis of symmetry suggesting itself as an ideal division in the graphic presentation of the duality of the instrument, as plastic reality and as geometric design. Where feasible, instruments are shown in the left-hand side of the main plates, with the customary fittings of bridge and tailpiece, any chin-rests being removed. Peg-shafts are indicated, but as original pegs rarely survive, and as their 'cylindrical' position is, by function, not fixed, the visually distracting peg-heads are not. Strings are also not drawn in (even where their original number and disposition remains), owing to the danger of visual confusion in a drawing where such linear forms perform a more important geometrical function. This, perhaps, will explain the physical impossibility, apparent in the drawings, of tables seemingly devoid of sound-boxes (the sound-holes are left white, rather than shadowed, for greater clarity of form) firmly fixed to necks, and bearing bridges and tailpieces secured 'in suspension' without the agency of strings.

Throughout the making of the drawings, the major criterion was that of visual clarity. An unforeseen pitfall, but one once identified soon rectified, was the remarkable degree to which humidity can affect the dimensions of paper, and therefore of recorded image.

The inevitable restrictions of format size may have caused some disorientation of scale in the main drawings (the plates), the images presented depicting instruments of overall lengths varying from approximately 500 mm to nearly 1300 mm. To provide a point of scale reference, a small, square-centimetre-based scale key is included in each plate, and is shown here actual size in Fig. 14.

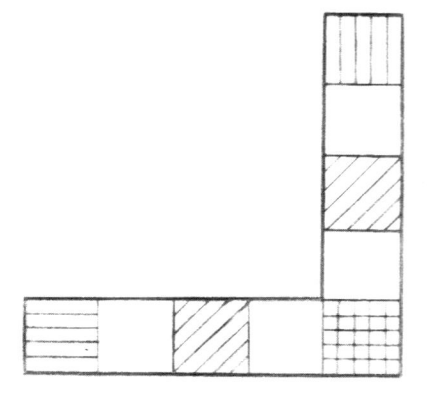

FIG. 14. Scale key (actual size)

The Analyses

Not surprisingly, the practical analysis of the instrument designs soon suggested the most suitable order and method for so doing and, although a universal approach to proportioning is certainly *not* attributable to the many luthiers whose work is here discussed, a universal investigative procedure did prove to be the most effective.

Having recorded the necessary outlines and checking measurements (and having rendered the left-hand side of the drawing), analysis was begun by first examining the overall measurements—body length, string length, upper-, middle-, and lower-bout widths, etc.—for proportional relationship; this would also entail estimating major ratios like the body-containing rectangle(s), and checking for possible grid-planning. Next, the body outline itself was broken down into its constituent single-radius arcs. The centres of these arcs were located by a simple device, made by engraving a series of concentric circles on a clear perspex sheet of suitable size, and drilling a small hole at their centre; this was laid against the contour in question and moved until the two curves coincided; the centre was then marked. In this manner, any multi-centred curve, or pseudo-ellipse, can be simply resolved into its component arcs. These separate vectors would be recorded, revealing any geometrical design processes such as grids, planning arcs or circles, vesicas, etc., while their arithmetical values, upon generation, might disclose the presence of a proportional scheme.

The whole procedure is a slow but not unexciting one, particularly when vectors derived by measurement from an instrument's geometry are arithmetically confirmed by calculation from its emerging system of proportion. Throughout the analyses, a general margin of error of 0.5 mm was employed, although where larger specimens exhibited measurements lying outside this tolerance, yet seemingly related by obvious intention to an overall scheme of proportions, they were so declared, together with the difference of their deviation.

In this way, the design make-up of each of thirty-three examples (thirty-one instruments and two instrument-drawings) was broken down into its component geometrical and proportional processes. To facilitate a general view of this necessarily lengthy exposition, a summary chart of the combined analyses follows the instruments themselves; it is fully explained then, but makes use of certain symbols to represent proportional and geometrical findings, and, as these are included as an additional summary in the individual instrument texts, it would be as well to give explanation of them here.

In order, they follow, more or less, the investigative procedure outlined above. There are thirteen symbols, which will fall into four main categories:

(i) significant linear and rectilinear ratios;

(ii) arc-based geometries;

(iii) proportional systems:
   (*a*) rational;
   (*b*) irrational;

(iv) spiral geometry of head.

These are:

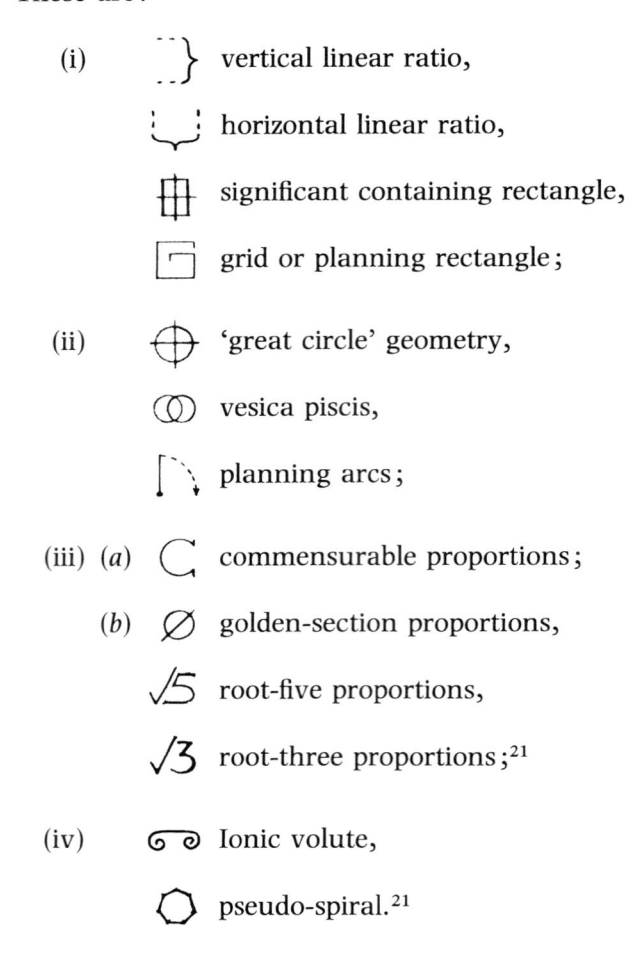

(i) ⟩ vertical linear ratio,

⌣ horizontal linear ratio,

⊞ significant containing rectangle,

▢ grid or planning rectangle;

(ii) ⊕ 'great circle' geometry,

◉ vesica piscis,

⌐ planning arcs;

(iii) (a) C commensurable proportions;

(b) ∅ golden-section proportions,

$\sqrt{5}$ root-five proportions,

$\sqrt{3}$ root-three proportions;[21]

(iv) ෆ Ionic volute,

⬡ pseudo-spiral.[21]

The use of dotted parentheses around a symbol indicates that, although present, the particular geometrical or proportional device is not of major significance within the scheme.

Categorization

The instruments, which technically speaking are all chordophones, are first simply organized into two groups—bowed and plucked—then subdivided into families following a generally accepted organological pecking order, that is:

Bowed
    (i) Viols (Exx. I–VI)
    (ii) Liras da Braccio (Exx. VII–IX)
    (iii) Violins (Viola, Violoncello) (Exx. X–XV)
    (iv) Violas d'Amore (Exx. XVI–XVII)
    (v) Kits or Pochettes (Exx. XVIII–XIX)

Plucked
    (vi) Lutes (Exx. XX–XXV)
    (vii) Mandore and Mandolines (Exx. XXVI–XXVIII)
    (viii) Citterns (Exx. XXIX–XXX)
    (ix) Guitars (Exx. XXXI–XXXIII)

The instruments are arranged chronologically within each section.
    Although the subtitle claims this to be a study of bowed and plucked

---

[21] Present in only one application.

string instruments, the reader may have noticed the absence of one or two stringed-instrument types covered by the above headings. This is because such instruments either were considered too difficult to analyse (as in the case of the harp, which, like the keyboard instruments and (dare I include?) the hurdy-gurdy, belongs to different traditions of design and manufacture from the one I hope to explore), or were just of too formidable a scale, or too delicate construction, for safe and/or practical handling and drawing (in which category I have had to place the violone, double-bass, and, regrettably, the baryton), or they were musicological variants of no great design significance or body-outline variance (e.g. the colascione), or quite simply are instruments which survive in only one example, which itself may not be typical (such as the orpharion and vihuela). Frequently far more than just one of these reservations have applied to an individual category, in addition to a further problem which, of course, has affected my selection of examples in all categories: that of accessibility.

Selection of Examples

For the luthier, the designing of a musical instrument is only part, though undeniably a vital part, of the complex task of actually producing enough instruments to keep himself. A design is conceived and drawn, and working patterns and moulds are made from it, to produce, if the design is successful, numerous versions, each of which will have, in addition to the original matter of the archetypal design, an individual spirit of its own, created by the spontaneous and unique fusion of two variables: the particular characteristics of the material and the particular mood of the maker. Depending on the working methods and the nature of the individual maker, these variables can evolve considerably away from the original design, leading to the formation of 'new' archetypes, or they can remain fairly static, until the model itself is superseded *in toto*.

Whether or not a design is given opportunity to evolve, our chief concern must be with the luthier's conceptual design-thinking, and that is going to be at its purest, or most evident, in an instrument nearer to the 'archetype'—a point confirmed by the analysis of many of the instruments which follow.

The selection of suitable examples has therefore been influenced by the following considerations:

(i) to cover as wide a field of the multifarious 'classic' body outlines as possible;

(ii) to study the earliest suitable form of each type or variant, in an approach to its archetype;

(iii) to cover as wide a geographical spread as permitted by (i) and (ii), bearing in mind that many instruments had either their origins or best manufacture in Italy, which is consequently well represented;

(iv) to offer as wide a chronological spread as (ii) allowed within the chosen period;[22]

(v) to include the work of renowned and influential luthiers, especially where they are associated with a particular form or variant;

(vi) to represent as many different pitch-size members within each 'family' of instruments as possible;

(vii) to select only examples in original constructional condition, although, where necessity dictates, to include those with known minor alteration to be identified and explained in the text.

[22] Very few European stringed instruments survive from before the date of our earliest examples—*c*.1550 (Exx. I and XXI)—although a design for a lute (*c*.1460) (Ex. XX) does. From the sixteenth century to the end of the eighteenth (our last examples are from the 1750s and '60s), the working/thinking processes of the luthier probably did not alter a great deal. The enormous social and technological turbulence which occurred at the end of this period, however, could be said to mark the end of a certain tradition of lutherie, and the beginning of a familiar division into either 'studio-' or factory-based manufacture, each governed by its own methodology.

6 Analysis of instrument examples

VIOLS

It is generally accepted that the viol family, as we know it, first appeared on the musical scene in the latter half of the fifteenth century, and, together with its plucked counterparts, the lutes, thereafter maintained a considerable influence on musical thought over an extensive period of time. Indeed, from their first introduction, viols, in one form or another, have been actively making music—as viols, until about the third quarter of the eighteenth century, and, if you accept the double-bass within the viol genealogy (a view which has been challenged), then the instrument's record of service could be said to be unbroken.

Early examples come mostly from Italy, and the three Italian viols which are discussed in detail below immediately illustrate the surprising variety of shape and form that marked the early development of the instrument, a characteristic which no doubt led to Gerald Hayes's oft-quoted description of the viol as 'a very Proteus among instruments'.[23]

Ex. I
Figs. 15–18, Pl. I

VIOL, BASS. ITALY, BRESCIA, c.1550
PELEGRINO DI ZANETTO
MUSÉE DU CONSERVATOIRE ROYAL DE MUSIQUE, BRUSSELS
Acc. No.: not known

The first of the six viols examined is a bass, of the cornerless, guitar-shaped, *fiedel* form with sloping shoulders and *alla gobba* back (literally 'hunchback', referring to the inward slope of the upper portion of the back). Despite this misleading description of 'sloping shoulders' and 'hunchback', the instrument is of handsome aspect, and now forms part of the extensive collection of the Conservatoire Royal de Musique in Brussels. It was made in Brescia by Pelegrino di Zanetto da Michelis (1520–?) and probably dates from around 1550; the original label, sadly, has been lost, although a photograph of it does survive, which I have been able to reproduce here (Fig. 15).

Its geometry, an analysis of which follows, reveals commensurable vectors governing the arc radii of the body outline, the string length, and bridge and nut positions. The value of the common factor, the unit u, is calculated as 32.75 mm, an amount which does not appear to conform, in either whole or simple part, to any likely system of measurement then used. This could be due either to a straightforward irrationality of the designer, or to the enlargement of a previously designed tenor or treble viol, the relative pitch, or the string length, itself generating the unit of commensurable proportion used in the rest of the instrument's design.

FIG. 15. Photograph of label, now missing, from Zanetto bass viol (Ex. I)

[23] This delightful mythological analogy seems first to have been applied to a keyboard instrument offering plucked string, organ, and regal timbres listed in the inventory (1664) of the collection of Manfredo Settala, where it is described, 'ne proteus inter instrumenta desit'.

ANALYSIS OF INSTRUMENT EXAMPLES

The overall proportions are examined in Fig. 16. All the brackets are multiples of the basic unit u. The string length AC is 655 mm or $20u$; divided in half (at the octave), it coincides with the top of the body, B, thus allowing an octave fret to be tied around the finger-board, which at this point leaves the support of the neck. BD, the body length, is in fact a little (3.5 mm) over $19u$,[24] and the distance from bridge-line, C, to tail, D, is therefore $19u - 10u$, or $9u$ (295 mm). The widths of upper and lower bouts are also commensurable: TT' measures 262 mm ($8u$), while QQ' is 327.5 mm ($10u$); they are therefore in 4 : 5 ratio.

No proportional significance was demonstrated in either the positioning of the fold in the instrument's back, or the depth (slightly varying) of the instrument's ribs.[25] The analysis of the body outline can be seen in Fig. 17. For the sake of clarity, only the right side of the symmetrical plan is discussed; this will be the usual procedure for all the following instrument analyses, and renders the dissection of the main instrument-drawing, through the small textual figures, more comprehensible.

The outline curves are initiated in Fig. 17 by arc $G'H'$, centred at I', radius measured as 33 mm. It can be assumed that this must be the common unit u (32.75 mm), which here makes its only appearance as a single factor. This small arc is then joined by straight line $H'J'$ to the main upper-bout arc $J'L'$ whose centre, K, lies on the centre line (BD). It is here that the true beauty of economy of the outline starts to become apparent, for the radius of this arc, 131 mm or $4u$, is common to upper, middle, and lower bouts. Thus the upper bouts are joined by the short straight line $L'M'$ to middle-bout arc $M'O'$, centre N', whose radius, as we have already mentioned, is $4u$, or 131 mm. The counter-curve of the lower bouts is directly connected to the arc of the middle bouts at O', arc $O'Q'$ being centred at P, on the horizontal QQ', the level of greatest width indicated in Fig. 16. The radius of this arc is 196.5 mm, or $6u$. The curve is continued by arc $Q'R'$, centre P' (the counterpart of P, PP' thus being $2u$ in length) and of the common bout-arc radius, 131 mm ($4u$). The lower bouts are completed by arc $R'D$,[26] centre C on the centre line, the bridge position. The radius, 295 mm, is equal to $9u$, and therefore gives a lower-bout arc-radius ratio sequence of 6 : 4 : 9.

The dashed circle, whose centre on the centre line is at F, passes through the four centrings of the f-holes. Its radius, 98 mm, equals $3u$. (3×32.75 mm actually equals 98.25 mm. In practice, however, anything less than 0.5 mm is scarcely measurable; any difference of 0.5 mm or less will therefore be regarded as acceptable margin of error.)

The arcs employed in the curves of the peg-box are, perhaps, not quite as carefully considered. The head is of slightly unexpected design—although thoroughly Brescian in character. It lacks a heel, and the abutment of head and neck is consequently somewhat weak, belying the otherwise decisive vigour and clear design of the head itself. The scroll is very well conceived, but deeply cut—so deep, in fact, that its resolution with the flat cheek of the peg-box relies not on the gentle 'ironing out' of the angled pitch of the scroll into the planes of the cheek, as we find in the standard head of the violin family, but rather on a frank contrast between the planes of the peg-box and those of the scroll, which meet in an incised, curved V, terminating at point V in Fig. 18. Indeed, this solution involves a nice adaptation of the classical Ionic volute—as we shall see, the most commonly used spiral for the design of scroll-heads.[27] The outer whorl of this spiral corresponds to the edge of the scroll (Fig. 18) from the eye,[28]

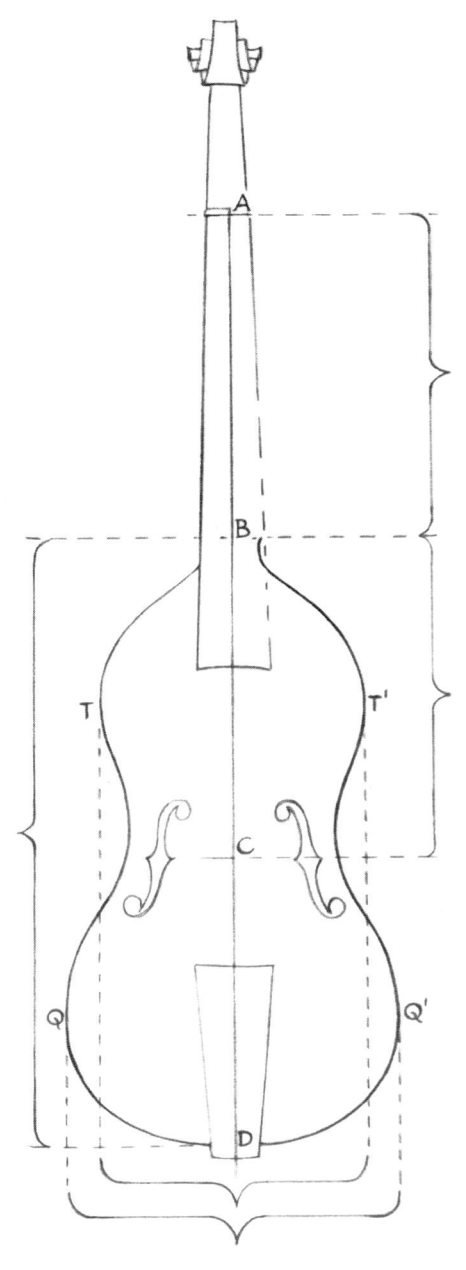

Fig. 16

---

[24] Although much in excess of the 0.5 mm margin of error, or difference, which will generally be adhered to in this study, the difference here was proportionally small enough (0.56 per cent) to mention the $19u$ division as the most likely rationalization of body length, particularly in view of the rest of the instrument's proportional scheme.

[25] As we have said, this last seems to be a factor common to all the viols and violins subsequently analysed.

[26] In later analyses the equivalent arc is referred to as the 'arc of origin' of the lower bouts.

[27] For geometrical construction, see p. 21 above.

[28] Confusingly also called the 'ear' of the scroll.

FIG. 17

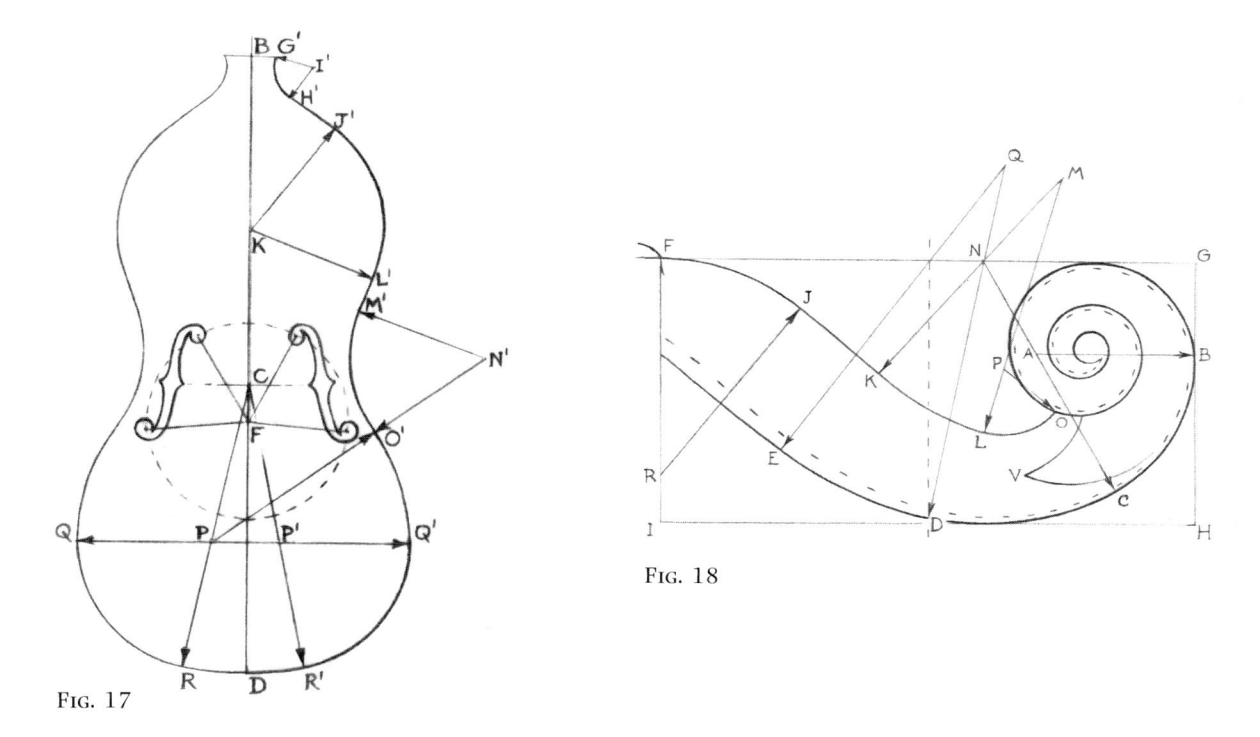

FIG. 18

unfolding to point B. In this head, however, the inner whorl, which, although staying closer to the outer line than in the classical example, corresponds to it, and forms the bevelled edge, continuing beyond point B, not deviating from the spiral, but ceasing at point V. The important outer edge is continued from point B by arc BC, centre A, radius 56 mm, which, like some of the other vectors in the peg-box, was not proportionally significant. The curve is continued by arc CD, centre N, on line FNG of the containing rectangle FGHI, its radius therefore equal to this rectangle's short side, i.e. 95 mm. With a long side of 190 mm and a short side of 95 mm, FGHI is a $\sqrt{4}$ rectangle, or double square. Its values, however, do not individually relate to the main scheme. The curve of the peg-box underside is continued by arc DE, centre Q, radius 131 mm; this, of course, is a vector common to the main commensurable scheme, although its isolated appearance in the head is probably a coincidence. E is extended by a straight line until the counter-curve of the head/neck join is met. The top curve of the peg-box is initiated by arc FJ, centre R (on line FRI of head-containing rectangle FGHI); its radius is 78 mm. The straight line JK joins this arc to arc KL, centre M, radius 95 mm (equal to FI and to the radius of arc CD, whose centre, N, lies on radius KM). The curve is completed by arc LO, centre P, radius 24 mm, and concludes the analysis of this bass viol by Pelegrino di Zanetto.

PLATE I

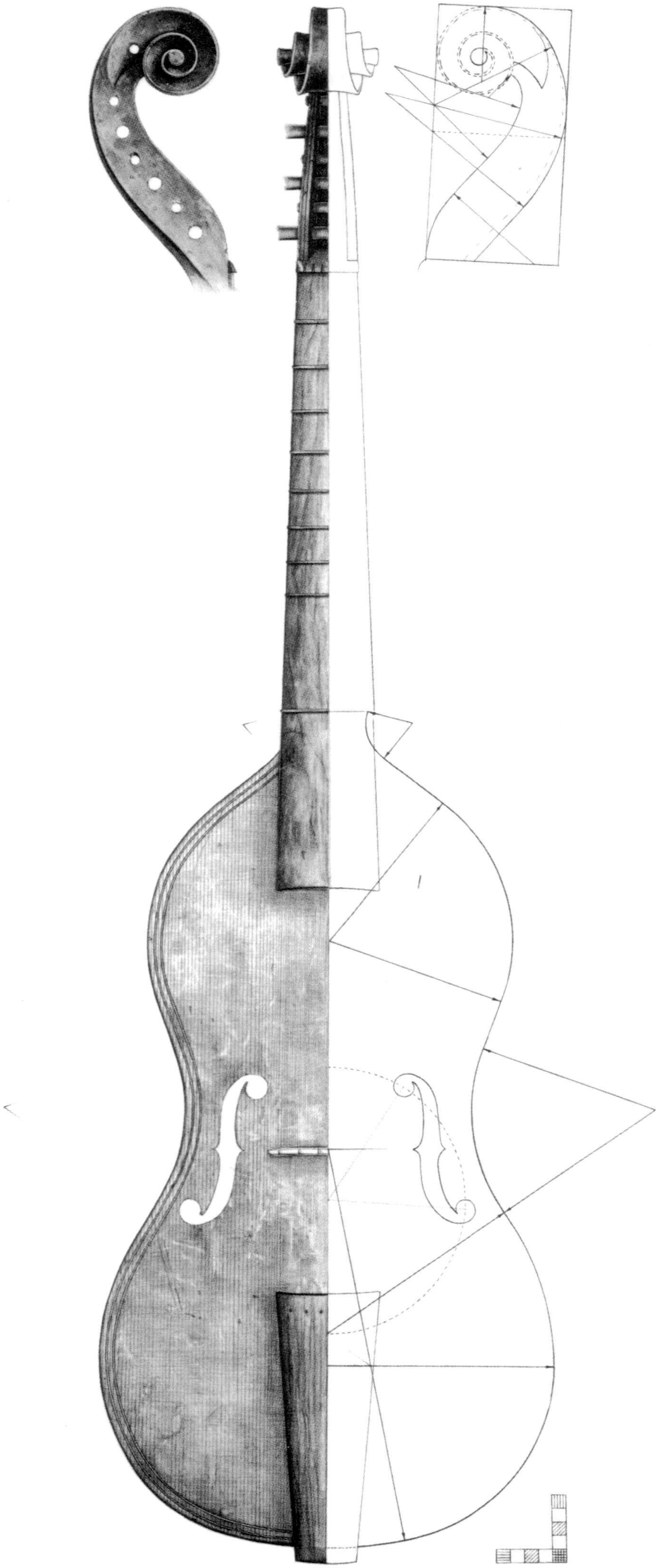

Ex. II
Figs. 19–22, Pl. II

VIOL, TREBLE. ITALY, VENICE, c.1575
GIOVANNI MARIA DA BRESCIA
HILL COLLECTION, ASHMOLEAN MUSEUM, OXFORD
Acc. No.: 1

This treble viol, forming part of the Hill Collection of instruments at the Ashmolean Museum, is of the early, cornerless, *fiedel* variety with 'squared' shoulders. It was most probably made in Venice by Giovanni Maria of Brescia around 1575, and not, as previously stated by Boyden, between 1520 and 1525.[29] Nevertheless it is one of the earliest treble viols to survive. An identical copy of this instrument by the luthier Leandro Bisiach, a former owner, can be found in the collection at the Castello Sforzesco in Milan, differing only in details of fittings.

The Ashmolean viol is fully described in the Boyden catalogue, although the measurements given are, for our purpose, grossly misleading, in that they include the curvature of modelled plates, and in this particular example a considerable error was made in the measurement of the middle bouts, which are given some 8 mm short.

Analysis of this treble revealed a very beautiful geometry, governed by an arithmetic series relating to $\sqrt{5}$ symmetry. The terms in this series express the ratios of the radii of the arcs used in the design of the outline. I shall call the terms, in ascending order of value, a, b, c, d, and e, where $a = 55$ mm, $b = 72$ mm, $c = 89$ mm, $d = 106$ mm, and $e = 123$ mm, and the unit of difference between each, u, $= 17$ mm. Their relationships and their $\sqrt{5}$ partiality are clearly shown in the following table:

	Radii in whole-no. mm
Extremes of series	$\dfrac{e}{a} = \dfrac{123}{55} = 2.236 = \sqrt{5}$
Divisions of terms by unit	$\dfrac{a}{u} = \dfrac{55}{17} = 3.23(5) = \sqrt{5}+1$
	$\dfrac{b}{u} = \dfrac{72}{17} = 4.23(5) = \sqrt{5}+2$
	$\dfrac{c}{u} = \dfrac{89}{17} = 5.23(5) = \sqrt{5}+3$
	$\dfrac{d}{u} = \dfrac{106}{17} = 6.23(5) = \sqrt{5}+4$
	$\dfrac{e}{u} = \dfrac{123}{17} = 7.23(5) = \sqrt{5}+5$

The close sympathy that $\sqrt{5}$ symmetry has with the golden proportion (ϕ) can be shown when the third term is divided by the first:

$$\frac{c}{a} = \left(\frac{89}{55}\right) = 1.618 \ (\phi).$$

Before demonstrating the use of these arithmetically proportioned radii in the instrument, it should be noted that the 'unit of difference', u ($= 17$ mm),[30] divides the body length by 21, the string length by 18.5, the head length by 7, and the head 'depth' (in Fig. 22, GH) by 3.

[29] Giovanni Maria was still living in Venice in 1591, as his witnessing to a document lately discovered in Venetian archives testifies.

[30] 17 mm approximately equals $\frac{1}{20}$ Venetian foot.

The overall proportions of length and width are shown in Fig. 19. Here the head length, EA, of 7u can be seen to divide the body length, BD, by 3. This length (BD = 356 mm) is twice the upper-bout width XX' (178 mm), so that rectangle QRST is a double square, or $\sqrt{4}$ figure. The middle- and lower-bout widths are also in whole-number relationship:

$$\frac{ZZ'}{YY'} = \frac{216 \text{ mm}}{144 \text{ mm}} = 1.5 = 2:3.$$

The body-outline geometry is drawn here in Fig. 20, where we see a most beautiful scheme. Here, for the first time, is what we shall call a 'great circle' geometry. The drawing is largely self-explanatory; the outline is constructed inside a circumscribed circle, which forms part of the outline (its centre, C, being also at the centre of the body-plane, BD) and which, in addition, acts as a planning circle for certain arc centres. The Maria scheme is further enriched by the use of a vesica piscis arrangement which combines with the great circle to determine the lower-bout configuration. The vesica piscis emerges as one of the most important, and constantly recurring, planning devices employed in musical-instrument design, as is revealed by the geometrical analysis of many of the following examples, and as such it has, of course, been examined in closer detail in an earlier chapter (p. 18) of this study.

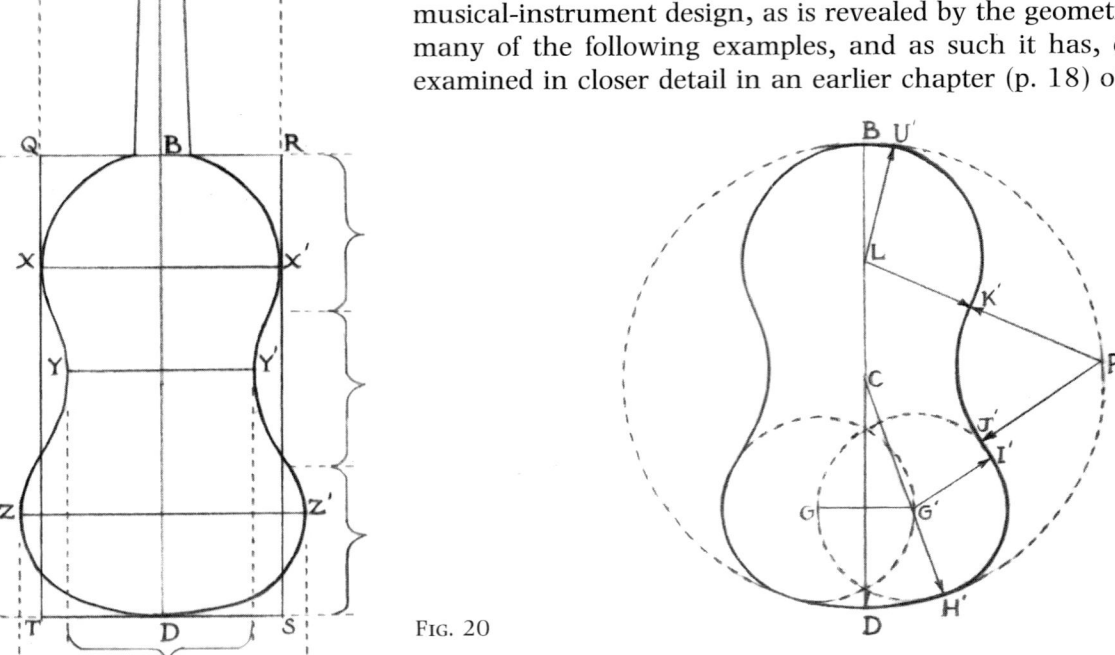

FIG. 19

FIG. 20

To return to the Maria viol and the outline drawn in Fig. 20: the arc of origin DH', as we have seen, forms part of the great circle centred at C; its radius is therefore 178 mm, which we can also express as 2 × 89 mm, or 2c, that is, $2u(\sqrt{5}+3)$, where $\sqrt{5}$ represents the ratio of the extremes of the arithmetic series: 123 mm and 55 mm (e/a). The curve is continued by an arc, H'I', forming part of the vesica piscis arrangement, centred at G and G'. Its radius, which is therefore one-third of the lower-bout width, measures 72 mm—factor b in the five-term series. A short straight line, I'J', connects lower to middle bouts (as a similar line joined the middle- and upper-bout curvature of the Zanetto viol), their curve delineated by arc J'K', centre P' on the great circle, and of radius 106 mm, or $d\ (u[\sqrt{5}+4])$.

The upper-bout section is formed by one sweeping arc, K'U', centred at L on the centre line, its radius measuring 89 mm, or $c\ (u[\sqrt{5}+3])$.

Fig. 21 gives the curves and positioning of the C-holes. As we have seen, the arc radius d that gave the middle-bout curve was centred at point P' on the great circle; a line drawn from this point through the notches of the C's and meeting the centre line at F forms the axis of the C-hole. C-hole centring is achieved by means of a circle, centre C, radius 72 mm (b), which touches the inner curve of the middle bouts and pierces the lower centring, and also by means of an intersecting arc, centre P', and radius 123 mm, or $e\,(u[\sqrt{5}+5])$. The main inner and outer curves of the C-holes themselves are formed by arcs whose centres, V' and W', lie on the FP' axis and whose principal radii measure 55 mm (a) and 72 mm (b) respectively.

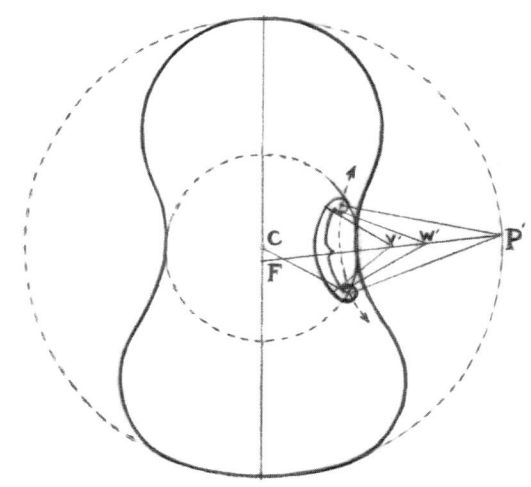

Fig. 21

At first sight, the head of this viol, shown in outline elevation in Fig. 22, is perhaps a little disappointing, particularly to eyes more accustomed to the exquisitely conceived and executed scrolls of the later Cremonese school of violin-making. Indeed, following the bold three-dimensionality of the Zanetto's scroll, the design of the 'Venetian head', found here and in the following example, appears to be flat and lifeless. Seen to advantage only from the side, the Ionic spiral of the scroll is carved in relief into the flat plane of the cheeks (see main drawing). This type of head is, of course, economical in both material and making-time.

Despite these initial reservations, which in any case should be thought of as generic idiosyncrasies, the analysis of the head-design of the Maria viol proved to be quite rewarding.

The arcs of the peg-box are given in Fig. 22, where the elevation is shown superimposed with its containing grid of 3×7 squares of side 17 mm, which, as the reader will recall, was the crucial 'unit of difference', u, between the important vectors of the body geometry. The arc BC, centre A, moves out from the Ionic spiral and is continued by arc CD, centre N, radius 85 mm, or 5 units of 17 mm. The lower peg-box curve is completed by counter-curve arc DE, centre P, radius 59.5 mm, $3\tfrac{1}{2}$ units of 17 mm. The upper peg-box curve is initiated by arc FJ, centre O (on FI produced), radius 102 mm, or 6 units of 17 mm. A straight line, JK, links this arc with final arc KL, centre M, radius 51 mm, or 3 units of 17 mm.

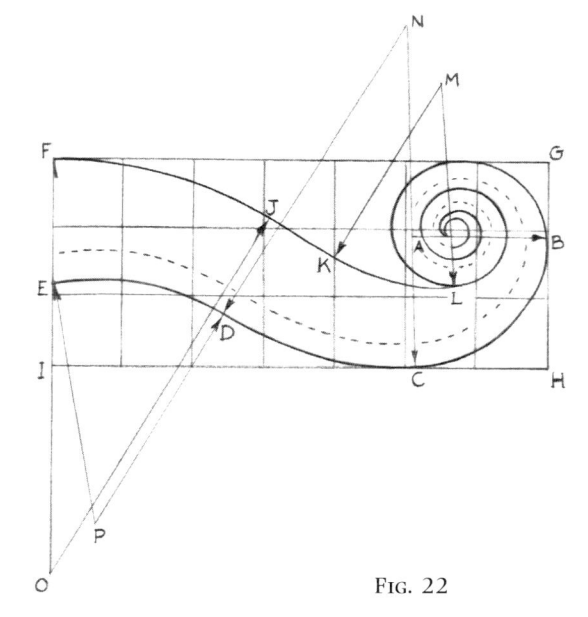

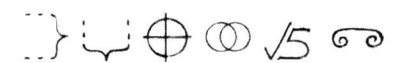

Fig. 22

Plate II

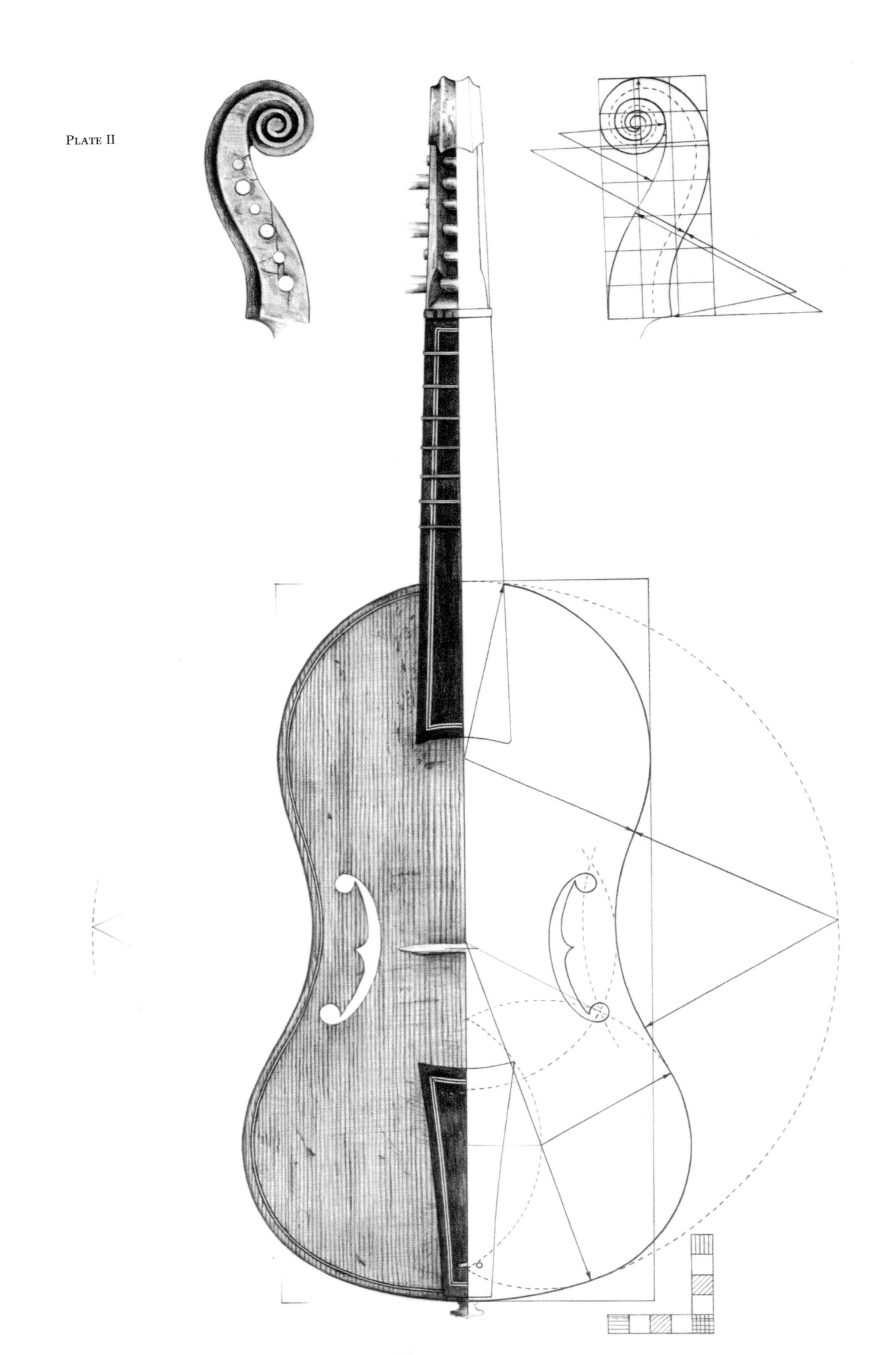

Ex. III
Figs. 23–29, Pl. III

VIOL, BASS. ITALY, VENICE, c.1590
BATTISTA CICILIANO
MUSÉE DU CONSERVATOIRE ROYAL DE MUSIQUE, BRUSSELS
Acc. No.: 1426

The Ciciliano[31] family were luthiers working in Venice throughout the sixteenth and seventeenth centuries, one of those Italian family dynasties whose many members, favouring the same few forenames, cause such confusion to historians. As we shall see later, it is interesting to note that a member of the Ciciliano family, one Gioanbattista, is mentioned by Silvestro Ganassi dal Fontego in his important treatise on the viol, *Regola Rubertina*, published in Venice in 1543.

The Ciciliano we are meeting here is Battista, as the label of this instrument, with its curious abbreviations, tells us: 'Batista fiel d'Ant⁰ Cicilian in Vª.'

The instrument, which dates from the last quarter of the sixteenth century, is a bass viol, now part of the collection at the Brussels Conservatoire Museum. It is of the early, four-cornered, sloping-shoulder variety. Perhaps not the most elegant of designs, with its disharmonious curves, ill-conceived areas, and disturbing imbalance between front and back plate,[32] its true significance lies in its position in the evolution of viol design, bearing as it does so many 'classic' features, albeit somewhat gracelessly. I should stress that these aesthetic defects are applicable to this variant form in general, and not only to this particular example, which, for all this, does possess a certain vigorous charm of its own.

The characteristic Renaissance preference for rational commensurable ratios is revealed in the instrument's geometrical scheme, where the majority of the controlling vectors are reduced to simple multiples of a basic unit. The unit itself is of great interest in that it would appear to originate in Brunswick inches, despite the fact that the instrument is from the Venetian school of making, and that its maker, Battista Ciciliano, like his father Antonio, worked in Venice, a centre with its own system of measurement unrelated to the Brunswick unit.

This unit of measurement, used to bring the design-vectors into commensurability, consists of $2\frac{1}{2}$ Brunswick inches (59.45 mm, taken here as 59.5 mm). As will be seen by the later examples discussed in this study, this desire for rational, whole-number relationships in design-vectors seems to be as much a guiding principle for the early luthier as it was for the architect, indeed, the 'nodal point of Renaissance aesthetics'.[33]

The metaphysical importance of this system lay in its analogizing visual proportions, particularly the relationships of the small integers (such as 1 : 2, 2 : 3, 3 : 4, 1 : 4, etc.) with the audible proportions of musical sound. (It was a Pythagorean revelation that the basic musical consonances are defined by small whole-number ratios.) The ultimate aim was not the transfiguration of the concrete visual arts by abstract music, but rather a deeper search for a cosmic order of mathematics, as reflected in all phenomena of beauty, giving measure, regulation, and harmony to all creation. The resulting proportions were used extensively by Renaissance artists and were often referred to by them in classical musical terms—an

---

[31] Sometimes given as Siciliano.
[32] The upper part of the back is wider than the table, causing a slight, and rather unaesthetic, slope of the upper ribs towards the front.
[33] R. Wittkower, *Architects' Year Book*, v (London, 1953).

FIG. 23. Fret-positioning and the musical proportions, Silvestro Ganassi, *Regola Rubertina*, 1543

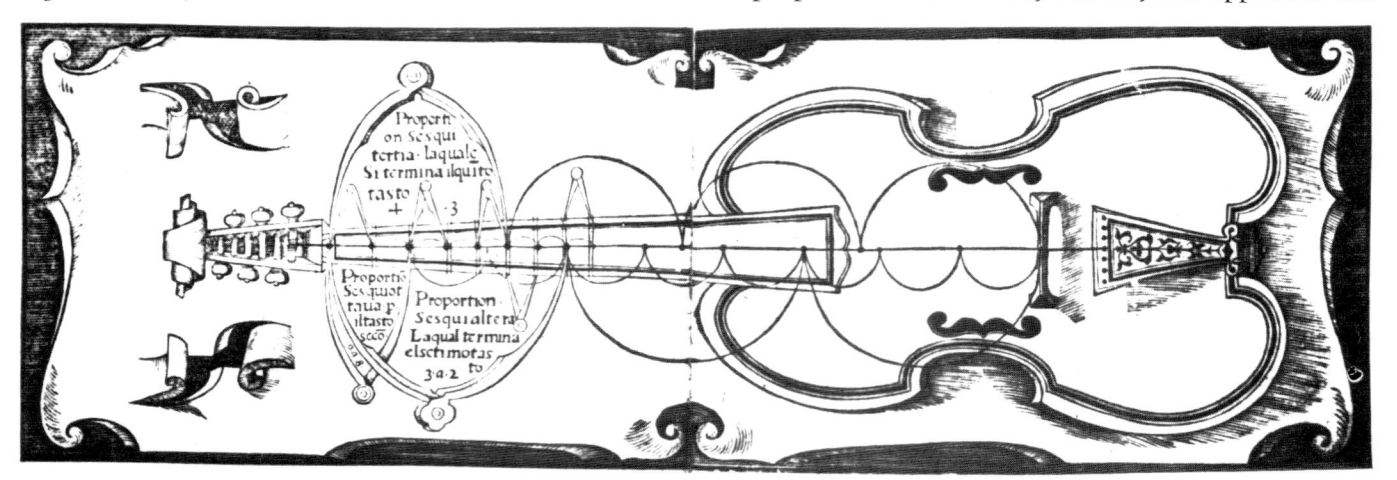

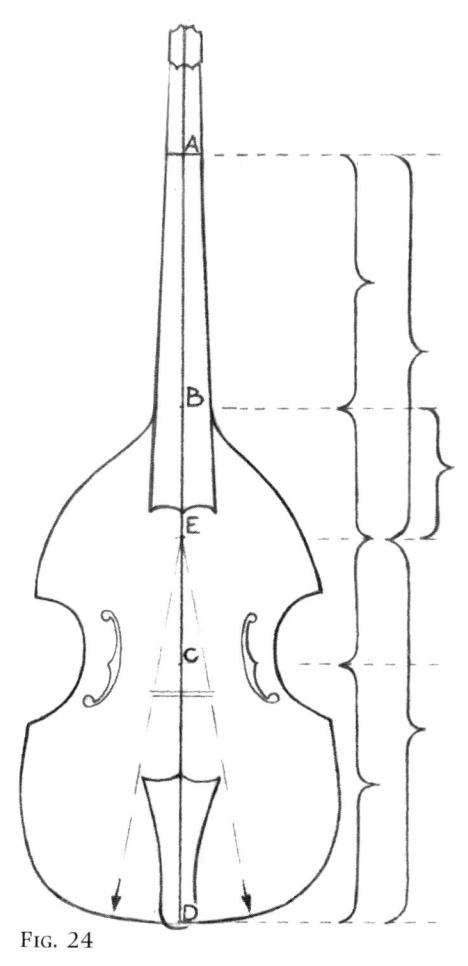

algebraic convenience with perhaps more metaphysical than acoustical relevance.

This has been discussed here because small whole-number ratios do occur in the main proportions of length of this early viol, although, of course, we have no way of knowing if its designer thought of them in musico-proportional terms. There is one piece of 'evidence', however, which suggests he may at least have been acquainted with the musical significance of these ratios. This is the Ganassi treatise on viol-playing, published in Venice in 1543, which I mentioned earlier (p. 39).

This important treatise bears a most interesting plate (Fig. 23) in which a few of the 'musical' proportions are named, defined, and applied to the string length of a viol, presumably for the regulation of the frets. It is also this treatise which mentions a member of this maker's family—Gioanbattista Ciciliano—so even as a piece of family history, not to mention sound commercial propaganda, this work, with its incidental proportional knowledge, was probably quite familiar to our designer. In the large drawing, I have consequently estimated the position of the bridge according to that indicated by Ganassi. This is lower than later advised by Christopher Simpson for the classical viol, but owing to the relative position of the middle bouts, the lower siting of the contemporary Ganassi would be more convenient and more likely from the point of view of bowing. Moreover, this bridge position yields some convincing whole-number (in Brunswick inches) magnitudes for both string length (642 mm = 27 Br. in.) and fret positions, where the second fret, which is the tone ('9 a 8', *sesquioctava*), is 71.3 mm (3 Br. in.), the fifth fret, which is the interval of a fourth ('4 a 3', *sesquitertia*), is 160.5 mm (6¾ Br. in.), and the seventh fret, which gives a musical fifth ('3 a 2', *sesquialtera*), is 214 mm (9 Br. in.).

It should be stated, however, that the use of whole-number ratios in a design as relatively complex as a musical instrument cannot possibly have the same visual immediacy that they would retain in the straight-line plane and simple volume experience of Renaissance architecture, where their use remains more evident.

Fig. 24 shows the basic proportions of length of the Ciciliano viol; it is these ratios which could be described as 'musical' in a Pythagoreo-Platonic sense. For the sake of demonstration, their musical nomenclature is here bracketed with them.

AD, nut to button, measures 892.5 mm, which is 15 units of 2½ Br. in. (59.5 mm). This is divided into 3 equal 5-unit parts, *AB*, *BC*, and *CD*. The

FIG. 24

ratio of neck- to body-length, $AB:BD$, is therefore $1:2$ (diapason or octave); similarly, the ratio of the radius of the arc of origin of the lower bouts, ED, $7\frac{1}{2}$ units, to overall length AD, 15 units, is also $1:2$ (diapason), whereas the same vector ED, $7\frac{1}{2}$ units, to body length BD, 10 units, is ratio $3:4$ (diatessaron or fourth—the *sesquitertia* proportion).

The difficulties of a 'musical' interpretation of proportion in musical-instrument design now become apparent within this analysis. To begin with, the concept of ratio, as I mentioned earlier, cannot have the same relevance here as it has for the architect who, at this time, was dealing primarily with the distribution and apportionment of static rectangles, which by definition are ratios in themselves. Conversely, the instrument-designer was dealing principally with the disposition of arcs, which, having a single vector of radius, have no such built-in relationship of ratio.

The point of reference in this commensurably proportioned design, as much as in the incommensurably proportioned instruments, inevitably becomes the smallest common factor. Here it is u, the unit of $2\frac{1}{2}$ Br. in.; in some later instruments it is ϕ, the smallest term of a golden-section series. All greater terms must then be discussed as generations of this 'mustard seed'.

To return to the Ciciliano analysis: the arc of origin was shown in Fig. 24 and its relationship with the overall proportions of length discussed in 'musical' terms. It is shown again in Fig. 25 as an arc HDH', radius $7\frac{1}{2}u$, centre E. It is continued by arc $H'I'$ (and arc HI) which is part of a vesica piscis arrangement centred at G and G'. This figure is itself a rational, commensurable one, containing the ratio $1:3$. The radius of the circles reveals the first of the minor inaccuracies of the instrument's mathematics, their radius being just over 2 mm short of $2u$.[34] This arc is continued by arc $I'J'$, centred outside the outline at S. It is of radius 368 mm, which is more than $6u$ (357 mm) but equal to a ϕ division of the overall body length, i.e. $\dfrac{10u}{\phi} = \dfrac{595 \text{ mm}}{1.618} = 367.7$ mm. This ϕ value may or may not be a coincidence—at any rate, it is the only appearance of the incommensurable golden section in the scheme of this viol.

An important property of these arcs, $J'I'$ and JI, is that, when produced from the lower corners J' and J, they cross on the centre line at point E, the centre of arc of origin HDH', and half division of AD (nut to button, see Fig. 24). This is the position occupied by a rose in many viol designs.

A secondary vesica piscis can be drawn (Fig. 26) across the middle bouts on the centre crossing, piercing the four corners L, L', J, and J', the centre of the two circles positioned where the backs of the C-holes cross the horizontal centre line. Point N' on the right-hand vesica circle, and N on the left-hand circle, are the centres for the main arcs of the simple two-arc middle bouts. On the right, this main arc is $J'K'$ and its radius is $1\frac{1}{3}u$. The remaining middle-bout arc $K'L'$ is centred at M' (on $K'N'$) and is the only occurrence, in this design, of the unit u alone. A circle, centre C, the centre of the model, and of radius $3u$, can be drawn, which, like the second vesica piscis, pierces the four corners of the instrument. The main curve of the C-holes is an arc centred at O', and of radius $1\frac{1}{2}u$.

The geometric construction of the upper bouts is very beautiful: the main vector, $4u$, is an important measurement, as we shall see. Here, Fig. 27, it forms the radius, VP', of the main arc $L'P'$, with its centre at the opposing upper C-hole centring (in Fig. 27, point V) and passing through key point E, on the centre line. The counter-curve, $P'Q'$, is centred at R',

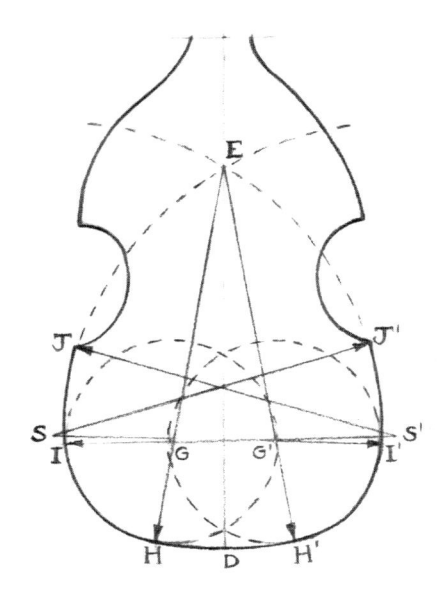

Fig. 25

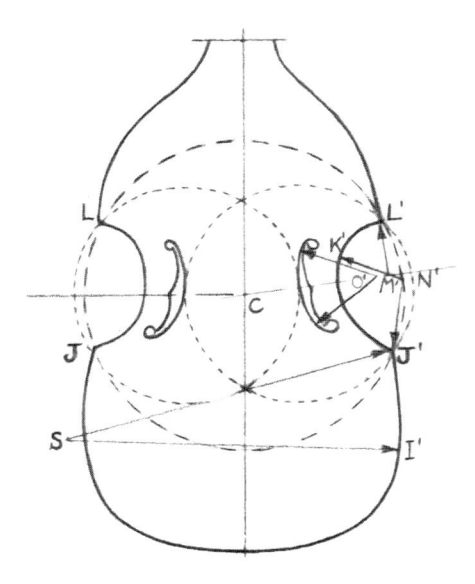

Fig. 26

[34] Although, as we have said, the general tolerance of inaccuracy here is 0.5 mm, this instrument is large, and not always carefully worked. It may well have been 'expanded' from a smaller design, thus magnifying an original error.

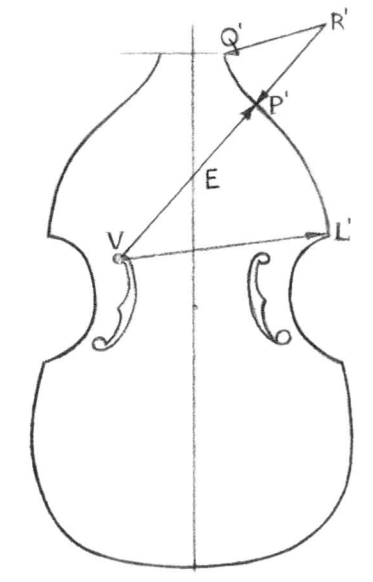

FIG. 27

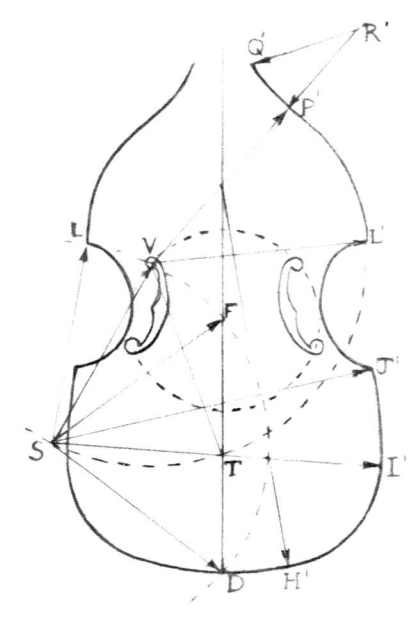

FIG. 28

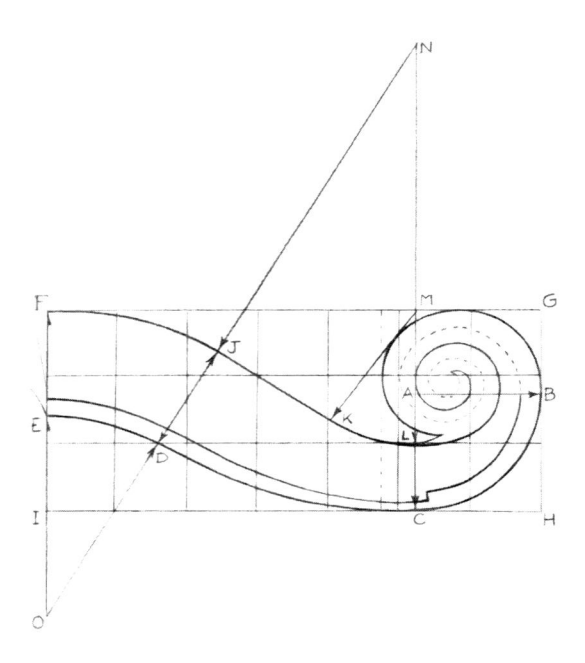

FIG. 29

and is of radius $2u$, which is, of course, half that of the main $4u$ upper-bout arc.

The geometrical importance of this $4u$ vector (238 mm, or 10 Br. in.) is shown in Fig. 28 where the main upper-bout arc $P'L'$ is produced, crossing the centre line at point T, the coincident crossing of radius $I'S$ (and IS') and passing through its centre point S. This point S can then be taken as the centre of a hypothetical arc, radius $4u$, which pierces the upper corner L, the upper C-hole centring V, the centre F on the centre line of a circle piercing the four C-hole centrings, and finally through D, the base-point of the model.

The head of the instrument is similar in form, and remarkably similar in geometry, to that of the preceding viol. It, too, is of typical Venetian form, with its spiral, again that of the classic Ionic volute, carved in relief into the extended plane of the cheek. Here, however, the vectors of the peg-box arcs, and indeed the overall proportions, bear no direct link with the rest of the instrument's scheme, the unit, u, making no appearance.

The head is, however, most definitely laid out in Brunswick inches. Like that of the Maria viol (Ex. II), the head of this instrument fits exactly into a 3×7 grid rectangle, and, in this case, the grid is of square Brunswick inches.

Fig. 29 depicts the geometry of the head, contained in the 3×7 rectangle $FGHI$. The Ionic volute terminates at B, the outer spiral being then continued by quadrant arc BC, centre A, radius 41.5 mm ($1\frac{3}{4}$ Br. in.) which is a quarter of the overall length of head, FG. This arc is continued by arc CD, centre N, radius 166.5 mm (7 Br. in.), again the overall head length. This is counter-curved by DE, centre O, radius 68.5 mm ($2\frac{7}{8}$ Br. in.). O is also the centre for the initiating arc FJ of the upper, or front, peg-box curve; its radius is $4\frac{1}{2}$ Br. in. This is linked by straight line JK to terminating arc KL, centre M (MK being tangential to the scroll) and radius 2 Br. in. (full).

Plate III

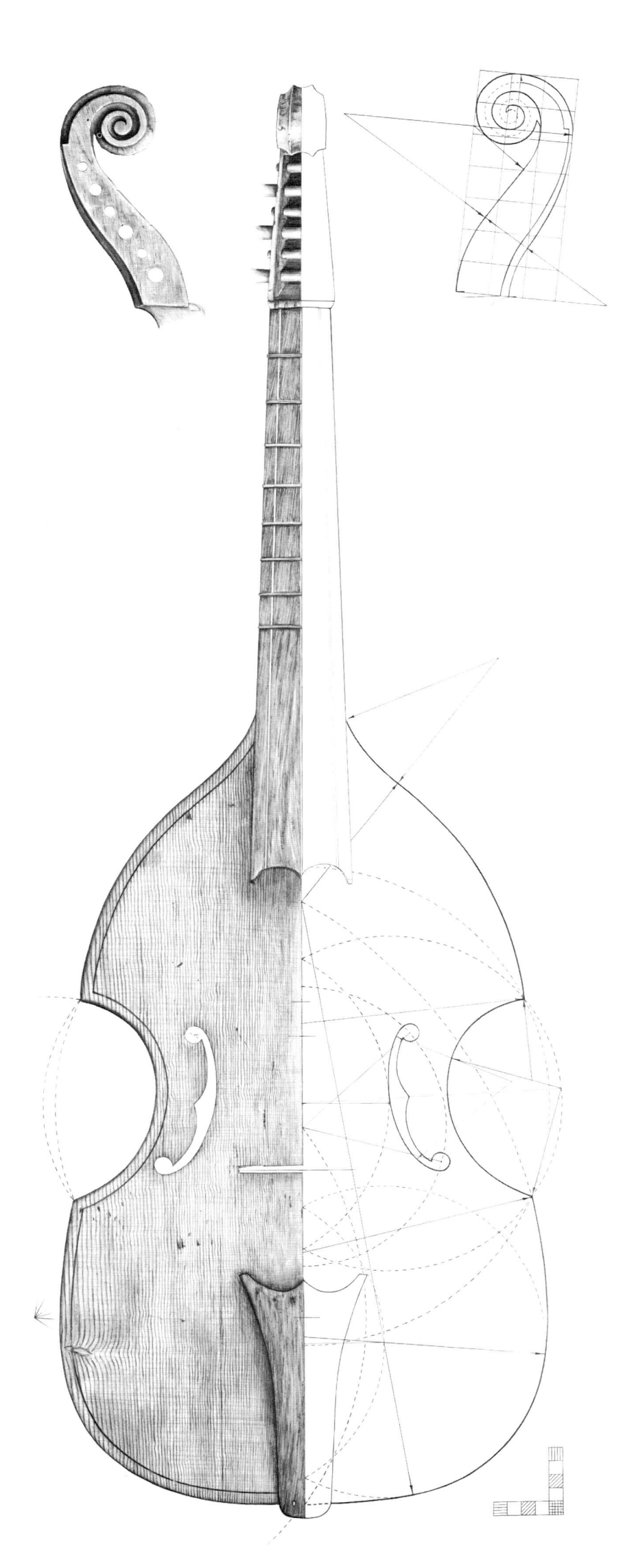

44 ANALYSIS OF INSTRUMENT EXAMPLES

Ex. IV

Figs. 30–34, Pl. IV

VIOL, SMALL TENOR. ENGLAND, LONDON, 1667
HENRY JAYE
VICTORIA AND ALBERT MUSEUM
Acc. No.: 173-1882

By the beginning of the seventeenth century, viol-making in England had reached a peak of refinement, with the evolution of a type of viol of extremely pure design, and one as yet free from the excesses of decoration found in many later Continental examples.

Thomas Mace, in his advice on the 'Best Provision' of viols, recommends the work of five English makers, there being 'no better in the world'.[35] Amongst this elect was Henry Jaye, whose fine tenor viol from the Victoria and Albert collection is here chosen to represent this 'classic' English tradition in viol design.

This particular instrument was mentioned by C. Stainer in his *Dictionary of Violin Makers* (1896):

> ... a tenor viol was exhibited at the South Kensington Museum, London, 1872, with the label 'Henry Jay in Southwarke, 1667'. It has six strings, tuned one-fifth higher than the bass-viol, catgut frets, and a beautifully carved scroll.

The date of 1667 makes it an extremely late work for Jaye, who was making viols 'in Southwarke' from about 1615 onwards.

The lower back of this beautiful instrument has suffered some later alteration, supposedly to allow it to be played on the shoulder (!)—but for our purposes, at least, the plan and geometrical construction of the instrument remain unspoilt.

One of the most beautiful features of the classic form of the viol is the 'sloping shoulder', which, by means of small outward-turning arcs between the neck and upper bouts, gracefully resolves their differences of direction. A less harmonious version of this counter-curved upper bout was seen in the early Venetian viol by Ciciliano (Ex. III), whose outline this classic model of Jaye's only superficially resembles. Geometrical analysis revealed, however, that the more likely design foundation of this sloping shoulder was the older squared shoulder of the guitar form found, for example, in the Maria treble viol (Ex. II). Indeed, it was not until this discovery was made that a 'design body-length'—one of the key measurements in instrument geometry—could be determined. In this case, the Jaye viol, the 'design body-length' was shorter than the actual top plate of the instrument, the exact difference being due to the aesthetic lengthening of the model by the additional, counter-directioned, curve of the upper bouts, as we shall see below. Hence the closer geometrical kinship between this and the squared-shoulder scheme (Ex. II) than with the superficially more like model of the Ciciliano (Ex. III), whose design body-length does equal the length of its top plate.[36]

The crucial design body-length of this viol was determined by the establishment of a point of upper limit to the body, a point later hidden by the instrument's developed design. This upper limit, in Fig. 30 point B, was easily located when the upper arcs of the upper bouts, which shared a common centre on the centre line of the instrument, were extended to join in a continuous arc, crossing the centre line at B. This divided the string

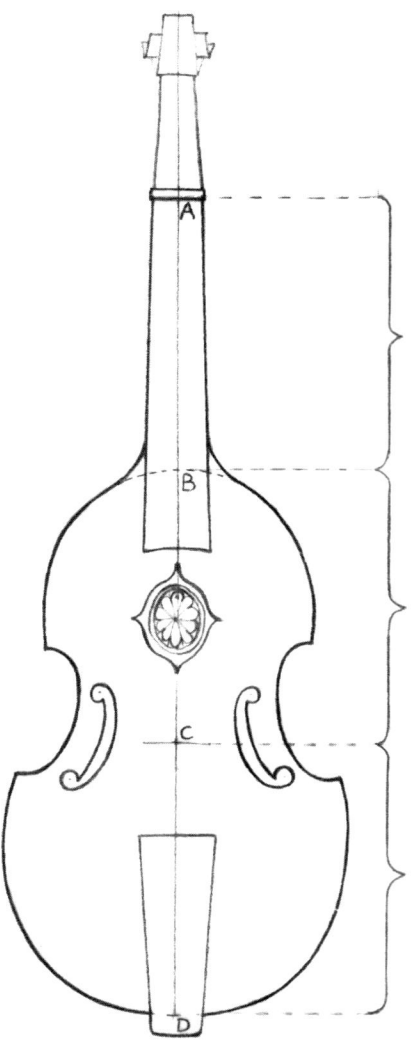

FIG. 30

[35] *Musick's Monument* (1st edn., London, 1676), Part III, chap. iv, p. 245.
[36] As indeed did the Zanetto's—an early viol (Ex. I) which yet incorporates the sloping-shoulder design.

length, nut (A) to bridge (C), in two, whilst the bridge itself divided this new, hypothetical, body length, BD, exactly in two, thus producing a tripartite division from nut to button, the unit $AB = BC = CD$ ($= 209.5$ mm) being the largest term, ϕ_2, in a ϕ series, which, together with a related, secondary ϕ series, governs practically the whole construction of the viol's plan.

As in the geometry of the older, cornerless, Maria viol, a great circle can now be constructed, radius ϕ_2, centre C (the bridge-line), crossing the centre line at points B and D (the lower extremity of the body), Fig. 31. Its full significance will be understood when the construction of the middle bouts is discussed.

The lower bouts are formed by three arcs. The first, the arc of origin DH', is centred at C—it therefore also forms part of the great circle, and has a radius of ϕ_2. The next arc, $H'I'$, centre G', is of radius 112 mm, the only major vector in the design which does not conform to the golden-section schemes. The final lower-bout arc is $I'N'$, which is centred at J and has a radius of 210 mm (allowing 0.5 mm error); this, too, is a ϕ_2 vector.

The middle bouts are constructed from point P' (and its lateral inversion) on the great circle (radius ϕ_2). The point is located by crossing the great circle with an intersecting arc of ϕ_2 radius centred at E, the geometrically significant point which is the centre of the instrument's rose. Point P', then, is the centre of the main middle-bout arc $R'Q'$; its radius, 129.5 mm, is ϕ_1 in the main series. The two minor middle-bout arcs, $N'R'$ and $Q'M'$, are of radius 36.5 mm and 26 mm respectively, neither value of ϕ significance.

The radii of the upper-bout scheme conform to the secondary, though related, ϕ series previously alluded to. This will be called ϕ_a, ϕ_b, and ϕ_c. It is related mathematically to the main series ϕ, ϕ_1, and ϕ_2 by its major term $\phi_c = 160$ mm $= 2\phi$.

The arc $S'L'$, which forms a large part of the upper bouts (and which originally gave the body length), is of radius ϕ_b, centre O, on the centre line. Arc $L'M'$, centre K, and radius 160 mm, ϕ_c ($= 2\phi$ of main series), shallows the curve for the corner, while the upper curve, the counter-curve $S'U'$, is of radius 61 mm, ϕ_a (61.1 mm) and centred at T'.

The position, and indeed the main curve, of the C-holes are plotted by the single value of ϕ. Firstly, a line is drawn (Fig. 32) from the centre of the rose (E) to the lower corner N'; this, incidentally, passes directly along one of the ten segmental divisions of the rose. The upper C-hole centring lies on this line EN' at V' so that $EV' = \phi$.

A second line, drawn from the upper corner M' through the upper centring V', meets the centre line at point F, so that $FV' = \phi$. Point F is in fact the centre for the circle, radius ϕ, which pierces both upper and lower C-hole centrings.

The principle arcs forming both the inner and outer curve of the C-holes are of radius ϕ, the centres offset so that the resulting opening narrows slightly towards the upper centring (see Fig. 32).

The decorative border of purfling around the oval rose also exhibits these golden-section values. The four 'pinched' points stationed, as it were, north, south, west, and east, from the centre, yield ϕ in the vertical, and $\frac{1}{2}\phi_1$ in the horizontal, plane.

The head of this tenor is of the open-scroll variety, where, true to the viol-maker's axiom of lightness, both visual and of construction, the 'ground' of the spiral is pierced through from one side of the head to the

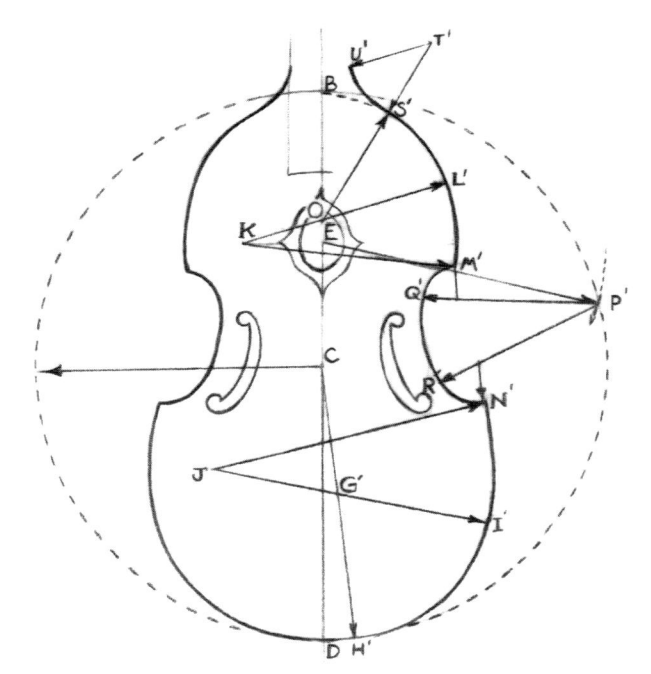

FIG. 31

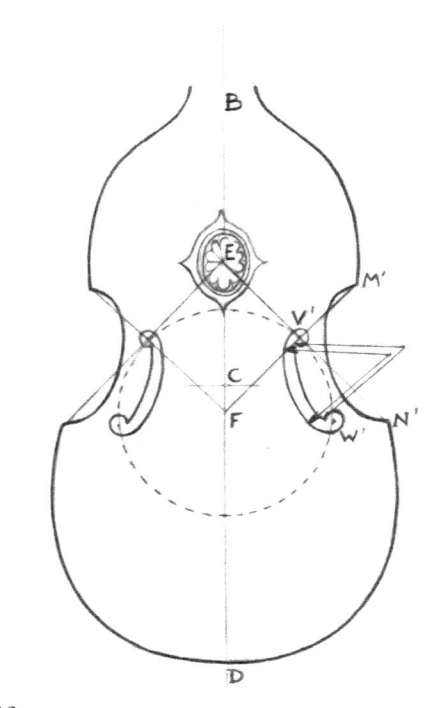

FIG. 32

other, unlike the scrolls found in members of the violin family. Elegant and airy though this is, the result is not the strongest use to be made of wood, as the unfortunate repairs in this splendid head testify. This late instrument of Jaye's shows no diminishing of his powers as a craftsman. The scroll, like the root of the neck, is festooned with fine relief carving of foliage, emerging, in the case of the cheek panels, from a grotesque in the form of a griffin's head.

The overall form of the scroll, however, seems somewhat unhappy; the generosity of the spiral as it emerges from the eye is not maintained as it flows into the curves of the peg-box. Indeed, it was this effect of tightening in the spiral as it uncurled that led me to investigate the possibility of its being a polygon-based pseudo-spiral, which in fact it proved to be. These pseudo-spirals are simply made with rule and compasses, and rely on the points and angles provided by the regular polygons as bases of augmentation for the arcs which shape them. The effect of 'tightening' as the spiral develops is, of course, due to the resultant diminishing proportion of its polygonal origin.

Fig. 33 shows the construction of the spiral used by the geometer of this instrument to design its scroll. It is based upon the geometry of the heptagon; a small heptagon was drawn, and, with compasses and rule, its sides were produced and used as radii for arcs which at each swing (of $360°/7$) were increased in radius by the length of one side of the heptagon. The arcs thus follow one of the rules for obtaining a smooth elliptical, or quasi-elliptical, curve, that of sharing a part of the coincident radius of the adjacent arc.

This spiral is shown in Fig. 34, the outline of the head in elevation, as the important outer volute of the scroll, the dotted line from A to B coinciding exactly with part of the spiral drawn in Fig. 33. The small section from A to the eye of the spiral is another section of the same spiral reiterated, as it were, to prevent the spiral of the scroll from closing too tightly. The inner curve of this spiral is not geometrically related but carved to give a suitable taper to the heptagonal spiral.

The traceable radii that form the curves of the peg-box relate exactly to the secondary ϕ series employed in the upper bouts of this instrument, and, as such, are discussed above.

In Fig. 34 the arc of the spiral flows from A to B, and then curves into an arc BC, radius ϕ_a, centre D, DC being the long side of the rectangle $DPQC$, which encloses the spiral of the scroll. Arc BC then flows into arc CE, radius ϕ_b, centre F. This rear curve of the peg-box is then completed by a short straight line, EG, connecting arc CE with counter-curved arc GH, radius ϕ_a, centre I, flowing into the heel of the head. Sharing part of a coincident radius with this arc is arc NM, again radius ϕ_a, centre O (rectangle $NPQO$ enclosing the entire head of the instrument); this arc initiates the upper, or front, curve of the peg-box. Straight line MK leads to counter-curve arc, KJ, which terminates the upper peg-box line, 'tucking' it under the scroll. KJ is centred at L, its radius relating to neither of the preceding ϕ series, but equalling the short side of spiral-enclosing rectangle $DPQC$.

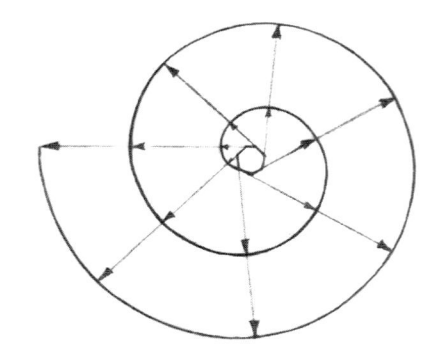

FIG. 33

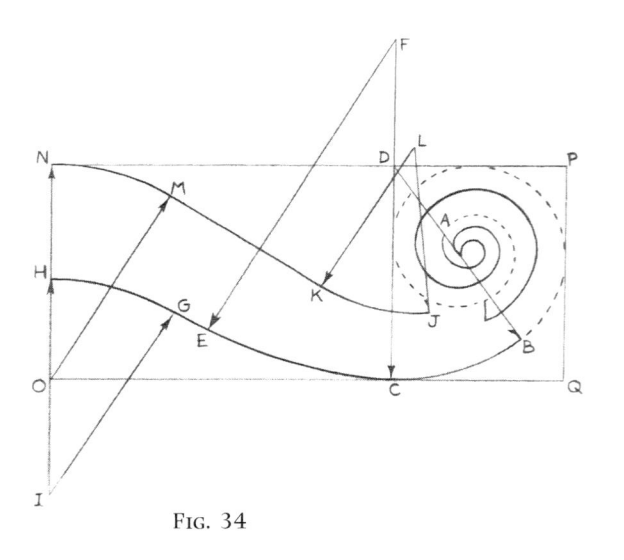

FIG. 34

Plate IV

Ex. V
Figs. 35–37, Pl. V

VIOL, BASS. GERMANY, HAMBURG, *c*.1700
JOACHIM TIELKE
VICTORIA AND ALBERT MUSEUM
Acc. No.: 168-1882

Within the history of musical instruments, the name Tielke is synonymous with elaborately designed and richly inlaid decoration. He was the key member of the Hamburg school (becoming a citizen of Hamburg in 1669), and his seductively lavish instruments soon won him the reputation of the most celebrated lute-maker of his time, his work achieving phenomenal prices: 'for one single lute 100 Mark or 50 Gulden'.

As well as lutes, his workshop produced some magnificent guitars, citterns (he was seemingly the innovator of the bell cittern, see Ex. XXX), and bass viols (by then the most commonly used member of the viol family). According to Hellwig,[37] some forty-seven bass viols by Tielke survive, amongst which, it could be said, are found some of the most spectacular examples of the art of lutherie.

Unfortunately, Tielke's decorative facility has quite dazzled the eye of popular judgement to his equally particular contribution to the formal evolution of viol design. His personal vision of the gamba outline is strikingly graceful, and, as we shall see in the following analysis, fastidiously planned. Most idiosyncratic is his treatment of the middle bouts, which have a notably open aspect, harmonizing the flow of upper- and lower-bout curvature. Tielke's pattern for the viol was continued by his followers[38] for the short time left to gamba manufacture, and the influence of its gentle curves can occasionally also be seen in a few of the later German violas d'amore.

This particular example, undated but thought to have been made *c*.1700, is no exception to the Tielke policy of lavish decoration; the back and sides bear allegorical scenes or 'triumphs' of inlaid and engraved sgraffito ivory, while the front is edged with ebony/ivory chequered purfling, and set with a fretted ivory rose, relief-carved with a figure of Orpheus singing to his harp. The finger-board and tailpiece are also richly decorated with ivory grotesques and arabesques inlaid into tortoiseshell, together with some rather strangely positioned rectangular panels of mother-of-pearl. The tailpiece itself is signed and dated (1835) by a previous owner of the instrument, the painter John Cawse. In the 1968 V. & A. catalogue, Baines suggests that Cawse may have been responsible for the alterations to the instrument's head. The original pegs have been replaced by early brass machines (by Baker of London), while the terminal itself appears to have been tampered with, for the rather uncomfortable scroll the instrument now bears is unlikely to be original. For this reason, no separate head elevation is given with this example, the discussion being limited to body plan, nut position (not shown in main drawing), and string length.

The geometrical scheme of the Tielke gamba is extremely complex and, as with many of the schemes here considered, can, owing to the nature of the mathematics involved, be expressed or explained in more than one way. This is particularly true of the irrational system used in this design,

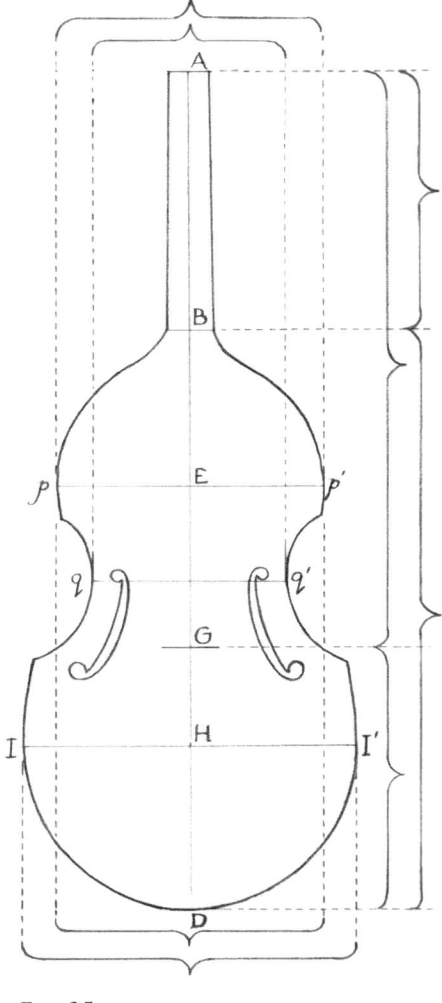

FIG. 35

---

[37] Günther Hellwig, 'Joachim Tielke', *GSJ*, vol. xvii, p. 31.

[38] See the magnificent bass viol (with its original bow) by Martin Voigt of Hamburg (1726)—V. & A., acc. no. 1298-1871.

that is, the 'symmetry' of $\sqrt{5}$, which, when governing a complex grid, as it does here, also realizes many golden-section and other $\sqrt{5}$-variant ratios.

Most of the overall proportions, both horizontal and vertical, are itemized in the explanation of the main grid, which includes the body-containing rectangle (Fig. 36). The separate ratios of body length, BD, and string length, AG, and the ratios of the bout widths are, however, first shown in Fig. 35.

Firstly, the string length and body length both measure 671 mm, that is, $AG = BD = 671$ mm; the neck, AB, measures 300 mm ($AD - BD$, or 971 mm $-$ 671 mm) which is the same as the upper-bout width pp'.

The ratio of string length to neck length, $\dfrac{AG}{AB}$,

or the ratio of body length to neck length, $\dfrac{BD}{AB}$,

or the ratio of body length to upper-bout width, $\dfrac{BD}{pp'}$,

all equal $\dfrac{671 \text{ mm}}{300 \text{ mm}} = 2.236$ or $\sqrt{5}$ (as do ratios $\dfrac{AG}{GD}, \dfrac{BD}{GD}$, etc.).

Although middle- (qq') and lower- (ll') bout widths do not relate in a very obvious way, $\dfrac{ll'}{qq'} = \dfrac{371 \text{ mm}}{217 \text{ mm}} = 1.710$, the other two permutations do indicate $\sqrt{5}$ harmony:

the ratio of lower- (ll') and upper- (pp') bout widths

$$= \frac{ll'}{pp'} = \frac{371 \text{ mm}}{300 \text{ mm}} = 1.236 = \sqrt{5} - 1$$

and the ratio of upper- (pp') and middle- (qq') bout widths

$$= \frac{pp'}{qq'} = \frac{300 \text{ mm}}{217 \text{ mm}} = 1.382 = 2.618 - 1.236 = (\phi + 1) - (\sqrt{5} - 1).$$

The main grid itself (Fig. 36) is a sophisticated network of squares, $\sqrt{5}$, $\sqrt{5}$ variant, ϕ, and $\sqrt{4}$ rectangles. It is perhaps best explored and examined by the reader's using the following check-list of the most important figures, their measurements in millimetres, consequent ratios, and schematic significance. 'Key' or 'parent' rectangles are underscored.

$\underline{aa'b'b} = \dfrac{671 \text{ mm}}{371 \text{ mm}} = 1.809 = \boxed{1} + \sqrt{5} - 1$ (body-containing rectangle)

or $aa'e'e + ee'b'b$

$aa'e'e = \dfrac{371 \text{ mm}}{371 \text{ mm}} = 1 = \boxed{1}$ (through bridge-line (G))

$ee'b'b = \dfrac{371 \text{ mm}}{300 \text{ mm}} = 1.236 = \sqrt{5} - 1$ (through lower sides and bridge-line (G))

$\underline{mm'b'b} = \dfrac{971 \text{ mm}}{371 \text{ mm}} = 2.617 \simeq \phi + 1$ (overall rectangle, nut to tail AD)

or $mm'f'f + ff'b'b$

$ff'b'b = \dfrac{371 \text{ mm}}{371 \text{ mm}} = 1 = \boxed{1}$ (contains lower bouts, with lower-bout arc IDI' produced to form circle, centre H, passing tangentially through middle bouts)

$\underline{cc'd'd} = \dfrac{671 \text{ mm}}{300 \text{ mm}} = 2.236 = \sqrt{5}$ (containing body length, BD, passing through upper bouts)

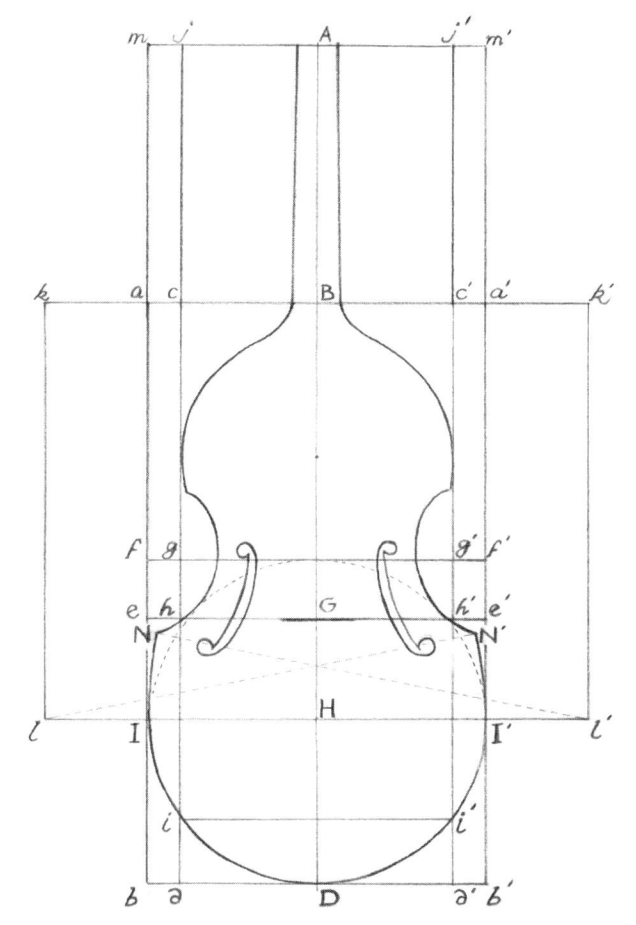

FIG. 36

ANALYSIS OF INSTRUMENT EXAMPLES

$$cc'i'i = \frac{60(1) \text{ mm}}{300 \text{ mm}} = 2.(003) \simeq \sqrt{4}$$ (body-top, cBc', through upper-bout sides to lower-bout curve, the double square bisected by ff' at gg', so that $gg'i'i$, $cc'g'g$, and $jj'c'c$ are all squares)

$$\left.\begin{array}{r}gg'i'i\\cc'g'g\\jj'c'c\end{array}\right\} = \frac{30(0) \text{ mm}}{300 \text{ mm}} = 1 = \boxed{1}$$

$$kk'l'l = \frac{600 \text{ mm}}{485.5 \text{ mm}} = 1.236 = \sqrt{5}-1,\text{ comprising rectangles:}$$

$$\left.\begin{array}{r}kBHl\\Bk'l'H\end{array}\right\} = \frac{485.5 \text{ mm}}{300 \text{ mm}} = 1.618 = \phi,\text{ plotting centres of lower-bout arcs }\left\{\begin{array}{l}I'N'\\IN\end{array}\right.$$

$$\left.\begin{array}{r}ka'I'l\\ak'l'I\end{array}\right\} = \frac{485.5 \text{ mm}}{485.5 \text{ mm}} = 1 = \boxed{1},\text{ plotting centres of lower-bout arcs }\left\{\begin{array}{l}I'N'\\IN\end{array}\right.$$

The body outline, which fits so snugly into this grid, is broken down into its component arcs in Fig. 37. Some of the component arc radii amounts we have already encountered by their coincidence with grid lines, and it is therefore not surprising that the scheme governing the body arc radii should also be $\sqrt{5}$ based. In fact, the radii are drawn from a geometric series in which the constant multiplication factor is $\sqrt{5}-1$, or 1.236. This gives a six-term progression, a, b, c, d, e, and f, in millimetre values measured as:

64.5, 79.5, 98, 122, 150, and 185.5.

Checked by calculation, the series reads:

64.4, 79.6, 98.2, 121.4, 150, and 185.5.

The outline commences in Fig. 37 with arc of origin DI', IDI' being a semicircle centred at grid point H; its radius, 185.5 mm, is the largest in the $\sqrt{5}-1$ series, that is $(\sqrt{5}-1)f$.

The lower bouts are completed by the shallow curve of arc $I'N'$, centred at l on the opposite side—this centre, too, occurs in the grid of fig. 36. The radius of arc $I'N'$ is 485.5 mm, which is four times the fourth term, $(\sqrt{5}-1)d$, of 121.4 mm (actually 485.6 mm), and, when divided by the previous term (485.6 mm/185.5 mm), produces 2.618, or $\phi+1$, or ϕ^2. All the remaining radii are single occurrences drawn directly from the $\sqrt{5}-1$ progression.

The middle bouts comprise three separate arcs: $N'R'$, radius 98 mm, $(\sqrt{5}-1)c$; $R'Q'$, radius 122 mm, $(\sqrt{5}-1)d$; and arc $Q'M'$, radius 64.5 mm, the smallest of the terms, $(\sqrt{5}-1)a$.

The upper, like the lower, bouts have only two constituent arcs: main arc $M'L'$, which is centred at E, the centre of the oval sound-board rose, and of radius 150 mm, $(\sqrt{5}-1)e$, and arc $S'U'$, centre T', radius 79.5 mm or $(\sqrt{5}-1)b$; the two arcs are connected by short straight line $L'S'$.

The oval rose has an outer border of purfling, which, measuring 76 mm × 57 mm, yielded the ratio $1.33\dot{3}$, or 4 : 3. This same ratio was found in the radii of the C-hole arcs, the shallower outer curve centred at V having a radius of 201 mm, while the inner curve, centred at W, a radius of 150 mm. This measurement, 150 mm, also occurs as term five, $(\sqrt{5}-1)e$, in the main series. The sound-hole centrings themselves are centred by a circle drawn in Fig. 37 at F; its radius, 122.5 mm, may also be considered as $(\sqrt{5}-1)d$ in the $\sqrt{5}-1$ progression, despite the small deviation in measurement.

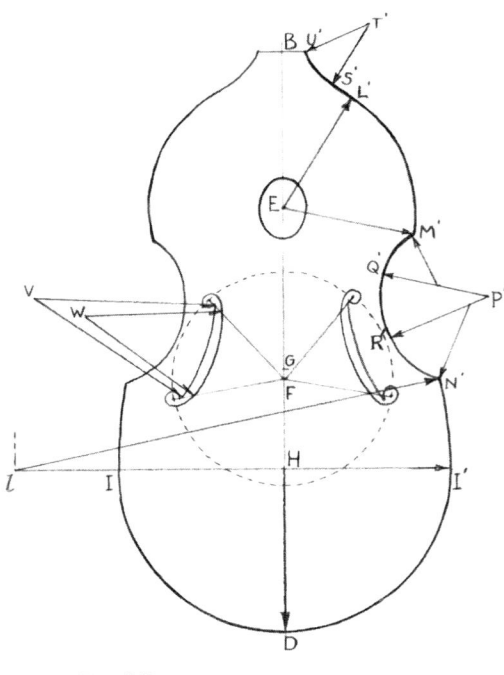

FIG. 37

PLATE V

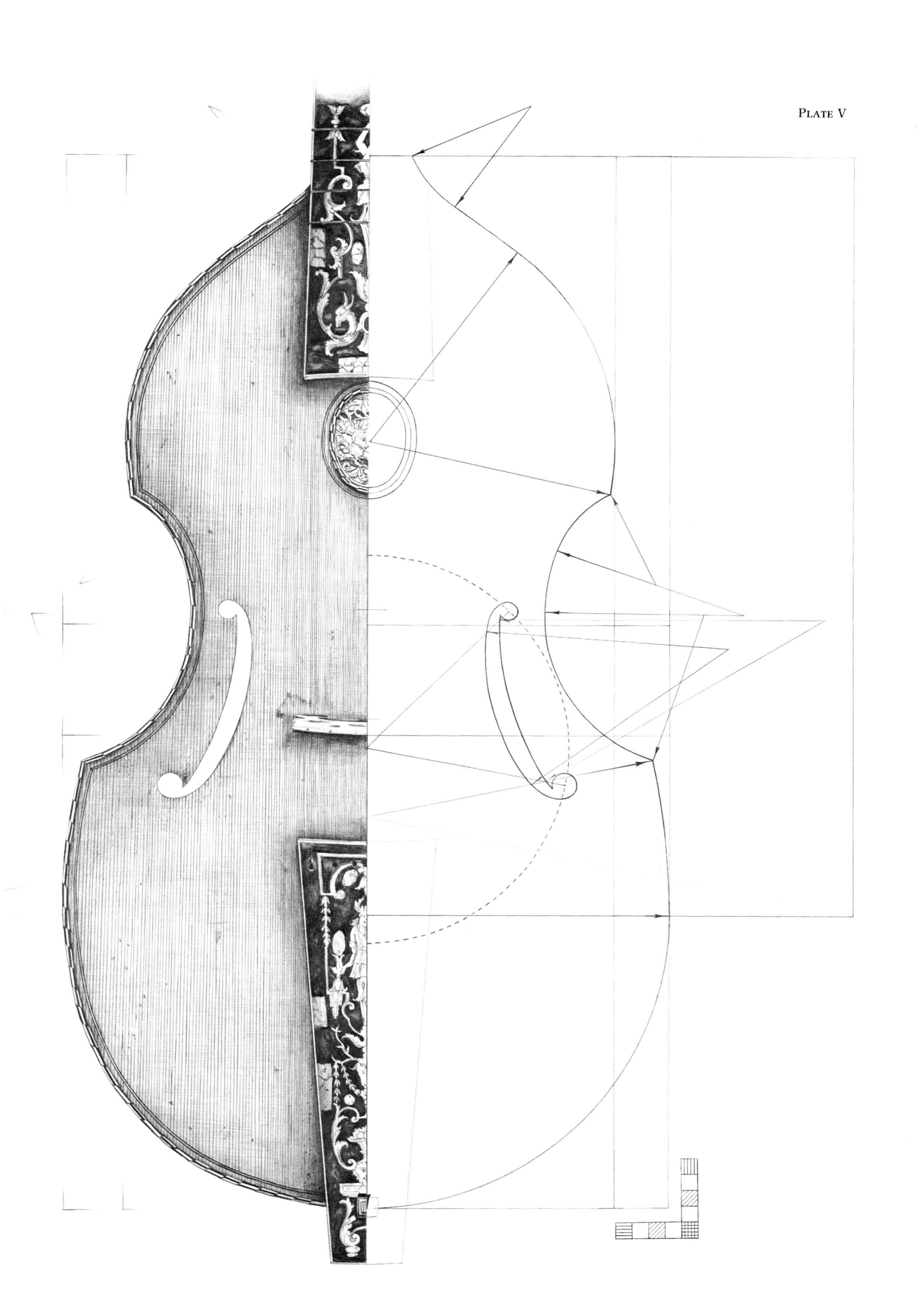

Ex. VI

Figs. 38–40, Pl. VI

VIOL, PARDESSUS. FRANCE, PARIS, 1759
LOUIS GUERSAN
DONALDSON COLLECTION, ROYAL COLLEGE OF MUSIC
Acc. No.: 149

For the last specimen of the viol family proper, I have selected an example of its youngest member, the eighteenth-century French innovation, the *pardessus de viole* ('pardessus' not here meaning 'overcoat', but literally an 'over-' or 'higher-'treble viol). Not generally regarded very seriously by musicologists, the pardessus had a brief life, inspiring little music, none of which is accounted notable. Like the hurdy-gurdy, the pardessus was in vogue for a short period in the eighteenth century, when, irrespective of its musical value, it was thought to be a suitably bucolic accessory to the pastoral pose of fashionable ladies. In these circles it also had a further cosmetic advantage—unlike the violin, its nearest musical equivalent, it is played 'downwards' on the lap, leaving the pretty head and *coiffure* free, and not marking the delicate white skin of the neck. Not surprisingly, it was of no further use after the Revolution.

The high social level of its French patrons ensured an equally high standard of manufacture and finish for these small instruments. Makers most noted for their output of pardessus were Paul François Grosset, Claude Pierray, and his pupil Louis Guersan. The present example is from the hand of this latter, and was made by him in 1759. It is of the usual five-stringed form, but is perhaps a little larger than the usual size. As can be seen from the drawing, it follows the 'classic' pattern encountered here in two previous examples, the Jaye and Tielke viols, and, indeed, established some 150–200 years earlier than the date of this Guersan.

In fact, the late date of this instrument, coinciding with the final decline of the viol family, could account for a similar decay in design-geometry, a deterioration only fully apparent when viewed comparatively with the preceding examples.

Nevertheless, numerical proportion has been carefully considered in the outline of this instrument, and, interestingly, the system selected was not the golden section but the related (and equally irrational) $\sqrt{5}$ proportion, which, the reader will remember, was also used in the Maria viol, Ex. II, and more significantly in Ex. V, the bass viol by Tielke.

As with the Jaye, the Guersan's actual body length, *BD*, was a measurement unrelated to any scheme or system used in the rest of the instrument (see Fig. 38). Whilst, however, the upper-bout arcs of the Jaye revealed a crucial 'design body-length', here no such device was to be found, the equivalent arc-centre in the Guersan not being on the centre line. Despite the absence of this 'point of upper limit'[39] the proportional principle attached to it, and shown in Fig. 30, still applies. Here, Fig. 38, the string length *AC* (nut to bridge), 305 mm, was found to be twice *CD* (bridge to tail), 152.5 mm.

Although here there is no, indeed can be no, great-circle geometry as found in the Maria and in the Jaye, a circle can be drawn, centre *C* (the true bridge position), which describes part of the lower bouts, the arc of origin *HDH'*. When produced, *HDH'* crosses the centre line at *O*, dividing the string length *AC* in two, thus giving the octave point.

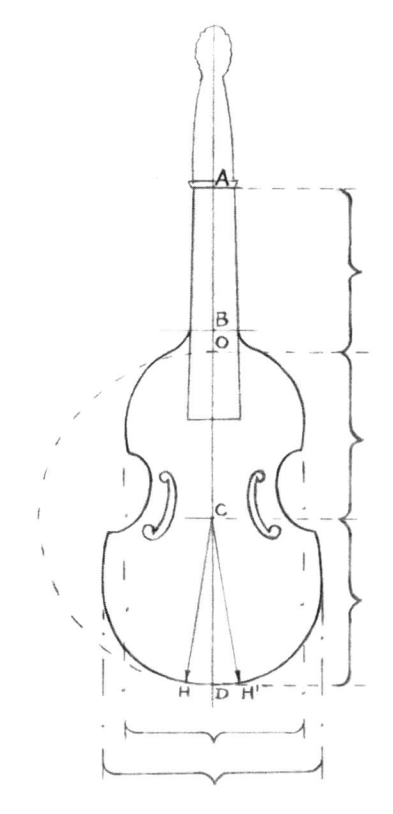

FIG. 38

[39] See p. 44 above, the Jaye viol.

A counterpart for the two related ϕ systems, used respectively for the upper and lower sections of the Jaye viol, can be seen here in the scheme of the Guersan. Based on an alternative $\sqrt{5}$ system, their most closely related terms are shown as the horizontal brackets in Fig. 38, that is, the width of upper and lower bouts. Their relationship, as measured, is not an exact one, but is close enough, given the $\sqrt{5}$ scheme of the instrument, to mention here: their ratio, 158 mm : 194.5 mm, is 1 : 1.23(1), 1.23(6) being $\sqrt{5}-1$. Both these vectors (158 and 194.5) are the major terms in separate $\sqrt{5}$ progressions, as we shall see.

Fig. 39 shows the outline analysed, with its component arcs. The arc of origin of the lower bouts, as we saw in Fig. 38, is centred at C, the true bridge position. Its radius is therefore 152.5 mm. The lower bouts are continued by arc $H'I'$, centre G', radius 87 mm. The curve is completed by arc $I'N'$, centre I (on the opposite edge), radius 194.5 mm. These two values have a $\sqrt{5}$ relationship, 87 mm : 194.5 mm being 1 : 2.236.

The middle bouts are rather more arbitrarily disposed: arc $N'R'$, radius 25 mm, is in 2.24 relationship ($\sqrt{5}$?) with main arc $R'Q'$, centre P', radius 56 mm, but the small arc $Q'M'$, radius 18 mm, does not relate proportionately to any other vector. The main middle-bout vector of 56 mm is not only the radius of the 'centring circle', which, centred at C, the bridge-line point, can be drawn through the C-hole centrings, but is also the main radius of the inner curve of the C-holes themselves. The outer curve is of radius 76 mm, again an unrelated number.

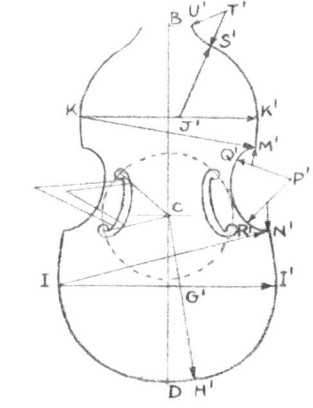

FIG. 39

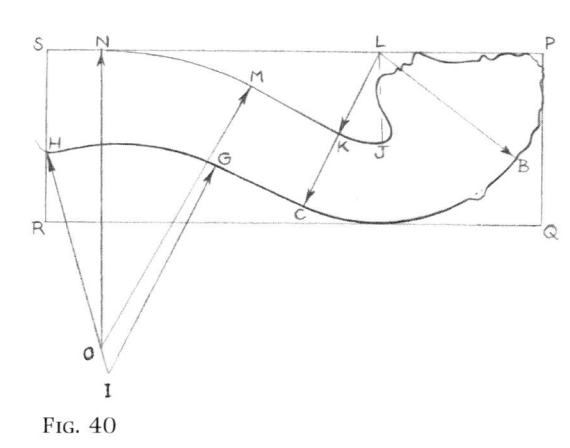

The three upper-bout arcs are governed by the second $\sqrt{5}$ progression. Arc $M'K'$, centre K on the opposite edge, is of radius 158 mm. The curve is continued by arc $K'S'$, centre J', radius 70.5 mm, and completed by the counter-curve of the shoulder, arc $S'U'$, centre T', radius 31.5 mm.

Thus, the values 158, 70.5, and 31.5 can be seen as a $\sqrt{5}$ progression:

$$158 : 70.5$$
being $\quad 1 : 2.2(41)$
and $\quad 70.5 : 31.5$
being $\quad 1 : 2.23(8),$

more precise millimetre values not being possible.

The head of this Guersan viol is surmounted by a well-carved female head with curling, flower-topped hair. The peg-box cheeks and back are also decorated, here with winding garlands carved in relief. Not as much care, however, has been taken with the proportional regulation of the peg-box curves as has been expended on the decoration. None of the vectors which govern these curves or the containing rectangle appears to relate to those used in the main scheme, or indeed to each other. They are drawn in Fig. 40, and an account of their values follows.

The carving of the hair ceases, and the curve of the peg-box back commences, at B, with arc BC, radius 48.5 mm; its centre, L, does however lie on line SP of the containing rectangle PQRS. A straight line, CG, links this arc to counter-curve GH, centre I, radius 65.5 mm. The main curve of the top of the peg-box is given by arc NM, centre O (on IH), radius 85 mm. This is connected, by straight line MK, to the small completing arc KJ, radius 26 mm, which shares a common centre on SP with arc BC at L.

FIG. 40

Plate VI

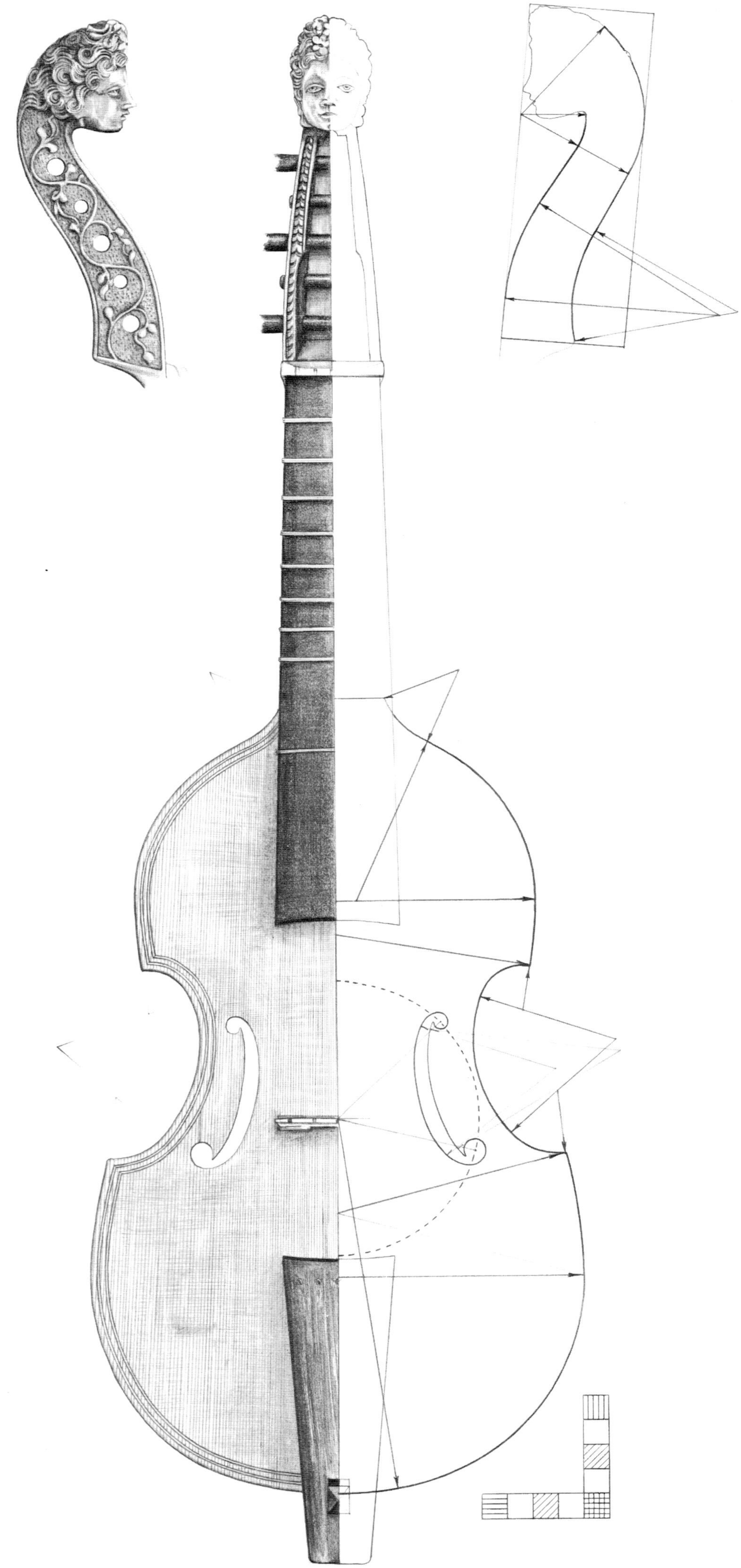

LIRAS DA BRACCIO

One of the few certain ancestors of the violin, the lira da braccio, was a sophisticated Italian instrument which first appeared at the end of the fifteenth century, a probable development from the medieval *da braccio* violas and fiddles. Few complete liras da braccio survive, which is surprising given the importance placed upon the instrument by the aristocracy and by the Neoplatonists, who quite erroneously judged it to be a link with the fabled lyre of the ancients. It was initially for the playing of this instrument that Leonardo was accepted into the service of Ludovico Sforza at Milan,[40] his lira being one of his own manufacture, made of silver (or, more likely, decorated with silver) and having the shape of a horse's head. Unfortunately, this instrument does not survive, although another 'cosa bizarra e nuova', by Giovanni d'Andrea of Verona, a lira of great anthropomorphic and symbolical extravagance, does, and is now in the Kunsthistorisches Museum of Vienna.

The first of our examples is of a more sober design. It is of the fully developed form, with two pairs of corners giving the customary three pairs of bouts of the violin family. From iconographical evidence it has been established that originally the lira, or 'viola', as it was first called, was of a cornerless guitar form, which later adopted first the lower and then both pairs of corners as in the present example. The bi-lobed lower bouts and flat peg-box are both typical features of the lira—the former being found only on the 'braccio' version and not in the lira da gamba. (One could therefore suppose that the resulting recess was to facilitate playing what is a quite sizeable instrument against the neck or shoulder.)

Ex. VII

Figs. 41–43, Pl. VII

LIRA DA BRACCIO. ITALY, VENICE, c.1575
GIOVANNI MARIA DA BRESCIA
HILL COLLECTION, ASHMOLEAN MUSEUM, OXFORD
Acc. No.: 8

This instrument is in the Hill collection at the Ashmolean Museum—it is the smallest of the surviving liras da braccio[41] and is fully described in the Boyden catalogue. There appears to be some doubt and mystery as to its provenance. At present it bears a label of Giovanni Maria da Brescia, 'Gioan maria bresiano in Venetia', which, most probably, it has not always possessed, as it seems likely that this instrument and the lira once owned and carefully described by Major Hajdecki in his important study[42] are one and the same. Hajdecki's lira, at that time, bore a false 'Duiffopruggar' (Tieffenbrucker) label. In any event, Boyden's information and consequent conclusions as to Giovanni Maria's dates would appear to be incorrect (see p. 35 n. 29 above), and if this, undoubtedly Venetian, instrument was made by him, its date would not be c.1525 but

[40] Giorgio Vasari, *The Lives of the Artists* (tr. George Bull, 1965; Penguin, 1978).

[41] A larger example of the same four-cornered type as the Ashmolean lira is to be found in the Donaldson collection and is illustrated in pls. 5 and 6 of Anthony Baines, *European and American Musical Instruments*. This is now thought to be a nineteenth-century impostor.

[42] *Die italienische Lira da Braccio* (Mostar, Hercegovina, 1892).

a good half-century later, which perhaps would seem to be a more likely dating for the Ashmolean lira, given its fully developed state.

Handsome though this instrument is, it does not, I feel, command the same aesthetic response as the Giovanni Maria treble viol (Ex. II), whose simpler, more homogeneous, design projects a sense of harmony which I find lacking in the, albeit more complex, less carefully made lira. Harmonically and geometrically the design of both instruments is interesting; and though differing in proportional system, each makes use of a 'great circle' to encompass the main middle-bout arc centres.

In practice, this lira proved to be one of the most difficult designs to analyse, not for any generic reason, but simply because the number of irregularities and asymmetries present in the outline clouded and confused many attempts to reveal its underlying geometry. The nature of the difficulties involved in tracing a scheme within a given outline is further discussed in connection with the fine Maggini viola (Ex. XIV) below. The chief difficulty in the present case was the frequent inconsistency between 'left-' and 'right'-hand factors. Despite this, a governing scheme is apparent and can be described, if somewhat cautiously.

The overall proportions, which do seem to have been given some consideration, are shown in Fig. 41. The commensurable scheme, which we shall encounter in the arc radii of the outline, is used from the outset, the common unit, u, being 15.5 mm. A body-containing rectangle is drawn in Fig. 41, $wxyz$, measuring 388 mm (body length BD) by 232 mm (lower-bout width II'); this, allowing a 0.5 mm margin of error, gives the ratio

$$\frac{388 \text{ mm}}{232 \text{ mm}} \left(\frac{387.5 \text{ mm}}{232.5 \text{ mm}}\right) = \frac{25u}{15u} = 1.66\dot{6} \text{ or } 3:5.$$

Incidentally, BD, 388 mm (387.5 mm), is also equivalent to $13\frac{1}{2}$ Venetian inches. The lower-bout width II' also has a harmonic horizontal linear relationship with upper-bout width WW' (WW' measures 187 mm, here indulgently read as $12u$):

$$\frac{232 \text{ mm}}{187 \text{ mm}} \left(\frac{232.5 \text{ mm}}{186 \text{ mm}}\right) = \frac{15u}{12u} = 1.25 \text{ or } 4:5,$$

WW', 187 mm, measuring $6\frac{1}{2}$ (6.52) Venetian inches.

The same system was found to govern the string length or nut and bridge positions. String length AV is measured as 325 mm or, allowing 0.5 mm error, $21u$ (325.5 mm), which is so arranged that neck length, AB, is $\frac{1}{3}AV$, or $BV = 2AB$. The length below the bridge, VD, is also commensurable to the main scheme: $VD = 171$ mm (170.5 mm) $= 11u$.

The great circle and component-arc radii are drawn in Fig. 42. In this scheme, the great circle is not so well integrated as it was in the Maria treble viol, where, as well as positioning the middle-bout arc centres, it also formed the lower-bout arc of origin, connecting the two vesica piscis arcs. Of course, the bi-lobed bottom of the lira precludes this particular arrangement, and the circle, whose radius is measured as 194 mm (193.75 mm $= 12.5u$), is centred at C, passing through the body-top B, middle-bout arc centre O, and across the lower-bout lobes to D.

Allowing for the rather badly fitted tail nut or 'saddle', the outline commences at d' with arc $d'H'$, centre E', radius 155 mm, or $10u$. It continues with quadrant arc $H'I'$, centre G', radius 62.5 mm (here taken as $4u$), and with arc $I'J'$, centre K on the centre line, radius half lower-bout width 116 mm, or $7\frac{1}{2}u$ (116.25 mm). The lower bouts are completed by counter-curve $J'M'$, centre L', radius 23 mm, or $1\frac{1}{2}u$ (23.25 mm).

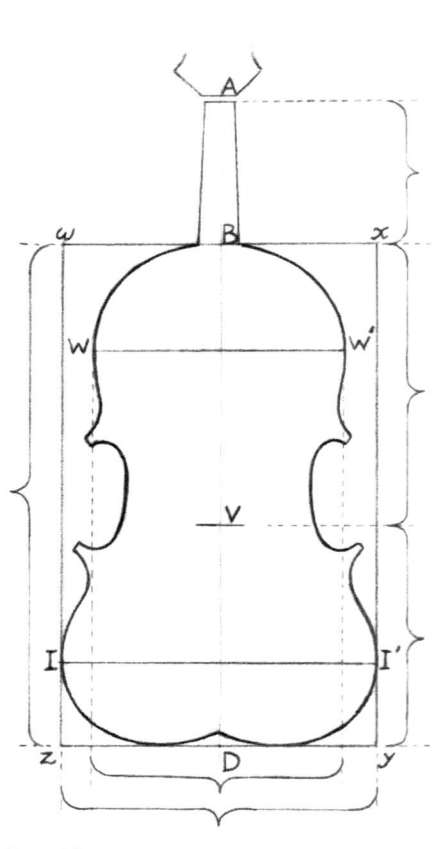

FIG. 41

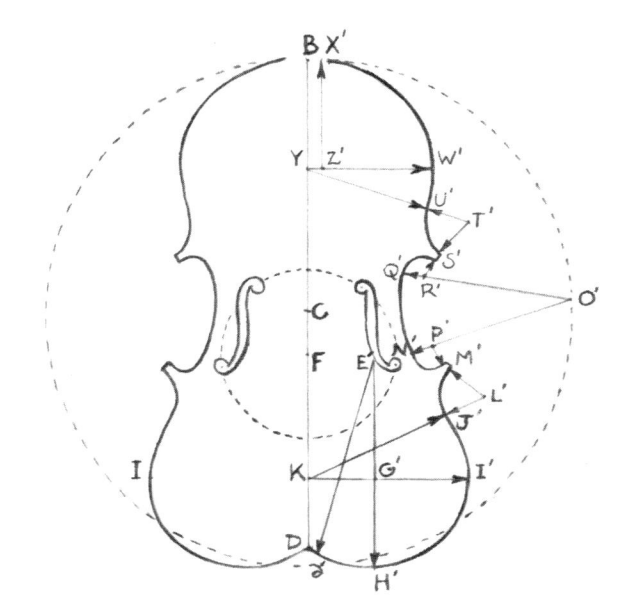

FIG. 42

Here, for the first time in this study, we meet the violin-type corner; the viol-type corners so far encountered are true geometrical points, in that the two arcs forming the corner actually meet, whereas in the case of the violin-type, the two corner-forming arcs never touch, but are separated, and linked, by a short, theoretically straight, line. Thus, in the latter case, two separate points of arc termination actually occur at the corners; for the sake of clarity, however, in such cases throughout this study only one 'common' corner-terminating letter will be given, as it was in a more traditionally correct methodology in the case of the viol-type corner.

The middle bouts are formed by three arcs: $M'N'$, centre P', radius 16 mm or u (15.5 mm); main arc $N'Q'$, centre O' on the 'great circle' with a radius measured as 124 mm (or $8u$) on one side, but as 128 mm on the other; and finally, arc $Q'S'$, centre R', radius 15.5 mm, or u.

The upper bouts, perhaps the most erratic part of the scheme, commence at S with counter-curve $S'U'$, centre T', radius 32 mm ($2u$?) on the right, but 36.5 mm on the left. The curve is continued by arc $U'W'$ centred at Y on the centre line (echoing the lower-bout construction) with a radius therefore of half the upper-bout width, that is, 93.5 mm, or $6u$ (93 mm), and completed by quadrant arc $W'X'$, centre Z' and of radius 82 mm on one side and 83.5 mm on the other, neither of which appears to relate to the emerging proportional scheme.

The circle piercing the f-hole centrings is centred at F on the centre line; its radius, 65.5 mm, is too large to be considered a unit vector, 62 mm, $4u$, being the closest term.

The beautifully decorated head, with its delicately painted Moresques recalling contemporary Italian harpsichord decoration, is here puritanically given in bare outline, in Fig. 43. Whilst no proportional significance was found in the ratio of the containing rectangle, or its components, the three arcs which form the convoluted sides of the peg-box revealed the same commensurable ratios as the main scheme. From top to bottom in Fig. 43: arc $A'B'$, centre C', has a radius of 46.5 mm, or $3u$; short straight line $B'D'$ connects this arc to arc $D'F'$, centre E on the opposite side, and of radius 78.5 mm ($5u$?—i.e. 77.5 mm); the remaining arc, $F'H'$, is centred at G', and is of radius 47 mm, again $3u$ (46.5 mm). (3 : 5 was the overall body ratio.) The peg-box side is completed by straight line $H'I'$.

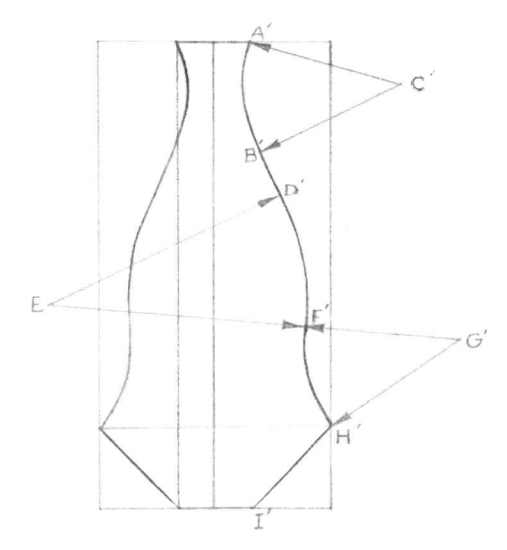

FIG. 43

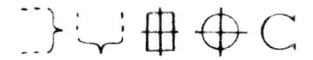

PLATE VII

Ex. VIII
Fig. 44, Pl. VIII

LIRA DA BRACCIO. ITALY, BRESCIA, c.1585?
GASPARO DA SALÒ
HILL COLLECTION, ASHMOLEAN MUSEUM, OXFORD
Acc. No.: 9

The two remaining examples of lira instruments to be considered are both Brescian, and though of radically differing scale, they have similar body outlines, that is, bi-lobed and two- rather than four-cornered.

The first, and smaller of the two, is attributed to Gasparo da Salò, and forms part of the Ashmolean Hill collection, wherein it is catalogued as lira–viola of 'hybrid form, found during the early evolution of the violin family and combining elements of the viola and lira da braccio'. Baines, too, groups this particular example with the modern development of the 'viola' as 'middle member of the violin group'. It seems quite as likely, however, that the present four-stringed state of this instrument is a later alteration brought about in the interests of prolonged use (Boyden vouches for the beauty and power of its tone), and that this Gasparo may equally well have originally functioned as a five- or seven-stringed lira da braccio. If such is the case, then the instrument before us would originally have possessed the characteristic leaf-shaped head, with a facility for drones or bourdon strings (see Pl. VII), rather than the more familiar scroll-head with four lateral pegs, which it now bears. The lira group, despite its importance in Renaissance music and culture, remains a mysterious, insufficiently researched area of organology; without further knowledge, the exact original state of an instrument such as this can only be a matter of conjecture.

Contemporary illustrations of the two-cornered lira form, however, are numerous, and an excellent analogous study of some of these graphics and of the few surviving instruments has been made by Laurence Witten.[43] In Witten's view, the date claimed by the label of this Ashmolean instrument—'Gasparo da Salò, in Brescia 1561'—is too early (the first record, or other 'record', of his working in Brescia being from 1565) and he prefers to date the instrument from 1600—which even by his own presented findings of graphic evidence seems perhaps a little late. The great rarity, and therefore the doubtful authenticity, of dated Gasparo labels is, of course, a point well heeded.

Whatever its date, there seems little doubt that Gasparo Bertolotti, called da Salò, *was* the author of this lira, whose powerful, forthright design is upheld by its equally robust workmanship. The curious wood used in the belly is cedar of Lebanon, of a vigorous 'cross-hatched' growth, which no doubt contributes to the instrument's somewhat austere countenance.

None of the measurements of overall height or width in either this or the following example was found to have been considered proportionately. This is unusual, although, as a glance at Summary Chart 1 on p. 158 will confirm, not exceptional. It is unfortunate that in both cases no reliable evidence of original string length, nut position, or exact bridge position exists to enlighten their geometries, which will therefore be considered in body outline only.

The body design of the Gasparo lira was found to be governed by a

[43] Laurence C. Witten II, 'Apollo, Orpheus, and David', *Journal of the American Musical Instrument Society*, i (1975).

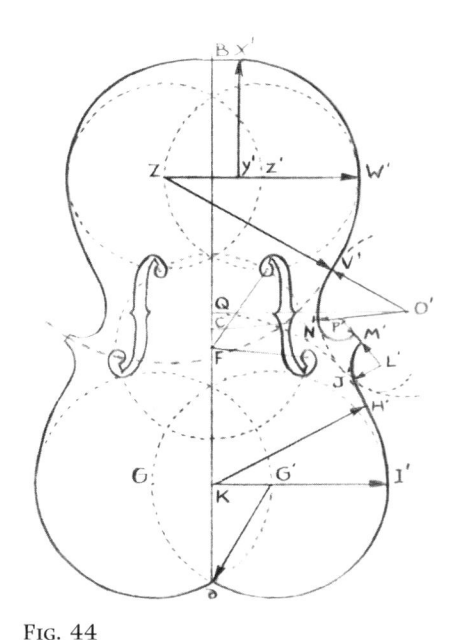

commensurable scheme based on not one, but two units, giving two scales of aggregation, which, peculiarly, are not obviously related to one another, although each is independently established by the same process.

The smaller unit, u, governs the upper-bout area of the instrument, as well as the positioning of the f-holes. It is calculated as 17.75 mm, and is one-twelfth of the upper-bout width, which is constructionally divided into three equal parts by a vesica piscis arrangement, each radius of which therefore measures $4u$, as we shall see.

The larger unit, U, governs the middle and lower bouts of the design; it measures 21.5 mm and is in turn one twelfth part of the lower-bout width, which is similarly divided into three equal parts of $4U$ by the vesica piscis device which provides the main arcs of the lower bouts.

Considering the ubiquitous nature of the vesica piscis construction, it is surprising that, out of the three examples chosen here, each having bi-lobed lower bouts (a design which immediately suggests the two interlocked vesica circles), only one, this lira of Gasparo, actually incorporates the device. This can be seen in Fig. 44, centred at G and G'. The outline begins with vesica arc dI', centre G', radius 86 mm or $4U$; it continues with arc $I'H'$, centre K on the centre line, radius therefore $6U$ (129 mm). A short straight line $H'J'$ connects this arc with corner counter-curve $J'M'$, centre L', radius 21.5 mm, or U.

The middle bouts, if such they can be called, begin with arc $M'N'$, centre P', radius measured as 16 mm, which, allowing a 0.125 mm 'error', proclaims this vector as $0.75U$ and therefore a quarter of the next vector, the radius of arc $N'V'$, centred at O', measuring 64.5 mm or $3U$. The arc, as well as having obligatory tangentiality with its two adjoining arcs, is also 'tangential' to arc $M'J'$ produced and to arc $I'H'$ produced, as can be seen in the drawing. Radius $O'P'N'$ produced will also cross the centre line at point C, the 'theoretical' model centre.

This is the stage where the smaller commensurable unit ($u =$ 17.75 mm) takes over the design. Arc $V'W'$ is centred at Z on the opposite side of the instrument, at a one-third division of the upper-bout width (see implied vesica in Fig. 44). Its radius therefore measures $8u$, or 142 mm, which incidentally is also the distance QO'. These arcs, when produced downwards, cross the centre line a little below point F, and thence intersect the opposite lower sound-hole centring, and the opposite corner. The upper bouts are completed by arc $W'X'$, centre Y', radius measured as 89 mm, which, allowing 0.25 mm error, equals $5u$ (88.75 mm).

The smaller-unit system is also used in positioning the f-holes. The circle piercing the four f-hole centrings is centred at point F; its radius, 71 mm, is $4u$. The upper f-hole centrings are pierced, too, by the upper, constructional, vesica circles, radius also $4u$. In addition, F is the point where the current bridge position crosses the centre line.

The head of this instrument, as we have already discussed, is a possible scroll replacement to what may have been a leaf form of peg-box. The present head, however, would seem not to be a restoration 'in the old style' as Boyden suggests, but an original, old, Brescian head, perhaps even from a tenor by Gasparo himself. Handsome though this cannibalized scroll is, with its fine Ionic volute, its geometrical scheme is of no relevance to the lira's original design, and is therefore not analysed here.

FIG. 44

PLATE VIII

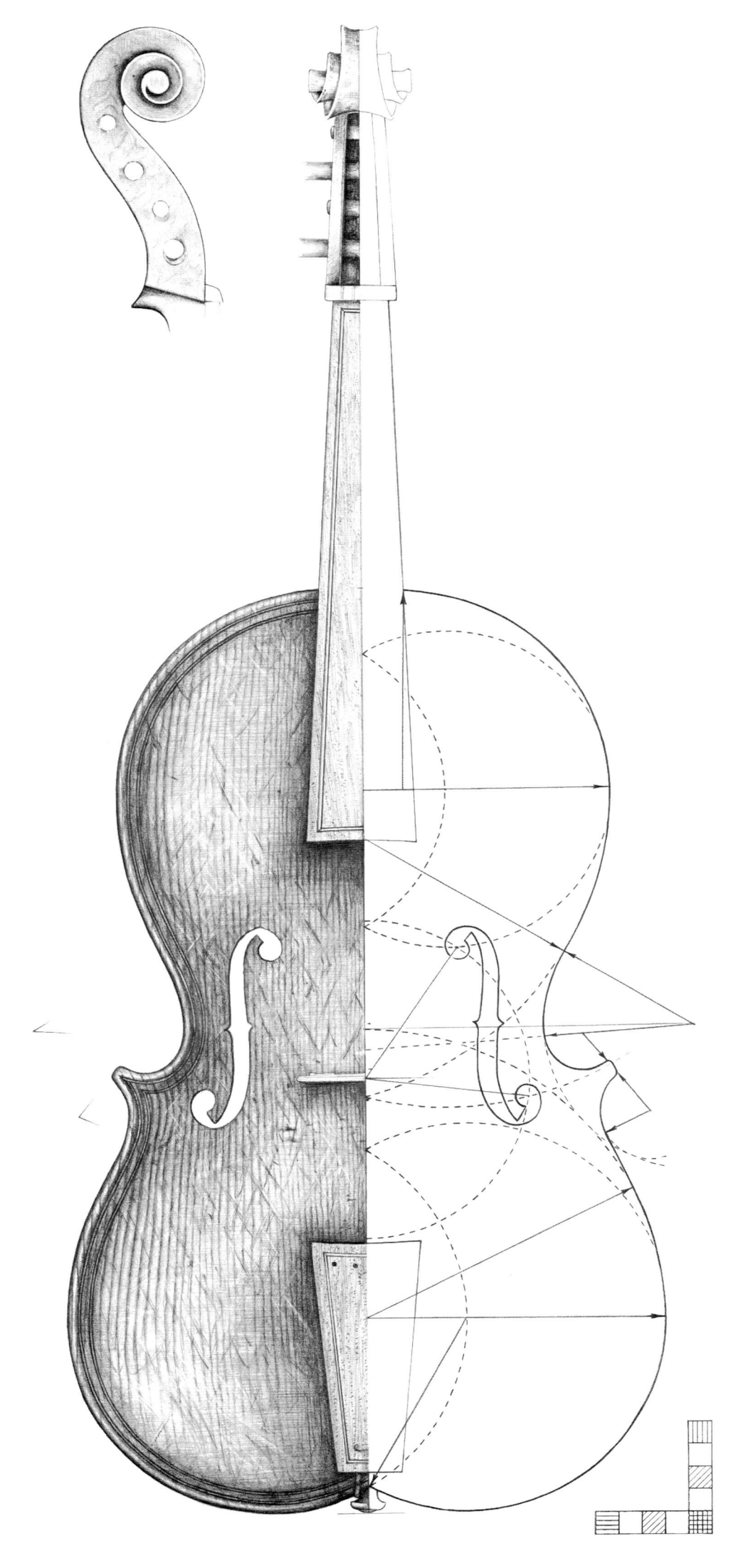

62 ANALYSIS OF INSTRUMENT EXAMPLES

Ex. IX

Figs. 45–46, Pl. IX

LIRA DA BRACCIO. ITALY, BRESCIA, c.1570
MAKER UNKNOWN
MUSÉE DU CONSERVATOIRE ROYAL DE MUSIQUE, BRUSSELS
Acc. No.: 1415

There is no adequate reason to doubt that this impressive specimen, despite its enormity, was once strung and played *alla spalla* as a lira da braccio. An idea of just how so large a lira was accommodated by a player can be understood from the figure of Apollo in Raphael's *Parnassus*, the preparatory study for which is given here as Fig. 45. The head of the lira ('lyre') which Apollo is playing is also clearly shown as the flat, leaf-shape type with seven pegs—both the mystical number of strings for Apollo's

FIG. 45. Drawing for the *Parnassus* Apollo, Raphael. (By courtesy of the Musée des Beaux-Arts, Lille)

archaic lyre, and, in consequence, the standard disposition for the sixteenth-century lira da braccio. The original head and fittings for this example have long since passed into limbo, along with any proportional information they may have disclosed, the instrument consisting of a body-shell alone when it was examined for this study.

As with the preceding example, the table has been made from cedar of Lebanon, a rather coarse timber apparently in plentiful supply in sixteenth-century Brescia. This instrument, like Ex. VIII, also bears a Gasparo da Salò label, although here it is an obvious, handwritten counterfeit. The true author of this giant lira is unknown; he was certainly Brescian (the previous attribution to Gasparo is, however, unlikely) and he was undoubtedly a skilled worker, as the admirable purfling designs of the back inlay demonstrate. A manufacture date within the period 1560–80 is perhaps the most likely.

In dealing with the geometry of the small Gasparo lira, it was mentioned apropos that no clear overall proportions of height or width resolved themselves in either that or the present example. Here, in the absence of these, or any traceable form of planning circle, rectangle, or other device such as the vesica piscis, only the commensurable scheme, which governs all but one of the component-arc radii, exists to disclose any proportional considerations of its maker.

The body outline, broken down into its constituent arcs, is drawn in Fig. 46. The lower bouts, which, as we have previously mentioned, are not formed by a vesica construction, commence at d, with arc dI'. This arc, whose centre is at G', is of radius 112.5 mm, which, in the commensurable scheme, measures $5u$, where $u = 22.5$ mm. The curve is continued by arc $I'J'$, centre K', radius 135 mm, or $6u$, and is terminated by counter-curve $J'M'$, centre L', radius 22.5 mm or u.

The middle/upper-bout outline is started with arc $M'N'$, centre P', radius also 22.5 mm, u, thus making the corner symmetrically curved. Point O' is the centre of the next arc $N'V'$ whose radius $O'N'$ is in line with point F on the centre line. This radius (of arc $N'V'$) measures 90.5 mm, which, allowing a 0.5 mm error, is taken here to be $4u$ (90 mm).

The upper bouts consist of just two arcs: $V'W'$ and $W'X'$. $V'W'$ is centred at Z on the opposite side, its large radius, 225 mm, being exactly $10u$. The last arc of the outline, the remaining upper-bout arc $W'X'$, centred at Y', is the only arc radius which does not relate to the unit scheme governing the rest of the instrument. Nor does this rogue measurement of 129 mm respond to any other part of the design, barring two minor exceptions: the first is its repetition as the interval GG' (Fig. 46) between the main lower-bout centres, and the second as the distance $S'O'$ on line $FS'O'$, point S' being where FO' intersects the sound-hole centring circle centred at F. No convincing rectangular or other planning rationale could, however, be justified for these coincident amounts.

The radius of the circle, centre F, piercing the four f-hole centrings was measured as 69 mm, which cannot quite be considered part of the commensurable scheme ($3u = 67.5$ mm). The distance between upper and lower sound-hole centrings (102 mm) was found to be the same as that between the two lower centring points.

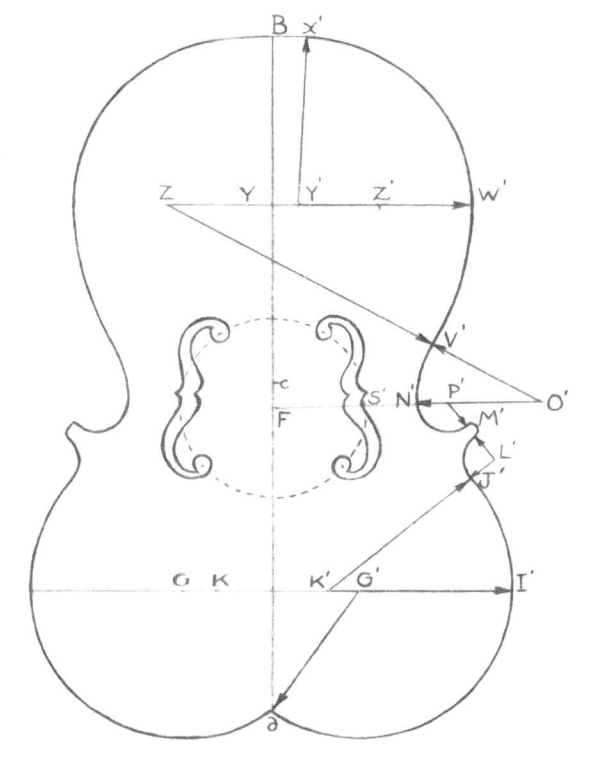

Fig. 46

PLATE IX

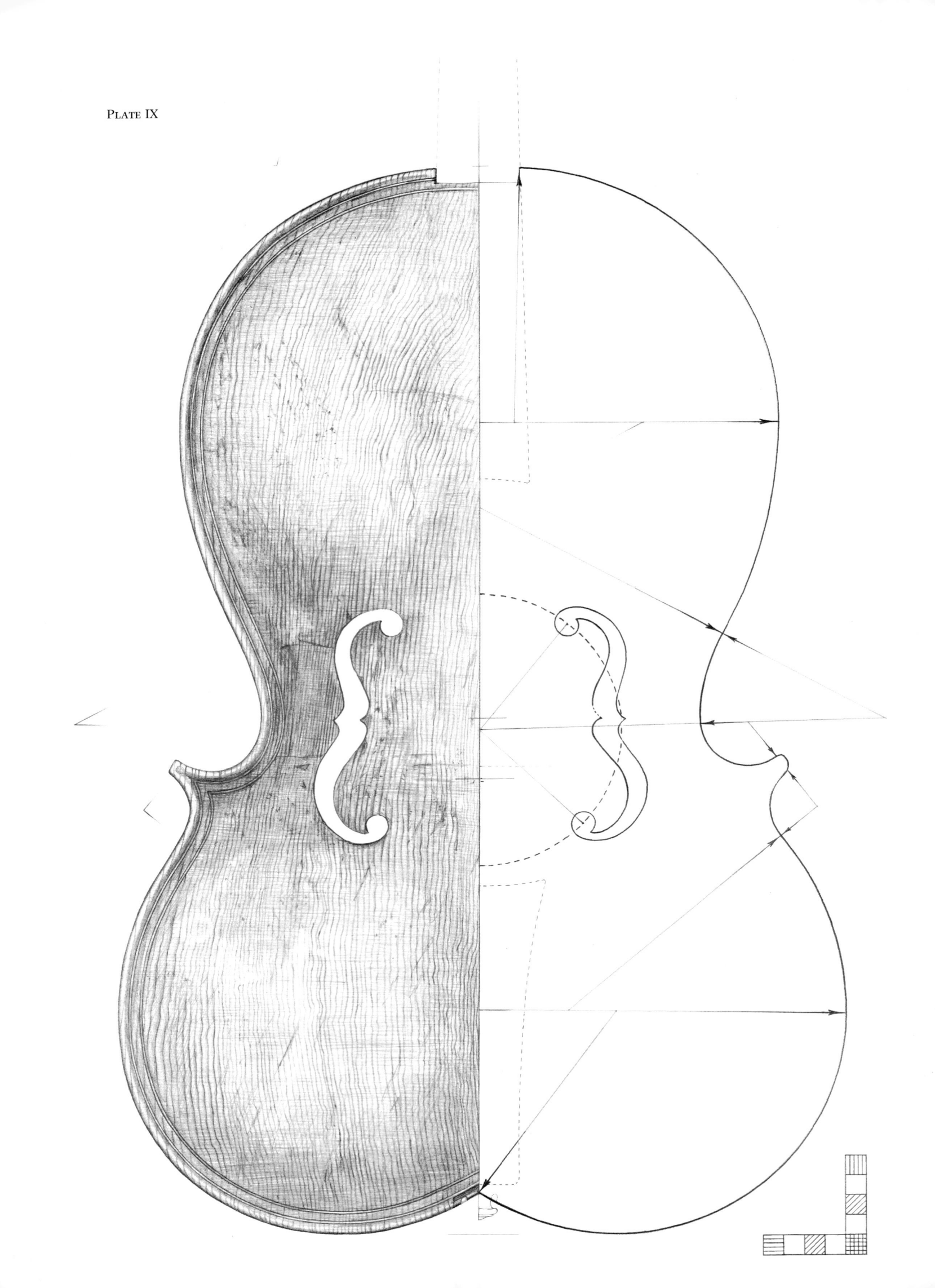

VIOLINS (VIOLA, VIOLONCELLO)

Perhaps no single event in the history of Western musical instruments has had greater impact on subsequent musical thought and practice than the emergence, in the sixteenth century, of the violin family.

The exact time-and-place circumstances of that appearance are still not fully established, although the belief is generally held that the family evolved from both the lowly rebec and the lofty lira da braccio, and that the first violins were of the 'viola' range, the other members of the family developing up and down in pitch-sizes from these. The first 'small violas' (the 'violinos') were, in fact, three-stringed, although no early violin in three-stringed state is known to survive.

There were also members of the family other than those which now form the classic quartet, that is, violin, viola, and violoncello (the double-bass is really a modified orchestral variant from the viol family,[44] there being no true contrabass violin). The extension of the tonal range of these three main divisions, however, meant that the intermediary instrument sizes, such as the tenor violas, the violoncello piccolo, and violino piccolos, were in effect made redundant.

The early violins, in England particularly, suffered tonal comparison with the gentle concord of the viols and viol consorts. At first, the violin's more incisive, vigorous voice was used in music of the dance, and that, according to the lawyer Roger North (1653–1734), at rather a low social level: 'the use of the violin had bin litle in England except by Common Fidlers', and even Mersenne (1636) thought that 'the violin is too crude'. Thomas Mace, whose enthusiasm for the viols we have already encountered, was equally scathing and reactionary. The 'scoulding violins' which made his 'Ears Glow' and filled his 'brains full of Friskes' were, however, a good deal less brilliant and penetrating in sound than the instrument we ourselves are used to hearing, a violin which in turn lacks something of the silvery mellowness and warmth of its baroque predecessor. Apart from the considerable acoustical developments accomplished by the great Cremonese masters, this difference in sound is, to a large degree, due to the major structural changes imposed upon the violin by the increasing technical demands, and changing tonal criteria and pitch levels, of its later players.

These structural modifications, which had been made by about 1800, included the replacement of the old bass-bar with a longer, stouter one, the lengthening of the finger-board, raising of the height and camber of the bridge (thus once and for all stressing the instrument's role as a melodic one), and, most crucial of all to the instrument's outward design, the lengthening, re-angling, and recontouring of the neck. This last is of great pertinence here, as such alterations to old instruments inevitably obscure some of the designer's original geometrical plan.

Tonally valued instruments rarely escaped this 'neck surgery', which either involved remodelling and re-angling, or, more frequently, complete replacement of the original neck, with the old head being grafted on to the new, extended, neck.

The unfortunate aesthetic aspects of this modification are demonstrated by Figs. 47 and 48, an original neck and a modified neck, respectively. It

[44] See introduction to Viols, p. 31 above.

will be observed at once that the organic harmony of head–neck–body is lost with this alteration. In Fig. 47 the join between the neck and the later discarded finger-board wedge is in line with the seam between table and ribs. In profile, the slope of board and neck each taper on either side of this line towards the head, the more organic taper of the original neck having greater sympathy with the curving taper of the head, from the cheeks round into the scroll. Moreover, the original wedge (supporting the older, more delicate finger-board) reconciled, by means of its arched underside, the curve of the table-arching with the straight line of the finger-board top—an aesthetic nicety that was overlooked with the 'improvement', Fig. 48, where the straight back of the new finger-board juts out unsympathetically over the contoured modelling of the table.

The Cremonese Violin

The extreme diversity of form which characterized the early development of the viol finds no true parallel in the formative years of the violin family. The essential shape of the violin was formalized early, with no subsequent deviant enjoying any measure of success.[45] The crucial evolution of the instrument, both acoustic and aesthetic, from the sixteenth to the eighteenth centuries was therefore accomplished within comparatively narrow and infinitely subtle constraints. Accordingly, I have decided to examine this gradual development through four instruments, dating from 1564 to 1703, instruments from three makers united by the most important and innovatory tradition of violin-making, the Cremonese school. The four violins are the Andrea Amati of 1564, a Nicola Amati c.1670, and two by Antonio Stradivari, one of 1666, and the 'Emiliani' of 1703.

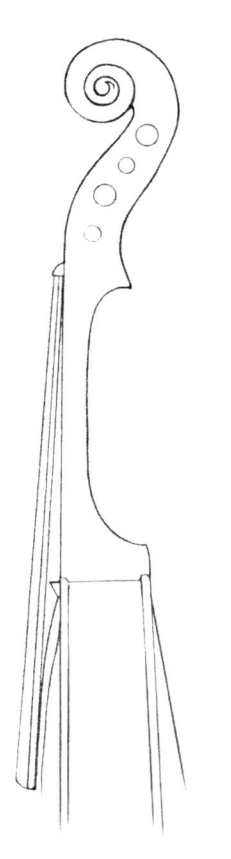

FIG. 47. Original form of violin neck and finger-board

Ex. X

Figs. 49–54, Pl. X

VIOLIN (SMALL MODEL). ITALY, CREMONA, 1564
ANDREA AMATI
HILL COLLECTION, ASHMOLEAN MUSEUM, OXFORD
Acc. No.: 10

Our first example selected from the violin family is one of the earliest of remaining stringed instruments. An exquisite violin from the hand of Andrea Amati, it dates from 1564, and is one of the thirty-eight instruments made by that great master for King Charles IX of France. The back and ribs bear traces of the painted royal insignia and motto, 'Pietate et Justitia', used by the young king (only fourteen years old when this instrument was completed) and his mother, Catherine de Medici, who most probably commissioned the 'thirty-eight' (twelve small violins, twelve large violins, six tenors, and eight basses) to be used by the musicians of the French court. The sound of this body of strings must have been 'royal' indeed. Alas, only a handful of these Charles IX Amatis survived the dispersal and destruction of court property brought about by the French Revolution.

---

[45] Attempts at 'redesigning' the instrument in the nineteenth century were made by respected luthiers such as Chanot, Savart, and Staufer. They consisted of reductions of the complex body outline to a more rational, cornerless form. Models produced by Chanot and Staufer were of guitar outline—a shape Stradivari himself had considered—while that of Savart was of trapezoid form. Both types are reported favourably in 'behind the curtain' acoustic tests, but, predictably, neither achieved any degree of acceptance in the aesthetically conservative world of the musician.

The Hill collection at the Ashmolean Museum, however, includes *two* Charles IX instruments: a magnificent large viola (one of the six 'tenors') and this beautiful instrument, one of the twelve small-pattern violins which would have played the upper-treble parts in the royal concerts.

Despite its extremely early date, this violin is a fully developed instrument, the product of over thirty years' experience of a master luthier, perhaps the first great violin-maker to gain widespread recognition for his work.

Its geometry is rather complex, lacking the elegant economy found, for example, in the design of the Maria treble viol, or the geometrical facility displayed in the more complex scheme of the tenor viol by Jaye. Like both these instruments, however, but unlike the other violins here to be discussed, this Amati still retains a trace of the great-circle geometry which we shall also encounter in the Brescian viola by Maggini. The great circle (radius $\frac{1}{2}$ body-length, centre C) is no longer used here as a centring guide for the middle-bout arcs, but does still provide the foundation of the outline, the arcs of origin, in Fig. 49 arcs HDH' and GBG'.

It is this term, radius CB, or CD, which becomes the largest term, ϕ_6, in a seven-part ϕ series governing the upper-bout design, and, to a lesser extent, the position of the f-holes and the radii of the minor arcs of the middle bouts. The vectors, in millimetres, of this ϕ series are:

ϕ_6: 171.5, ϕ_5: 106, ϕ_4: 65.5, ϕ_3: 40.5, ϕ_2: 25, ϕ_1: 15.4, ϕ: 9.5.

Fig. 50 shows the scheme for the upper bouts. The composite curve $G'S'$ is initiated by the upper arc of origin BG', centre C. C is also the centre of the model, and thus the radius of arc BG' is half body-length, 171.5 mm or ϕ_6. Point E' on radius CG' is a ϕ division, and is the centre for arc $G'M'$, radius ϕ_4 (CE' is the ϕ_5 radius of an important construction circle which is discussed below). The upper-bout curve then shallows with arc $M'N'$, centre L on the centre line, and therefore of radius half upper-bout width. This radius, like that of the small counter-curve arc $N'S'$, has no numerical relationship to either the ϕ series or any other major vector used in the design.

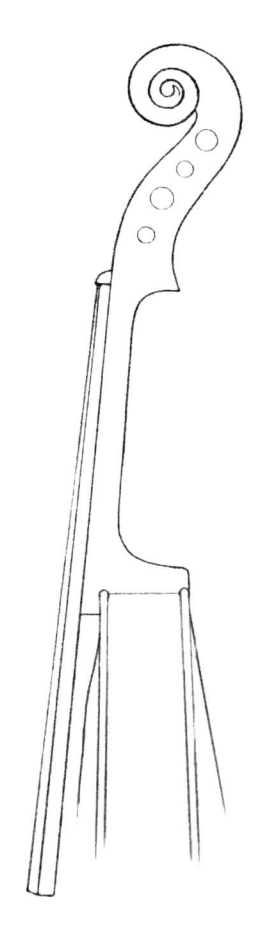

FIG. 48. Modification of violin neck and finger-board

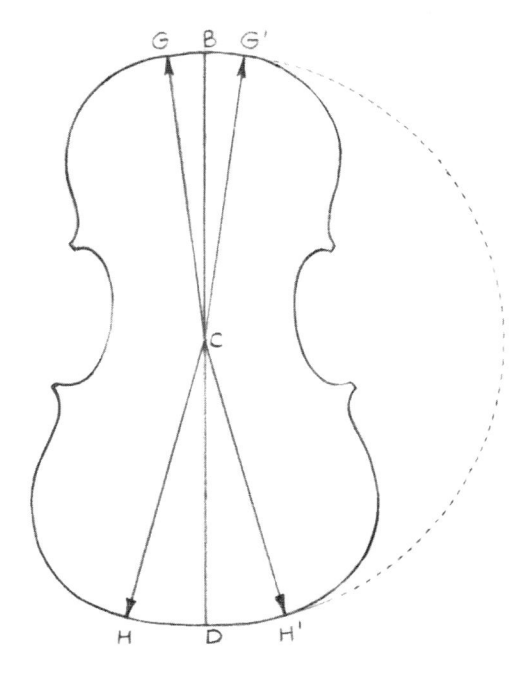

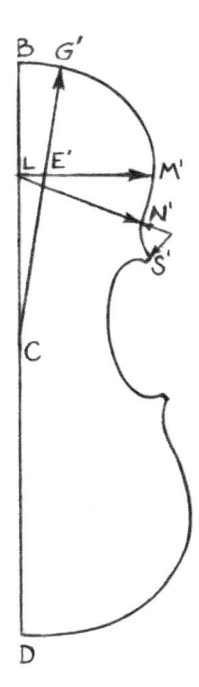

FIG. 49

FIG. 50

Fig. 51 examines a further use of the ϕ series. A circle of radius ϕ_3, centre C, pierces the f-hole at its centre V' between the middle notches, whilst a circle of radius ϕ_4, also centre C, pierces the lower f-hole centring, W'. The important ϕ_5 circle mentioned earlier is shown here as arc $E'P'O$ which together with the body length defines the hypothetical vertical aggregation of four ϕ rectangles (for clarity, only half the symmetrical plan is shown), whose diagonals, BP' and DP', pierce the corners S' and T' respectively. The establishment, in this way, of point P' (and, of course, its lateral inversion, P) is of great importance in determining the vector which is to complete the plotting of middle and lower bouts, as we shall see.

This vector could be described as being distantly related to the ϕ series discussed above. Mathematically, it is in fact $\frac{2}{3}$ of ϕ_5 ($\frac{2}{3} \times 106$ mm = $70.66\dot{6}$ mm, or 70.7 mm), with an additional commensurable relationship with the body length of which it is one-fifth ($\frac{1}{5} \times 353$ mm = 70.6 mm). Geometrically its value, and relationship to the body outline and the ϕ series, is demonstrated in Fig. 52 by drawing the vesica piscis on the horizontal centre line, between the two corner-piercing ϕ-rectangle diagonal points P and P' (i.e. on line PCP'). The common radius of the vesica piscis circles is equal in value to the vector that we seek. The relationship between the ϕ_5 radius circle, the vesica piscis, and the outline is shown in Fig. 52 by the lines of intersection—$QQ'Q''$ and $RR'R''$.

The lower and middle bouts are completed in Fig. 53 with this major vector of 70.7 mm. The arc $H'R''$, radius 70.7 mm (measured as 70.5 mm), centre K', continues the 'great circle' arc of origin DH'. The counter-curve $R''T'$ completes the lower bouts. The radius of this arc, like its upper-bout counterpart, is mathematically unrelated to the other values used in this instrument.

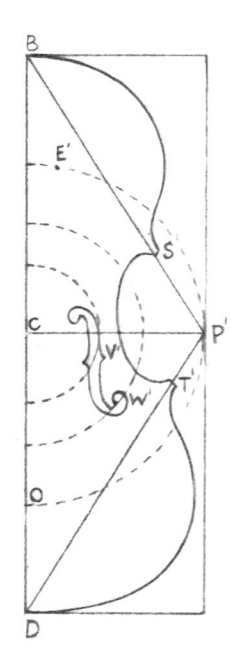

FIG. 51

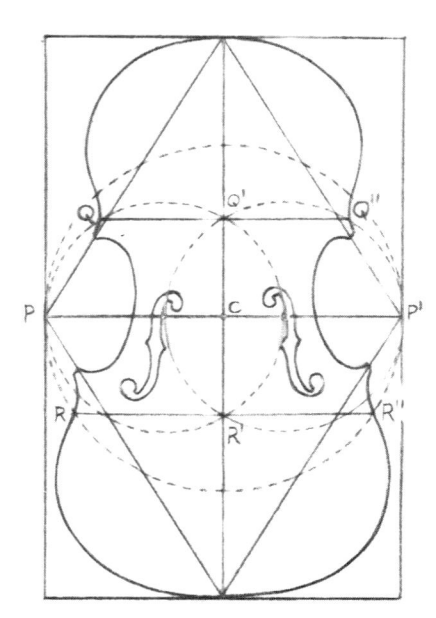

FIG. 52

If arc $H'R''$ and its lateral inversion HR, radii 70.(7) mm, centres K' and K respectively, are produced to form circles, they will cross on the centre line at point F. This point is the centre of a circle piercing the upper and lower centrings of the f-holes. Its radius is 53 mm, which is the distance KK', and, incidentally, twice the 'equivalent' distance EE' (see Fig. 50) in the upper-bout construction.

The middle bouts are also analysed in Fig. 53. The main arc $Y'Z'$ is of radius 70.5 mm (70.7 mm?) which, as discussed above, is the radius, too, for main lower-bout arc $H'R''$. The minor arcs completing the curve of the middle bouts, $S'X'$, $X'Y'$, and $Z'T'$, all have radii of ϕ-series values: ϕ, ϕ_2, and ϕ_1, respectively.

This completes the analysis of the somewhat tortuous geometry of this instrument's body design.

The neck of this Amati, like that of so many other fiddles, has been lengthened and repositioned according to modern practice.[46] In the main drawing (Pl. X) its present position is shown to the left of the centre line; to the right I have indicated its probable original length (approximately 5 mm shorter than present condition). No geometry was found to correlate the total length, nut position, or string length to the schemes used in the body design.

The head of this instrument has a crisp, delicate beauty, suggesting an illusion of its growth out of the wood, rather than its having been carved from it. Traces of the original painted decoration remain in the spirals of the scroll. The head, like the other parts of this violin, seems to demonstrate a ruggedly independent geometry; none of the radii of its arcs has any relationship with the various vectors of the body scheme—it is a complete and separate conception.

The analysis of the head is shown in Fig. 54, where it is contained within two rectangles of the same (1.342) proportion, annexed long side to short side: $QRST$, which contains the spiral of the scroll, and $PQTU$, which contains the peg-box. The spiral itself is that of the usual classic Ionic volute, traced in Fig. 54 by the smaller dotted line (the larger dashing representing the bevel of the scroll, which corresponds visually to the inner line of the volute). Its conformity with classic models ceases at A

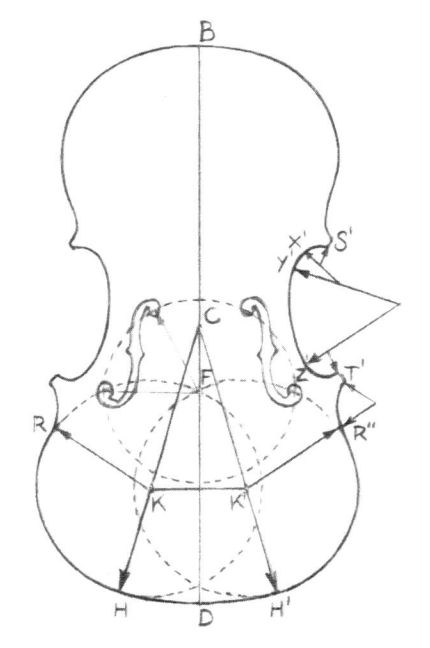

FIG. 53

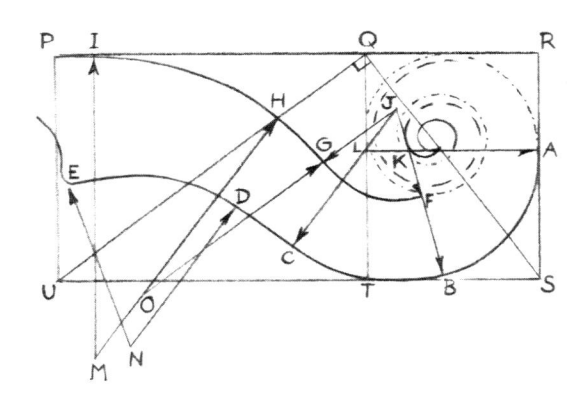

FIG. 54

(rectangle $ASTL$ is also 1.342 in proportion). Thence, the radii of the subsequent arcs conform to a 1.342 series based on the sides of this system of rectangles. The progression in whole-number millimetre values is: 19, 26, 35, 47, 63. Thus, the spiral is continued by arc AB, radius 26 mm, centre K; arc BC, radius 35 mm, centre J; short straight line CD, to counter-curve arc DE, radius 35 mm, centre N. The upper curves of the peg-box are equally elegant of construction: arc FG, radius 19 mm, centre J; counter-curve arc GH, radius 47 mm, centre O; and finally arc HI, radius 63 mm, centre M.

[46] See introductory note to the violin group (pp. 65–66 above) with reference to Figs. 47 and 48.

Plate X

Ex. XI

Figs. 55–58, Pl. XI

VIOLIN. ITALY, CREMONA, c.1670
NICOLA AMATI
PRIVATE COLLECTION, LONDON

Between the last violin and this present example lies a period of about one hundred years of development, and two generations of the Amati family. Nicola was the grandson of Andrea, through Hieronymous (of the 'brothers' Amati, Antonius and Hieronymous), and is the most universally celebrated member of this illustrious Cremonese family. This fame arises not only from his magnificent instruments, and the great tonal advancement they represent, but also from the considerable influence he was to have as teacher and model for the succeeding generation of luthiers, who were to bring the Cremonese school of violin-making to an unrivalled zenith.

Music itself had hardly stood still during the century or so which separates these two Amatis. The increasing demands for greater power and brilliancy from its players are reflected in the broader proportions and lower arching of the later violin. This example, which misleadingly bears an earlier label of 1664, is a so-called 'grand-pattern' Amati, and it was probably made in 1670 when the master was well into his seventh decade.

As with the previous example, the neck has been lengthened, here probably by about 5 or 6 mm; this supposed original position of the head, as well as the original outline of the right-hand upper bout (somewhat reduced by wear and repairs), are therefore given in the main drawing.

There is a markedly more relaxed approach to the geometrical planning of this instrument than there was in the complex harmonic organization of vectors found in the Andrea Amati previously discussed. It was discovered that the body plan of the Andrea was governed by a seven-term ϕ series, with the important lower-bout and middle-bout arc (in that small pattern, 70.7 mm) being mathematically related to it, *and* commensurably related to the body length. In this instrument, as we shall see, the minor vectors are not incorporated in the smaller four-termed ϕ progression, but, like the equivalent lower-bout term (here 71.5 mm), appear to resolve themselves into whole-number and simple fractions of a unit relating to, and here expressed in, Brunswick inches, the resulting scheme being a somewhat unlikely mixture of rational and irrational mathematical values.

The other great difference in planning occurs with the centring of the lower-bout arc of origin. In the Andrea it was centred at C, the centre of the model, and therefore related to the great-circle geometry found in contemporary and later viols (Exx. II and IV). In the Nicola Amati, however, this centre has shifted upwards on the centre line to a golden-section division of the model, thus giving a shallower start to the lower-bout curves and a deeper start to the upper-bout curves.

This centring point is shown, point E, Fig. 55, governing the arc of origin of the upper and lower bouts (GBG' and HDH'). E divides the body length, BD (355 mm or ϕ_3), into two ϕ values: $ED = 219.5$ mm or ϕ_2, and $EB = 135.5$ mm or ϕ_1. This last term, ϕ_1, is the radius of upper-bout arc of origin BG', and halved (allowing 0.25 mm error) gives the

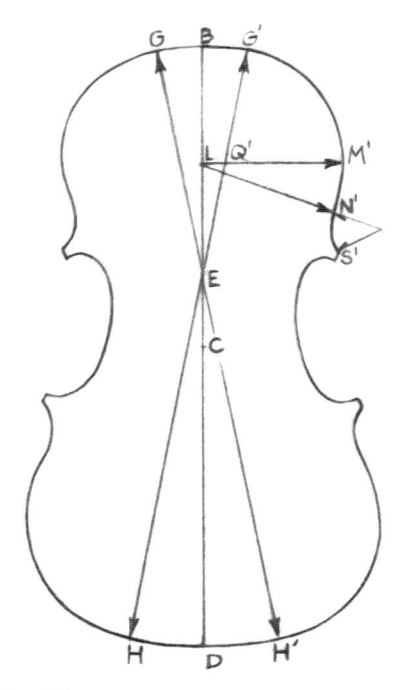

FIG. 55

radius, measured as 68 mm, of the following arc, $G'M'$, centre Q' ($\frac{1}{2}\phi_1 = 67.75$ mm). The curve then shallows with arc $M'N'$, centre L on the centre line, and of radius 84 mm, the value ϕ, which completes the four-term ϕ series:

$$\phi_3: 355 \text{ mm}, \phi_2: 219.5 \text{ mm}, \phi_1: 135.5 \text{ mm}, \phi: 84 \text{ mm}$$

(all values taken to nearest 0.5 mm). The curve is then completed by counter-curve arc $N'S'$, radius 30 mm, which can be interpreted as $1\frac{1}{4}$ Br. in., the first of the smaller vectors, harmonically unrelated to the main series.

These simple fractions of Brunswick inches are also found (Fig. 56) in the radii of the minor arcs of the middle bouts: $S'X'$, radius 12 mm ($\frac{1}{2}$ Br. in.); $X'Y'$, radius 30 mm ($1\frac{1}{4}$ Br. in., and equal to upper-bout counter-curve $N'S'$); and the lower arc $Z'T'$, radius 18 mm ($\frac{3}{4}$ Br. in.). The main arc, $Y'Z'$, of the middle bouts is of radius 68 mm, which is the same as that of the main upper-bout arc $G'M'$, that is, $\frac{1}{2}\phi_1$. It is centred at J', a point equidistant from ϕ-point E and centre-point C on the centre line (see locating arcs in Fig. 56). A line drawn from J' across to the centre line

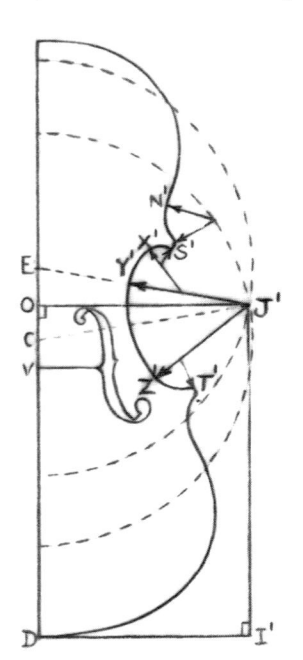

FIG. 56

meeting at O, and a line dropped from J' to the base line meeting at I', form a hypothetical rectangle of ϕ proportion, $J'I'DO$, whose sides relate to the instrument's bridge and nut position. The long sides of this rectangle, OD and $J'I'$, measure 195 mm, which is also equal to the important bridge-locating factor, BV (see also Fig. 57). The probable original nut position, A, approximately 6 mm lower on the centre line than at present, would also be in ϕ relationship to BV, so that

$$AB = (120.5 \text{ mm}) : BV = 195 \text{ mm}$$
$$\text{as} \quad OJ' \text{ (or } DI'\text{)} : OD \text{ (or } J'I'\text{)}.$$

The construction of the lower bouts roughly corresponds, in its disposition of radii and arcs, to that of the upper bouts (their proportional interrelationship is, of course, quite different). This differs from the scheme used by Andrea Amati in the small-pattern violin previously analysed, where the main lower-bout arc ($H'R''$ in Fig. 53) continued from the arc of origin to the counter-curve of the lower corner. Here, in Fig. 57, the

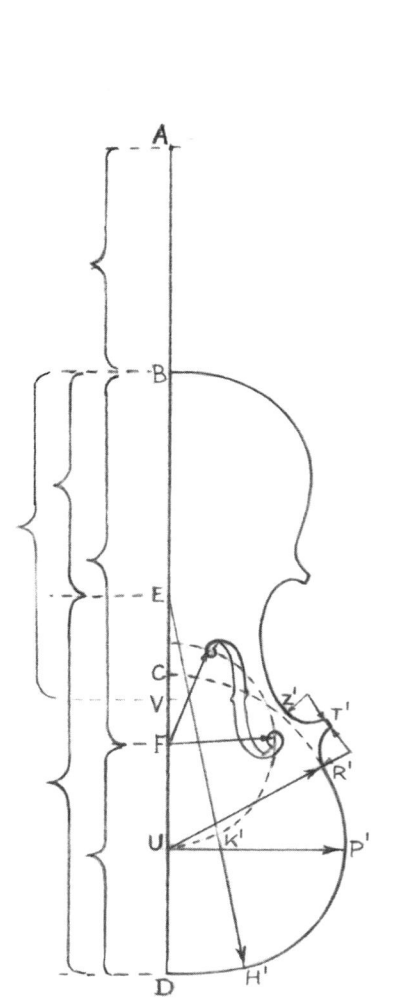

FIG. 57

corner counter-curve $T'R'$ mirrors its middle-bout neighbour, $Z'T'$, having the same radius, 18 mm ($\frac{3}{4}$ Br. in.), and leading into an intermediary arc, $R'P'$, centred, like its upper-bout cousin, on the centre line, at U. This arc, half the lower-bout measurement = 208 mm ($8\frac{3}{4}$ Br. in.), can be produced to the centre line, where it crosses at C, the centre of the model. The principal lower-bout arc, $P'H'$, centre K', is of radius 71.5 mm (measured), which, though unrelated to the ϕ progression, *is* expressible in Brunswick inches (3 Br. in. = 71.34 mm), and again, as in the previous violin, will divide the body length by 5 (here, $\frac{1}{5} \times 356$ mm = 71.2 mm).

The lower bouts of the instrument are completed by arc of origin DH', centre E, radius 219.5 mm, or ϕ_2, the only main-series harmonic value to occur in the lower-bout scheme. The main ϕ division of the body length, BD, which gave point E, can also be inverted; this gives point F, the centre of the circle which pierces the upper and lower centrings of the f-holes.

The head-design of this Nicola, like the planning of the body outline, betrays a rather more casual approach to schematic geometry than we found in the Andrea Amati. The work itself is careful enough, and the result very beautiful, though of a different character from the marvellous 'Alard' scroll of 1649; perhaps in the later scroll one can see something of the Stradivari heads to come.

Fig. 58 shows the head outline contained in two annexed rectangles: scroll, $QRST$, and peg-box, $PQTU$. In the Andrea Amati, the equivalents of these two rectangles were found to be of the same proportion, and together with a third, inscribed, rectangle of similar ratio provided a series which governed the radii of the head and peg-box. Here there is no such organization. The two annexed rectangles are harmonically unrelated, as are the radii of the various component arcs, whose centres, like the Andrea scroll, take no heed of the containing rectangle.

The Ionic volute of the scroll represented in Fig. 58 by the dotted lines terminates at A, where it is continued by quadrant arc AB, centre K, radius 27.5 mm. Arc BC is centred at J and is of radius 46.5 mm; a short straight line, CD, connects BC with the countercurve arc, DE, centre M, radius 31 mm. Point M is also the centre for upper peg-box arc IH, which is therefore partly concentric with arc ED; IH has a radius of 54 mm. The peg-box design is completed by straight line HG and terminating arc GF, centre L, radius 13 mm. No mathematic or harmonic scheme could be found to unite these values, which, with the exception of line RS, the depth of the head (48 mm or 2 Br. in.), also failed to comply with whole or simple fractions of Brunswick inches of the kind seemingly used in the smaller vectors of the body scheme.

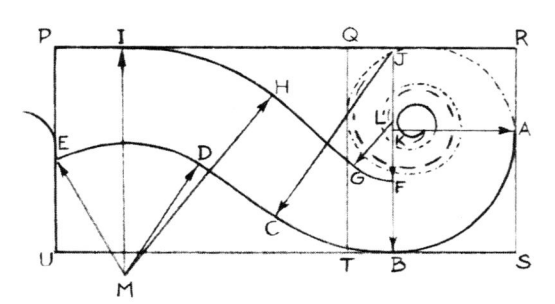

Fig. 58

One interesting factor to emerge from the head analyses of the first three examples (Exx. X, XI, and XII) of violin here given is that the length of the head was found to be half the maximum width of the lower bouts.

Plate XI

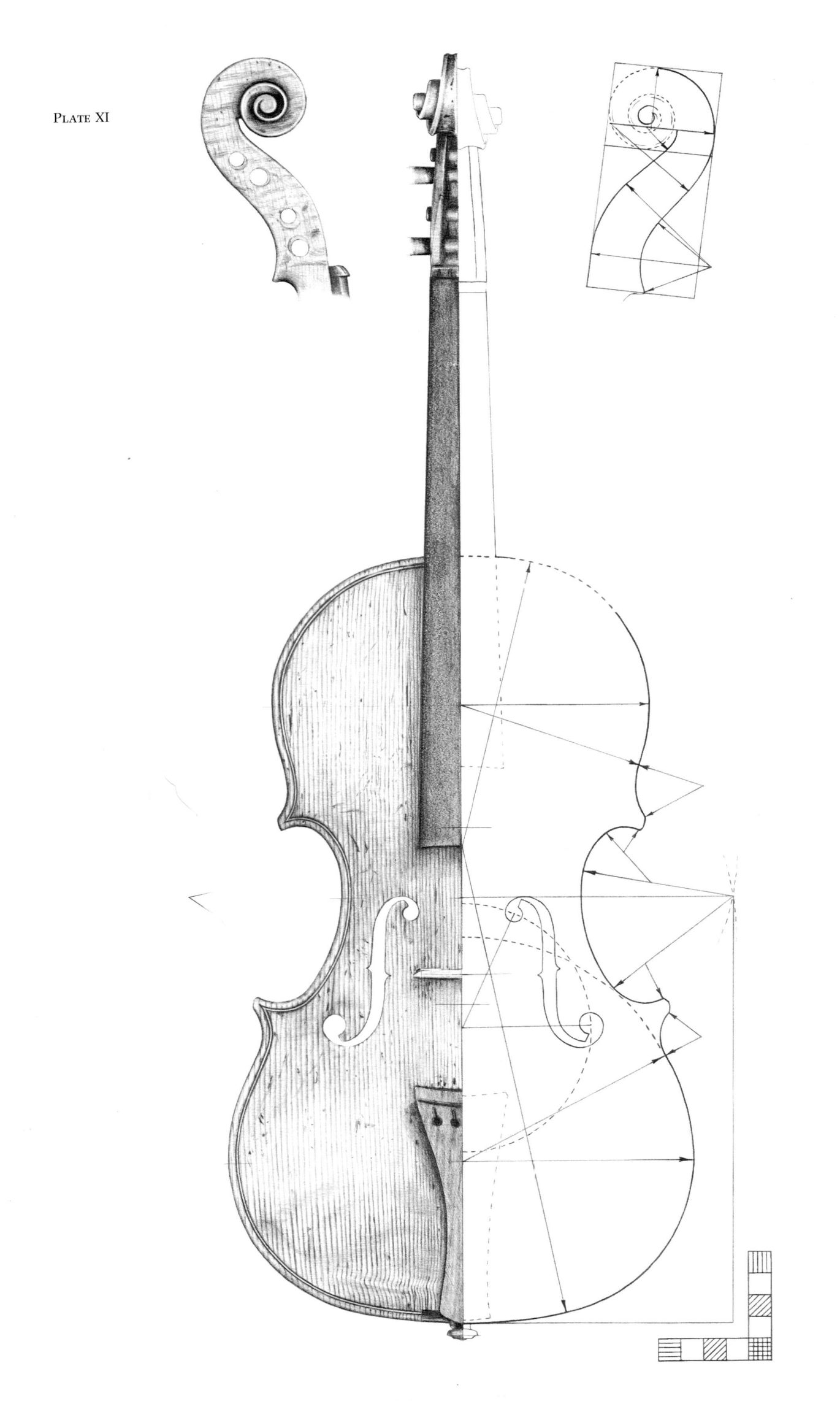

Ex. XII
Figs. 59-62, Pl. XII

VIOLIN. ITALY, CREMONA, 1666
ANTONIO STRADIVARI
PRIVATE COLLECTION, LONDON

Much has been written about Antonio Stradivari, a man whose contribution to the development of the violin, and thereby to music itself, is inestimable, and whose profound artistry, unerring intuition, and limitless energy became as legendary in his long lifetime as did his consequent and unspoiling wealth.[47] Given, then, his 'key-figure' status, I have decided on two contrasting Stradivaris to complete the developing sequence of Cremonese violins; the first is a rare early work of 1666 (the year before his first marriage), the second a celebrated violin of 1703, an instrument which reflects the full illumination of his genius.

Despite the most exhaustive researches, much of Stradivari's early life still rests in obscurity. From the instruments of his old age, where the master proudly declares the total of his years beneath the date of making,[48] it has been established that he was born in 1644, but no definitive account of his early training has yet been made. From the character of his early work, it has been concluded that, like many of his gifted contemporaries, he must have been a pupil of Nicola Amati. This is supported by the label of this early Stradivari, which reads:

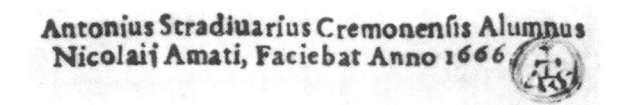

> Antonius Stradiuarius Cremonenfis Alumnus
> Nicolaij Amati, Faciebat Anno 1666

the 'ALUMNUS' meaning 'foster-son' or 'disciple'. Indeed, the debt to Nicola can be plainly seen in the design analysis of this violin, together with the younger man's own emerging personality: accepting some elements, while questioning and rejecting other parts of the inherited pattern. Comparing the contemporary Nicola violin with this 1666 Stradivari, the impression is that they are at once like and very unlike. Already there is a feeling of length and elegance[49] in the latter work, although it is only a fraction longer and narrower than the Amati. The effect, as the geometry reveals, is made almost entirely by the more shallow treatment of the middle bouts.

The young Antonio's attitude towards *proportional* geometry, like his master Nicola's, appears to be freer than Andrea's, for once more we can trace no attempt to organize the small vectors harmonically, as were organized those of the very early Amati. Nevertheless, the handling of the geometry is rather more careful than that of the Nicola. The main golden-section body division (point E, Figs. 55 and 59), for example, is the focus, in the case of the Stradivarius (Fig. 59), for two converging lines which pass exactly through the upper and lower *f*-hole centrings, whereas the same focus in the Nicola Amati occurs 2–3 mm above point E.

In the Stradivarius, too, the maker's regard for the basic proportions of length is demonstrated by the harmonic organization of overall length to body length, a disposition not considered in either of the two Amatis here

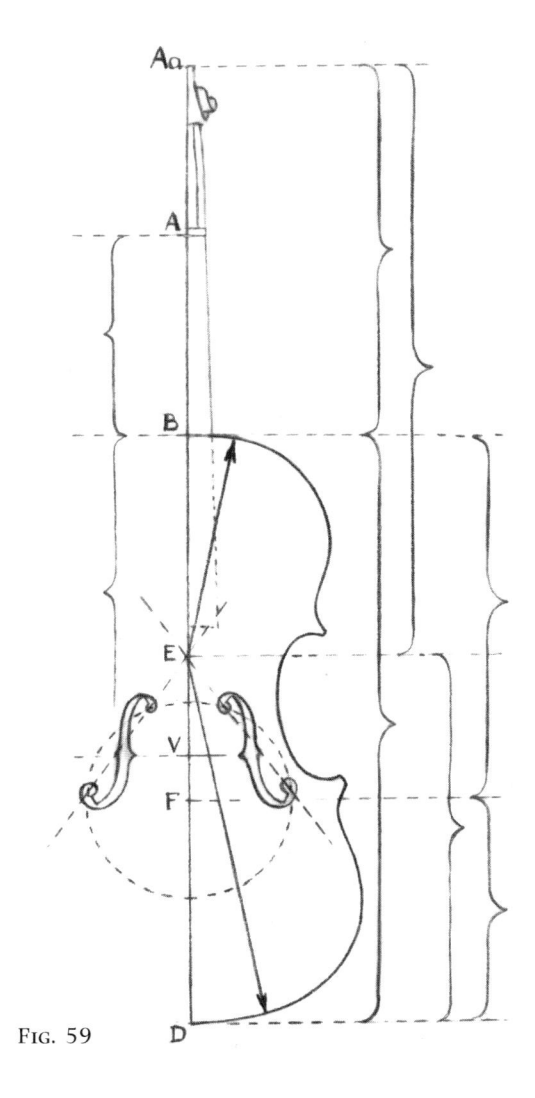

FIG. 59

---

[47] 'Ricco come Stradivari' actually entered the Cremonese vernacular.

[48] One such instrument, which was finished the year before his death, is inscribed 'anno aetatis 92', and another, of 1737, 'D'anni 93'.

[49] Stradivari himself is described as tall and lean.

analysed. This organization, the most sustained and beautiful use of ϕ proportion found in the instrument, utilizes four out of the five terms in the progression:

ϕ_4: 576 mm, ϕ_3: 356 mm, ϕ_2: 220 mm, ϕ_1: 136 mm, ϕ: 84 mm

(the last term in practice recorded as 83.5 mm). In Fig. 59, the overall length from the top of the head (here shown in its original position), Aa, to the button or base line, D, measures 576 mm, ϕ_4. It is divided in ϕ proportion at B, BD being the body length ϕ_3, which in turn is divided by ϕ at E, and inversely at F. E is the important centring point for the upper- and lower-bout arcs of origin; its position, at the ϕ division of BD, so that $BE = \phi_1$ and $ED = \phi_2$, was seen in the Nicola Amati, but not in the Andrea. The ϕ division F, where $BF = \phi_2$ and $FD = \phi_1$, is the centre of a circle, piercing the upper and lower f-hole centrings; its radius, 59.5 mm, illustrates the same puzzling tendency to simple fractions of Brunswick inches, which were found in the Nicola and which are continued here, 59.5 mm = $2\frac{1}{2}$ Br. in. (therefore also one-sixth of the body length, 356 mm (full) = 15 Br. in.).

A secondary use of the ϕ proportion is disclosed by original nut position A, where a ϕ division of the string length, AV (in plan, 315.5 mm), occurs at B, the point where neck and body meet, so that $AB = 120.5$ mm and $BV = 195$ mm.

The construction of both upper and, particularly, lower bouts closely follows that of the contemporary Nicola Amati violin. The main ϕ series is again used in the upper-bout scheme, which is shown here in Fig. 60. The upper-bout arc of origin, BG', is centred at ϕ-point E giving a radius of 136 mm or ϕ_1. Its neighbouring arc $G'M'$ is centred at Q', half-way along radius EG', thus arc $G'M'$ is of radius 68 mm—$\frac{1}{2}\phi_1$. The curve then shallows with arc $M'N'$, centre L on the centre line, radius 83.5 mm (or, allowing an error of 0.5 mm, ϕ). The counter-curve $N'S'$, centre a', is the only measurement in the upper-bout scheme of the Stradivarius which deviates significantly from that of the Nicola. Here the countercurve is deeper and the corner shorter than in the previous instrument, but again its harmonically unrelated radius is easily expressible as a Brunswick inch fraction, in this case $\frac{3}{4}$ Br. in. as against the $1\frac{1}{4}$ Bri. in. radius used in the Amati. As we shall see, an arc of exactly the same radius is used in the equivalent counter-curve of the lower bout, a practice not followed in either of the preceding instruments.

But the major divergence by the young Stradivari from the model of his master arises, as we have observed, in the increased radius and consequent shallowing of the main middle-bout arc. The curve of the middle bouts, Fig. 61, is initiated by arc $S'X'$, radius 10 mm, and, like the other middle-bout arcs, is harmonically unrelated to the main series. $S'X'$ is continued by arc $X'Y'$, radius 24 mm (1 Br. in.), which shallows the curve into the main arc. The centre, J', of the main arc, $Y'Z'$, is still equidistant from ϕ-point E and centre-point C, as the large locating arcs in Fig. 61 demonstrate, and, although harmonically unrelated to the main scheme, the exact radius of the arc appears to have been decided by a ϕ division, where $J'Y' : Y'E$ as $1 : 1.618$. The middle bouts are terminated by arc $Z'T'$, radius 18 mm or $\frac{3}{4}$ Br. in., denoting a return to the model used by Nicola, to which the lower bouts conform.

Symmetrically curved lower corners are achieved, once more, by using the same small radius of $Z'T'$ for the lower-bout counter-curve $T'R'$, centred at b'. Incidentally, a circle drawn with its centre at C, the centre of

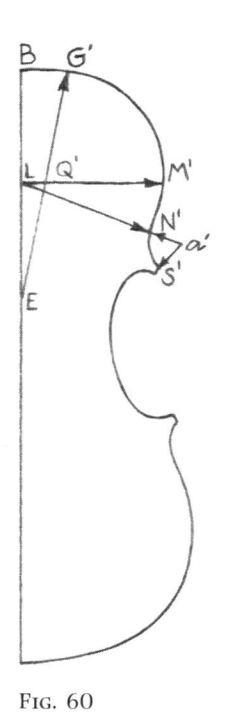

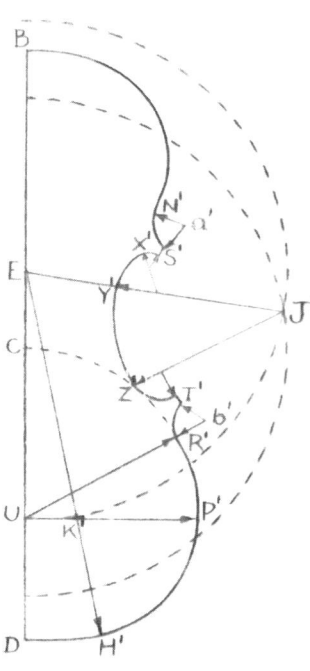

FIG. 60

FIG. 61

the model, will pierce the counter-curve arc centres a, a', b, b'. (This is further discussed in Appendix B, q.v.). Lower-bout construction is continued by arc $R'P'$, centre U on the centre line, and of radius 103.5 mm (0.5 mm shorter than the Amati), an arc which, when produced, crosses the centre line at C. The main lower-bout arc $P'H'$ is centred at K' and is of radius 71.5 mm (3 Br. in.)—again a one-fifth division of the body length. The centre, K', is also pierced by the middle-bout centre-locating arc centred at E. E is, of course, in its turn the centre of the lower-bout arc of origin DH', radius ϕ_2, which completes the lower-bout scheme. The outline geometry of this instrument and that of its original mould are further discussed in Appendix B (p. 172).

Fig. 62 is the geometrical plan of the rather assertive head of this violin—a head which, though lacking the calm suavity of the Nicola Amati, presents a more than compensatory vigour and masculinity. Aside from the manner of its execution, much of this boldness is traceable, in design terms, to the powerful, uninterrupted main upper peg-box arc IH. Again, the two containing rectangles, $PQTU$ and $QRST$, are of differing proportion, and there is no attempt to harmonize the separate radii in the design. The customary Ionic volute is represented in Fig. 62 by the dashed line, which terminates at A, to be continued by the quadrant arc AB, centre K, radius 27 mm. The centre J of the adjoining arc BC now lies on the side of the containing rectangle, unlike both the preceding violin heads, where it lay inside the rectangle. The radius of BC is therefore 49 mm, the depth of the head. A straight line, CD, leads to the terminating arc DE, centre N, radius 31.5 mm. The main arc of the upper curve, previously mentioned, is IH, centre M, radius 73 mm. It forms the whole of the peg-box top apart from a short, initiating, straight line, PI, and a small counter-curve, HG, centre F.

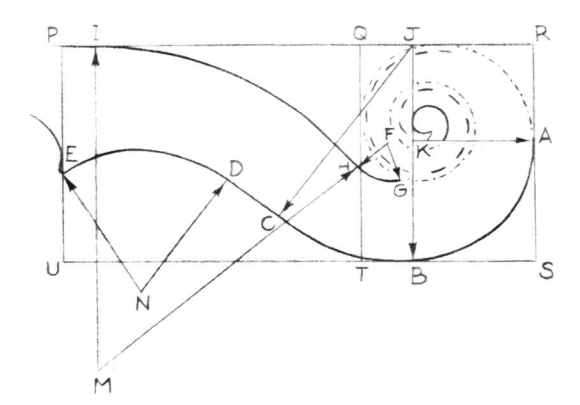

FIG. 62

Perhaps more remarkable than the strange concoction of irrational and rational systems employed in both the preceding and the present examples is the apparent use of the Brunswick inch in a centre which possessed its own unit of measurement, the Cremonese *oncia*, or inch.[50] The explanation for this most probably lies in coincidence, in that the overall body length, being a whole-number Brunswick inch factor (15 Br. in.),[51] means that other measurements in a commensurable, or part-commensurable, scheme will also be likely to coincide with whole, or simple fractions of, Brunswick inches.

[50] For policy on measurement systems, see Chapter 4, p. 22 above. The Cremonese inch has been a particularly difficult unit to define; various sources give it a value varying from 39.25 mm to 40.3 mm.

[51] 15 Br. in. = 356.7 mm. The body length of the Nicola Amati actually equals 355 mm, as measured, while that of the 1666 Stradivari equals 356 mm.

Plate XII

Ex. XIII
Figs. 63–65, Pl. XIII

VIOLIN. ITALY, CREMONA, 1703
ANTONIO STRADIVARI
PRIVATE COLLECTION, LONDON

The fourth, and last, violin that will be considered in our examination of the Cremonese development is also undoubtedly the most elegant: the Emiliani Stradivari of 1703. Made at the beginning of the master's so-called Golden Period, it is a fine classical example, much akin to the famous 'Betts' (1704). Alas, no black-and-white drawing can even suggest that marvellous luminous amalgam of wood and varnish, light and colour, which is so much a part of the undeniable charisma of these great instruments; but a comparative glance at the two drawings of the 1666 and 1703 examples (Pls. XII and XIII) should at least convey some of the repose and exquisite grace of the later instrument. Here there is a greater feeling of resolution; the curves and counter-curves of the outline flow without check through the divisions of upper, middle, and lower bouts, whilst the refinement of the f-holes now casts upon the physiognomy an air of calm beauty. In short, the instrument is a complete and perfect expression of Stradivari's personal vision of the luthier's art.

It should be stressed that the full essence of the difference separating these two products of Stradivari can only really be comprehended in terms of plastic quality. Differences of quantity, of measurement, are of course discernible, and are in some ways more easily discussed, but finally it has to be admitted that no evocation of the spirit was ever achieved through a mere description of the body. Nevertheless, an examination of the design make-up of this instrument, viewed against those of its precursors, does offer some modest insights into its creator's methodology.

Again we may proceed with an examination of the overall proportions, shown here in Fig. 63, which should be compared with Fig. 59, the equivalent stage of analysis of the 1666 instrument. It can be seen at once from this comparison that the instances of vertical proportioning are not as extensive in the later instrument, though it could be argued that where the golden-section ratios do remain they still govern the more important points of division, that is, point E, the centre for the arcs of origin and the focus of the f-hole centrings, and the neck : string-length relationship, $AB:AV$.

If the overall dimensions of this violin evince less proportional planning than the preceding example, the same cannot be said for the organization of the vectors governing the body outline. Here, as a glance at Appendix C (a summarized chart-analysis of the four Cremonese violins) will show, by slight alteration to a few of the radii the two seemingly opposing modes of proportion, the commensurable and the incommensurable, present in the other designs, are, in the 1703 instrument, far more positively integrated, suggesting an interpretation which to a further extent reconciles these rational and irrational factors. Furthermore, the rational proportions in the present scheme move away from their coincidence with 'Brunswick inch' values to a firm basis in a unit of commensurability, here measured as 17 mm.

An analysis of the body outline is shown in Fig. 64. The arc of origin, as we have seen, is still centred at ϕ-point E, which divides the body length BD, 354.5 mm (ϕ_2), into BE, 135.5 mm (ϕ), and ED, 219 mm (ϕ_1). Thus

FIG. 63

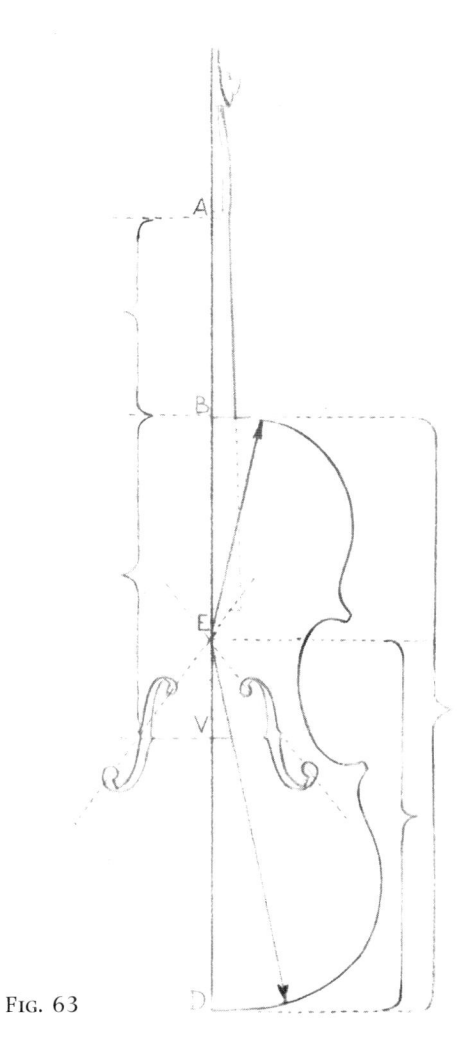

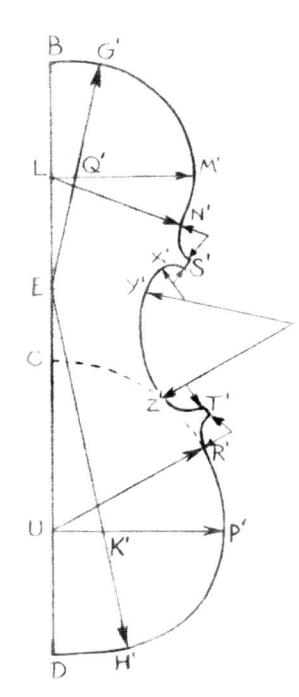

FIG. 64

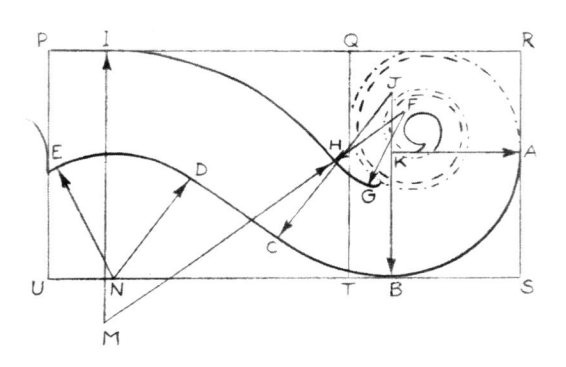

FIG. 65

the lower-bout arc of origin HDH' has a radius ϕ_1, or 219 mm. The curve continues with arc $H'P'$, centred at K'. This arc is of radius 71 mm (70.9 mm?), which again was read as being in commensurable (1 : 5) ratio with the body length BD. The next arc is $P'R'$, centre U on the centre line, and of radius 102.25 mm (the maximum width PUP', being twice UP', is measured as 204.5 mm). This is the first of the vectors that responds to the main commensurable scheme of arithmetic means, which is based upon the unit of 17 mm: in this case the radius can be expressed as $6u$ (102(.25) mm/17 mm = 6(.01)). The lower bouts are completed by counter-curve $R'T'$, radius 17 mm (u).

The middle bouts are also started with an arc, $T'Z'$, of this 'u' radius, which once again ensures that the lower corner is symmetrically curved. The main arc, $Z'Y'$, is also of radius commensurable to this scheme of arithmetic proportion: it measures 85 mm, which divides, 85 mm/17 mm, to $5u$. The remaining two smaller vectors, arcs $Y'X'$ and $X'S'$, have radii of 24 mm and 10 mm respectively, neither of which relate to any traceable scheme.

The upper bouts are initiated by arc $S'N'$, also radius 17 mm, or u. The curve is continued by arc $N'M'$, centre L, on the centre line, radius 83.5 mm (half the maximum width), equal to ϕ, and approximately equal to $5u$. The main upper-bout arc, $M'G'$, centred at Q', is of radius 68 mm, which is exactly $4u$ (68 mm/17 mm = 4). The outline is completed by the upper-bout arc of origin $G'B$, centre ϕ-point E, and of radius 135.5 mm (ϕ).

In this body outline we see a far fuller amplification of the whole-number resonances, only partially declared in the previous two violins. And, as the following analysis shows, the proportional scheme found in the head proves it to be a worthy crown to the body-geometry.

The main drawing shows something of the compact power of this masterly scroll—a head much grander in proportions than those previously examined. Fig. 65 gives the breakdown of the peg-box curves into their component arcs. The large containing rectangle $PRSU$ measures 105 mm by 52 mm, giving a ratio of 2.019, which might be taken as a $\sqrt{4}$ rectangle, or double square (a solution also found in the head of the Zanetto viol, Ex. I). The constituent rectangles $PQTU$ and $QRST$, however, did not relate in ratio either to one another or to the parent rectangle. The superbly carved Ionic volute is traced in Fig. 65 by the outer broken line, finishing at A. The spiral is continued by the usual quadrant arc, AB, radius 28.5 mm, centred at K; thence by arc BC, centre J, radius 42.5 mm; straight line CD, and counter-curve DE, centred at N on $PRSU$, radius 28.5 mm. The upper peg-box curve has the same bold, one-arc sweep as the master's early violin previously analysed. This is arc IH, centre M, radius 63.5 mm, and it is finished off by small counter-curve HG, centre F, radius 19 mm.

Thus the millimetre vectors for the peg-box are, in progression: 19, 28.5 (twice), 42.5, and 63.5, which, allowing a small margin for the inexactitudes of measurement, reveals a beautiful geometric progression tuned to the ratio of 2 : 3:

$$\frac{28.5 \text{ mm}}{19 \text{ mm}} = 1.5 \left(\frac{3}{2}\right); \quad \frac{42.5 \text{ mm}}{28.5 \text{ mm}} = 1.49; \quad \frac{63.5 \text{ mm}}{42.5 \text{ mm}} = 1.49.$$

A summarized analysis of these four Cremonese violins, presented as one development, is given in Appendix C (p. 174) in the form of a chart of comparative arc radii of the four body outlines.

Plate XIII

Ex. XIV

Figs. 66–69, Pl. XIV

VIOLA. ITALY, BRESCIA, c.1610
GIOVANNI PAOLO MAGGINI
PRIVATE COLLECTION, LONDON

Following the tradition that a good pupil should surpass his master, Giovanni Paolo Maggini ennobled in his work the vigorous originality of his teacher, Gasparo da Salò, with a grandeur still entirely masculine and thoroughly Brescian in character. He was truly the apogee of the Brescian school, and no further separate development was to follow his death, probably of the plague, in 1632. The quintessential Brescian qualities of strength and vigour remained, however, as indispensable agents in the evolution of the more refined and reposeful ideals of the Cremonese school, and, without these Dionysian influences, a del Gesu would certainly never have arisen from the Apollonian academies of Cremona.

Analysis of this particular Maggini, a superb, exceedingly rare, contralto viola, c.1610, did reveal a very fine commensurable geometry, but it also entailed a confrontation with three of the principal problems encountered when obtaining and processing proportional information from an elderly instrument:

(i) Distortion and asymmetry.
(ii) The incidence of a point 'just missing' in an otherwise complete and convincing scheme, owing to either:
   (a) wear to the fabric; or
   (b) a making- or drawing-error; or
   (c) a 'last minute' arbitrary or intuitive decision of the maker.
(iii) Our use of a decimal system (here with a 0.5 mm smallest factor) to express, and discuss, quantities (based on a host of differing units)[52] undoubtedly originally conceived as fractions, which, although far less convenient and universally applicable than the decimal ratio, nevertheless beautifully and finitely express their *quality* of relationship, as well as their quantity.[53]

Very often, as in the case of the lower bouts of this instrument, all three problems are involved at once. This became apparent when the lower-bout width was measured as 1 mm short, overall, of what is obviously, according to the support of the rest of the scheme, the true and intended width of the original design. Or, as in the case of the most common problem, number (i) on the above list, distortion and asymmetry, the problem can be isolated, as it was found to be in the lower corners of this instrument, which consequently proved to be a little difficult to resolve.

Therefore, with my primary directive in mind, that of producing an exposé of the use of geometry and numerical proportion in these designs, the following analysis treats the lower-bout width not as 245 mm (measured) but as 24(6) mm (planned). This 0.4 per cent margin, I feel, is amply justified by the resulting homogeneity of the scheme. The use of parentheses around the last digit of a figure indicates a vector based on, or a subdivision of, this 'resolved' measurement.

The third problem, too, arising from the necessary use of the decimal system, became apparent at an early stage in the analysis. Here, the usual proviso of a 0.5 mm minimum quantity can become restrictive,

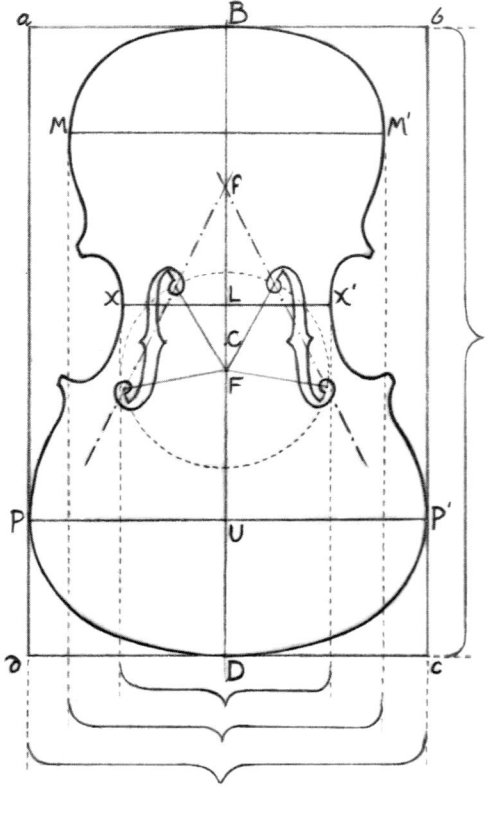

FIG. 66

[52] See Chapter 4, p. 22 (and also p. 77 n. 50).

[53] It must be appreciated, however, that our task being one of comparative study, the use of any system other than our own, familiar metric/decimal system would be unpractical.

because, while it is impractical to measure an amount smaller than 0.5 mm, a calculated quantity might well necessitate the use of a smaller division. Such a situation occurs in the unravelling of the scheme of commensurable proportion which governs this instrument. Here a basic unit was discovered common to all the major vectors, and was calculated as 16.4 mm (u).

This unit was found to govern the basic overall proportions, vertical and horizontal. In Fig. 66 the body outline is drawn in its containing rectangle, $abcd$, which measures 410 mm × 24(6) mm, or $25u \times 15u$, giving the ratio 5 : 3 (1.66̇6̇). The widths of upper, middle, and lower bouts (MM', XX', and PP') also have the same unit commensurability:

$MM' = 196.5$ mm $= 12u$ (allowing 0.3 mm error)
$XX' = 131$ mm $= 8u$ (allowing 0.2 mm error)
and $PP' = 24(6)$ mm $= 15u$ (0.4 per cent error, discussed above),

the amounts 12 : 8 : 15 yielding two simple ratios of 3 : 2 and 4 : 5.

Fig. 67 is drawn to show the basis of the body-geometry. The centrally placed axis-point, C (coinciding with the bridge position), immediately suggests great-circle resonances, although here such a figure is not used as a planning circle. A similar arrangement was found, without the beautiful vesicas, in the first Cremonese violin analysis, that of the Andrea Amati (Ex. X) of 1564. Another similarity with that example is the use of the same vector for main lower-bout and middle-bout arc radii.

One aspect common to all the violins analysed, as can be construed from Appendix B, was the 5 : 1 ratio of body length to the main lower-bout arc radius; this rule was also found to apply to the Maggini viola, where it formed part of the comprehensive commensurable plan.

The outline itself is initiated, Fig. 68, with the arc of origin DH', centre C, radius 205 mm, $12.5u$. It is continued by arc $H'P'$, centre K', the major vesica piscis arrangement, whose radius, 8(2) mm (one-fifth body length), equals $5u$. The curve is shallowed by arc $P'R'$, centre U, on the centre line, radius 12(3) mm or $7.5u$. The lower bouts are terminated by countercurve arc $R'T'$, centre J', radius measured as 24.5 mm, $1.5u$ (allowing 0.1 mm error).

The middle bouts comprise three arcs: $T'Z'$, $Z'Y'$, and $Y'S'$. $T'Z'$ is centred at W'; its radius, 22 mm, appears to relate to the scheme by being a third of the minor upper-bout vesica radius, which would give it a 'u-rating' of 1.33̇3̇. The main middle-bout arc, $Z'Y'$, centre O', as we have said, equals in radius the principal lower-bout arc $H'P'$, i.e. the major vesica radius (KK') of $5u$. Fig. 68 shows that a line drawn horizontally from point L on the centre line passes through X' (with X, the point of minimum middle-bout width) and on to O'. This line, $LX'O'$, is an aggregate of the minor and major vesica radii, which govern respectively the upper- and lower-bout schemes, here appropriately coming together in the middle bouts. LX' is 65(.5) mm, the upper vesica radius, while $X'O'$ is 82 mm, the lower vesica radius, demonstrating the 4 : 5 relationship of the two parts. LO' is also the short side of rectangle $LO'E'D$, which, measuring 229.5 mm × 147.5 mm, is also commensurable to this scheme, being a rectangle $14u$ (229.6 mm) × $9u$ (147.6 mm)—rectangle decimal ratio, 1.55̇5̇. The middle bouts are completed by arcs $Y'S'$, centre V', radius measured as 16(.5) mm, or u.

The upper bouts start with arc $S'N'$, centre I', of the same radius as arc $T'Z'$, that is, 22 mm, one-third of the minor, upper-bout vesica radius. The curve then changes direction with arc $N'M'$, part of the upper vesica

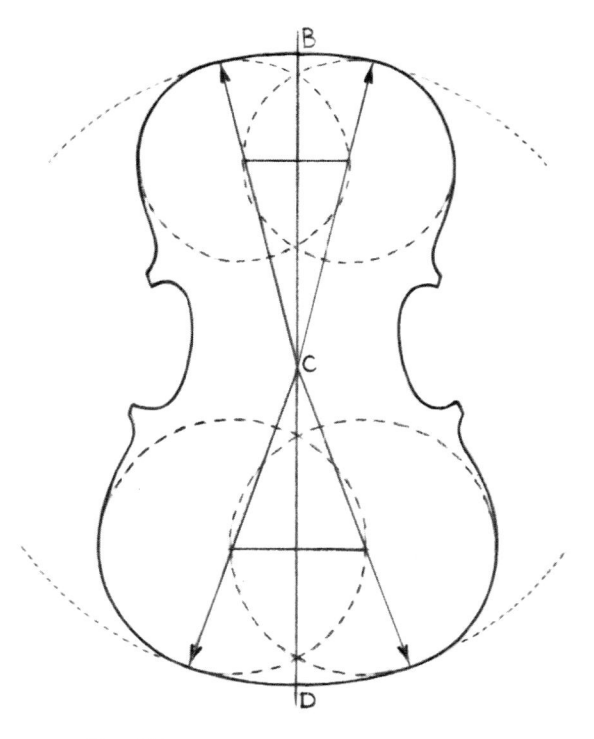

FIG. 67

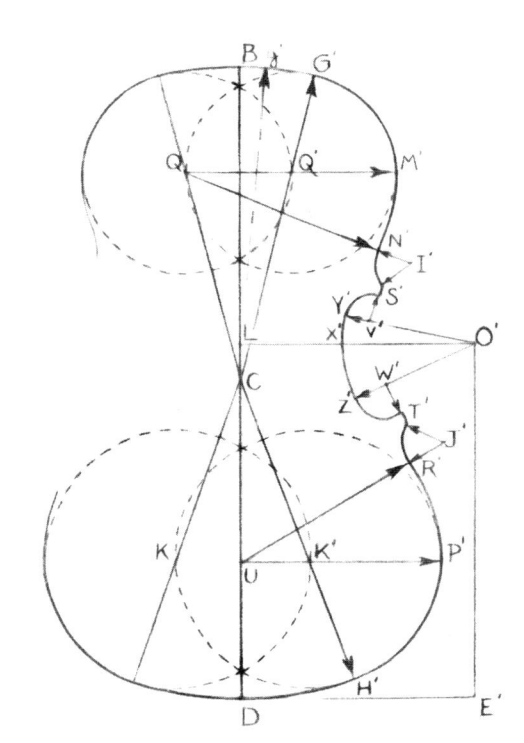

FIG. 68

arrangement, the centre for this right-side curve being at Q, the centre of the left-side vesica circle; its radius is therefore two vesica radii, or 131 mm as measured (131.2 mm as calculated), that is $8u$. Arc $M'G'$, part of the vesica construction, is centred at Q', its radius, 65(.5) mm, being $4u$. The outline is completed up to the neck by arc $G'g'$, centred at C, radius therefore equal to that of the lower-bout arc of origin, that is, 205 mm, or $12.5u$.

The positioning of the *f*-holes is shown in Fig. 66. The circle which pierces the four centrings has its centre at F; its radius of 63 mm did not correspond to the proportional scheme. Lines drawn through the two centres, however, converge at point f on the centre line; fD measures 307.5 mm, and Bf 102.5 mm, f being a 3:4 division of the body length, BD.

The boldness and assertion exhibited in the body design of this splendid viola is not quite as evident in the head. This is almost entirely due to the slender, under-massed character of the peg-box, which imparts an unexpected (and unwanted) impression of delicacy where one was led to anticipate strength. Nevertheless, the head has much of beauty to it, and is certainly one of the most beautifully conceived heads to be analysed for this study.

The geometry, traced in Fig. 69, demonstrates a careful regard for the containing and component rectangles which, together with the arc radii, respond to simple commensurable ratios, a scheme not directly related to the 16.4 mm unit which governed the body plan.

The main rectangle, $PRSU$, is 132.75 mm (132.5 mm as measured) × 59 mm, which gives a ratio of 2.25 (9:4). The scroll-containing rectangle, $QRST$, is a one-third vertical division of $PRSU$, and thus measures 59 mm × 44.25 mm, ratio $1.33\dot{3}$ (or 4:3). It leaves a 'remainder', the peg-box-containing rectangle, $PQTU$, which measures 88.5 mm × 59 mm, ratio 1.5 (or 3:2). A further rectangle is implied by one of the arc centres, M; this is $IROM$, 118 mm × 78.6 mm (78.5 mm as measured), which also yields the ratio 1.5 (3:2).

The arcs analysed in Fig. 69 begin with the continuation of the Ionic volute, by quadrant arc AB, centre G, radius 35.4 mm (35.5 mm as measured). This vector has a 4:5 (1.25) relationship with QR (44.25 mm), and a 3:5 ($1.66\dot{6}$) relationship with the radius of the next arc, BC, which is centred at J on PR, its radius therefore equalling head depth RS, that is, 59 mm. A straight line, CD, connects this with counter-curve arc DE, centre N, radius also 35.4 mm. The top side of the peg-box is initiated by straight line PI, leading into main arc IH, centre M (see above), radius 78.6 mm (2 Cremonese inches?)[54] which has a 4:3 ($1.33\dot{3}$) relationship with head depth RS. The outline is completed by counter-curve HF, also centred at J, and, once again, an arc of 35.4 mm radius.

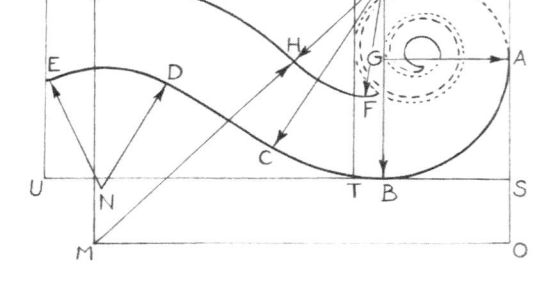

FIG. 69

[54] See p. 77 n. 50 above.

Plate XIV

Ex. XV
Figs. 70–72, Pl. XV

VIOLONCELLO (SMALL MODEL). ENGLAND, LONDON, 1718
BARAK NORMAN
PRIVATE COLLECTION, LONDON

The last member of the violin family to be dealt with here, the violoncello, was also the last of the group to enjoy an individual solo career. Before it could leave its role as 'bass violin' and challenge the solo position of the tenacious gamba, the violoncino, or violoncello as it was to become, had first to reduce its dimensions to a more manageable and 'flexible' size. This appears to have been accomplished by the end of the seventeenth century, one of its most important authors being Antonio Stradivari.[55]

In England the move towards a smaller model cello occurred not much later than the Italian development—possibly the outcome of similar, though quite separate, circumstances. The present example is just such an instrument, a small cello from the English school, made by Barak Norman 'at the Baſs Violin [usually written, or read, as 'at the Bass Viol in ...'] St. Paul's Church y^d, London'. It is dated 1718, and bears his ingenious monogram of a BN calligraphically intertwined with its own inversion, purfled in the centre of the back, as well as an inlaid floral device on the front. In his *Dictionary of Violin Makers* Stainer mentions such a cello of Barak Norman dated 1718 (possibly even this example) which 'was valued at 15 guineas in 1790, but now [1896] the price is higher'.

Geometrically this instrument was a little disappointing. Only a few tantalizing echoes of proportional thinking were found, with no one line of thought asserting itself sufficiently to proclaim it to be the system used.

The same number and disposition of arcs form its body outline as other violin family members here analysed, although it cannot be said that they have been used as carefully, or indeed if they have even been used consciously at all. The radius, UP', of lower-bout arc $R'P'$ (Fig. 71), for example, here deviates from the horizontal—the result of either a careless (or ignorant) formation of the model, or, as I suspect, an arbitrary alteration of curvature, that is, an alteration to the model or design archetype previous to this example's manufacture, thus negating any original, proportionally based geometrical construction present.

Viewing more positively what nevertheless is a handsome instrument, it is only fair to add that some proportional relationships did emerge and these are discussed below.

In Fig. 70, the overall proportions, vertical and horizontal, are shown. No significant 'containing' rectangle was found, although upper- and lower-bout widths did relate:

$$MM' : WW'$$
$$349 \text{ mm} : 419 \text{ mm} \ (= 1.2006)$$
$$\text{or} \qquad 5 : 6.$$

These two 'maximum-width lines' (MM' and WW')—lines which also intersect the corner-curve arc centres of upper (Q and Q') and lower (K and K') bouts—can be connected by a square of side 419 mm (maximum lower-bout width, WW'); in Fig. 70, this is square $VV'W'W$. The two annexed rectangles, $WIDJ$ and $IW'J'D$, each measure 157.5 mm × 209.5 mm ($= 1.330$), giving them a 3 : 4 ratio.

---

[55] W. H., A. F., and A. E. Hill, *Antonio Stradivari*: 'The excellence of Stradivari's violoncellos is even more remarkable than that of his other productions; in fact, we can unhesitatingly say that his finest examples stand without rivals. ... He fixed once and for all the standard proportions and dimensions of the violoncello.'

Despite these commensurable ratios, there occurs, once again, an isolated golden-section factor; here it is the centring at E of the lower and upper arcs of origin, E being a ϕ division of BD:

$$\frac{BD}{ED} = \frac{711 \text{ mm}}{439.5 \text{ mm}} = 1.6177 \ (1.618).$$

One more ratio is indicated in Fig. 70, although it must be stressed that this is a hypothetical one. The cello has unfortunately undergone the usual process of neck alteration; I have therefore had to estimate its original string length (or nut position). It was achieved by generation and calculation from measurements taken from a similar size and type of cello[56] still possessed of its original neck. This suggested a string length between 7 mm and 17 mm shorter than at present. In fact, the extreme figure of difference, 17 mm, would give a string length of 650 mm—exactly twice the distance from bridge to tail:

$$AO : OD$$
$$650 \text{ mm} : 325 \text{ mm}$$
$$2 : 1,$$

the same proportions being present in the Jaye and Guersan viols. It should, however, be repeated that this is an estimated measurement.

Given the paucity of proportional material present in the radii of the component arcs, it would be a needlessly unproductive exercise to give the customary commentary to the accompanying outline figure. Instead a table or list of the component arcs drawn in Fig. 71 is given, which will allow any patient reader to search further should he so wish; he is cautioned, however, for although a few hopeful 'leads' were found, no one factor or system unites all, or even a convincing majority, of the vectors.

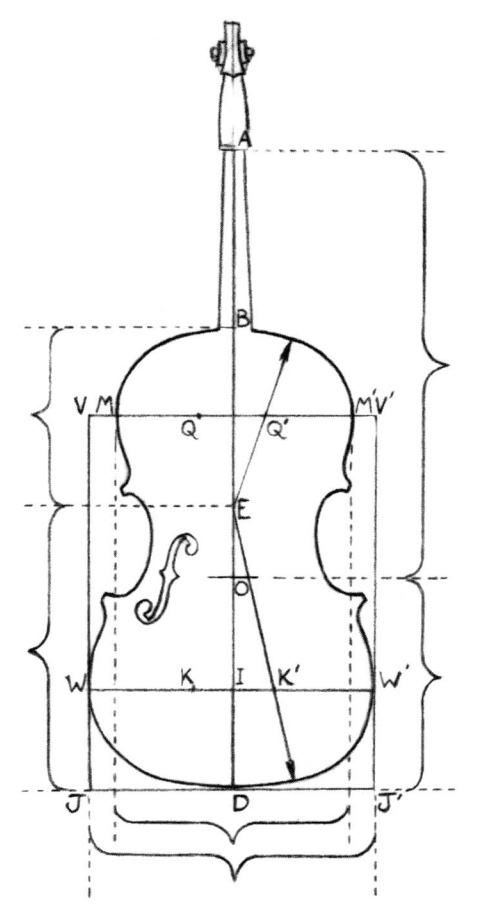

FIG. 70

Arc	Radius in mm
$\begin{bmatrix} b'G' \\ G'M' \\ M'N' \\ N'S' \end{bmatrix}$	271.5 (ϕ) 126 223 (centred in opposite centre of previous arc, GM) 27
$\begin{bmatrix} S'X' \\ X'Y' \\ Y'Z' \\ Z'T' \end{bmatrix}$	21 63 184 44.5
$\begin{bmatrix} T'R' \\ R'P' \\ P'H' \\ H'D \end{bmatrix}$	27 209.5 149 439.5 (ϕ)
Circle piercing f-hole centrings	135

The splendid head was a little more rewarding to analyse, although here again difficulties, due to a seeming carelessness in the sequence of 'organic' curves, were encountered. Like the body plan, the analysis of the head of the Barak Norman revealed some overall commensurable proportions, but also the absence of a containing rectangle of significant ratio. Thus, the length of the head (in Fig. 72, PR), as in several violins also measured, equalled half the width of the lower bouts (PR actually measures 210 mm, and the lower bouts 419 mm). This distance, that of

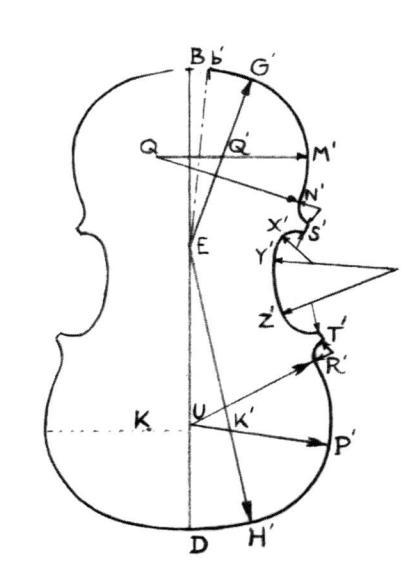

FIG. 71

[56] Maker Johann Theodorus Cuypers, c.1775, no. 18 in the van Leeuwen Boomkamp collection (now in the Gemeentemuseum).

88 ANALYSIS OF INSTRUMENT EXAMPLES

the horizontal plane of the head-containing rectangle, *PRST*, is divided in the analysis by two verticals: *QU* partitions the scroll (*QR*, of *QRSU*, is approximately a one-third division of *PR*: 210 mm/69 mm = 3.043); and *VB* is a vertical on which lie three arc centres—one that of the quadrant arc *AB*. *VB* cuts the head-containing rectangle (*PRST*) at exactly a quarter division. This gives the quadrant arc *AB*, centre *K* (on *VB*), the curve leading from the beautiful volute, a radius of 52.5 mm ($\frac{1}{4}$ head length).

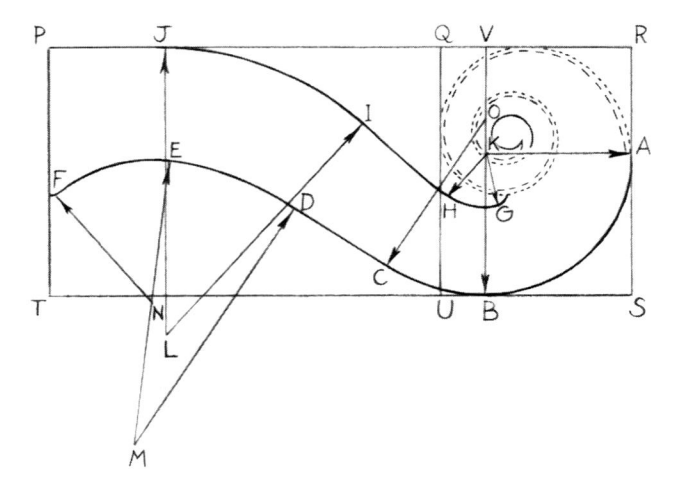

FIG. 72

Arc *BC*, centre *O* (on *VB*), radius 65 mm, continues the curve, meeting straight line *CD*. Counter-curve *DE*, centre *M*, has a radius of 105 mm ($\frac{1}{2}$ head length), and this connects with arc *EF*, centre *N*, radius 52.5 mm, matching, once again, quadrant arc *AB* ($\frac{1}{4}$ head length). The upper peg-box outline begins with straight line *PJ*, linked with main arc *JI*, centre *L*, radius 105 mm ($\frac{1}{2}$ head length). Straight line *IH* connects this main arc with the small, final, counter-curve arc *HG*, centred, like the quadrant arc, at *K*, and of radius 20 mm.

Plate XV

VIOLAS D'AMORE

> The lovely viola d'amore deserves its beautiful name, for it expresses much languishment and tenderness. Its sound is argentine or silvery, and exceptionally agreeable and sweet. It is a pity that its use is so limited.[57]

Few would disagree with Mattheson that so sweet an instrument merited as sweet a name as the d'amore, but exactly how it achieved such a title is an interesting and long-unsolved question.[58] Opinion is divided between those who take viola *d'amore* to mean 'viol of love', and others, maintaining an Eastern origin, who claim viola *da More* as 'viol of the Moors'. The former, and more generally accepted explanation (perhaps by reason of the sympathetic timbre of the instrument), is given cultural support by the tradition of ornament for the long peg-box, which often includes the carved head of a suitably blindfolded Cupid, and sometimes a 'scroll'-heel formed of a scallop shell—the attribute of Cupid's mother, Venus Aphrodite, goddess of love. The second, 'Moorish', derivation is given organological credence by reason of the d'amore family's chief, and amongst Western instruments practially unique,[59] characteristic, the set of sympathetic strings, which lie passively responsive beneath the bowed strings—a system quite common amongst Middle and Far Eastern instruments. The peculiar sound-holes, too, have, in all their 'flaming sword' variations, more than a little of the East in their calligraphy (Fig. 73).

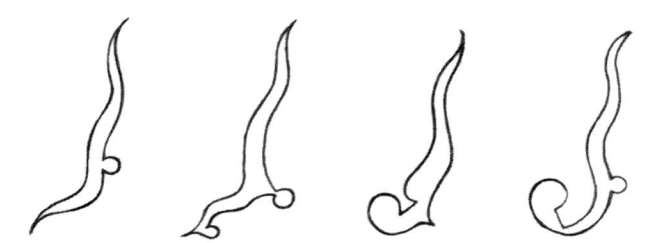

FIG. 73. Viola d'amore sound-hole designs

The tuning of the sympathetic strings is generally accepted to correspond to that of the bowed strings. This brings us to yet another peculiarity of the instrument, for while most other stringed instruments of the late seventeenth and eighteenth centuries had one standard tuning, the chameleonic d'amore adopted an old system of tuning the strings, 'lyra way', according to the demands of the music, *scordatura*, which usually meant having the open strings (bowed and sympathetic) tuned to the tonic chord of the piece to be performed; hence Mattheson's reservation 'that its use is so limited', for the poor player has to know as many different 'fingerings' as the major and minor keys in which he is likely to play. In practice, this actually means seven or eight tunings, although one early authority, Joseph Majer,[60] offers as many as seventeen, whilst another, Eisel,[61] after laborious but valiant explanations of the instrument's tunings, finishes in a tone of defeat, with the advice: 'they may do as they wish—let every sensible judge of music tune it in the way it suits him best.'

The form of the body itself is equally unstandardized. There are six-stringed and seven-stringed violas d'amore equipped with sympathetic

---

[57] Mattheson, *Das Neu-eröffnete Orchester* (Hamburg, 1713).

[58] Filippo Bonanni, writing in 1716: 'Another . . . instrument which some people use is called the viola d'amore, for which I have been unable to discover the reason for its having such a name.'

[59] Practically unique in the sense that the use of sympathetic strings in the baryton and occasionally in pochettes d'amour is likely to be a 'dispersal' from their original use in the viola d'amore. Sympathetic strings have also been used in the Norwegian Hardanger, or folk fiddle, from about the middle of the seventeenth century onwards.

[60] *Neu-eröffneter theoretisch und practischer Music Saal* (Nuremberg, 1732).

[61] *Musicus autodidactus* (Erfurt, 1738).

strings numbering from the usual six, on the more common six bowed-string instrument, to as many as twenty-four on some of the more extravagant so-called 'English Violets'. Body lengths, too, vary, from violin-size moderates to arm-crippling giants. There are, however, two clear types of outline employed: the viol form, and the so-called 'festooned', or multiple-bouted, pattern. Both are represented here in the two examples chosen: a six bowed, six sympathetic, viol-outline viola d'amore, and a seven bowed, sixteen sympathetic, 'festooned' form English Violet.

Ex. XVI

Figs. 74–75, Pl. XVI

VIOLA D'AMORE. BOHEMIA, c.1750
MAKER UNKNOWN
PRIVATE COLLECTION, LONDON

The first of the two violas d'amore to be discussed is a fine instrument, regrettably unsigned, but probably made by one of the makers of the Bohemian school about 1750. The body outline, although different in feeling, owes much to the classical form of the viol which was met with earlier in this study: Exx. IV, V, and VI, by Jaye, Tielke, and Guersan. Here, of course, the usual viol body construction is given greater strength by the high arching of the upper plate, a very un-viol-like characteristic—but a reinforcement essential to such a structure, loaded as it is with two sets of strings at fairly high tension.

The necks of instruments of the viol family are proportionally longer than those of the violin group, and, in two of the classical examples mentioned above, this, combined with the higher position of the bridge, resulted in the distance from nut to bridge, or string length AC, being twice the length between bridge and button, or tail, CD; see Figs. 30 and 38. In the viola d'amore this ratio is of great importance owing to the sympathetic strings. As I mentioned earlier, these are situated *below* the playing strings—in fact, they run from the upper peg-box, bypassing the lower, passing over their own nut (below A) through a tunnel beneath the finger-board, through holes in the bridge and thence to the tail, over another nut, to be anchored in pins in the bottom block. Thus they have not one but *two* sounding lengths: that is, above the bridge, AC, and below it, CD—hence the importance of this ratio, for if $AC = 2CD$, then the result will be two choirs of sympathetics, one 'sounding' an octave above the other. In this case, however, although the bridge is in the centre, C, of the body, BD, the neck (nut A) cannot be, and is not, measured as half the body length, so that $AB = BC = CD$. AB is in fact a little shorter, which is accounted for by the thickness of the two nuts, at A and D, and the bridge at C (at the centre of the body when the two 'sides' of the sympathetic strings are in octaves). This explains why, given this octave principle, the nut point, A, is not included in the vertical proportions shown in Fig. 74, which therefore consist only of $BC = CD$ ($= 178$ mm). The horizontal linear proportions are also shown in Fig. 74:

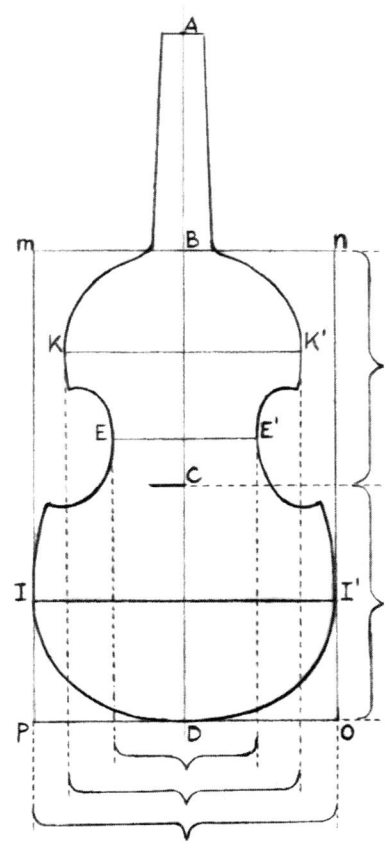

FIG. 74

the lower-bout width, *II'*, is 222.5 mm; the middle bouts, *EE'*, 111 mm; and the upper-bout width, *KK'*, is 177.5 mm. This gives ratios of:

II' : *EE'*
222.5 : 111
2 : 1 (2.004)

EE' : *KK'*
111 : 177.5
5 : 8 (1.599)

II' : *KK'*
222.5 : 177.5
5 : 4 (1.253).

This last ratio, as we shall see, governs the relationship between the two commensurable schemes which rule the lower and upper parts of the design. The 5 : 8 ratio also applies to the rectangle *mnop* which 'contains' the sound-box (356 mm/222.5 mm = 1.6 = 5 : 8).

Further planning of the body outline is given in Fig. 75. As well as the familiar arc radii, the reader will notice the use of planning squares, and the return of the great circle (see Exx. II, IV, VII, X, and XIV). There also appears to be a Brunswick inch resonance in many of the separate vectors. Only the points relevant to the analysis of the right-hand half of the instrument are given.

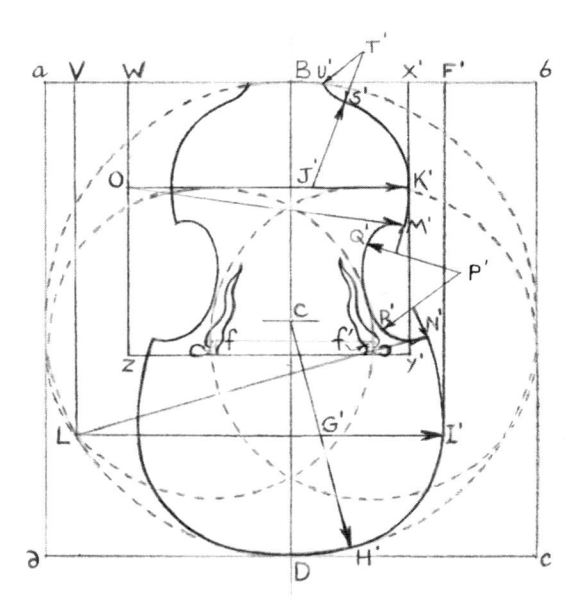

FIG. 75

The outline is initiated by great-circle arc of origin *DH'*, centre *C*, radius 178 mm (half the body length—*BD* : *CD* = 2 : 1). It is continued by arc *H'I'*, centre *G'*, radius 89 mm, repeating the ratio 2 : 1 (*CH'* : *G'H'*). The lower bouts are completed by arc *I'N'*, centre *L*, which lies outside the outline, on the great circle; this radius, *I'L*, is 267 mm, and gives ratios of 3 : 2 (267 mm : 178 mm) and 3 : 1 (276 mm : 89 mm) with the other lower-bout arc radii mentioned above. A square, *VF'I'L*, can be constructed, using radius *I'L* as its base, its top, *VF'*, passing through point *B*, the top of the body. Thus, the three vectors of the lower bouts could be expressed as multiples of the smallest term, a quarter division of the body length, which for clarity we will call a major unit:

178 = 2 maj. units;   89 = 1 maj. unit;   267 = 3 maj. units.

The middle bouts mark the change-over from the 'major unit' commensurable system of the lower bouts to the 'minor unit' commensurable system of the upper bouts. This latter is based on a unit of 71 mm, a fifth division of the body length, giving a lower : upper bout ratio of 89 mm : 71 mm (1.253), or 5 : 4, which was revealed earlier by the overall proportions of width. The first middle-bout arc, $N'R'$, still relates to the lower (major) scheme—its radius is measured as 26.5 mm which, allowing for measurement 267 mm : 26.5 mm (10.075), gives a ratio of 10 : 1 with the preceding major term.

The main middle-bout arc, $R'Q'$, centre P', is of radius 71 mm, or 1 minor unit of the upper scheme. The small arc $Q'M'$, completing the centre curve, has the same relationship with the large upper-bout radius, OM', as $R'N'$ had with large lower-bout radius LN', that of 1 : 10. $Q'M'$'s radius measures 21.5 mm, while that of the upper-bout arc $M'K'$, centred at O, is 213 mm, or 3 minor units. Again, a 'planning square' (here $WX'Y'Z$) can be drawn, although here there is no relationship with the great circle; the top of the square, side WX', passes through B; side WZ passes through arc centre O; and side ZY', the base of the square, passes along the bottom of the sound-holes. The upper bouts are continued from $M'K'$ by arc $K'S'$, centre J', and of radius 71 mm, or 1 minor unit, u. The counter-curve $S'U'$, centre T', is of radius 35.5 mm ($\frac{1}{2}u$), giving upper-bout vector ratios of 3 : 1 (6 : 2) and 2 : 1. In both upper and lower bouts the main unit was related to the overall bout width as 2 : 5, that is:

$$\text{upper } \frac{177.5 \text{ mm}}{71 \text{ mm}} = 2.5$$

$$\text{and lower } \frac{222.5 \text{ mm}}{89 \text{ mm}} = 2.5.$$

The whole proportional planning of the body-outline vectors has therefore been very beautifully managed; the two simple commensurable schemes, major and minor, are commensurably integrated, both with each other and with the overall proportions, being a quarter and a fifth respectively of the body length:

$$\frac{356 \text{ mm}}{89 \text{ mm}} = 4; \qquad \frac{356 \text{ mm}}{71 \text{ mm}} = 5(.014).$$

A further geometrical device is drawn in Fig. 75, the vesica piscis. If this is centred at points f and f' in the sound-holes (118.5 mm apart as measured), the resulting figure fits inside the containing square $abcd$, touches radius OK' (and, of course, KO'), and passes through centre L (and L') on the great circle.

The beautifully carved heads of both this and the following instrument were not drawn in elevation for analysis, since the curves of their peg-boxes were extremely shallow, and therefore thought unlikely to yield any accurately measurable information.

PLATE XVI

Ex. XVII
Figs. 76–78, Pl. XVII

ENGLISH VIOLET. GERMANY, MUNICH, 1724
PAULUS ALLETSEE
GEMEENTEMUSEUM, THE HAGUE
(Ex Carel van Leeuwen Boomkamp, No. 8)

Over a dozen violas d'amore made by Paulus Alletsee are known to survive, and most of them are mentioned by Harry Danks in his survey of known instruments, 'Makers of the Viola d'amore',[62] appended to his invaluable profile, *The Viola d'Amore* (Bois de Boulogne, 1976). The present specimen, which has, however, eluded Mr Danks's net, is an 'English Violet' dating from 1724 and bearing seven bowed and sixteen sympathetic strings. It is from the Carel van Leeuwen Boomkamp collection, which is now housed at The Hague in the Gemeentemuseum.

No satisfactory explanation has ever been found for the name 'English Violet'. In the first instance, violet, or *violetta*, would normally describe a small viola, and yet instruments called English Violet are always larger than the average viola d'amore: and, of course, there is nothing remotely 'English' about the violet, or the viola d'amore, which were both quite definitely evolved in what we would now call Germany. Danks puts forward Kinsky's view that *englisch* may have been a contemporary (Leopold Mozart?) misnomer—*engelhaft*, meaning angelic, having been the intended adjective, an explanation which at least conforms to the celestial image of the instrument. Whatever its origins, the name 'English Violet' is usually reserved for a subtype of larger viola d'amore, with an increased number of sympathetic strings, and which are more commonly of multiple-bouted, or festooned, outline.

As we have seen, and indeed shall see, practically all the instrument-designs analysed in this study are harmonically governed, to greater or lesser extent, through the proportions of their component-arc radii, sometimes with, as it were, 'positional planning' by means of the vesica piscis (Exx. II, III, VIII, X, XIV, and XVI), the great circle (Exx. II, IV, VII, X, XIV, and XVI), or grids in the form of planning squares or containing rectangles, etc. (Exx. V, VII, XIV, XV, and XVI). The numbers indicate relevant instrument examples *previously* analysed in this study—for overall data, see Chapter 7, main Summary Chart 1, p. 158.

In the geometry of this instrument, however, the emphasis is radically changed away from the proportional regulation of arc vectors toward a more vigorous and complete positional planning of arc centres, using planning circles and, most notably, an extremely comprehensive rectangular grid.

The reader will observe, from the main drawing, the great complexity of the Alletsee's body outline. The increased number of arcs, and the great stress laid on their positioning by planning circles and rectangles, as well as the grid itself, result in rather a bulky knot to unravel for the analysis. Because of this, I shall discuss the geometry in two 'layers'. The first will be the by now familiar process of examining the principal measurements (string length, nut- and bridge-positions, body length, and bout widths) for overall proportional relationships, followed by a vector-by-vector harmonic exposé of the outline, while the second 'layer' will consist of a summary of the all-important grid system used by the instrument's

[62] This survey also lists the previous instrument, Ex. XVI.

FIG. 76

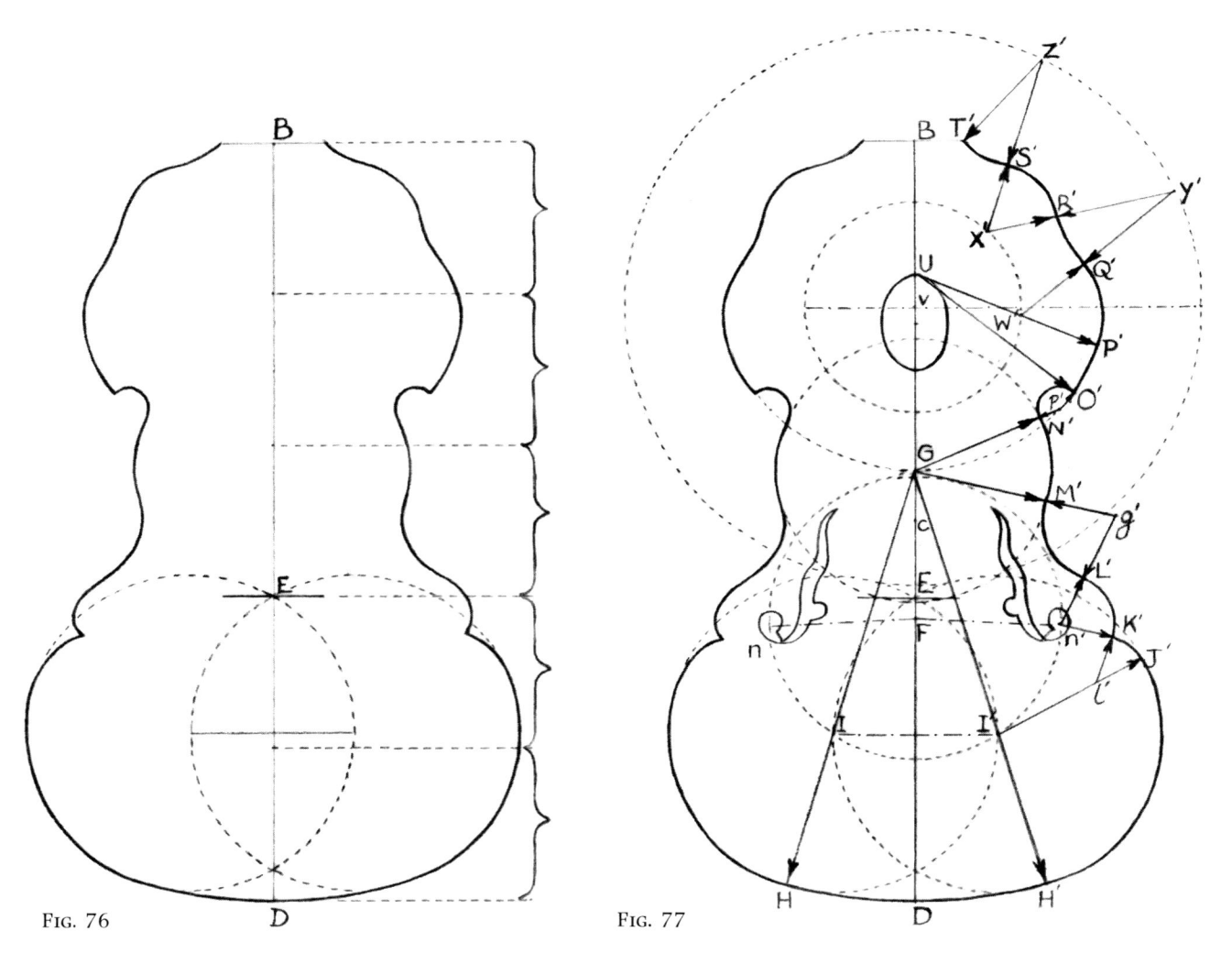

FIG. 77

geometer. It must be remembered, however, that this two-layered approach is merely an analytical convenience, the two systems or processes being homogeneously conceived, interdependent, and constructionally inseparable.

Fig. 76 shows the outline of the violet, its vertical axis *BD*, and its bridge position *E*. As the brackets convey, the length, *BD*, can be divided into five equal parts (each of 85 mm), with the bridge-line falling on a $\frac{2}{5}$ division from the bottom. This is also the upper point on the centre line, where the two vesica piscis circles, which are part of the lower-bout construction, cross and intersect each other. Apart from two planning circles, whole-number relationships do not occur elsewhere in the design, which is otherwise golden-section regulated. Other vertical and horizontal ratios are dealt with later in the discussion of the grid.

Apart from the vesica piscis arrangement, other circles are employed to plan and unify symmetrically the outline (see Fig. 77). As many of these circles just miss having a centre–circumference relationship with one another, the scheme is not as scrupulously composed as its companion grid, but is nevertheless quite handsome. The radii of these circles, like the radii of the outline arcs themselves, bear few traces of harmonic consideration, apart from the two upper 'planning circles' centred at *V* (which are of radius 155 mm and 59 mm, which may relate by $\phi+1$, i.e. 155 mm/59 mm $= 2.627 \simeq 1.618+1$) and the circle centred at *F* (which pierces the two vesica centres *I* and *I'*, the lower sound-hole

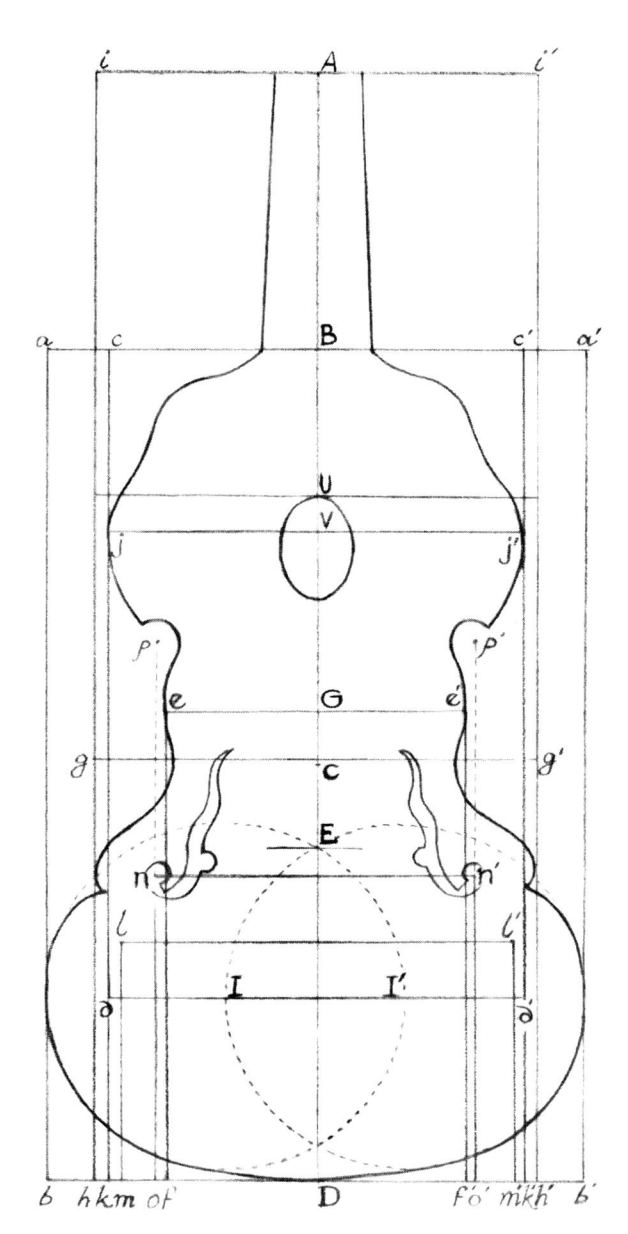

Fig. 78

centrings n and n', and just misses centre G of the middle circle), whose radius, 77.5 mm, is half the radius of the large circle centred at V (155 mm).

G is also the centre of arc of origin $(H)DH'$, radius 239.5 mm, which initiates the instrument's outline. The lower bouts are continued by vesica arc $H'J'$, centre I', radius 87.5 mm, and completed by arc $J'K'$, centre l', radius 27 mm; the use here of a lower-case locating letter indicates its presence in the grid scheme discussed hereafter.

The middle-bout section could be said to start at K', with arc $K'L'$, radius 27 mm (the same as the preceding lower-bout arc) and centre n', neatly placed at the lower sound-hole centre. The curve is continued by $L'M'$, centre g' (again a grid point), radius 38.5 mm. The main middle-bout arc $M'N'$ is provided by main circle centre G, radius 74 mm, which passes just below the bridge-line, and the section closes with arc $N'O'$, centre p', radius 11.5 mm.

The upper bouts are initiated by arc $O'P'$, centre U (the top of the sound-board rose), radius 108 mm. When produced, this arc pierces the centre, p' (and p), of the top middle-bout arc, and narrowly misses G (centre of main circle). The undulating curves of the upper bouts begin their sinuous motion with arc $P'Q'$, centre W', radius 44 mm; W' is situated on the smaller planning circle (radius 59 mm) which, like its larger companion, is centred at V. The curve of the bouts takes an inward dip with arc $Q'R'$, centre Y' (on the larger planning circle, radius 155 mm) and radius 62 mm. It bulges outwards again with arc $R'S'$, centre X', on the smaller circle, and radius 38.5 mm (an amount encountered earlier as a middle-bout vector), centred at g', and here having a ϕ relationship with its two neighbouring radii (62mm/38.5 mm $= 1.610 \simeq \phi$). The final arc of the outline is again an incurving one, $S'T'$, centre Z', again on the larger planning circle, radius, as mentioned, 62 mm.

The grid itself, which is a reticulation of overlapping ϕ rectangles and squares, is given in Fig. 78. The diagram is largely self-explanatory, and the component rectangles and squares will therefore be more easily followed from a check-list than from a descriptive text. Before giving such a list, however, it will probably be of help to mention a few of the major figures included in the drawing. First, the whole body is outlined by a containing rectangle $aa'b'b$, of ϕ ratio. The sides of this rectangle pass through the top, B, and bottom, D, of the body, and touch, tangentially, the lower bouts at the point of maximum width. The same method is applied to the upper bouts, where rectangle $cc'd'd$ passes again through the top, B, and, on each side, through the point of maximum width of the upper (j and j') and middle bouts, having its base line dd' intersecting the centres, I and I', of the lower-bout vesica arrangement. Rectangle $ee'f'f$ frames the middle-bout width and main circle diameter with the base line, fDf', while the square, $gg'h'h$, gives centres for the middle-bout arcs LM and $L'M'$ (gg' passes a little above true centre C). $gg'h'h$ is also the external companion square of ϕ rectangle $ii'g'g$, which links the body plan to the nut position, A.

The following is a check-list of these, and other, rectangles, giving measurements, ratios, and summarized significance. Once again, many of the vectors of this scheme appear to relate to the Brunswick inch:

$$aa'b'b = \frac{425 \text{ mm}}{262.5 \text{ mm}} = 1.619 \quad \text{overall body-containing rectangle}$$

$$cc'd'd = \frac{331 \text{ mm}}{206 \text{ mm}} = 1.607 \quad \text{upper and middle bouts, vesica piscis centres}$$

$$ee'f'f = \frac{239.5 \text{ mm}}{148 \text{ mm}} = 1.618 \quad \text{middle bouts}$$

$$gg'h'h = \frac{216 \text{ mm}}{216 \text{ mm}} = \boxed{1} \quad \text{arc centres for middle bouts}$$

$$ii'g'g = \frac{349 \text{ mm}}{216 \text{ mm}} = 1.616 \quad \text{nut position}$$

$$jj'k'k = \frac{331 \text{ mm}}{206 \text{ mm}} = 1.607 \quad \text{upper and middle bouts, upper-bout planning-circle centre, } V$$

$$ll'm'm = \frac{196 \text{ mm}}{121 \text{ mm}} = 1.6198 \quad \text{lower-bout arc centres}$$

$$nn'o'o = \frac{155 \text{ mm}}{155 \text{ mm}} = \boxed{1} \quad \text{sound-hole centrings.}$$

PLATE XVII

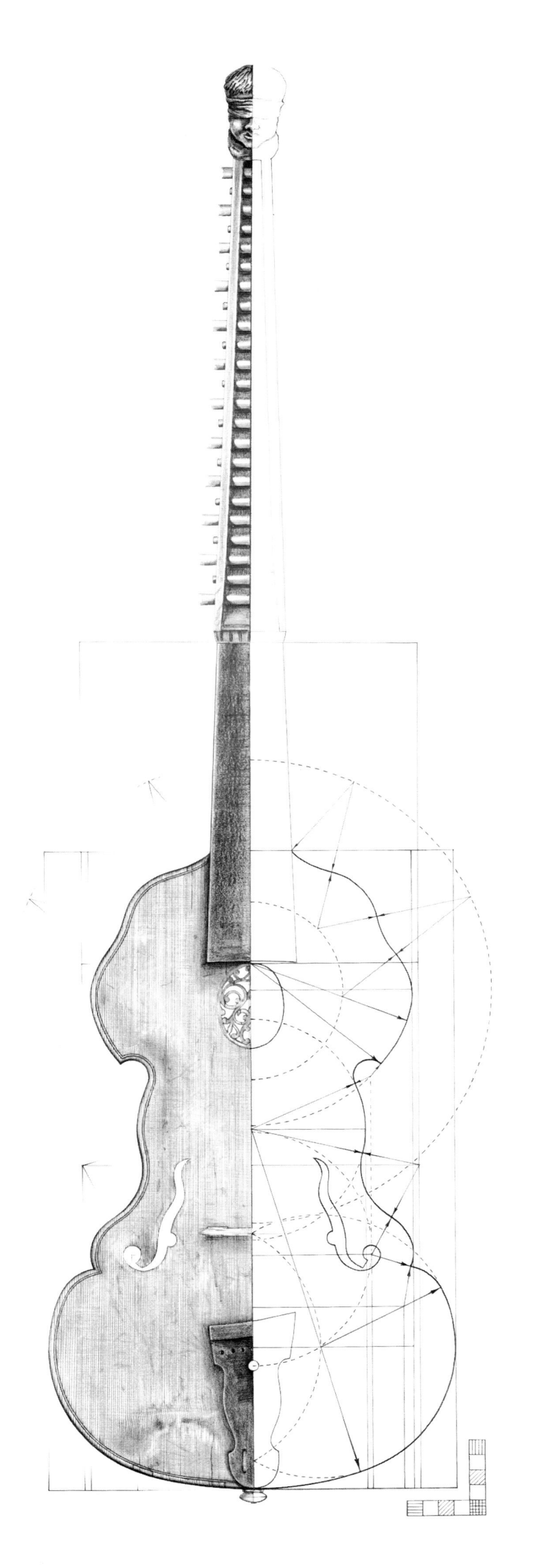

KITS OR POCHETTES

The kit, or pochette, was the tiny instrument used by dancing-masters of the seventeenth and eighteenth centuries discreetly to mark time and tune for their pupils. In essence it is a highly portable, literally pocketable, violin, carried with its tiny bow in a tubular case inside the long pockets of the teacher's coat. The usual form of the instrument was the so-called 'rebec' shape, sometimes also called a *sordine*, which was straight-sided, narrow, and truncheon-like (hence the tubular case), although many survive with miniature violin bodies, sometimes festooned in outline like our first example, dating from 1686. More rare is the type represented here by the second specimen, of c.1760, which, like the preceding violas d'amore, has an arrangement of sympathetic strings below the fingerboard. Later examples were made to collapse, or perhaps assemble, with bow, into a hollow walking-stick, as were some flutes and clarinets, as well as the more expected swords, guns, and drinking-flasks of the early nineteenth century.

One characteristic common to most kits, however, is the archaic 'E' form of sound-hole (see Exx. II and III), used here no doubt to minimize the weakening effect of the openings to the very narrow sound-boards.

Ex. XVIII

Figs. 79–80, Pl. XVIII

KIT or POCHETTE. BELGIUM, BRUSSELS, 1686
GASPAR BORBON
MUSÉE DU CONSERVATOIRE ROYAL DE MUSIQUE, BRUSSELS
Acc. No.: 2764

Although it seems to be an unusually complex outline for such a modest little instrument, this arrangement of convolutions is also found in pochettes other than this example of Borbon's. One such is the pochette, thought to be Italian and once attributed to Stradivari, which is in the Donaldson collection. This has the same body outline, but a different head, bearing a conventional scroll-head instead of the volute and escutcheon of the Borbon. The temptation to attribute the Donaldson pochette to Stradivari is understandable, for amongst the many paper patterns of instrument outlines left by the master are a number of kit designs of varying forms, two of which are similar to this 'festooned' form. It was interesting to compare the outline of the Borbon (1686) with the two Stradivari patterns (c.1700?), copies of which were made from the originals in Cremona. None of the curves was found to correspond in any of the designs, whereas the height of the middle-bout complex, that is, distance *RK* (see Fig. 79), was found to be the same in all three cases—the only common measurement.

The body geometry of the Borbon pochette is shown in Fig. 79. As can be seen, it reveals a further example of great-circle planning, although here, as in the Jaye viol (Ex. IV), the circle does not coincide with the arc of origin, as in Ex. II (Maria treble viol) and Ex. XVI (anonymous Bohemian viola d'amore). The radii of the outline arcs were governed by a simple commensurable scheme based on a unit (u) of 9.5 mm, which was the unit radius of the smallest arcs in Fig. 79, given the lower-case letters of a', b', c', d', and e' for their centres. The top, like the bottom, of the instrument's outline is defined by a miniature vesica piscis, an arrangement which, as it were, 'anchors' the two symmetrical halves of the instrument at each of its extreme ends. The top vesica arc is $W'U'$, centred at V', radius 19 mm or $2u$. The curve is then inflexed by main upper-bout arc $U'S'$, centre T', positioned on the great circle, and radius 47.5 mm or $5u$. The curve is closed by the first of the small arcs, $S'R'$, centre e', radius u. Small arc $R'P'$, centre d', radius u, makes the corner, which is turned by inverse arc $P'O'$, centre c', also radius u. The next arc, middle-bout arc $O'N'$, is centred at Q', and is of radius 28.5 mm or $3u$. When produced, this arc and arc $U'S'$, centred at T', touch 'tangentially' (see dotted line in Fig. 79). The middle bouts are continued by straight line $N'M'$, and then turn inwards with arc $M'L'$, centre g', radius 38 mm, $4u$, and are completed by small arc $L'K'$, centre b', in the lower sound-hole centring, radius u.

The lower bouts also start (or end) with a small arc—$K'J'$, centred at a', radius also u. They curve inwards with main arc $J'H'$, centred at Z' (outside the great circle) and of radius 66.5 mm, or $7u$. The outline is completed by the echo vesica piscis arcs of the top, although here they are beautifully connected by the arc of origin, which is centred at the upper intersection of the two arcs (E). Owing to wear, or an error in drawing or making, this lower vesica is a fraction smaller than the upper one: $H'G'$, centre I', has a radius of 18.5 mm (0.5 mm short of $2u$), which makes diameter EG', the radius of arc $G'D'$, 37 mm. Regarding this as wear, or error, the final two outline vectors would be $2u$ and $4u$, respectively.

The sound-hole centrings are pierced by a circle drawn from F on the centre line; its radius is 37 mm, just short of $4u$, which would have given a radius of 38 mm. The centres of the curves of the sound-holes have also been drawn in Fig. 79. The outermost curve is centred at X' on the great circle, while the inner curve is centred at Y'. Their radii, 107 mm and 82 mm, are not related to the commensurable scheme. The only linear measurement, vertical or horizontal, to yield to the 9.5 mm unit, apart, that is, from the above radii, proved to be the string length which, being 304 mm, divides 304/9.5 to $32u$.

The diminutive head of the instrument is shown in outline profile in Fig. 80. Here again the radii of the arcs were found to be multiples of the basic unit, u, of 9.5 mm. Once more, the overall proportions (e.g. the containing rectangle $WXYZ$) have not been considered proportionately. The under-curve of the volute is started with arc AB, centre O, radius 19 mm or $2u$, continued by arc BC, centre D, radius 66.5 mm ($7u$) and completed by short straight line CE and counter-curve EF, centre G, radius again 19 mm or $2u$. The top side of the peg-box consists of large arc HI, centred at J, and of radius 66.5 mm ($7u$), short straight line IK, and the inner curve KL, also centred at O, and of radius 6.5 mm.

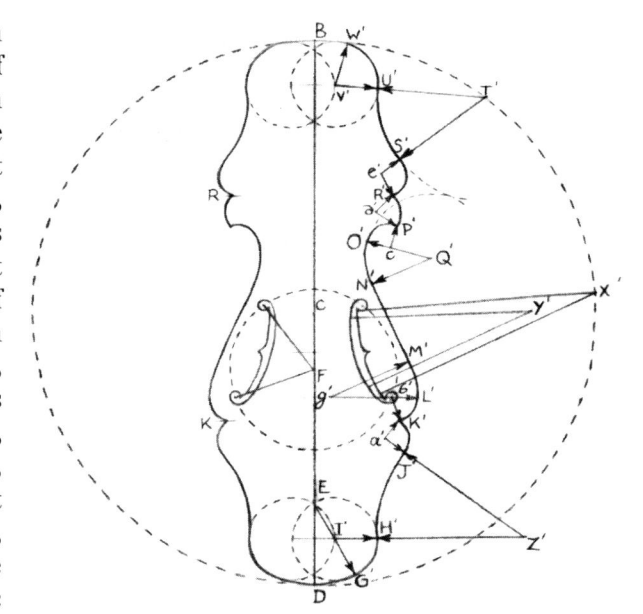

FIG. 79

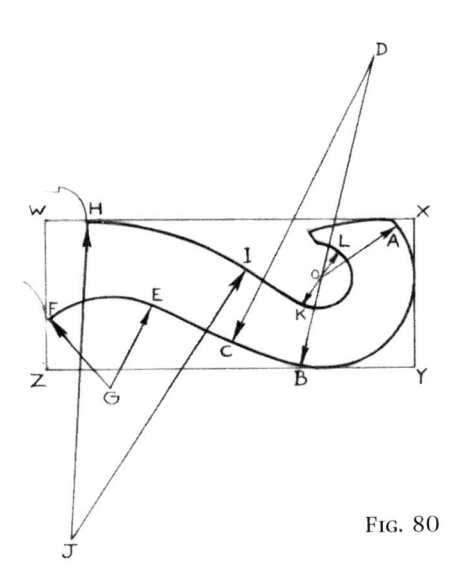

FIG. 80

Plate XVIII

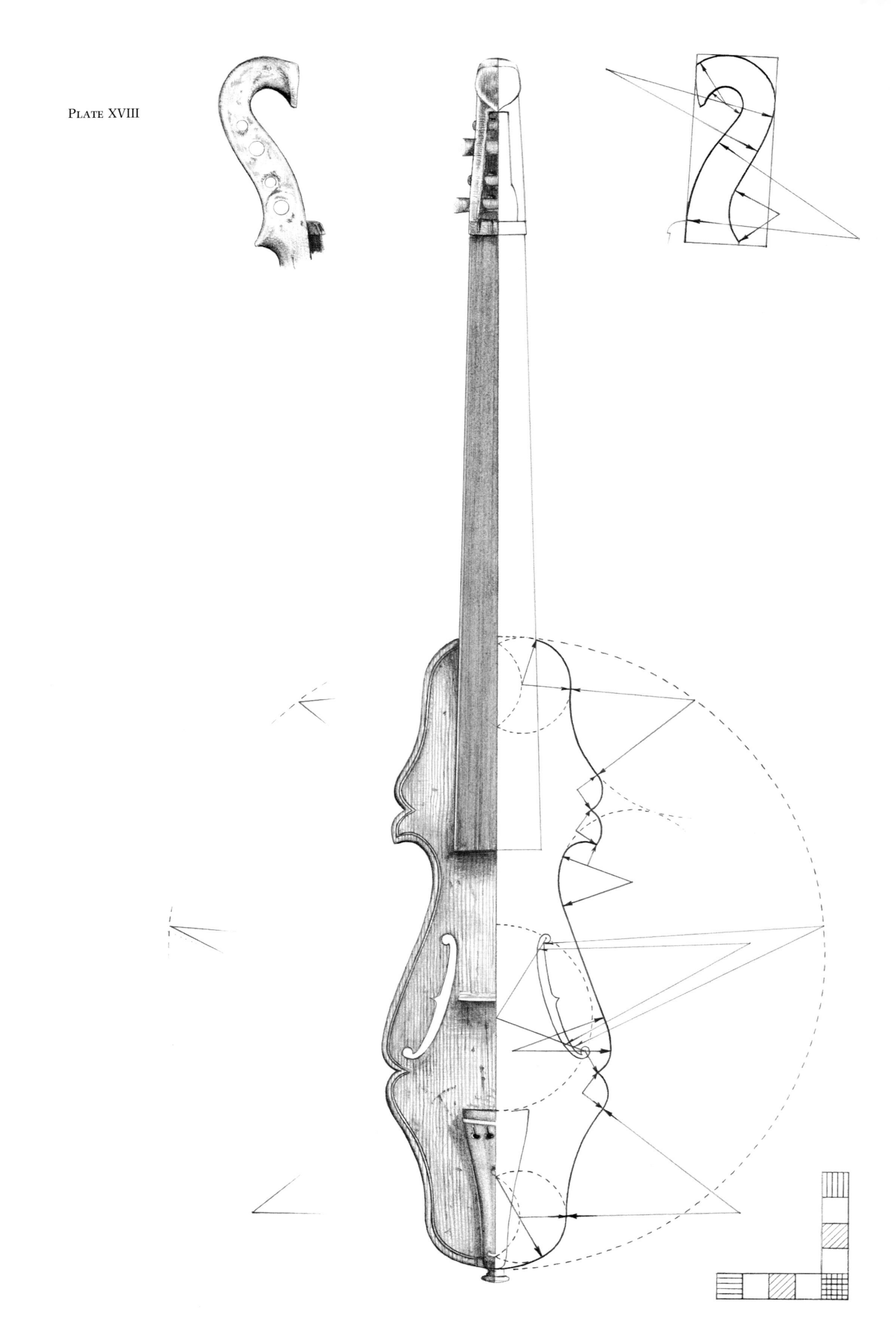

Ex. XIX

Figs. 81–83, Pl. XIX

POCHETTE D'AMOUR. ITALY, TURIN, c.1760
BATTISTA GENOVA
DONALDSON COLLECTION, ROYAL COLLEGE OF MUSIC
Acc. No.: RCM 38

The idea of a pochette d'amour is intriguing, for one is inclined to suppose that such a tiny, ribless sound-box as in this instrument of Battista Genova would be an insufficient resonator to amplify and transmit the gentle vibrations of sympathetic strings, but apparently it is, and the resulting sound is described as 'silvery'. Although rare, and indeed its maker little known, this example is not unique, there being an exotic 'festooned' pochette d'amour with 'flame' sound-holes in the collection of instruments at Budapest, while the Metropolitan Museum of Art (New York) has two fine specimens, one of which, bearing a carved Cupid's head of exceptional beauty, is of similar overall outline to our own instrument.

Genova actually worked in Turin, where he had been a pupil of Gian Francesco Celoniati. The present example, which was made probably c.1760, bears the same golden-yellow varnish that his teacher used, and has a graceful little body of viol outline.

Although of different form, time, and place, the proportional system used in this design is very similar to that used in the previous example, the Gaspar Borbon pochette, that is, a simple, commensurable scheme, based on a small unit, u, which here equals 9 mm. It can be seen regulating the widths (horizontal linear proportion) of the upper, middle, and lower bouts in Fig. 81. WW', the upper bouts, measure 90 mm across, or $10u$; the middle bouts, VV', are 54 mm wide, or $6u$; and HH', the lower bouts, measure 108(.5) mm or $12u$ (twice the middle-bout measurement—see also Ex. XVI, Fig. 74), which gives bout ratios of:

$$10:6:12$$
$$\text{or} \quad 5:3:6.$$

The outline itself is broken down into component arcs and radii in Fig. 82. Here the lower bouts are seen to have the same semicircular start as those of the Tielke viol (Ex. V). This is arc DH', centre G, which has a radius of 54(.25) mm (HH' measuring 108.5 mm), or, allowing the 0.25 mm as margin, $6u$. The centre of the next, and only other, lower-bout arc is positioned on the opposite edge of the instrument, so that arc $H'I'$, centre H, has a radius of 108.5 mm, $12u$, twice that of arc DH'.

The middle bouts comprise three arcs: $I'J'$, centre M', radius 13.5 mm, equalling $1.5u$; main arc $J'K'$, centre L' (not, however, positioned by either circle or grid), radius 36 mm or $4u$; and finally $K'O'$, centre N', radius also 13.5 mm ($1.5u$). The upper bouts, like the lower bouts, are also part-formed by an arc centred on the centre line; this is arc $O'Q'$, centre P, radius 45 mm or $5u$. The curve continues with arc $Q'S'$, centre R, radius 55 mm (the same as radius GH') or $6u$, and the outline is completed by counter-curve $S'T'$, centre U', radius 27 mm, which equals $3u$.

Again the sound-holes are of the archaic 'E' type, and slightly uncomfortably placed, as though the too-near upper centres should have been connected to their lower circles by 'ƒ's and not by the old 'E's. The circle piercing these four centres is centred at F on the centre line; its radius, 33 mm, does not relate to the unit system; its circumference is

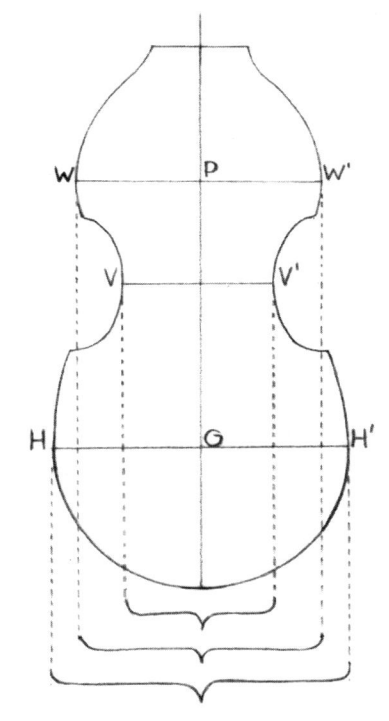

FIG. 81

FIG. 82

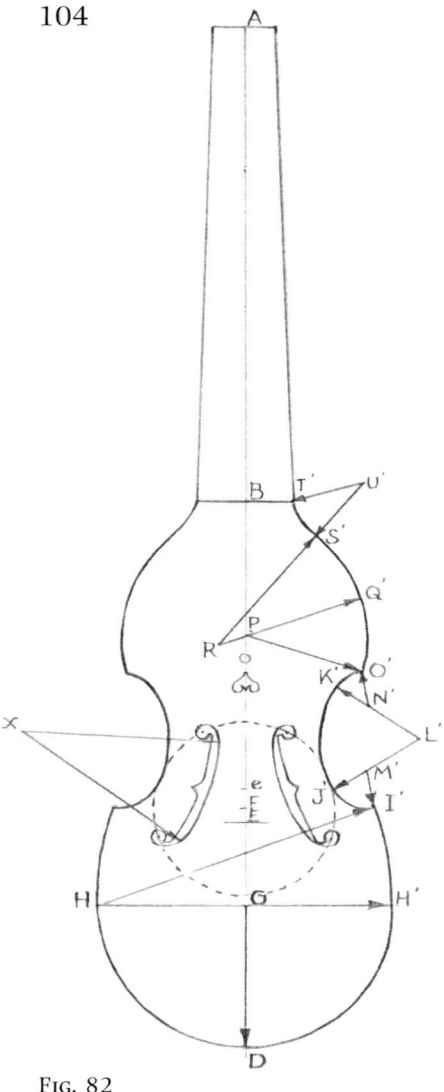

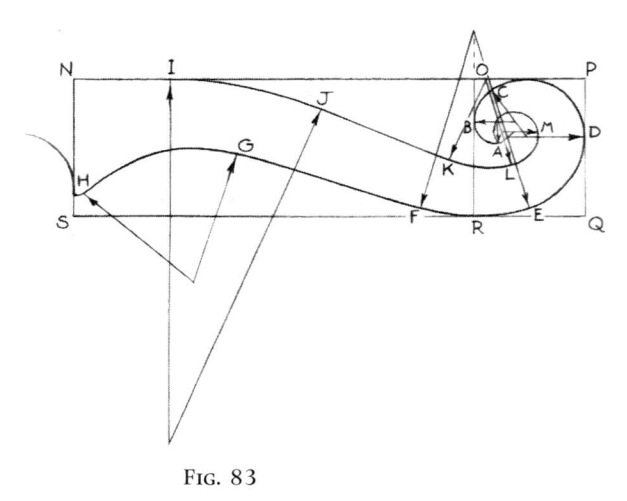

FIG. 83

[63] That is, on a line intersecting the point of weight equilibrium of the plate.

'tangential' to the middle-bout curves. The inner curve of the sound-hole itself does, however, correspond to the commensurable scheme—it is shown in Fig. 82 with its centre at x, its radius, 72 mm, being twice the main middle-bout arc radius and equalling $8u$.

The question of string length and bridge position is a tricky one. At present the instrument is set up with its bridge at E, no doubt the 'position of greatest use', that is, where the marks and wear to the belly indicate, by a sort of majority vote, where the bridge has always been. Bearing in mind that these little pochettes rarely conform to normal luthier practices, it should, however, be mentioned that the notches in the sound-holes, which would normally indicate the ideal bridge position,[63] suggest a higher placing (in Fig. 82, e), a position which gives the sympathetic strings a harmonically tuned string length on both sides of the bridge, so that $Ae : eD$ is as $3 : 1$, a consideration not at present catered for with the bridge at E. In practice, however, the luthier, in adopting these sound-holes and positioning them so closely, has reduced the width of belly at this point (e), so that there is scarce enough room to stand a bridge, not to mention the paucity of wood remaining for the essential vibration. Had the existing centres been connected by 'f's rather than by 'E's, this problem would not have arisen, and the harmonically, and aesthetically, more likely bridge position would then have been possible. I therefore suspect that the design archetype of this instrument may well have differed in this respect.

The incorporation of sympathetic strings, with their additional tuning-pegs, has meant a much longer peg-box for this pochette than for that of the Borbon. As with the body design, there is a feeling of organic grace about the head, with its volute terminal, which has been curve-analysed in Fig. 83. The vortex of this drawing is inevitably crowded and confusing; to avoid greater muddle, I have therefore not loaded the figure with added letters denoting the centres of arcs, centres which the reader should still be able to find from the identity of the arc alone.

The overall containing rectangles, $NPQS$, $NORS$, and $OPQR$, again were not found to have any proportional significance, although once or twice a radius did correspond to an isolated measurement. Neither did the unit scheme of the body design ($u = 9$ mm) appear in the planning of the head.

The arithmetic mean ($b = \frac{1}{2}(a+c)$), however, was used, and the important outer volute of the head is so governed. The arcs whose radii comprise this arithmetic progression are AB, BC, CD, and DE, and their radii in millimetres respectively read $5.5, 10.5, 15.5,$ and 20.5. The curve is then shallowed by arc EF, whose centre lies on head-containing rectangle side RO produced, and whose radius measures 51.5 mm, which is 0.5 mm short of being the sum of the preceding volute radii, but is also half of measurement NO. The under-curve of the peg-box is then continued by straight line FG and counter-curve GH, whose radius, 37 mm, equals the height, PQ, of the head rectangle $NPQS$.

The top curve of the peg-box commences after straight line NI, with arc IJ, whose radius, 99 mm, equals $\frac{3}{4}$ of NO. Straight line JK then connects this with the curves of the inner volute arc KL, centred on line NP, radius 24 mm, arc LM, radius 9.5 mm, and centre arc MA, radius 6 mm—curves whose radii have a more arbitrary relationship than did the arithmetically organized arcs of the outer volute.

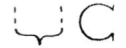

PLATE XIX

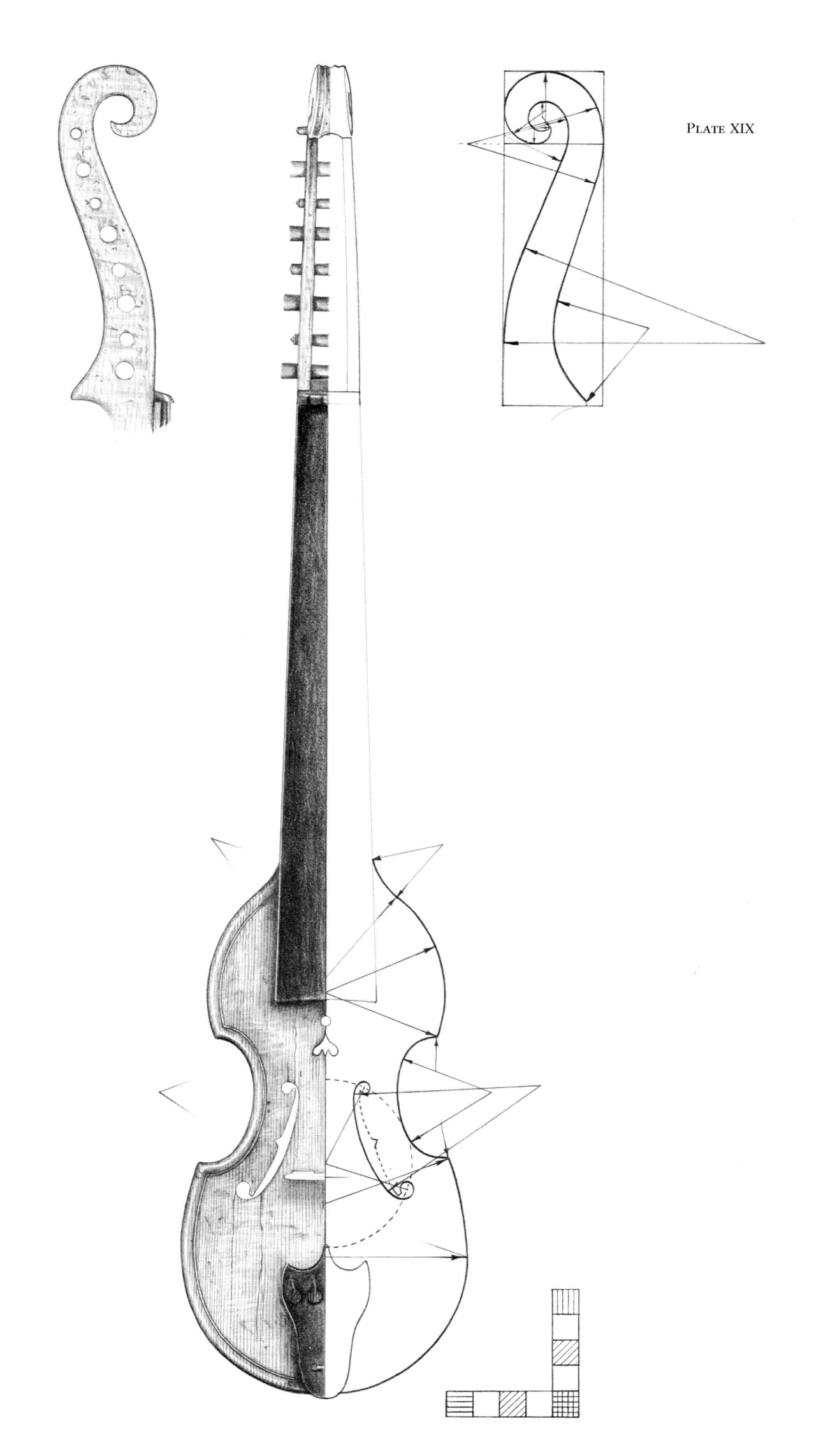

LUTES

The singular importance of the lute as a key musical instrument of the Renaissance is attested to not only by the enormous wealth of music it engendered, but also by the poets, writers, and painters who found inspiration in the gentle magic of its sound, or in the pure and deceptively simple beauty of its form. This prime position, however, is not substantiated by the number of early lutes to survive, which is lamentably few. From inventories, such as that taken from the working stock of the master luthier, Lucas Maler, at his death,[64] we know that lutes, and highly valued ones at that, were produced in what seem to be astonishing quantities by the German colonies of lute-makers then working in northern Italy. Alas, the remarkably fragile nature of these instruments, which helped to give them the resonant tonal qualities for which they were so prized and consequently so widely used, has meant that, of the thousands of master-instruments made in the sixteenth century, scarce a handful survive, even in part. That almost no sixteenth-century lute remains to us in the form and condition that it left its maker, however, is due not just to their inherent fragility, but also to the continual changes in the nature of the music itself, with the increasing demand for a deeper register to the instrument. Thus, good lutes, which usually meant old lutes (Samuel Johnson's *Dictionary*, 1755, discloses that a lute might take up to eighty years to reach its best tone)[65] were constantly being fitted with new necks, heads, bridges, and bars, to keep apace of musical fashion, at a rate which left even Praetorius a little dazed: '... from year to year, so many changes are being made that nothing very definite can be written'.[66]

In short, the old, highly prized lute bodies were considered by subsequent players to be interchangeable, and the string-stop, neck, and head type were considerations to be custom-fitted to the players' musical needs: witness the correspondence between the 'English' lutenist Jacques Gaultier and Constantin Huygens in Holland (1647-8):

> There is certainly here another kind of lute of Bologna for accompanying singing. It is one of the large lutes of Sconvel. If you would please let me know in what fashion you would like the neck to be, and whether you would like it to be both for the playing of pieces and also for singing, I will have it put into playing order.[67]

Many fine lutes have therefore had working careers throughout the whole period of the instrument's use, sailing, if not under different colours (to use the old phrase), then certainly by means of different riggings. When the lute finally went out of fashion in the eighteenth century, surviving bodies were often yet again re-used, either in the manufacture of hurdy-gurdies, or, later, in conversions to guitars and even mandolones. The nineteenth-century forgers of 'antique' artefacts also did their share of lute body-snatching in order to cannibalize diverse remains and fragments into suspiciously over-decorative 'collector's pieces', many of which have regrettably found their way into some important public collections, to be displayed as genuine sixteenth- or seventeenth-century instruments.

It is therefore out of caution that I have decided, in this section, to confine my analyses to the primary aspects of body design, although

---

[64] M. W. Prynne, 'Some Remarks on Old Lutes', *LSJ* vol. 1. See also 'The Old Bologna Lute-Makers', *LSJ* vol. 3, by the same writer.
[65] Prynne, *LSJ* vol. 3.
[66] *Syntagma Musicum*, Part 1, chap. xxv.
[67] J. D. Roberts, 'The Lute: Historical Notes', *LSJ* vol. 2, p. 21.

where string lengths or nut or bridge positions are thought to be original, then, of course, these too are taken into consideration.

The bodies of the bowed instruments that we have discussed so far have backs designed on the same two-dimensional plan as the front,[68] with a section of vertical ribs, sometimes parallel, sometimes almost imperceptibly tapered, forming the sides of the sound-box, thus enclosing the essential volume of air. For our purpose, this has needed no discussion, in plane geometry terms, beyond that of the body plan itself (and, where relevant, an elevation of the head design). With the lute form of body, however, the two-dimensional body outline rises into a vault of seemingly complex, three-dimensional curves, which can, however, be rendered back into the two-dimensional plane geometry in which they were undoubtedly conceived.[69] To this end, I have analysed the only consistently definable measurements which could be taken from the vault; a longitudinal profile, together with a horizontal cross-section at the widest point.

Ex. XX
Figs. 84–85

LUTE (DRAWING). HOLLAND, *c.*1460
HENRICUS ARNAULT OF ZWOLLE
BIBLIOTHÈQUE NATIONALE, PARIS
Acc. No.: 7295

Perhaps the two most significant instrument-examples in this section are the lutes by Hans Frei and Giovanni Hieber, which mark the change in development of the 'classic' instrument from the exquisite Bolognese 'pearl-mould' form, with its long, shallow curves, to the fuller, broader shape of the later sixteenth-century Venetian lutes. Before discussing both these and the other lutes, however, we have a unique opportunity to examine the design of a fifteenth-century lute, through the concise working drawing left by the Dutch scholar Henricus Arnault of Zwolle. It is given, with instructions for the forming of the outline and the making of the interior mould, on a single sheet, which forms part of a manuscript treatise on musical instruments (mainly keyboards) now in the Bibliothèque Nationale in Paris.

This sheet is shown here in Fig. 84. The paper on which it was written has stretched a little in the vertical axis, resulting in a slight distortion in the drawing. Arnault seems to have made one or two errors, which he rather charmingly corrects: for example, the left-hand figure is the correction for a section incorrectly drawn in the mould end-view on the right of the page. He also started his drawing too high on the page, for when he came to draw in the surprisingly long neck[70] he ran out of paper; unperturbed, he explains:

> Item—the neck should have the length of the line *ik* to the nut, but here it is too short, because the paper is not long enough.

Arnault mentions no measurements as such, but clearly defines the proportions that the lute should have, which are all derived from simple, whole-number ratios. For the sake of clarity, I have redrawn Arnault's lute according to his written instructions, omitting those lines pertaining to the mould construction, Fig. 85 (my construction and lettering).

[68] An arguable exception perhaps would be the *alla gobba* back of the viols and, more particularly, that found in the sloping-shouldered type, such as the Ciciliano (Ex. III).

[69] For corroboration of this view, see the following analysis of the Buechenberg chitarrone (Ex. XXIII).

[70] See Ian Harwood's remarks on his discussion of this lute in 'A Fifteenth Century Lute Design', *LSJ* vol. 2, pp. 7–8. This useful article also provides a full English translation of Arnault's Latin text.

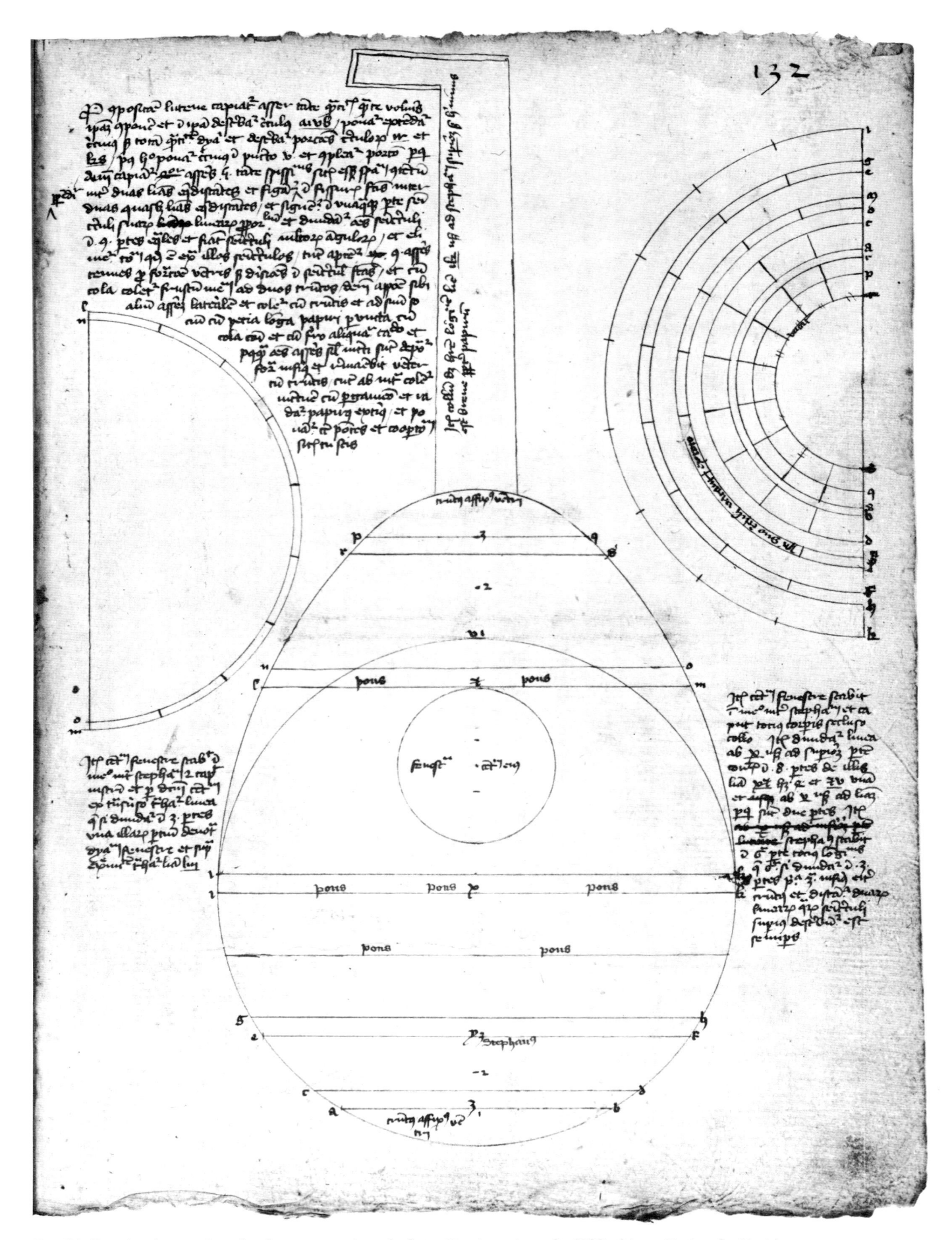

FIG. 84. Drawing instructions for the construction of a lute, Henricus Arnault. (Bibliothèque Nationale, Paris)

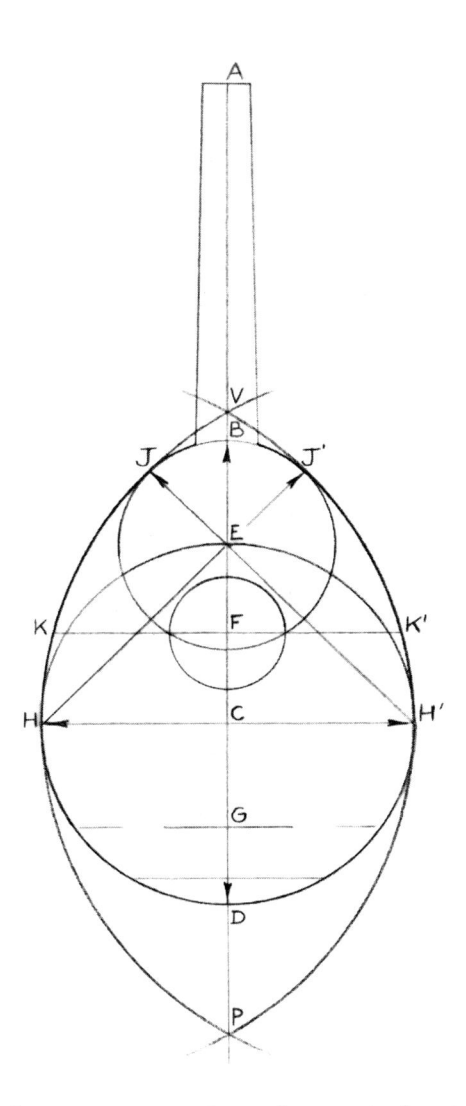

FIG. 85

A circle is first drawn, centre C on the vertical axis. The horizontal diameter HCH' is then constructed, and arcs HJ, centre H', and H'J', centre H, are completed, the radii HJ' and H'J crossing at the point where the centre line and large-circle circumference meet. This becomes the centre E for the arc JBJ', which completes the body outline. The radii EJ and EJ' are thus determined by 'tangency' to the larger arcs.

The radii of these two circles, centre E and centre C, have a ratio of $7:12$. All other measurements are developed from whole-number, vertical or horizontal, divisions of this body outline. Thus, the neck AB is given as being equal to the body width HCH'; the bridge position, G, on the centre line, as a one-sixth division of BD, and of GD, the lower third to be the bottom block; the sound-hole is centred at F, half-way between the top and the bridge ($\frac{1}{2}BG = F$), and its diameter is to be one-third of the horizontal piercing its centre, KFK'.

Apart from this commensurable approach to ratio, the other important design factor to emerge from the drawing is the large vesica piscis, VP, in which the whole lute body is inscribed (main arcs HJ and H'J' being produced from the main diameter HCH'). Interestingly, the use of this significant design device is not alluded to in the text.

Ex. XXI
Figs. 86–89, Pl. XX

LUTE, TENOR. ITALY, BOLOGNA, c.1550
HANS FREI
WARWICK COUNTY MUSEUM
Acc. No.: 67/1965

The deep-bodied, rounded lute of Arnault's drawing, utilizing the same curve for outline and cross-section alike, was superseded in the early sixteenth century by a slimmer, more sophisticated shape—the so-called 'pearl-mould'[71] form of the early Bolognese school. Due homage is paid to the artistry and skill of the two most prestigious luthiers of this development in Mary Burwell's *Instruction Book for the Lute*,[72] written in the 1660s:

> Laux Maler [Mauller] and Hans Frey [Hunts Frith] have been the two chiefest lute-makers that have lived at Bologna, who have rendered their names immortal by the melodious sound of that famous instrument, and will still make them resound through all the earth as long as it will please God to maintain the harmony of the universe.

And John Evelyn, on a visit to Bologna in 1645, long after it had ceased to be a centre of lute-making, wrote:

> This place has also been celebrated for lutes made by the old masters, Mollen [Maler], Hans Frei, and Nicholas Sconvelt, which were of extraordinary price; the workmen were chiefly Germans.[73]

Indeed, these instruments have always been in great demand, despite their consequent 'extraordinary price'. Mace[74] speaks of Maler lutes, 'pittiful Old, Batter'd Crack'd Things', valued at one hundred pounds apiece (1676), when a fine new lute, '... far more taking to the common eye', would cost but three or four pounds.

It has been estimated[75] that Maler's output of instruments may have been as high as 4,000 lutes during his working lifetime, but of these only three examples survive; similarly, only three Frei lutes are extant, while of Sconfelt, sadly, no instrument remains to illuminate the hearsay of a considerable reputation.

I have chosen, then, to represent this important school with a lute made by Hans Frei in about 1550. It is the instrument once owned by Eric Halfpenny, but which is now lodged in Warwick County Museum (Accession No.: 67/1965). The condition of the instrument is surprisingly good, although its present eleven-course condition is not original, the neck, head, and bridge being later, probably seventeenth-century, replacements of the earlier, shorter neck and fittings, which most likely would have carried only six or seven courses. Only the body scheme itself will therefore be considered, and an account of its geometry follows.

Fig. 86 shows the body outline or the table of the lute inscribed in its containing rectangle, *EFGH*. The ratio of this rectangle is, of course, that of the vertical and horizontal axes, *AD* and *NN'*, of the lute plan itself, and it comes as no surprise, given the harmonious aspect of the instrument, that this ratio should prove to be 1 : 1.618—the golden ratio:

$$\frac{AD}{NN'} = \frac{497.5 \text{ mm}}{307.5 \text{ mm}} = 1.618.$$

---

[71] Thomas Mace, *Musick's Monument* (London, 1676), Part II, chap. iii, p. 49.
[72] Quoted in *GSJ* vol. xi.
[73] Quoted in *LSJ* vol. 3.
[74] *Musick's Monument* (London, 1676), Part II, chap. iii, p. 48.
[75] Prynne, 'The Old Bologna Lute-Makers', *LSJ* vol. 5, p. 20.

It is interesting, as we shall see, that Frei, having selected this most beautiful, but mathematically irrational, scheme for his basic proportion, should then revert in the remaining traceable proportional decisions to the rational, commensurable ratios of the kind used by Arnault a century earlier (see earlier discussion). This is shown almost immediately: in Fig. 86 the arc of origin, IDI', is drawn, centred at point A, where the centre line meets the upper limit of the table. Its radius is therefore the body length, 497.5 mm, and the radii AI and AI' pierce the centres C and C' of the ubiquitous vesica piscis construction, whose two circles form the continuation of this lower arc, from I to J and from I' to J' (for the sake of clarity, only the right-hand side of the symmetrical plan is analysed in Fig. 86). The radius of these circles is an important vector in the design, demonstrating the first of Frei's commensurable ratios, being 1 : 5 of the overall length AD ($AD/CI = 497.5$ mm/99.5 mm $= 5/1$).

The remaining curves of the outline are completed (Fig. 86) by arcs $J'M'$ and $M'L'$. Arc $M'L'$ is extremely shallow, centred at O, with a radius of 765 mm, for which no harmonic resolution could be extrapolated from the vectors of the body scheme.

This brings us to Fig. 87, which deals with the design decisions made within the outline—the position of the bridge, and the size and placing of the rose. This last question of the rose is an intriguing one, for it is now thought quite likely that the cutting of lute roses was a specialized occupation, undertaken by skilled south German craftsmen, and that the great Italian lute-makers of the sixteenth century purchased their rectangular lute-belly 'blanks' from the north, with the roses already cut. It would then remain for them to construct their outlines around this existing feature. Unfortunately, no real light can be thrown on this quite plausible theory by the geometry of these early lutes, except that from the examples analysed it would appear that greater attention is paid to the linear proportion radiating from the circular border itself (i.e. from the circumference of the rose to the body outline and bridge position) than to either (a) the position of its centre within the vertical axis, or (b) the harmonic relationship of its size, radius or diameter, to the overall proportional scheme. This thought-process is demonstrated here in Fig. 87, where, quite independently of the actual size of the rose (which is not harmonically related to the main scheme) or indeed the position of its centre, the proportions around its circumference and within the body outline, with the incorporation of the bridge position, are elegantly disposed by means of the simple, whole-number ratios of 1 : 1, 1 : 2, 2 : 3, and 1 : 3. These are best expressed in terms of units, in this case 81 mm in length. Thus, in the vertical axis AD, there are two units between A, the top of the table, and the top of the rose, as there are equally two units between the bridge, B, and the lower edge of the rose, leaving one unit between the bridge-line at B and the lower edge of the table, D, and similarly one unit between the left and right sides of the rose and the adjacent edges of the table. This is demonstrated more clearly by the dotted concentric circles radiating out from the rose in Fig. 87, in each case the radii being increased by one unit of 81 mm.

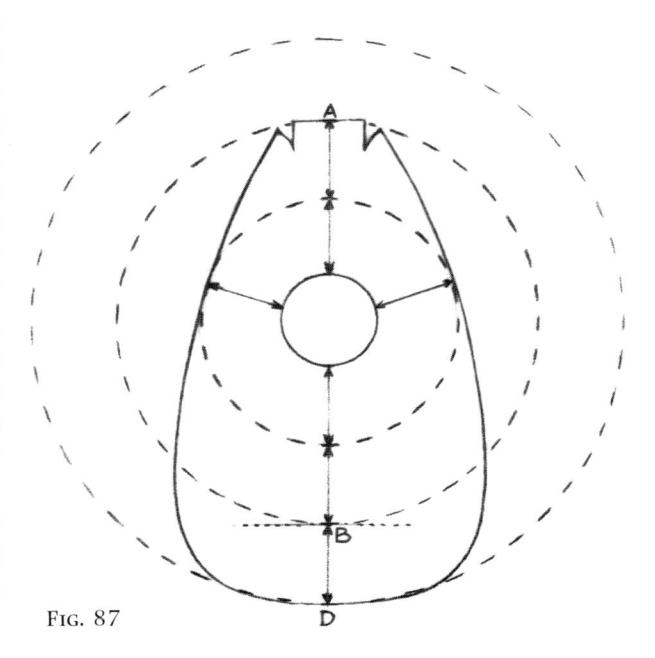

FIG. 86

FIG. 87

Unlike the lute of Arnault's drawing, the longitudinal section of this design is not the same as half its plan. Nevertheless, its depth is equal to half its width. Fig. 88 shows the vertical, or longitudinal, section, which can be inscribed in two annexed golden-section rectangles, $AA'P'P$ and $PP'D'D$, which are therefore related to the main outline-containing ϕ-rectangle, $EFGH$, in the ratio $1:4$. The lower of these two rectangles contains the square $QQ'D'D$, which, as can be seen, is of great importance.

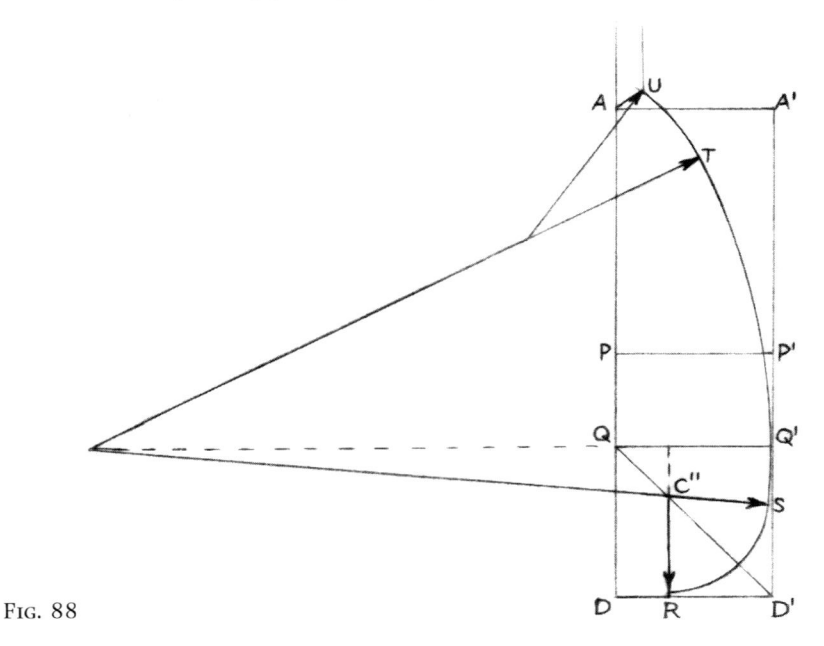

Fig. 88

The diagonal, QD', of this square passes through the centre, C'', of the lowest arc, RS, whose radius, 99.5 mm, exactly equals that of the corresponding vesica piscis arcs, JI and $I'J'$, used in the front of the instrument, where this important vector was shown to have a $1:5$ relationship with the overall length AD. A vertical line drawn through centre C'', in Fig. 88, meets the base line, DD', at R, that is, the point where the ribs of the vault rise away from behind the strengthening 'lace', shown in cross-section as DR. Here another commensurable ratio is found, as $DR:DD'$ equals $1:3$. The lowest arc, RS, is continued by the main arc, ST, whose centre lies on $Q'Q$ produced, and completed, meeting the back of the neck at U, by arc TU, of radii 672 mm and 187 mm respectively. Neither of these last values was found to relate harmonically to the rest of the scheme.

The cross-section taken at the widest point is shown in Fig. 89. As I mentioned above, although it is not semicircular in section like the lute of Arnault, this Frei lute's depth (QQ') is half its width (WW'). $QW'VQ'$ is therefore a square, containing the smaller square $XZVY$, which in turn yields the quadrant arc defining the joints of the ribs. This arc, ZY, is centred at X, and its radius, 132.5 mm, is again related to the important vector, 99.5 mm, of the vesica piscis arcs and longitudinal cross-section, here in the ratio 99.5 mm $:$ 132.5 mm $=$ 132.5/99.5 $=$ 1.33(2) $\simeq$ 3 : 4.

Fig. 89

Thus, although broadly planned to the overall accommodation of the golden ratio, the detailed planning of this most beautiful instrument is entrusted to the rational, whole-number, so-called 'musical'[76] ratios such as $1:1$, $1:2$, $1:3$, $1:5$, $2:3$, and $3:4$.

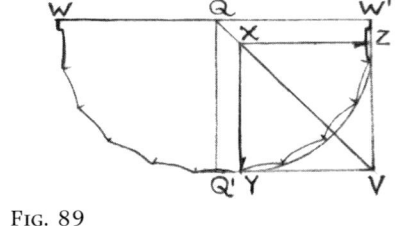

[76] See discussion of the Ciciliano viol, Ex. III.

Plate XX

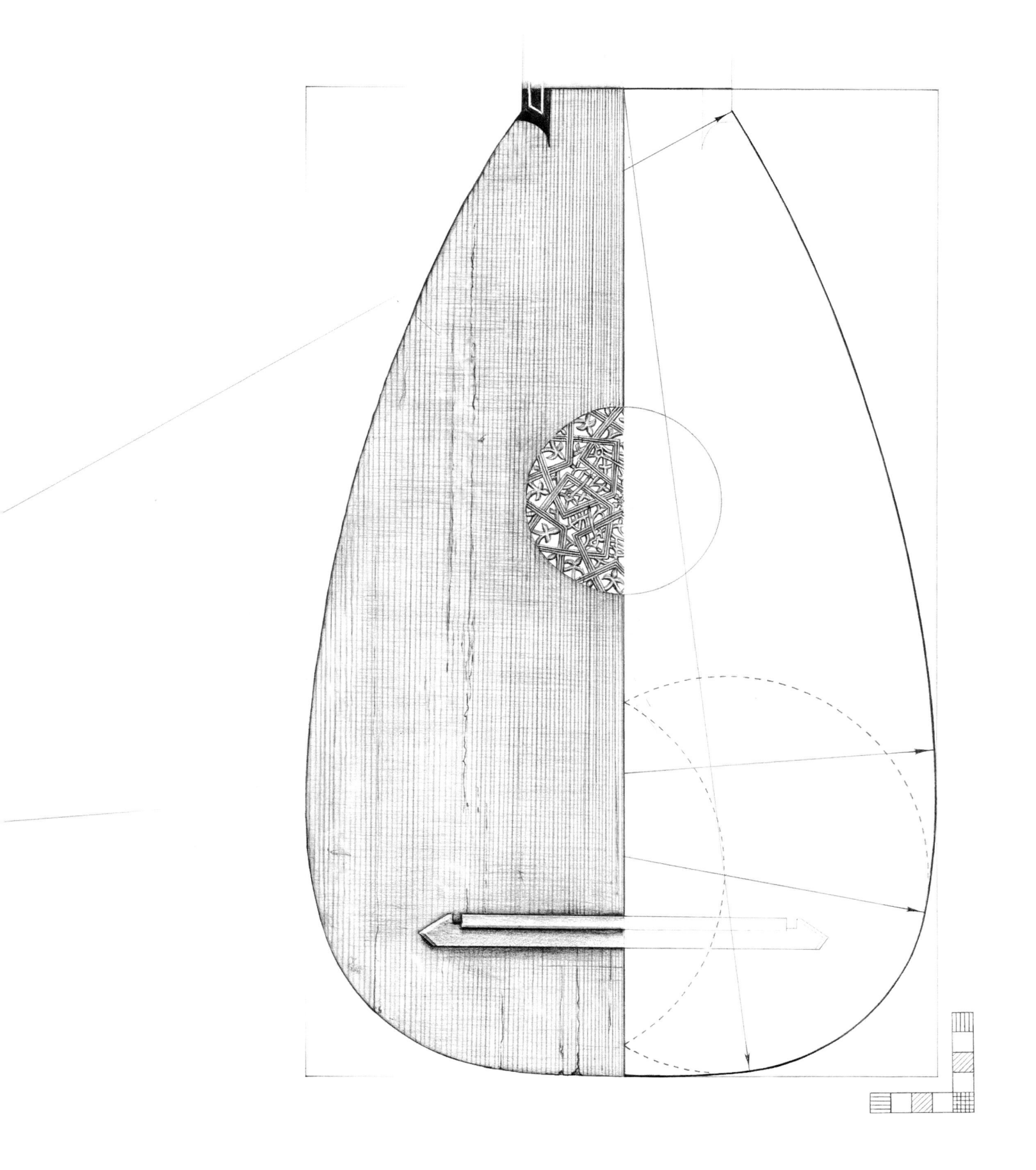

Ex. XXII
Figs. 90–94, Pl. XXI

LUTE, ALTO. ITALY, VENICE, c.1580
GIOVANNI HIEBER
MUSÉE DU CONSERVATOIRE ROYAL DE MUSIQUE, BRUSSELS
Acc. No.: 1561

Unique among the instruments discussed in this section, and indeed practically amongst all other surviving sixteenth-century lutes, this instrument, made in the last quarter of the century by Giovanni Hieber of Venice, does retain its original head and neck—a fact which is satisfyingly confirmed by the analysis of its geometry, explained below. Apart from the verification of the head and neck's authenticity, the analysis also reveals the full extent of the later alterations, and effective shortening of the lower part of the body (some idea of which can be gained from examination of the instrument itself), and establishes what must have been the original bridge position, before the lower part of the table sustained its distorting damage and repair. This can be seen most clearly in the main drawing, where the present flattened state of the lute's base (which, regrettably, has been thought by some modern luthiers to be a particular feature of the instrument, and one to be faithfully replicated) is drawn within the reconstructed original outline. That this is correct is clearly supported by (*a*) the remaining outline geometry, (*b*) the instrument's type, and, with the reinstatement of the true bridge position, (*c*) the typical commensurable proportions then found in the lute's plan.

Indeed, the establishment of the original bridge-line was the initial thread in the unravelling of the Hieber's design geometry,

> Untwisting all the chains that tie
> The hidden soul of harmony.

By this repositioning, not only were the harmonic proportions within the table itself resolved, but the consequent original string length was then also found to be in commensurable relationship with the table length. This information, too, is given in the main drawing: on the left-hand side, the present, altered position of the bridge is shown, together with the appropriate fret positions, while on the right-hand side I have drawn the supposed original bridge-line, and the revised fretting.

The complete, pre-alteration, body outline is shown, with the neck, in Fig. 90, where AD is the body length (A being the top of the table) and E the nut of the instrument. Here, no proportional significance was found in the rectangles containing the body outline, or the neck and body together, as was the case with the body area of the Frei lute, which, as the reader will remember, was precisely defined by the elegant, though schematically isolated, golden-section rectangle. Linear proportion, however, has been considered, for we find that overall length to body length, i.e.

$$ED : AD$$
$$676.5 \text{ mm} : 451 \text{ mm},$$
is $\quad 3 : 2;$

or, alternatively, body length to neck length

$$AD : AE$$
$$451 \text{ mm} : 225.5 \text{ mm}$$
equals $\quad 2 : 1.$

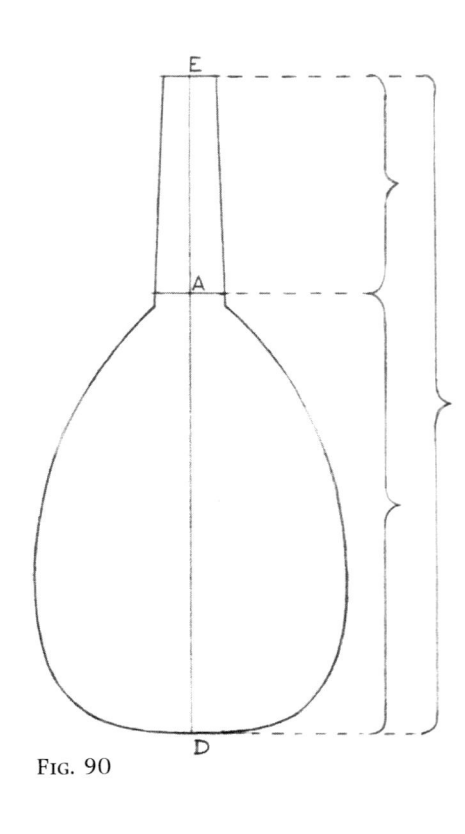

FIG. 90

ANALYSIS OF INSTRUMENT EXAMPLES

The geometry of the body outline (Fig. 91) follows the same pattern as that found in the Frei lute, although the proportional relationship between the various vectors is different.

The arc of origin IDI', now obscured by damage, is almost certain to have been centred at A. (As we have said, this is corroborated by previous example (cf. Frei), the remaining arcs, and the consequent commensurable cohesion of the instrument's proportions.) The radius of this arc would therefore be the body length AD, 451 mm. The next arcs were provided by two circles, in vesica piscis arrangement, centred at C and C', which two points lie on the lines produced from the edges of the neck (see Fig. 91). Arc $I'J'$ is thus centred at C', and is of 97.5 mm radius. This is contained, as in the Frei lute, by an arc, $J'K'$, centred at M, on the opposite edge of the table at the widest point, giving an arc radius of 309 mm (body width). The main arc is $K'L'$, which is centred at N. Its radius, 390 mm, is commensurably related to the vesica piscis arc radii, centred at C and C' (97.5 mm), in the ratio $4:1$.

The rose position, bridge-line position, and string length are examined in Fig. 92. Again, greater regard is paid to the space surrounding the circumference of the rose than to the positioning of its centre. Following both the Frei and the Arnault, the distances above and below the rose are again equal, i.e.

$$AR = R''B = 142.5 \text{ mm.}$$

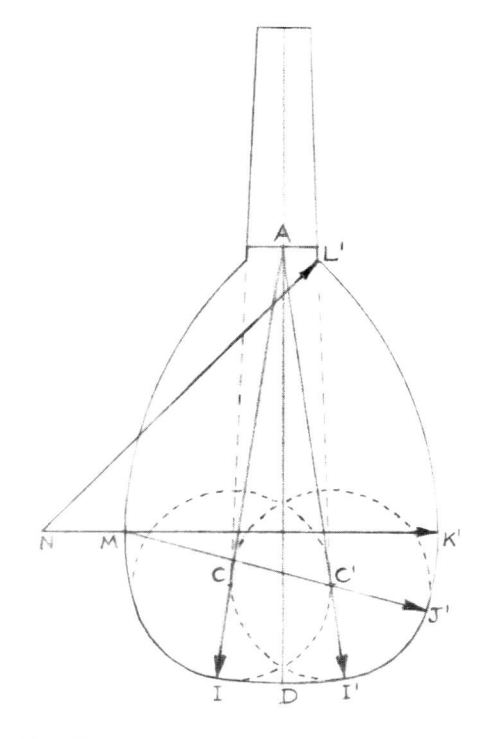

FIG. 91

This is related to $R'F'$ (95 mm) in the now familiar ratio

$$142.5 : 95$$
$$3 : 2$$

while the remaining space below the bridge, BD, is, in turn, related to $R'F'$ in the ratio

$$76 \text{ mm} : 95 \text{ mm}$$
$$4 : 5.$$

The line GG' is equal in length to the rose diameter RR''.

The true string length, EB, was also found to be in simple, whole-number relationship with both the body length, AD, and the overall length, ED, that is:

$$AD : EB$$
$$451 \text{ mm} : 601(.3) \text{ mm}$$
$$3 : 4$$

and
$$ED : EB$$
$$676.5 \text{ mm} : 601(.3) \text{ mm}$$
$$9 : 8.$$

Thus, by the resolution of these rational proportions, the original plan of this important instrument becomes apparent, its design made whole, desite the ravages to its fabric. Regrettably, the nature of the damage and repair, which partly obscured the lower front of the instrument, resulted in distortion of the vault, which consequently caused some difficulty when the relevant cross-sections were measured. The following vectors, however, would appear by their interrelationship to be correct.

Fig. 93 is the longitudinal section of the Hieber. The dashed line in the lower section traces the present damaged profile of the bottom of the vault. Like the Frei, this lute is as deep as half its width, its deepest point, Q',

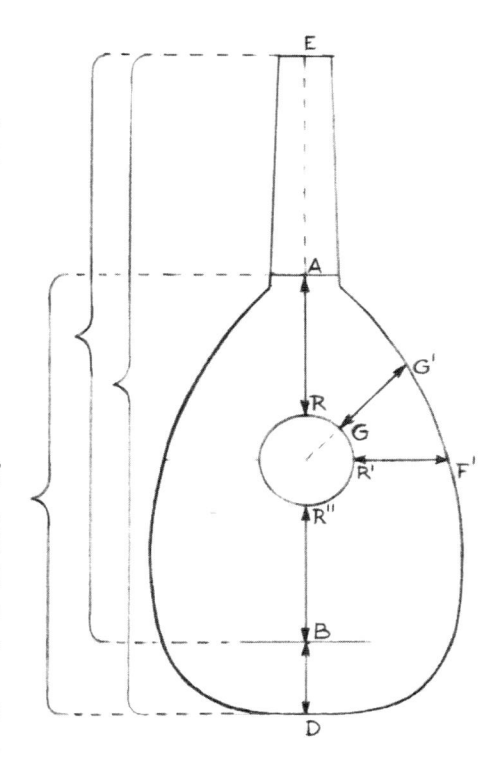

FIG. 92

FIG. 93

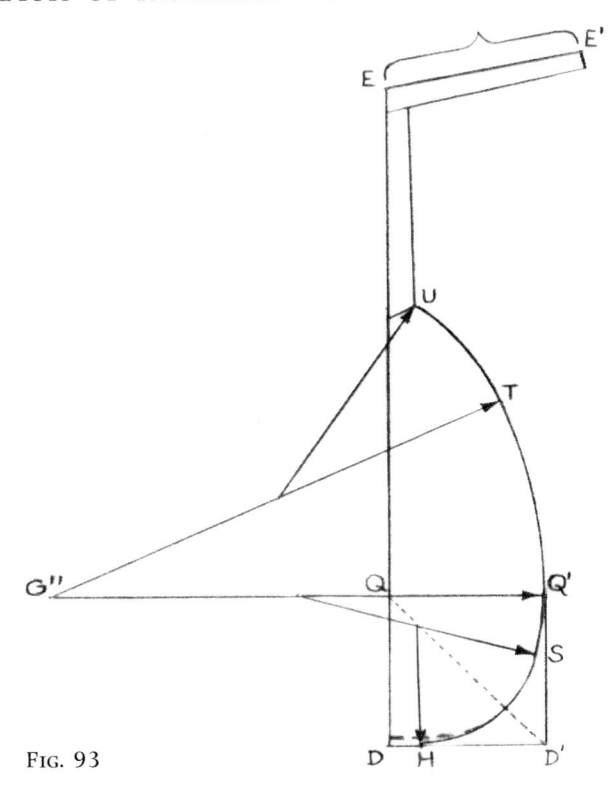

being the corner of a square, $QQ'D'D$, which contains, and defines, the lower arcs. The present lace depth, DH, is related to the overall depth, DD', in the ratio

$$DH : DD'$$
$$1 : 5.$$

The centre of the arc HS lies on the diagonal, QD', of this square, and its radius is 122 mm. This relates to the vesica arcs of the plan in the ratio

$$122 \text{ mm} : 97.5 \text{ mm}$$
$$5 : 4.$$

The arc is continued by arc SQ', radius 244 mm, which is in 2 : 1 ratio with arc SH and 5 : 2 ratio with the vesica arcs. The main arc is $Q'T$, centred at G'', of radius 487.5 mm. This is in exactly 5 : 1 ratio with the vesica arcs, and again (here allowing for a 0.5 mm margin of error) 2 : 1 ratio with its preceding arc SQ'. The profile of the vault is completed by arc TU, radius 244 mm, which thus mirrors arc SQ'. Fig. 93 also includes the head profile which measures, EE', 195 mm, which is 2 : 1 to the 'key' radius of the vesica piscis arcs.

The horizontal cross-section taken at the widest point is shown in Fig. 94. The depth being half the width, $QW'VQ'$ is a square. It contains the smaller square, $XZVY$, bearing the rib-seam-defining quadrant arc ZY, centre X. The radius of this arc relates to the larger square in the ratio 8 : 9.

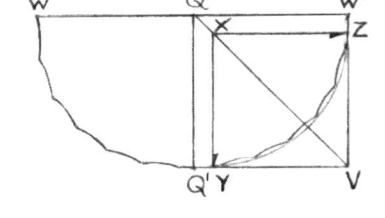

FIG. 94

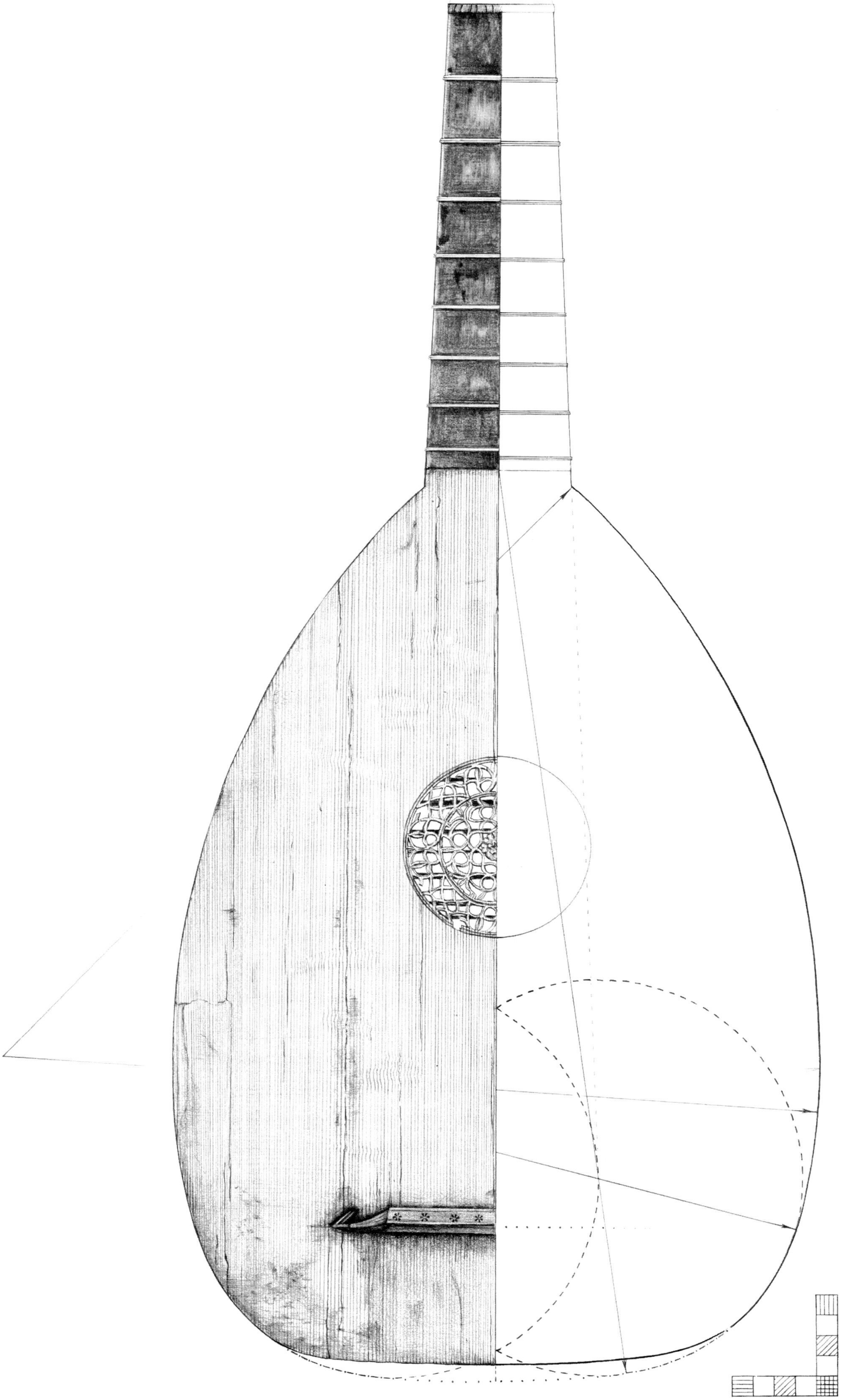

PLATE XXI

Ex. XXIII
Figs. 95–98, Pl. XXII

LUTE, CHITARRONE. ITALY, ROME, 1614
MATTEO BUECHENBERG
VICTORIA AND ALBERT MUSEUM
Acc. No.: 218-1882

By the turn of the sixteenth century, the need for lutes with an extensive bass register, primarily for the accompaniment of singing, resulted in the introduction of the rather unlikely-looking, but musically effective, long-necked bass lutes, called *chitarroni*. This development coincided with the shift of the centre of lute-making from Venice—as, earlier, it had moved to Venice from Bologna—to Padua and to Rome. Thus, it was the makers of Rome who became associated with the early development of the chitarrone (referred to by Praetorius as the 'Roman theorbo') and of these, Matteo Buechenberg, the maker of our third example, was perhaps the most famous.

Constructionally, one of the major innovations found in the instruments of this school is the increased number of ribs forming the vault. Previously, as we have seen, nine-, eleven-, or thirteen-ribbed vaults were most often employed, whereas this vault is constructed from no fewer than forty-one narrow ribs, each cut from a piece of pine with dark to light shading in the grain, achieving a *trompe-l'œil* effect of fluting.

An idea of the size of the chitarrone is gained from Fig. 95, where the additional long neck, which brings the instrument's total length to over six feet, can be seen. Unfortunately, this 'bass' neck has been repaired and spliced, which is why its present string length of approximately 1590 mm has not been included in the following analysis.

The commensurable proportions which were found in the preceding lutes are also evident in this fine design of Buechenberg's. Here the whole-number proportions are based on one unit, with remarkable consistency. In fact, this unit of 127.5 mm is the radius of the customary vesica piscis lower-bout construction, which was also found in this lute and which is discussed below.

The commensurable proportions of length can be seen in Fig. 95, the vertical distance between each set of horizontal lines being one unit of 127.5 mm. *ED* comprises eight such units. Thus, the ratio of neck length to body length

$$EA : AD = 3 : 5$$

and the ratio of string length to body length

$$EB : AD = 7 : 5.$$

The bridge-line, *B*, is placed at one-fifth of the body length from *D*, while the centre line, *R*, of the main lower roses, in the triple rose cluster, is half-way between the body top *A* and bridge *B*, *RD* being three-fifths of *AD*, and *AR* two-fifths of *AD*.

The rectangle containing the body outline has no proportional significance, as was the case with the Frei's body plan (which, as the reader will remember, was inscribed within a golden-section rectangle, although the lute as a whole was found to be governed by commensurable

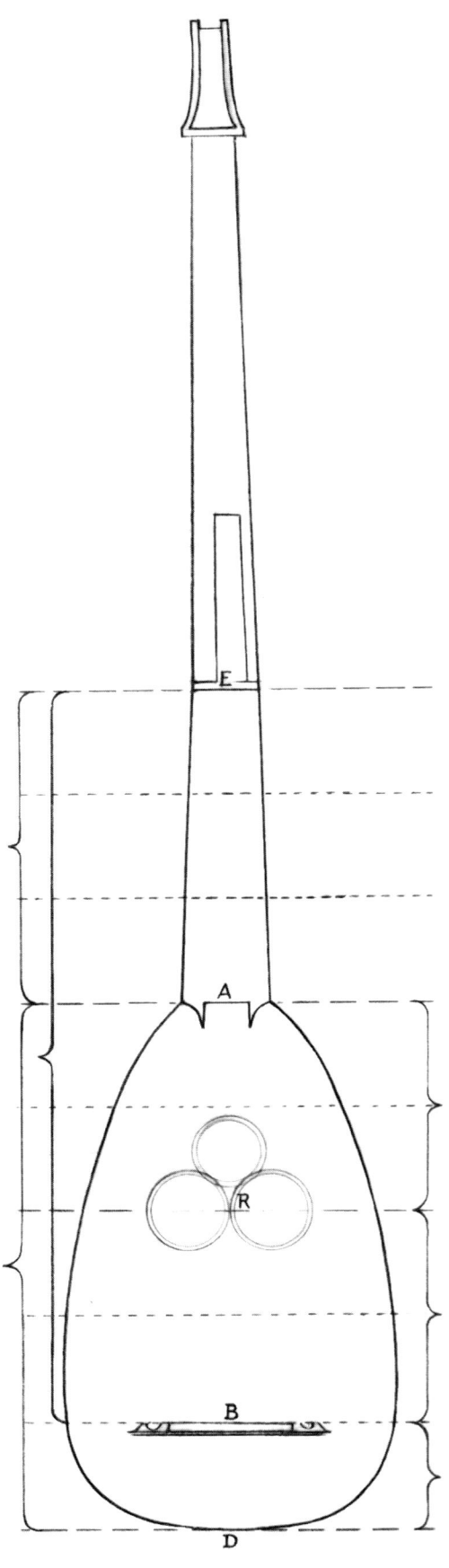

FIG. 95

ratios). The present design, using only rational, whole-number ratios of the same unit, makes no attempt to rationalize the body width (and therefore the containing rectangle), the type of body-outline construction precluding a proportional solution that utilizes the same system.

The geometry of the Buechenberg's body outline is drawn in Fig. 96. The arc of origin, IDI', is still centred at A, the radius therefore equalling the body length, 637.5 mm, which is exactly five units. The outline is continued by arc $I'J'$, centre C', radius 127.5 mm. This arc and, of course, its twin, IJ, are formed by the vesica piscis construction centred at C and C'; as we have said, its component radii of 127.5 mm form the key unit to the whole-number ratios of the design. It was of great importance, too, in the other lutes so far discussed and, like the Frei lute, its ratio here to the body length is 1 : 5. In agreement with the preceding lutes, too, is the arrangement of the next arc, $J'K'$, whose centre, M, again lies on the opposite edge of the instrument, at the point of maximum width. The main arc, $K'G'$, is centred at N; its radius, 892.5 mm, is equal to the main string length, that is, seven units. The rounder shoulders of this large-bodied lute are provided by an additional arc, $G'H'$, centre F, radius 255 mm, exactly two units, which completes the body outline.

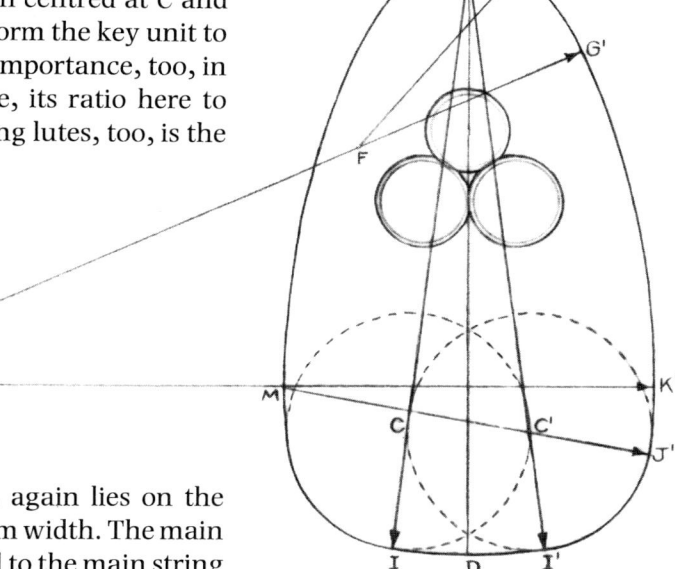

FIG. 96

The explanation of the positioning of the roses does not require, as before, a separate diagram, as their centring was shown quite clearly in Fig. 95. In this instrument, however, two departures from the practice of rose-positioning shown in the last two lutes were found. The first was the harmonic placing of a rose centre (see Fig. 95) where previously the circumferences alone were found to be of prime harmonic importance. The second was the harmonic consideration of the rose diameter. The main drawing shows how the upper rose is smaller than the lower two; its outer border, however, touches, and 'leads into', the inner borders of the lower two, and these three circles, which thus form a trefoil, are of the same diameter, 85 mm, which is related to the main unit of 127.5 mm in the ratio 2 : 3.

In so large an instrument, it should be of no surprise that its depth is less than half its width (depth = $\frac{1}{2}$width is a principle found in the Arnault, the Frei, and the Hieber); nevertheless, the point of maximum depth, Q', in Fig. 97, lies in plane QQ', at a distance from the bottom of the instrument, i.e. QD, which is equal to half its width, so that $QD = 195$ mm.

DP is the 'lace', or capping strip, which is a little distorted with age and repair. The vault section is commenced by arc PS, whose radius again equals that of the vesica piscis arcs of the plan (127.5 mm). It is continued here by arc SQ', radius 637.5 mm; this equals the body length, and arc-of-origin radius, of five units. The main arc, $Q'T$, continues the curve of the vault from the point of maximum depth. This arc is of radius 1020 mm, which equals the overall length from main nut

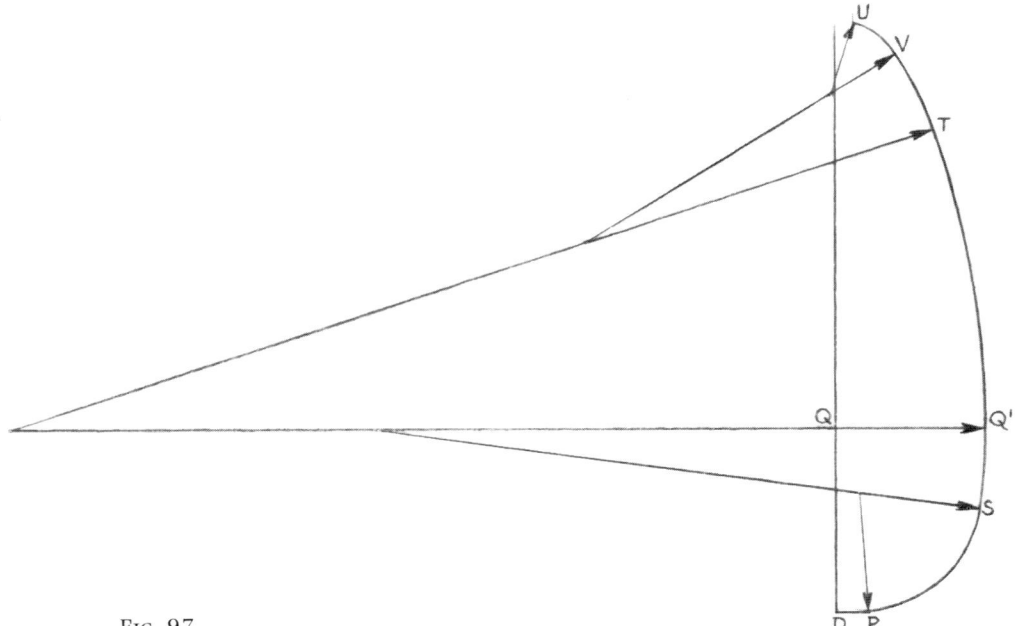

Fig. 97

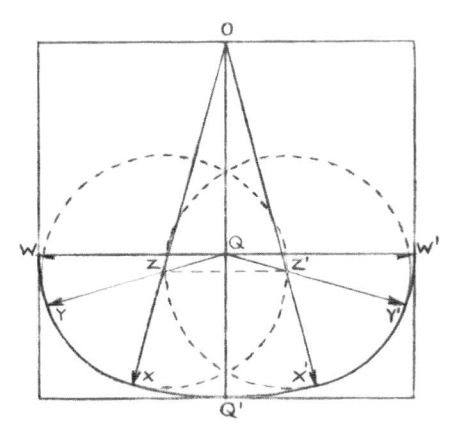

Fig. 98

to button (*ED* in Fig. 95), that is, eight units. The arc *TV* continues this curve; its radius is 382.5 mm, which equals the main neck length of three units. The sectional curve of the vault is completed by a further arc, *VU*, whose radius, 85 mm, we have also encountered before as the common rose diameter, which equalled two-thirds of a unit.

The section taken at the maximum width and depth of the lute is shown in Fig. 98. It is quite different in geometrical plan from the two preceding instruments, as visual comparison will show.

The remarkable degree of proportional homogeneity found in this instrument, however, extends quite notably to this section. Although, as we have seen, its depth, QQ', is not equal to half its width (WW'), the width and half-width values are still used here. Indeed, the whole section is related to the design of the body plan in an extremely beautiful solution, which can be inscribed in a square of side 390 mm, the maximum width of the instrument. Thus, the curve of the section is initiated from the edge of the table by arc $W'Y'$, which is centred at Q; its radius is therefore 195 mm, half the body width. It is continued by arc $Y'X'$, centred at Z', whose radius is 127.5 mm, and, as can be seen from the diagram, forms part of another vesica piscis arrangement, which echoes the construction used in the plan of the instrument, and indeed in the longitudinal cross-section. The vesica arcs are joined by arc $XQ'X'$, centred at O, and of radius 390 mm—the width of the instrument. This beautiful figure, which, above all, conclusively proves the plane geometry derivation of the three-dimensional lute vault, concludes the discussion of one of the most homogeneously conceived and mathematically satisfying instruments to be examined so far.

PLATE XXII

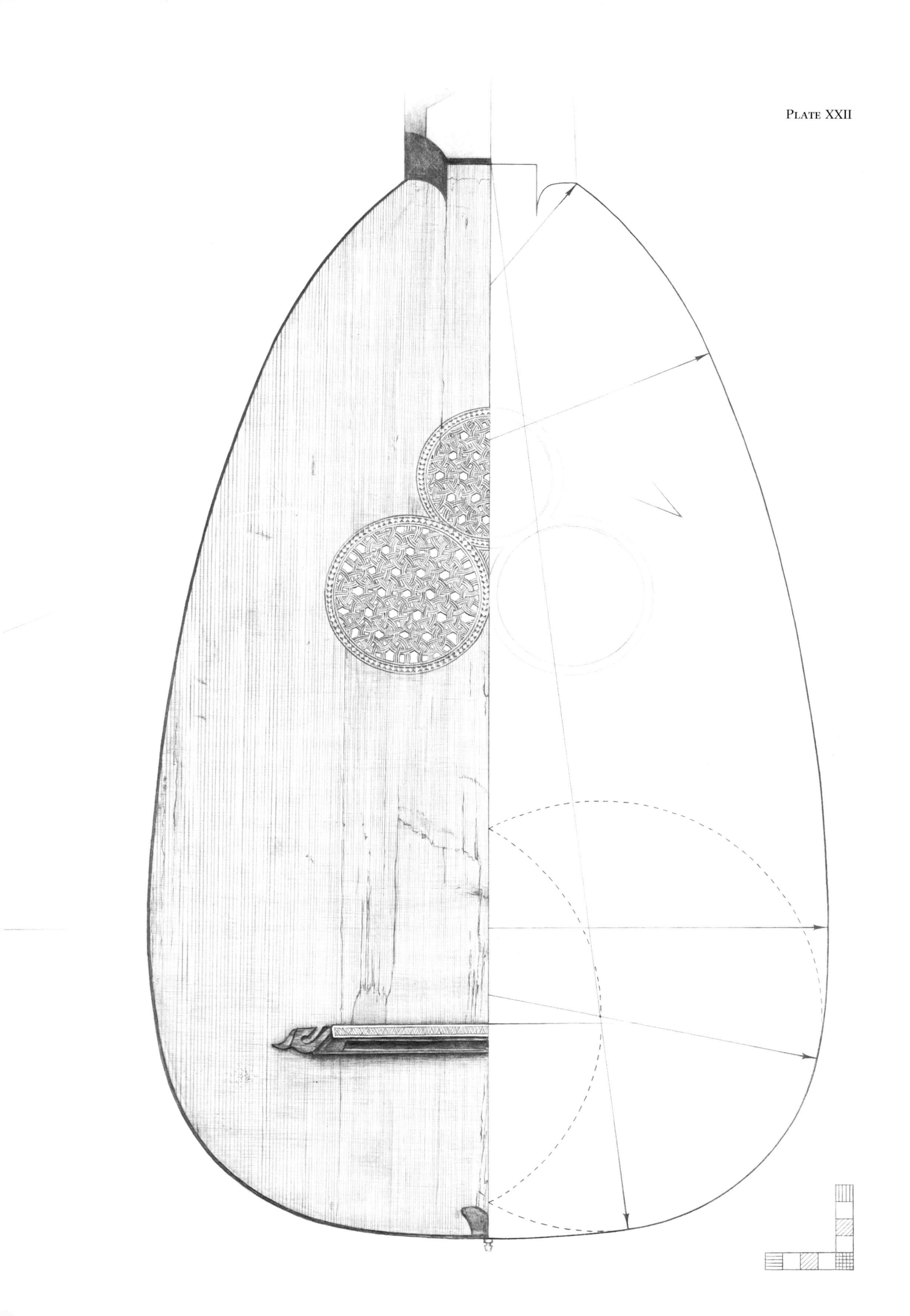

Ex. XXIV
Pl. XXIII

LUTE, THEORBO. GERMANY, HAMBURG, 1734
JACOBUS HENRICUS GOLDT
VICTORIA AND ALBERT MUSEUM
Acc. No.: 4274-1856

Ex. XXV
Figs. 99–102, Pl. XXIV

LUTE, THEORBO. ENGLAND, LONDON, 1762
MICHAEL RAUCHE
VICTORIA AND ALBERT MUSEUM
Acc. No.: 9-1871

The many fine lutes to come from Germany in the early eighteenth century reflect the great explosion of interest which occurred there, whilst elsewhere the instrument was in its final recession. These 'baroque lutes' tended to follow the elongated proportions of the early, Bolognese, instruments, and their makers, the Hoffmanns, Jauck, Schelle, etc., were worthy craftsmen. One such instrument, by Jacobus Henricus Goldt, was made in Hamburg in 1734, and is now in the Victoria and Albert Museum collection. It is extremely well made, and bears rich marquetry on neck and finger-board. The body, however, is of rather dull and stolid design, lacking that exquisite, gentle tension between the curves of the outline, which marks a well-conceived design. Neither is there inspiration, nor even sensitivity, to be found in the ponderous, rather bloated, form of the vault. It was measured, drawn, and analysed, but yielded disappointing proportional information. A drawing (Pl. XXIII) is included for the sake of visual comparison with the other lutes, but no geometrical *exposé* is necessary, the instrument lacking any traceable harmonic scheme, its vectors seeming arbitrary in value and disorganized in arrangement. Even the ubiquitous vesica piscis construction for the 'lower bouts'[77] was not used, thus flouting an unwritten law for the relationship of the crucial lower curves of one side of the outline to the mirror-image curves of the other.

Another lute, also a theorbo, was therefore selected from the Victoria and Albert Museum collection to present an eighteenth-century development of the instrument (Pl. XXIV). Perhaps not quite as typical as the Goldt, this fine lute by Michael Rauche was, in fact, of even later date, 1762, and was made, as the rather graphic cartouche on the back of its neck proclaims, in Chandos Street, London. Its design, although arguably betraying the more relaxed attitude of the eighteenth century towards geometrical and proportional planning in design, nevertheless belongs to the same design tradition as the lutes of the previous two centuries, with their characteristic employment of commensurable ratios.

A few simple ratios can be seen in the overall planning of the instrument in Fig. 99, although again no harmonic significance was found in the body-containing rectangle, as was the case of the Frei lute. For example,

---

[77] The term is here used to describe the lower section of the lute body, although of course there are no true 'bouts' to the unidirectional curves of a lute outline.

PLATE XXIII

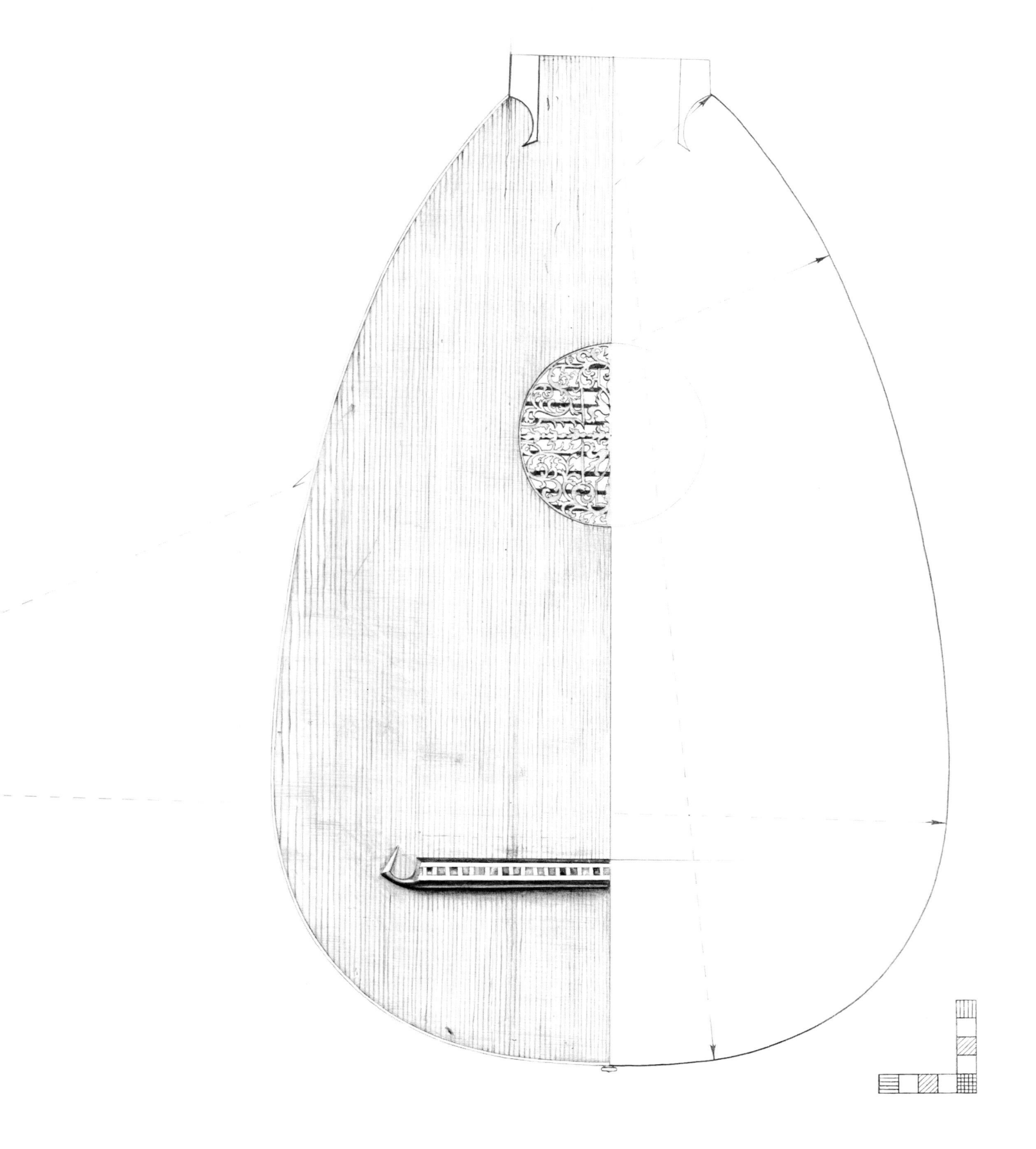

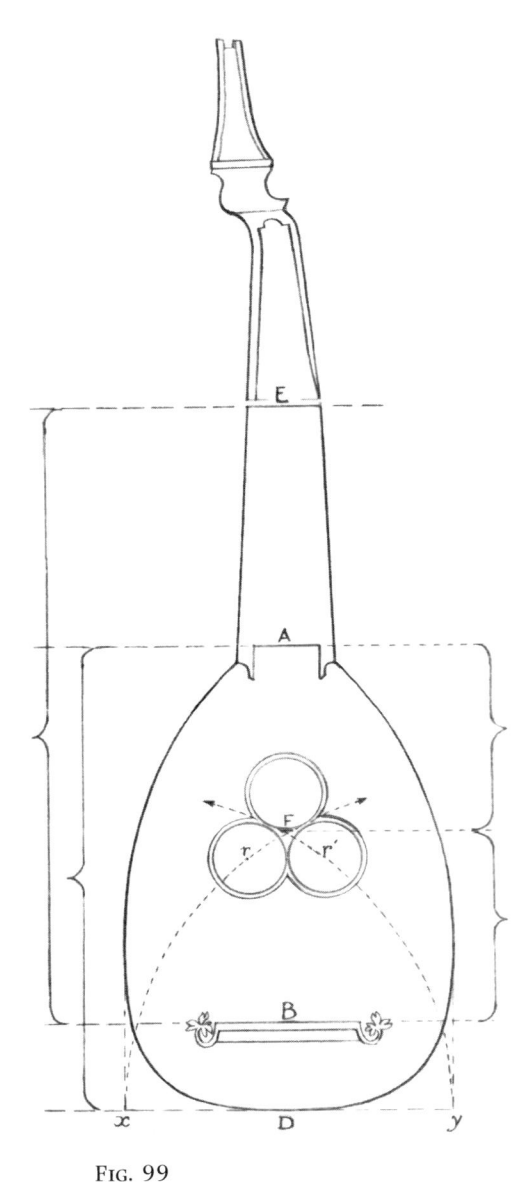

the main string length, EB, 712 mm, is in simple ratio with body length, AD, 535 mm, that is:

$$EB : AD$$
$$712 \text{ mm} : 535 \text{ mm}$$
$$= 4 : 3.$$

The positions of the bridge and rose cluster are also shown in Fig. 99. The bridge-line, B, misses having a 1 : 5 relationship with the body length, AD, by 2 to 3 mm, whereas the rose cluster, this time positioned by the lower tangential edge of the upper hole, point F, is still centred half-way between body-top, A, and bridge-line, B, i.e. $AF = FB$. The roses are also positioned by an arc-swing up from the base line, xy, and therefore of radius 366 mm, the overall width of the body; the arc passes through the lower rose centres, r and r' (Fig. 99), and thence through point F.

The geometry of the body outline is analysed in Fig. 100. The lower-bout[78] construction, as can be seen, is the classic 'vesica piscis/arc of origin' combination, which seems to have been the customary solution.

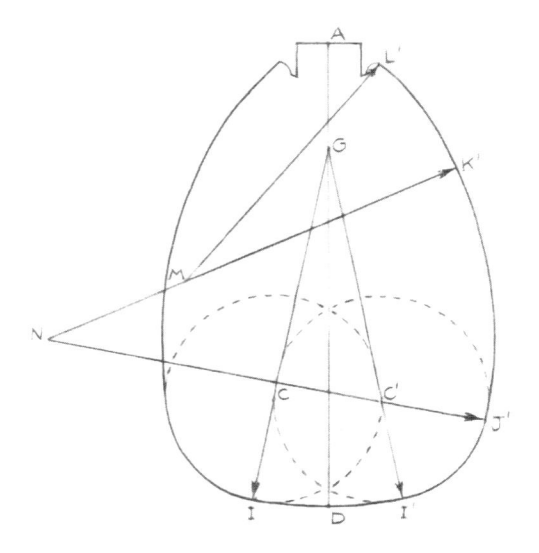

Fig. 99

Fig. 100

It differs, however, from the preceding analysed lutes both geometrically and harmonically. Unlike those of its forebears, the arc of origin is not centred at A (which would give a radius equal to body length AD), but instead it is positioned somewhat lower on the centre line (more akin to its position in violin geometries), shown here at G. This gives the arc-of-origin radius, GD, the value of 415 mm, which is the first of the commensurable radii of the body outlines, related, not as previously to the vesica piscis radii (here 116.5 mm, and harmonically isolated), but to the inner, inlaid radius of the roses, that is, 83 mm. Thus, the radius of the arc of origin, IDI', is related to this unit, 415 mm : 83 mm or 5 : 1.

The vesica piscis figure is shown centred at C and C', its arc, $I'J'$, connecting the arc of origin, DI', with the main arc of the outline, $J'K'$. This is centred at N, and is of radius 498 mm, which is equal to six units of 83 mm, and is therefore in 6 : 5 ratio with the arc of origin. The outline is concluded by arc $K'L'$, centre M, radius 332 mm, which is another vector commensurable to the unit of 83 mm, 332 mm : 83 mm, that is, 4 : 1. It therefore follows that this arc is in 332 : 498 ratio to its neighbour, that is, 4 : 6 or, if you prefer, 2 : 3.

[78] See p. 123 n. 77 above.

The geometry of the splendid, ivory-ribbed vault of this lute is described in the following two sections. The longitudinal section is drawn in Fig. 101. The straight 'lace' rib is *DH*, from which the curve is initiated by arc *HS*, radius 116.5 mm, which relates directly to the vesica piscis arc of the body plan, and thus conforms, in this detail, to practically all the lutes previously analysed here, and realizes a design tradition spanning more than two centuries. This arc, *HS*, is continued by arc *SQ*, radius 415 mm, which, as in the Buechenberg, is the same as the arc of origin (although in this case not also equal to the body length). As we have said, 415 mm is five units of 83 mm. The curve continues with arc *QT*, radius 498 mm, again relating to the front of the instrument, 498 mm being the main arc of the plan, and six units of 83 mm. The curve is completed by arc *TU*, radius 166 mm, which is, of course, two units of 83 mm.

166 mm is also the maximum depth, *W'V'*, of the vault, as is shown in the cross-sectional drawing, Fig. 102, taken at the point of maximum width, *WW'*, 367 mm. This, as in the cross-section of the Buechenberg, is

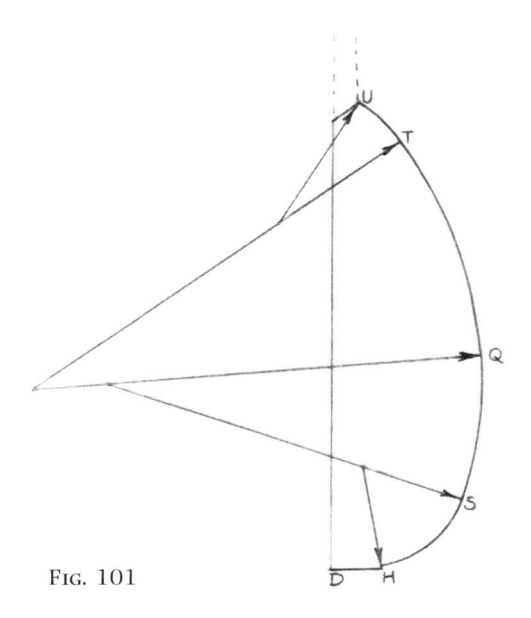

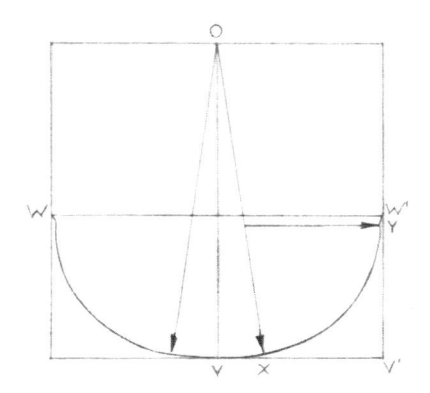

FIG. 101

FIG. 102

also the radius, *OV*, of arc *VX*, the lowest curve of the cross-section of the vault. This figure can therefore also be constructed within a square. The curve is completed by arc *XY*, radius 150 mm, a value not harmoniously integrated to the rest of the Rauche's geometry.

PLATE XXIV

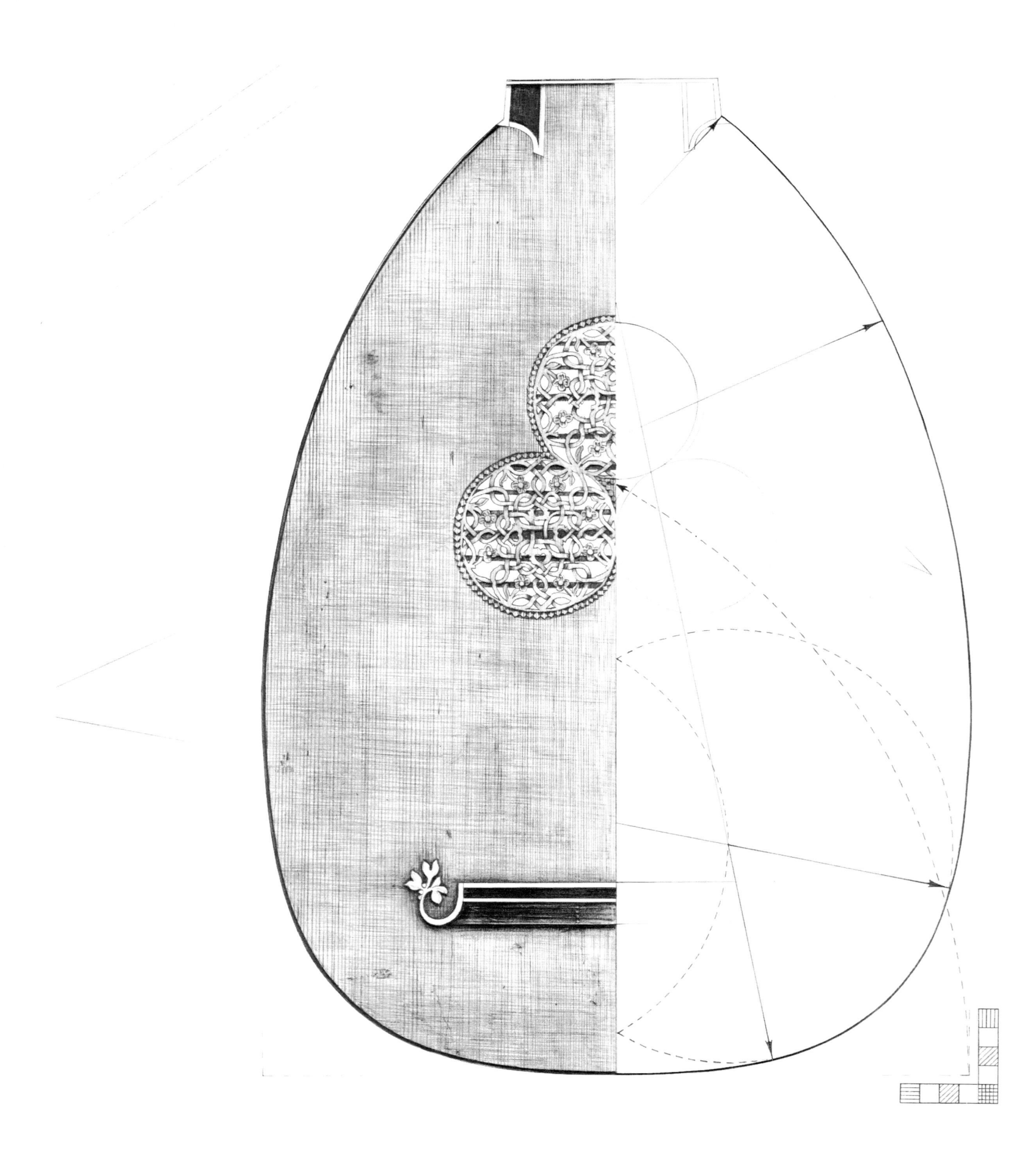

MANDORE AND MANDOLINES

The mandore and mandolines are here grouped together, as diminutive cousins of the lute family of instruments, some features of which, to a greater or lesser degree, they all possess.

Both names, mandore and mandoline, or mandolino, share a common origin in the Italian *mandorla*, meaning 'almond', an obvious allusion to the instrument's body shape. The origins of the instrument type, however, lie with the four-course mandore of the Renaissance, in effect a simple, miniature lute, which was sometimes added to a consort of lutes to brighten the texture, often, it would seem, to the detriment of the larger instruments: 'it so preoccupies the ear that the lutes have trouble in being heard'.[79]

In fact it was this mandore, represented here by an attractive, seventeenth-century, Italian specimen (Ex. XXVI), which became the most important founder-member of that group of instruments usually called the mandoline family. Ironically, the word 'family' here is used in a different organological sense from what it is taken to imply with regard to the families of instruments in the Renaissance. In this instance, the mandoline 'family' describes the many different regional variants and hybrids of mandoline which emerged in eighteenth- and nineteenth-century Italy; in the other, earlier sense, the family of instruments meant the range, in different sizes and pitches, of one type of instrument. The use of the word is ironic, because it was this crucial change, away from the concept of a graduated group as the governing order for musical instruments, which, in effect, afforded the mandore (and therefore its descendant, the mandoline) an opportunity to prosper. With the breakdown of the 'family' concept, the orphaned survivors tended to be those members found at the extremes of the pitch range, instruments now valued and developed for their individual timbre, rather than as separate parts of an 'unbroken' whole. One such was the mandore, which, throughout the seventeenth century, gradually increased its own range from four courses to six, at the same time undergoing a change of name to *mandolino*. This instrument, with carved and fretted rose, tied frets, reclining peg-box with horizontal pegs, and bridge-tied strings, became what we now call a Milanese mandoline (cf. Ex. XXVII), one of the two principal members of the mandoline group, the other being the Neapolitan mandoline, the more familiar, violin-tuned instrument first developed in the eighteenth century by the Vinaccia family (cf. Ex. XXVIII).

[79] Marin Mersenne, *Harmonie Universelle* (Paris, 1636).

Ex. XXVI

Figs. 103–107, Pl. XXV

MANDORE, FOUR-COURSE. ITALY, VENICE? *c.*1640
MAKER UNKNOWN
CONSERVATOIRE DE MUSIQUE, PARIS
Acc. No.: E.222, C.235

Perhaps not surprisingly, it is rare to find the decorative restraint of the violin, or the unembellished formal purity of the lute, in the more 'social' instruments, and in almost all the remaining examples in this study, great emphasis is placed by their makers on their decorative qualities, and their appeal as objects of virtu, as much as their function as musical instruments.

This delightful four-course mandore is no exception to this policy. Largely made from ivory, banded in head, neck, and vault with ornamental double-stringing of ebony, it presents a dazzling visual effect, a decorative scheme which, by contrast, stresses the organic, refractory qualities of the wood of the table, and bestows upon it an air of preciousness far above even that of the costly ivory which surrounds it. Great care, too, has been taken with the many-layered, sunken rose, a beautiful, organic accretion of fantastic, Gothic intricacy.

The Gothic mode appears to have continued in use, as the most suitable stylistic medium for the roses of musical instruments, long after it had ceased to be of interest in other fields of the decorative arts. This was, no doubt, due to an almost matchless facility for its providing ornamental, pierced tracery within a circle. Indeed, such was the eclecticism of the musical-instrument maker that a keyboard instrument might well display a severely Classical case, defined by academically correct mouldings, lined with all the Eastern riches of gilded Moresques, while in the sound-board there will lie a rose of the purest Gothic.

This present instrument, whose rather beautiful geometry is discussed below, was made by an unknown luthier, working in Italy (possibly Venice?) in about 1640. The overall proportions have been very carefully considered. The body plan fits exactly into a $\sqrt{4}$ rectangle, or double square. This, in Fig. 103, is WXYZ, WZ, or BD, measuring 249 mm, and ZY, or HH′, measuring 124.5 mm. This last, the body width, is also the length of the head (seen from the front) from the top, T, of the ornamental crest to A, the nut. The positioning of the sound-hole, centre F, is by means of a most beautiful method, one similar to that used in the Rauche theorbo (Ex. XXV); the line WX, short side of body-containing rectangle WXYZ, is dropped down on to the long side (XY or WZ) to point C′ or C; the resulting arcs (WC′ and XC) intersect the centre line at F, the exact centre of the rose. The bridge position, E, within the body-plane, BD, adopts the same proportioning as did the Buechenberg chitarrone (Ex. XXIII), that is, at a point one-fifth from the bottom of the instrument, so that $BE : BD = 4 : 5$.

The vectors used in the rest of the instrument's design are all directly, or indirectly, related to a commensurable unit, u, the smallest outline arc radius, which was first measured as 46.5 mm, but, by calculation, was confirmed as being 46.66̇ mm. In fact, $\frac{1}{3}u$, or 15.55̇ mm, also accounts for the overall measurements of body height and width, which can then be expressed as being $\frac{16}{3}u$ and $\frac{8}{3}u$ respectively. This unit also seems to be

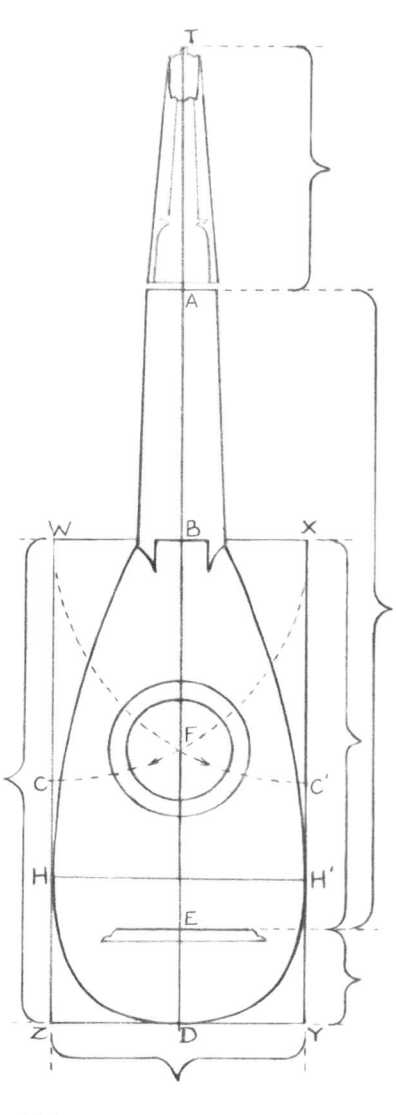

FIG. 103

present in the string length, AE, measuring 327.5 mm, which is probably intended as $7u$ (actually 46.666 mm × 7 = 326.666 mm).

The body outline is resolved into its component arcs in Fig. 104. The arc of origin, DI', is centred at O on the centre line, so that $DO : OB$ is 3 : 5. Its radius is therefore three-eighths of the body length, or, in terms of the unit of commensurability, $2u$ (93.333 mm). The next arc, arc $I'J'$, is centred at G', which is situated on the bridge-line (one-fifth of the body height from D), its radius being 46.666 mm, or u. The following arc, $J'K'$, is centred on the opposite edge of the instrument at H, the point of maximum width, its radius (half BD) therefore being 124.5 mm, or in terms of u, $\frac{8}{3}u$. When produced upwards, this arc, with its symmetrical opposite, centred at H', forms part of a vesica, the top of which 'tangentially' passes through the outer border of the rose. The largest, most shallow arc is $K'L'$, centre M, radius 420 mm, that is, exactly $9u$.

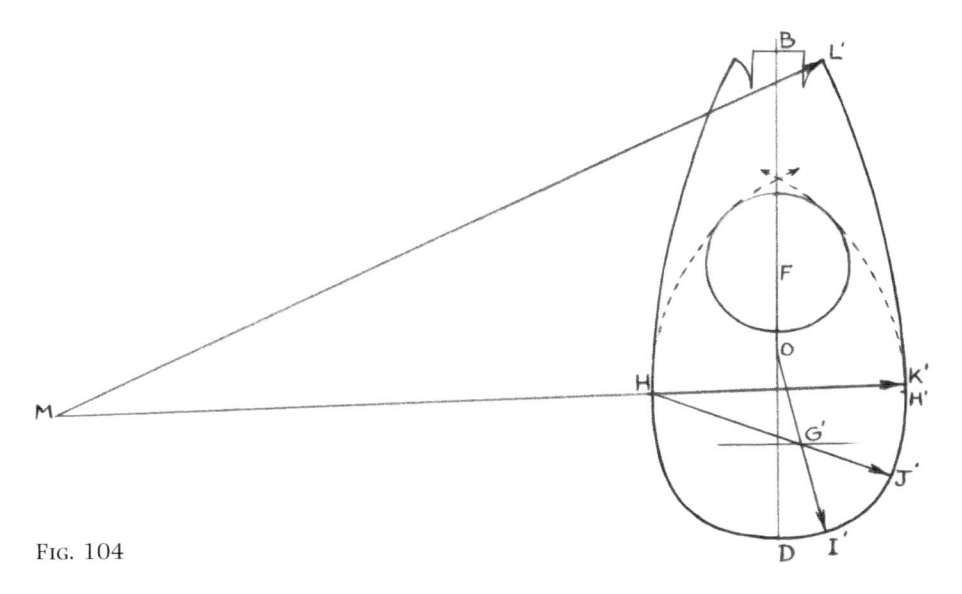

Fig. 104

With great beauty of economy, the composite curve of the body plan just discussed was found to be repeated in the longitudinal profile (Fig. 105). The body is, however, slightly deeper than half its width, as the cross-section (Fig. 106) later makes clear. After the lace, in Fig. 105 DI'',

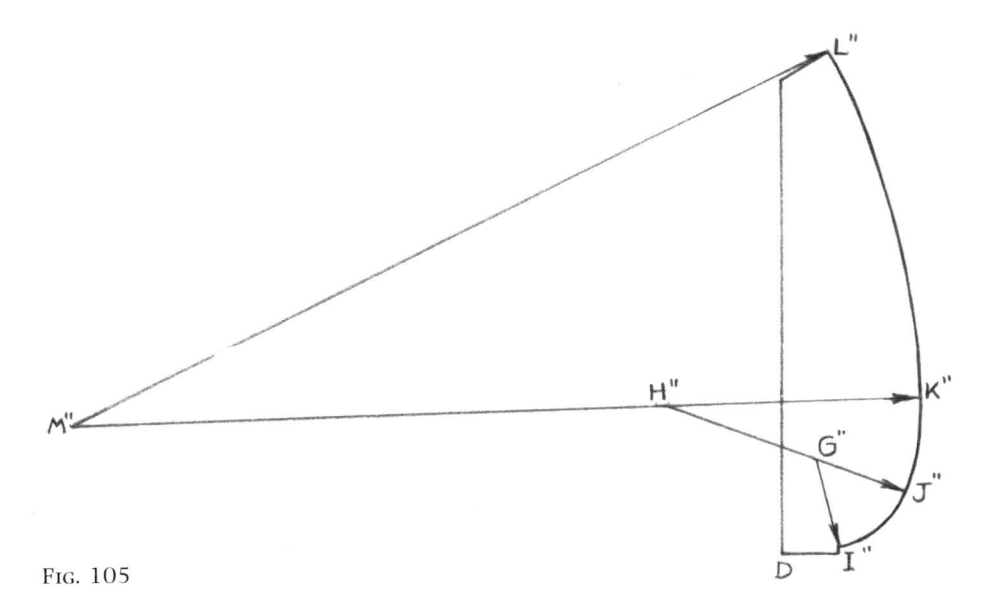

Fig. 105

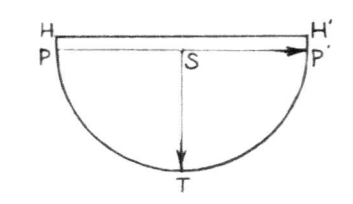

FIG. 106

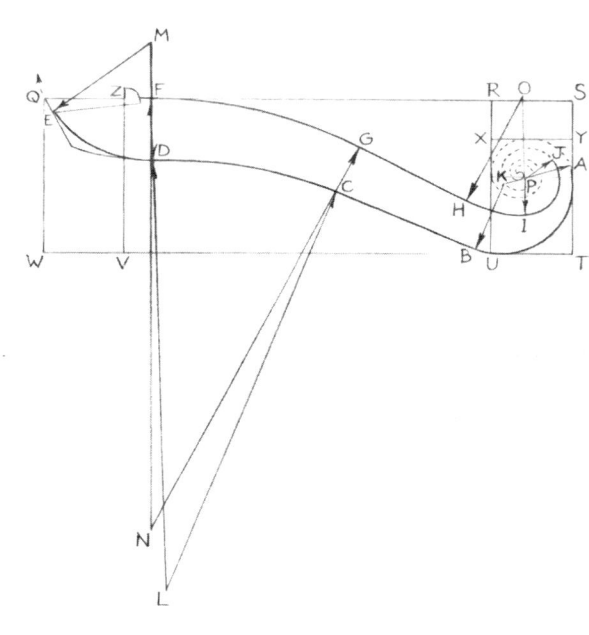

FIG. 107

the arcs exactly correspond to their Fig. 104 body-plan counterparts, the respective radii for arcs $I''J''$, $J''K''$, $K''L''$, being u, $\frac{8}{3}u$, and $9u$.

The cross-section taken at the widest point, HH', is drawn in Fig. 106. $H'P'$ is a straight line, whilst arc $P'T$ is a quadrant arc centred at S (PTP' being a semicircle), its radius, half the width, therefore being 62.25 mm ($\frac{8}{6}u$).

The difficulties of working in ivory, as opposed to wood, become more apparent in the head carving of this mandore. The tight, pierced spiral of the scroll begins to reveal signs of technical strain, while the little face, carved into the front of the scroll, considerably lowers the otherwise high standard of work, and could even be interpreted as later, 'amateur' interference, which I suspect, however, it is not. The uncertainties of the working of the upper part of the volute also made the geometrical analysis of the elevation considerably more difficult. The essential head outline is shown in Fig. 107, without the extra, ornamental features. It will be seen at once that the relationship of the scroll to the head-containing rectangle is radically different from the scroll-heads previously examined. Here, the line of the neck plane (continued as side QS of containing rectangle $QSTW$) does *not* pass tangentially through the top of the scroll spiral. Instead, the scroll lies in the bottom corner, STW, of the rectangle, with the centre, or eye, of the volute positioned on a horizontal plane passing exactly half-way through the short side, ST. The main rectangle, which measures 160 mm × 42 mm, is internally annexed at each end by two similar $\sqrt{4}$ rectangles standing vertically: $QZVW$, 21 mm × 42 mm, marking the position, Z, of the nut, and $RSTU$, also 21 mm × 42 mm, which borders the scroll itself. This last rectangle is further subdivided by horizontal XY, so that $XYTU$, 21 mm × 31.5 mm (a 1.5 or 2 : 3 rectangle), exactly contains the spiral of the scroll. Again, the classical Ionic volute is used, here ceasing on the outer curve at A, to be continued by arc AB, centre K, radius 18.5 mm (seemingly not schematically significant). The underside peg-box line is continued by straight line BC, and then by arc CD, centre L, and radius 118 mm, this being the distance between the two internal $\sqrt{4}$ rectangles, that is, ZR, or VU. The line is terminated by arc DE (produceable to Q), centred at M, and of radius 31.5 mm, equal to the long side of the spiral-containing rectangle, $XYTU$. The upper peg-box curve commences at F, with arc FG, centre N, radius 118 mm, echoing that of the main lower arc, CD. A straight line, GH, connects this with arc HI, centre O, radius again 31.5 mm, and small arc IJ, centre P, radius 9.5 mm, marries the upper curve to the inner Ionic spiral.

Plate XXV

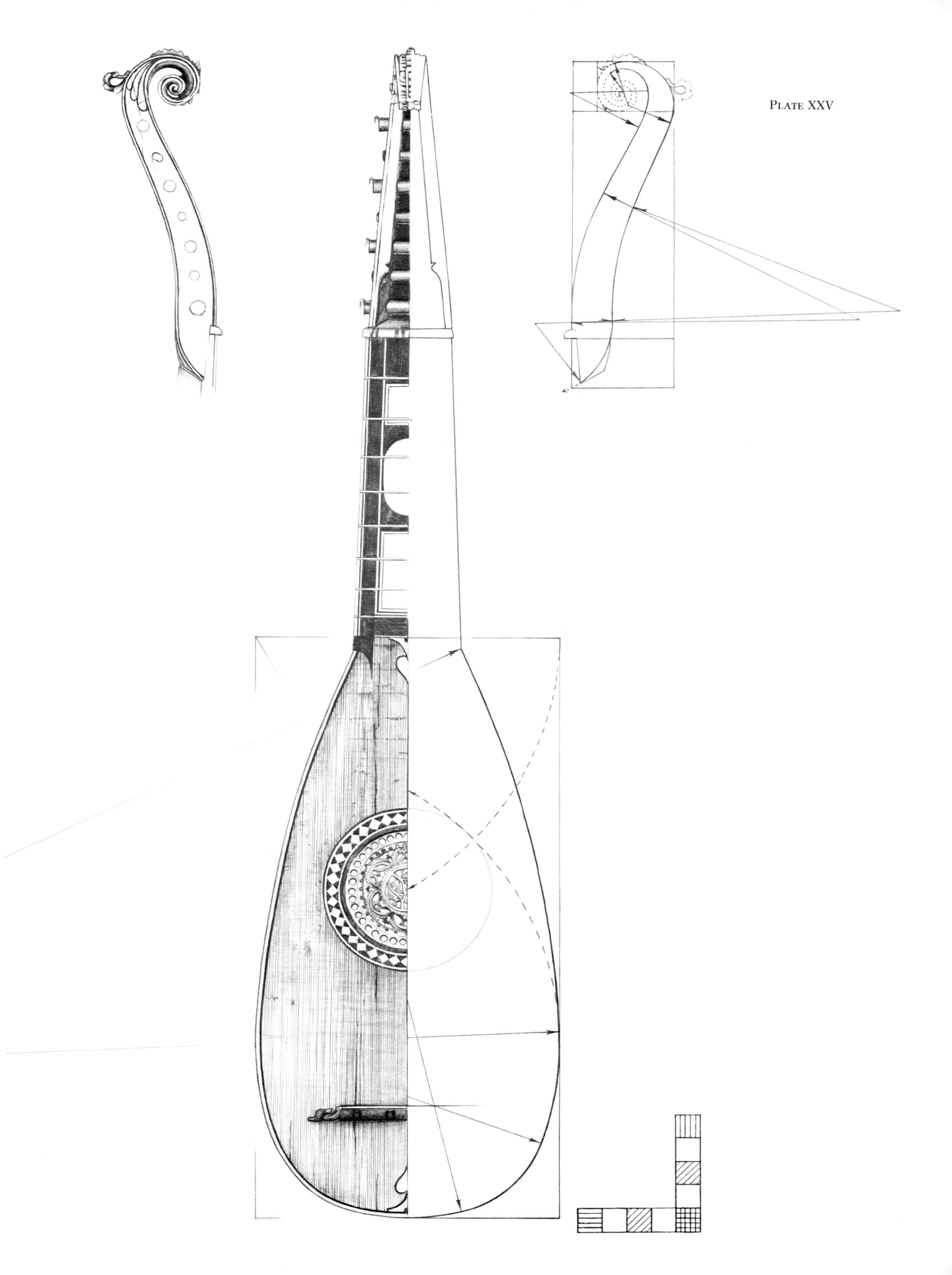

Ex. XXVII
Figs. 108–112, Pl. XXVI

MILANESE MANDOLINE—MANDOLINO CORISTO,
FIVE-COURSE. ITALY, CREMONA, c.1710
Attr. ANTONIO STRADIVARI
PRIVATE COLLECTION, LONDON

The main drawing firmly proclaims this mandoline to be the exception to the decorative tendency of plucked-instrument design remarked upon in the introduction to this section. There, I said it was rare to find the decorative restraint of the violin, and here, in this example, we have precisely that: a tiny plucked instrument, which we could call a Milanese mandoline, of plain and reserved design. This unusual sobriety is immediately explained on consideration of the instrument's authorship: for the handling of the wood, the carving of the head, and, particularly, the unmistakable brilliance of the surviving varnish, all point to one man—Antonio Stradivari. A direct check of the outline with the master's original patterns preserved in Cremona provided further confirmation, pattern No. 420,[80] a 'Mandolino Coristo',[81] being a counterpart in body outline, bridge position, and string disposition (four double courses, one single), although some deviation in rose position and finger-board width was evident. Moreover, decorative restraint was, of course, an essential characteristic of Stradivari's mature aesthetic. As far as this study is concerned, however, perhaps the most interesting clue was that found in the geometry itself, the head of the mandoline utilizing a geometric progression of 2 : 3, a system used in the head of the Emiliani violin of 1703 (Ex. XIII), although not in the very early violin of 1666 (Ex. XII). Thus, further analyses could possibly be of use in pin-pointing the date of the mandoline, which at present is estimated to be within the first twenty years of the eighteenth century.

The body-geometry of the Stradivari mandoline broadly follows the same patterns as the preceding mandore, although in this case the body-containing rectangle was not of any significant proportion. The elegant method used in the mandore of positioning the rose centre by dropping the rectangle sides arc-fashion across the centre line was also absent. Some linear proportions, however, were present, and are shown here in Fig. 108. Again, the bridge was positioned at a 1 : 5, 4 : 5 division of the body length ($BE : BD = 4 : 5$), although here the mathematics were not quite as precise:

$$BE : BD = 198.5 \text{ mm} : 248.5 \text{ mm} = 1.2518.$$

The other linear proportions which occur in Fig. 108 are the string length, AE, 319 mm, and the overall width, HH', 116 mm. They have an 11 : 4 ratio (2.75) which is mentioned here, as HH', a vector in the body outline, appears to have no other proportional significance, and, like the corresponding vector in the previous example, and in many of the lutes, is something of a rogue quantity.

The rest of the body design is governed by a commensurable scheme based on a unit, u, of 49.5 mm, again equal to the smallest outline arc radius. The body outline, showing the constituent arcs, is drawn in Fig. 109. The arc of origin, DI', is centred at O on the centre line, its radius, 99 mm, therefore being $2u$. This is continued by arc $I'J'$, centre G', on the

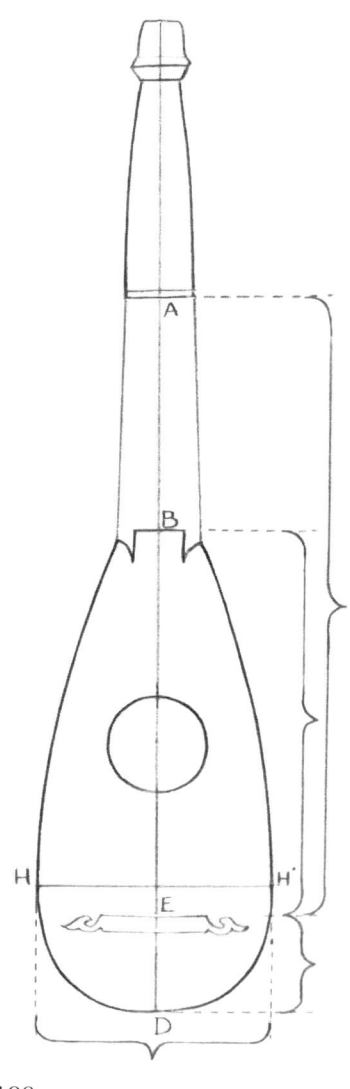

FIG. 108

[80] N420 is the catalogue number given by Sacconi in his *I 'Segreti' di Stradivari*. The pattern in question is illustrated in fig. 175, p. 238. There seems, however, to be an error in compilation, as the corresponding text, p. 239, does not seem to refer to this pattern.
[81] Stradivari's inscribed description.

ANALYSIS OF INSTRUMENT EXAMPLES

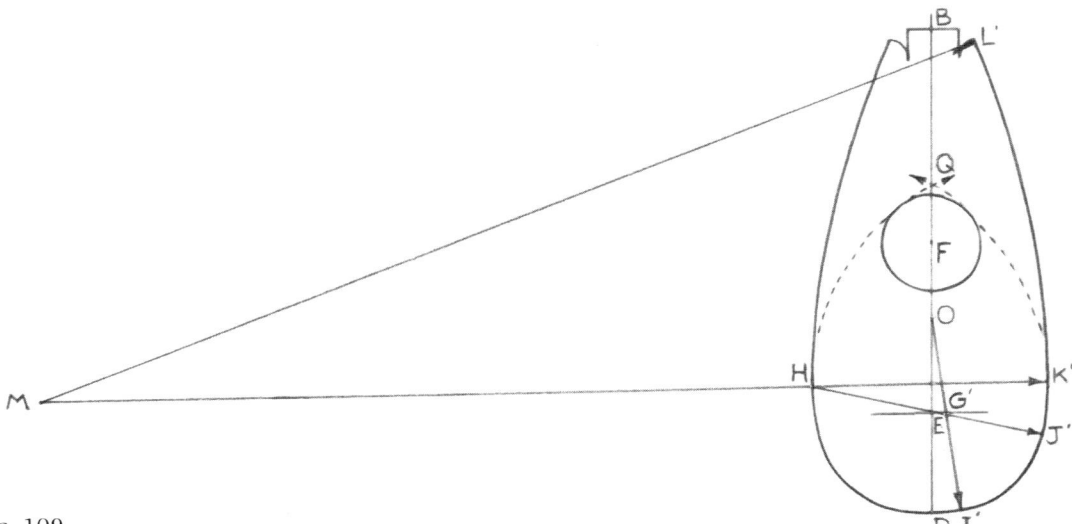

FIG. 109

bridge-line, and of radius 49.5 mm, or u. The next arc, $J'K'$, is centred at H, on the other side of the outline; its radius is therefore the width of the instrument, HH', which, as mentioned above, does not relate to the main commensurable scheme; like the previous example, however, when produced, these arcs, $J'K'$ and JK, form part of a vesica piscis, which 'tangentially' touches the outer circle of the rose, and here crosses the centre line at point Q, so that $QD:BD = 2:3$. The body outline is completed by arc $K'L'$, centre M, whose radius of 496.5 mm was here taken as $10u$.

The economy of form in the mandore, which applied the same curve to body plan and longitudinal profile, is evident here (Fig. 110), and again the body is slightly deeper than half its width. DI'' is the capping lace; arc

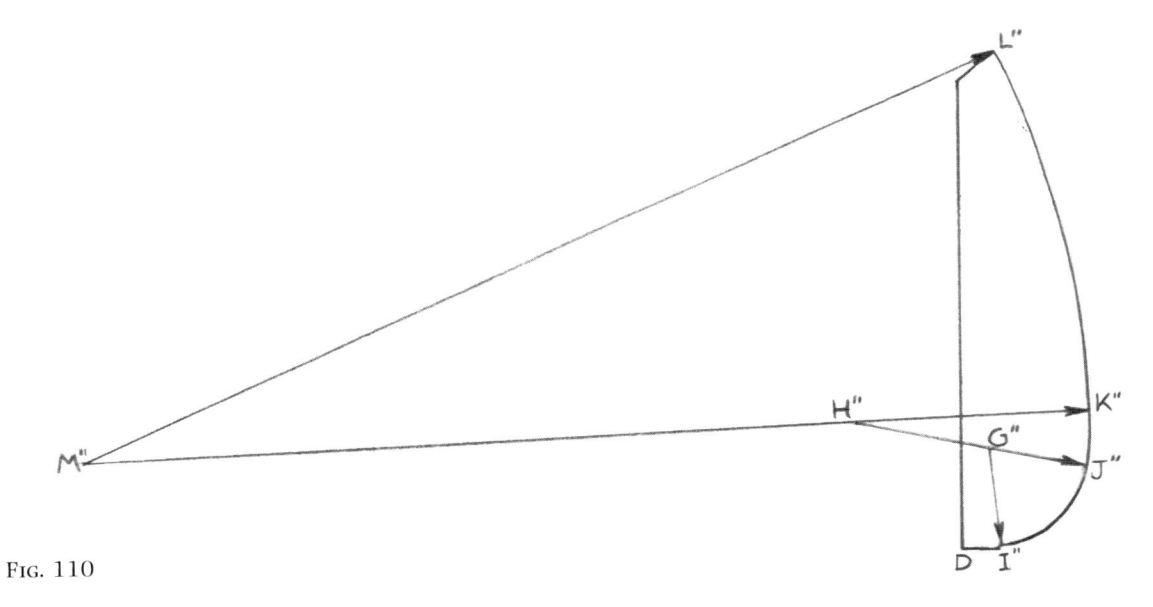

FIG. 110

$I''J''$ is centred at G'', radius 49.5 mm, or u; arc $J''K''$, centred at H'', is of radius 116 mm (the overall width); and arc $K''L''$ is 495 mm, or $10u$.

The cross-section taken at the widest point, HH', is given in Fig. 111. HP and $H'P'$ are the ledges of the capping rib. The curve of the rib section is semicircular, centred at S; arc $P'T(P)$ is of radius 56 mm, a vector not related to the unit scheme.

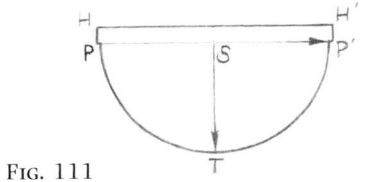

FIG. 111

The volute-and-escutcheon type head, with its beautifully curved peg-box, is drawn in profile in Fig. 112. Here, too, no proportional significance attaches to the ratio of the containing rectangle; height, ST, however, was found to equal the diameter of the body rose. The length from the top of the volute to the nut, SZ, equals 141.5 mm. Here, allowing for a 0.5 mm margin of error, this distance, 142 mm, is the major term of

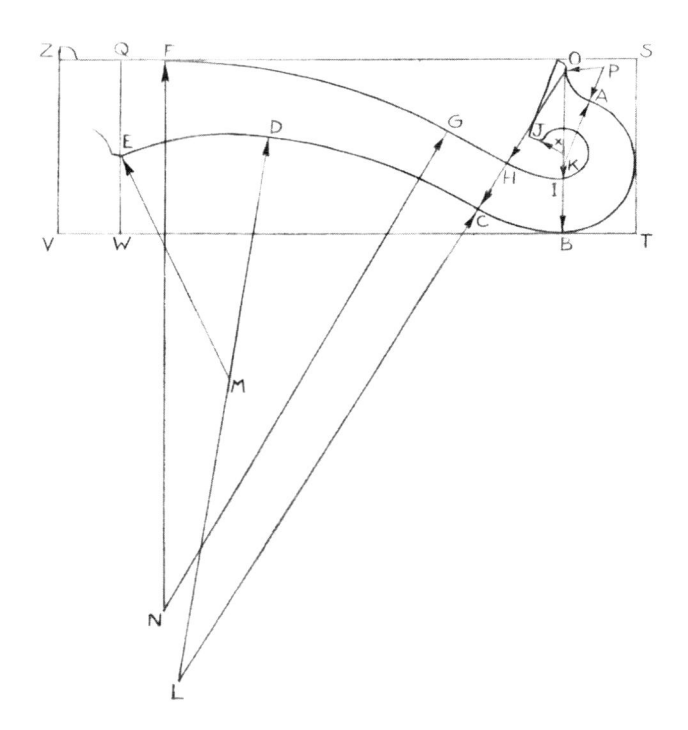

Fig. 112

a 2 : 3 (1.5) geometric progression, which governs the arc radii of the peg-box curves, although not those of the volute. The series consists of the following millimetre values:

28, 42, 63, (94.6), and 142.

The outer curve of the head starts at O, with counter-curve arc OA, centre P, radius 10 mm. The main outer volute curve, AB, then follows, and this is centred at K, and is of radius 17.5 mm; it is related to the next term, the radius of arc BC, in the ratio 5 : 12, arc BC, centre O, having a radius of 42 mm, the first of our 2 : 3 progression vectors. It is followed by the large arc CD, centre L, radius 142 mm (2 : 3), and finally by arc DE, centre M, radius 63 mm (2 : 3). The upper peg-box contour is initiated by straight line ZQF, leading to main arc FG, centre N, radius once again 142 mm (2 : 3). A short straight line, GH, links this to arc HI, centre O (shared with BC), radius 28 mm (2 : 3). The volute then completes the head with inner arc IJ, centre X, radius 6.5 mm.

Plate XXVI

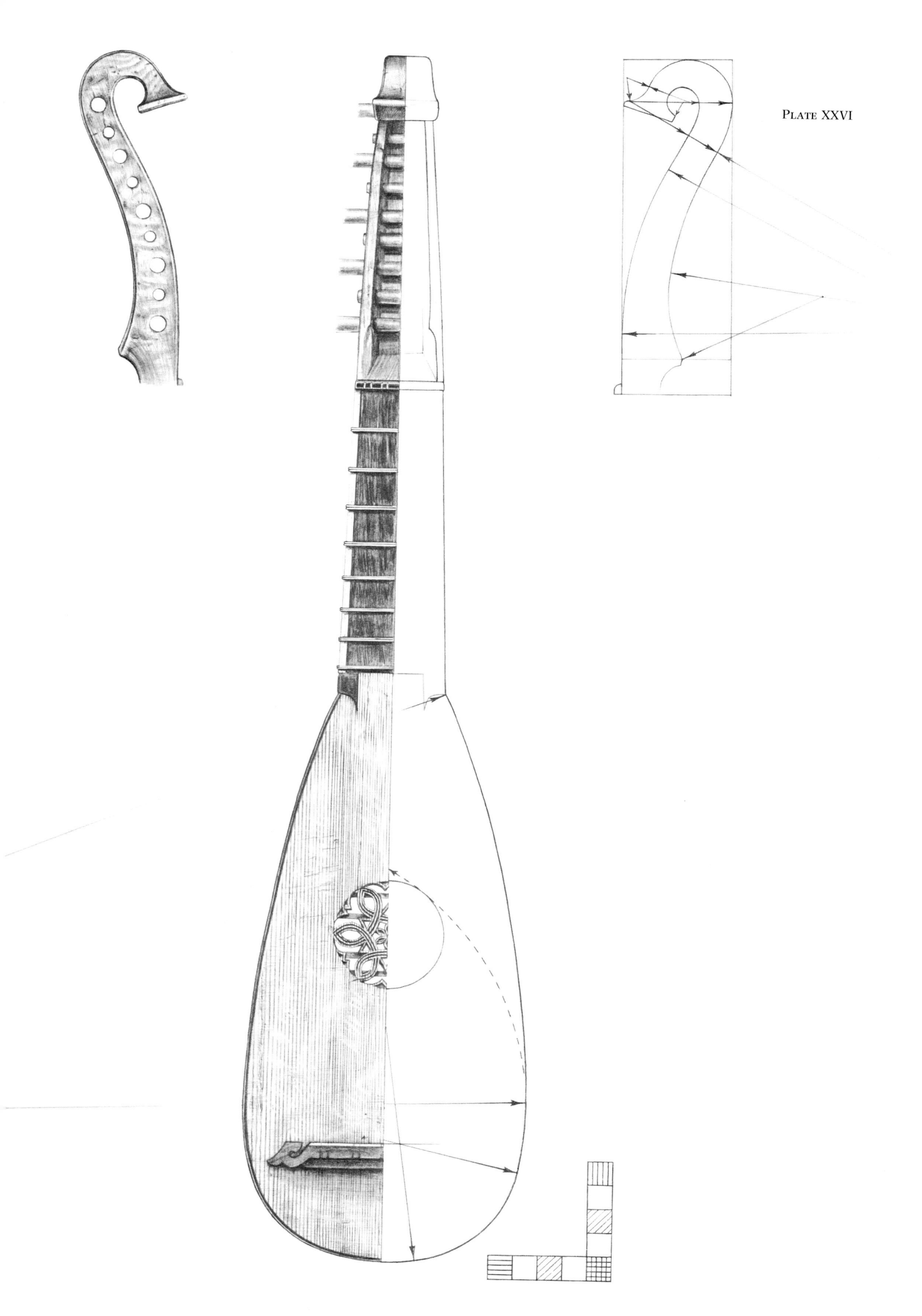

Ex. XXVIII
Figs. 113–118, Pl. XXVII

NEAPOLITAN MANDOLINE. ITALY, NAPLES, 1753
JOHANNES VINACCIA
PRIVATE COLLECTION, LONDON

The creation of the Neapolitan mandoline at once brings to mind the old story that the camel was a horse designed by a committee. Of course, the Neapolitan mandoline was probably developed (or should it be synthesized?) by one man, most likely a member of the Vinaccia family of luthiers, but it represents such a case of organological eclecticism that it is small wonder that the parallel of the camel story should suggest itself. The instrument's design is little more than an amalgam, a sort of cocktail, of previously separate ideas and features, combining violin tuning with lute stringing, the body form and tessitura of the mandore, the peg-, neck-, and head-systems of the guitar, together with the raked sound-board and string anchorage of the chitarra battente. These last two features, concerning the stringing system used (i.e. raked sound-board, with button fixture and peg-board with posterior pegs), were not, however, unprecedented features in mandoline design—they can be found in the Genoese mandoline, an early eighteenth-century *battente* variation of the Milanese instrument.

Why such a synthesis as the Neapolitan mandoline occurred is a musicological question which does not concern us here. What makes the instrument an interesting and important candidate for proportional study is its comparatively recent birth, in this form *c.*1740, which, firstly, gives us an opportunity of finding an example very near to the design archetype and, secondly, provides evidence of mid-eighteenth-century proportional thoughts, which, if present in the design, would have had to be applied actively, rather than just maintained as part of a passive design tradition not necessarily fully understood.

Even more interesting is the fact that a still-careful application of proportional knowledge should be made during a period when the quality of design, of decoration, and of manufacture was beginning to decline into a state of factory-produced decadence.

In Naples the Vinaccia family themselves were active as makers of violins, mandolas, mandolones, guitars, and mandolines from the beginning of the eighteenth to the end of the nineteenth centuries. This dynasty is a mightily confusing one to unravel, embracing as it does numerous father–son, uncle–nephew–cousin, relationships, all paying genealogical respect one to another by passing around the same few Christian names. Of their work, it is fair to say that, while the violins they produced are rather poorly conceived and executed, their original creations, the mandolas, mandolines, and their development of the guitar,[82] when from the hands of the more sensitive members of the family, are fine instruments, both in choice of materials, manufacture, and decoration, and, as will be revealed by the analysis of the following example, also in design conception.

During a period of only thirty or forty years the Neapolitan mandoline passed, in these and other Naples family workshops, from a carefully made and decorated, small-bodied instrument to an increasingly decadent form, with careless, mass-produced ornament, and ever more corpulent shape.

---

[82] One member of the Vinaccia family has been credited with the change to single, as opposed to double, stringing on the guitar. Of course, such a claim is practically impossible to verify; the Vinaccias, however, were certainly remarkable innovators.

A few good-quality examples have been available for study and have revealed some surprising and valuable information. During the first three decades of its existence, the Vinaccia Neapolitan mandoline, as I have said, underwent a considerable change in body contours, presumably in order to increase the volume of air contained, and thus supposedly increase the volume and depth of sound produced.[83] There seem to be three clear stages in this process, and the three outline types, each in production for about ten years, are shown here in Fig. 113; the intriguing link between these three differing outlines (*a*, *b*, *c*) is that they share a common vertical/horizontal ratio of 1.666—all three outlines can be 'contained' in a 3 : 5 rectangle.

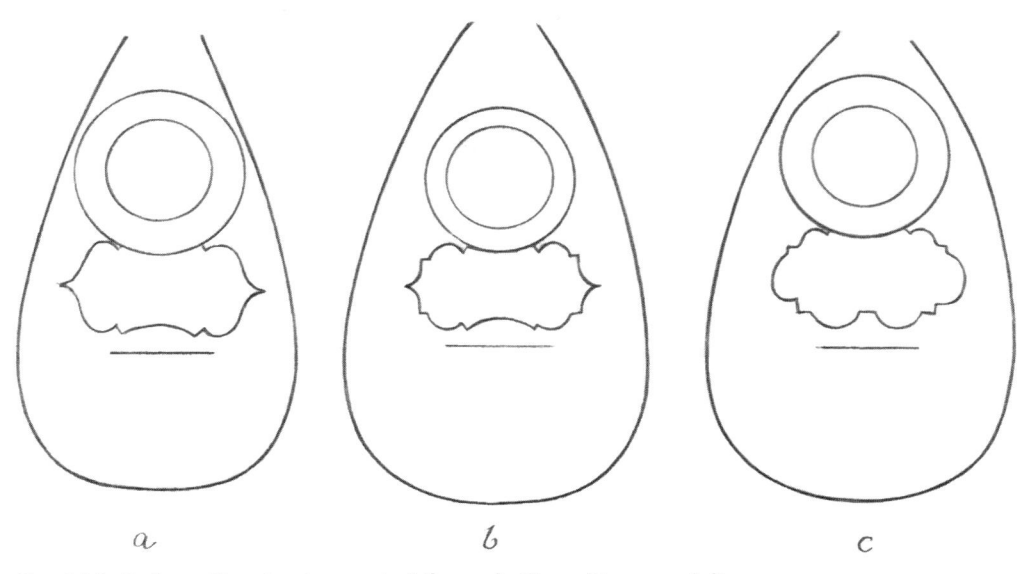

FIG. 113. Body-outline development of the early Neapolitan mandoline

Unfortunately, there is not room here to analyse fully more than one example of Vinaccia mandoline, and a final choice had to be made between two models: a fine example by perhaps the most accomplished of the Vinaccias (Fig. 113*b*), made in 1765 by Antonio Vinaccia, or an earlier one of 1753 (type Fig. 113*a*) from Johannes Vinaccia. This last, in the conception and execution of its decoration, lacked the sophistication of the Antonio, but, the Johannes's being so near to the design archetype (it is the earliest Neapolitan mandoline I have been able to locate) and having a most impressive proportional scheme, my choice was made.

The design of this instrument is governed by two separate commensurable systems: one specifically used in the containing rectangle and inscribed grid for the front of the instrument, the other in regulating the vertical/linear proportions; both are used in the radii of the component arcs. Rather beautifully, both units, major and minor, are given in the rose of the instrument. The minor unit, 27.25 mm, is the radius of the inner sound-hole opening, and the major unit, 47.5 mm, is the radius of the outer rose-border.

The rectangular grid containing the body is drawn in Fig. 114; *abcd*, as we mentioned earlier, is a 3 : 5 rectangle, measuring 273 mm × 163.5 mm (1.669). As well as the usual central vertical axis, there are three horizontal divisions, *ef*, *HH'*, and *ij*; *ef*, or *eCf*, passes tangentially through the sound-hole at *C*, the centre of the arc of origin, dividing *abcd* into square *efcd* and 1.5 (2 : 3) rectangle *abfe*. The square is bisected by horizontal *HEH'*, which, apart from being the widest point of the

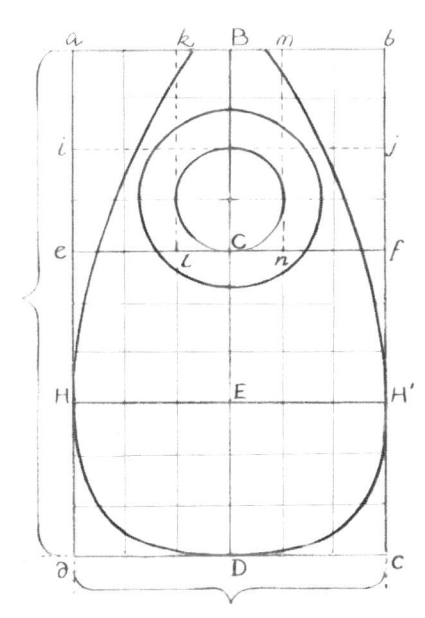

FIG. 114

[83] Personal practical experience with various examples negates this theory.

instrument, is also the exact position of the horizontal 'crease' of the raked sound-board and the bridge-line.

The other horizontal, *ij*, and two short verticals, *kl* and *mn*, are further internal divisions of the 2 : 3 rectangle *abfe*. In Fig. 114 they are drawn as dotted lines, and divide the area into squares, which exactly circumscribe the sound-hole opening; they are therefore squares of side 54.5 mm—two minor units, *u*. The four squares, which are quarters of *efcd*, are all of side $\frac{1}{2} \times 163.5$ mm = 81.75 mm or $3u$.

The major unit, U, 47.5 mm, regulates the vertical/linear proportioning shown in Fig. 115. *AE*, the string length, measures 332.5 mm, or $7U$; it is divided at *B*, so that *AB*, the neck, measures 142.5 mm, $3U$, and *BE* 190 mm, or $4U$. This last, 190 mm, or $4U$, is also the distance *FD*, rose-centre to tail. The last two ratios, bracketed in Fig. 115, are the diameter of the outer rose-border itself, *op*, 95 mm, or $2U$, and the distance *pD*, which like the neck, *AB*, measures 142.5 mm, or $3U$.

Fig. 116 gives a breakdown of the outline into component-arc radii. The arc of origin, *DI'*, is centred at *C*, *efcd* being a square (Fig. 114); its radius is therefore equal to the maximum body width, *HH'*, that is, 163.5 mm, or $6u$. The next arc, *I'J'*, centre *G'*, marks a return to the familiar vesica piscis lower-bout construction, which, however, was not present in the later Vinaccia models which have been examined. The radius of this vesica arc is 52 mm, which does not relate to either unit-commensurable system.

The curve is continued by arc *J'K'*, centre *H*, on the opposite edge, following the common practice dating back to Arnault of giving the arc, at the point of maximum width, a radius equal to the maximum width. Here it is 163.5 mm, or $6u$, and therefore also equal to the radius of the arc of origin; when produced upwards, arcs *J'K'* and *JK* enclose the inner sound-hole in the upper part of a vesica—see the previous two examples. The main curve of the outline, arc *K'L'*, is centred at *M*, and is of radius measured as 409 mm; this is two and a half times the width of 163.5 mm (408.75 mm), or $15u$.

The longitudinal profile, proportionately much deeper than the preceding mandore and Milanese mandoline, is drawn in Fig. 117. *DP* is the wide capping rib or 'lace'. The curve of the vault is initiated by arc *PQ*, a quadrant arc, centred at *O*, and of radius 47.5 mm, that is *u*. The main

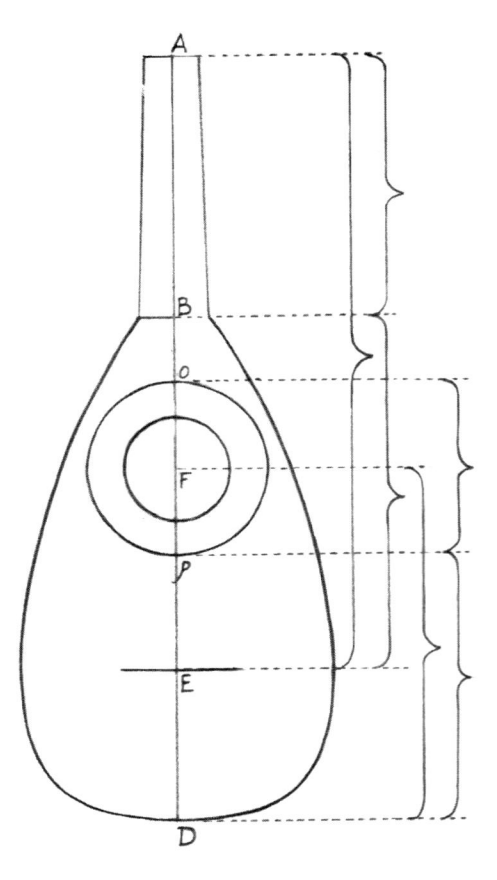

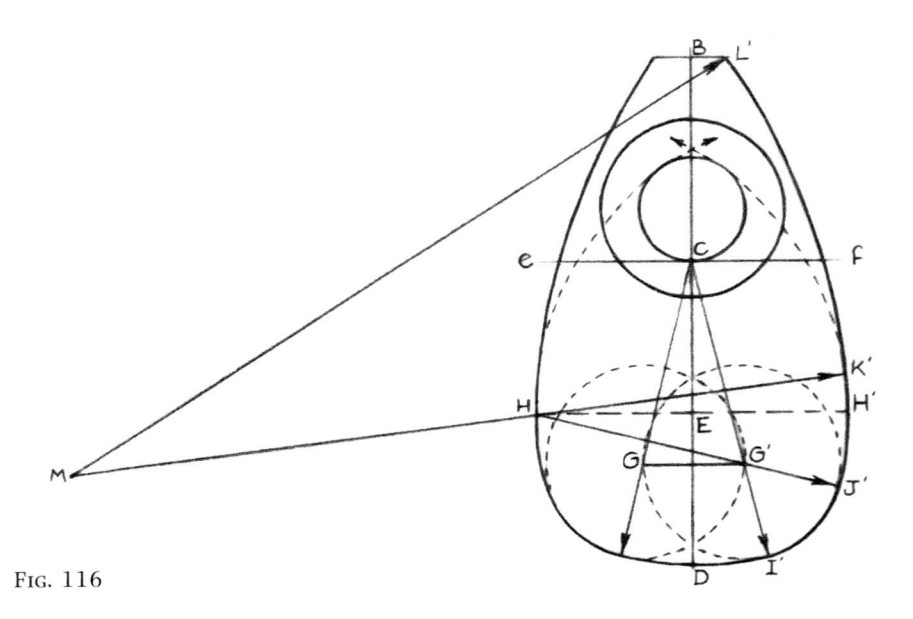

FIG. 115

FIG. 116

FIG. 117

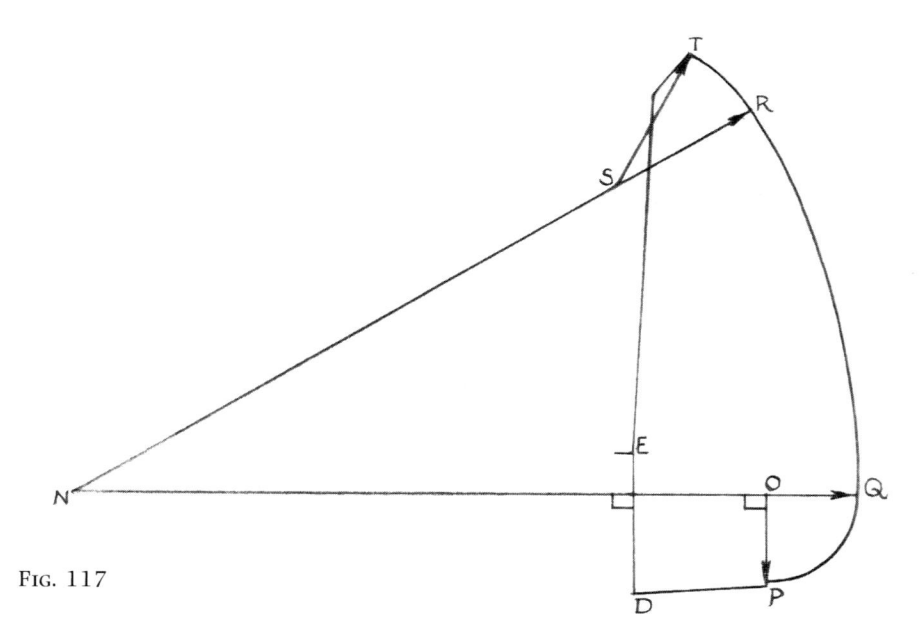

curve then continues with arc QR, centred at N, and of radius 408.5 mm, or $15u$ (408.75 mm)—the same as the main arc of the front of the instrument. The radius, NQ, of this arc passes through the rake of the sound-board, ED, at 90°. The curve of the profile is then completed by arc RT, centred at S, and of radius 82 mm, or $3u$ (81.75 mm).

Finally, Fig. 118 is the cross-section made at the point of maximum width. Here again, a vesica construction has been used—only once before found in a vault construction, that of the geometrically equally beautiful chitarrone by Buechenberg (Ex. XXIII). Arc ZX' is the cross-section arc of origin, centred at E; its radius, 119 mm, equals $2.5U$ (118.75 mm). Arc $X'W'$, centre Y', is the vesica arc and, like the small lower arc, PQ, of the profile, measures exactly 47.5 mm, or U, in radius. A shallow curve, $W'U'$, centre V, finishes the section before the lace $U'H'$; its radius measures 163.5 mm, the same as HH', the width of the model, that is, $6u$.

The head of this mandoline is of the flat, guitar type, with posterior pegs. It is mounted at the usual shallow angle to the neck (about 150°), but, to avoid confusion and distortion, has been depicted 'flat' in the main drawing, in the same plane as the neck and table of the instrument. This method has been adopted for this type of head, and the guitars which follow have all been so treated.

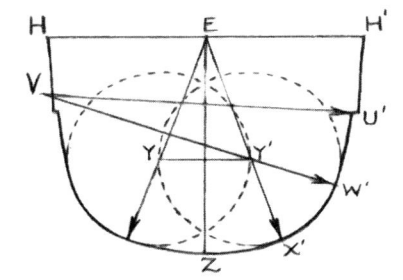

FIG. 118

Plate XXVII

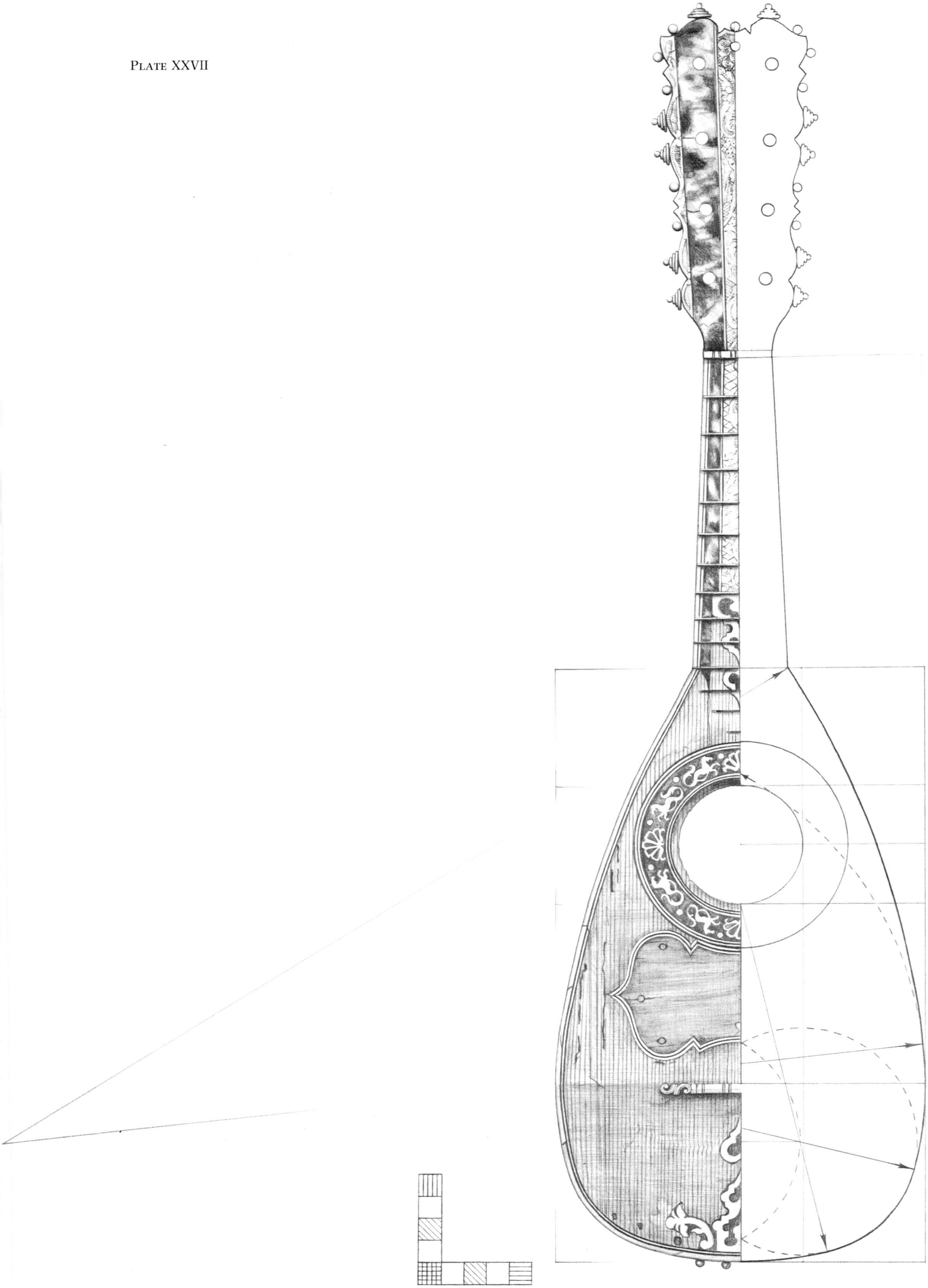

CITTERNS

'A rather ignoble kind of instrument played by cobblers and barbers' was the sentence passed on the cittern by Praetorius in 1619.[84] Other contemporary references, often rich in bawdy analogy, also stress this rather lowly status, one apparently arising from the enterprise of the barbers of the seventeenth century, particularly those in England, who provided a cittern for the casual diversion of waiting customers. Unfortunately, the advantages of stable, strummable, metal stringing, providing bright toned accompaniment or merry tunes, eminently suited the instrument to this somewhat promiscuous usage, which in turn prompted the inevitable parallels of easy virtue: 'a barber's cittern for every serving-man to play upon'.[85]

In fact, history has been unkind to the cittern, for it would appear that its origins were of a very different nature from that which it represents. Of all the instruments that had Neoplatonist pretensions to ancient lineage (and they were not a few), the cittern seemingly has the most convincing, and, even in a very refined and consciously designed instrument such as our first example, balusters, or scrolls at the stock of the neck, still remain as the supposed rudimentary vestiges of the wings, or arms, of the kithara, or ancient Greek lyre. Its relatively simple and robust structure meant that the cittern was cheaper to buy than the more intricately constructed lute, while its wire stringing assured easier and cheaper maintenance, particularly in the torrid Italian climate, where, like so many other instruments, it was first developed. Yet, despite its consequent popularity, the cittern was at first no less regarded than the lute, and thus enjoyed, from the middle of the sixteenth century, a fairly extensive printed repertoire of its own.[86]

Ex. XXIX
Figs. 119-120, Pl. XXVIII
CITTERN. ITALY, BRESCIA(?), c.1650
MAKER UNKNOWN
CONSERVATOIRE DE MUSIQUE, PARIS
Acc. No.: E.1271, C.1053

The decorative richness and costly workmanship of our first cittern example are further testimony to the instrument's noble status in seventeenth-century Italy. In overall form, and in many details of its superbly carved decoration, it follows the magnificent design developed by Girolamo di Virchis[87] in the second half of the sixteenth century. This cittern, from the Paris Conservatoire collection, and its sister in the Ashmolean are undoubtedly of later date, though perhaps not quite as late as that of 1700 occasionally given. Sometime before 1888, when it was described in *Musical Instruments*,[88] the Paris cittern had acquired, no doubt owing to its prodigious craftsmanship, both an attribution to, and indeed a label of, Stradivari. At that time (1888) it was stated as belonging to the great violinist Alard, who, it should be remembered, was the son-in-law of the important nineteenth-century luthier and violin connoisseur, Jean Baptiste Vuillaume. I suspect this period of its history to be the origin of the attribution, and possibly also that of the label—in any

---

[84] *Syntagma Musicum*.
[85] Thomas Dekker, *The Honest Whore* (quoted in Munrow, *Instruments of the Middle Ages and Renaissance*).
[86] See George A. Weigand, 'The Cittern Repertoire', *EM* vol. 1, no. 2 (April 1973).
[87] Cittern by Girolamo di Virchis, Brescia, 1574. Sammlung alter Musikinstrumente, A.61, Kunsthistorisches Museum, Vienna.
[88] A. J. Hipkins and W. Gibb, *Musical Instruments, Historic, Rare and Unique* (Edinburgh, 1888).

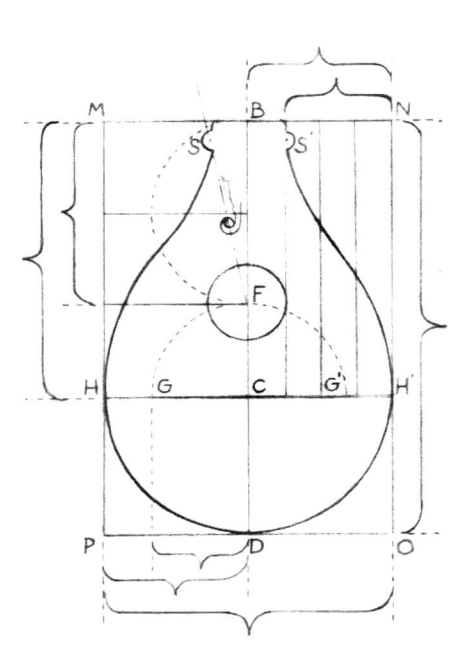

Fig. 119

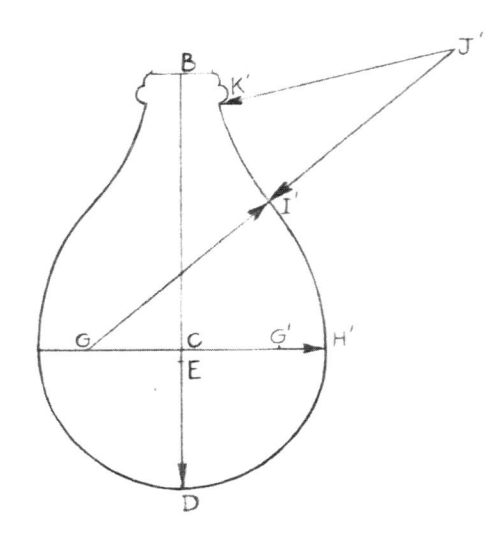

Fig. 120

event, it is a great loss to the history of lutherie that the true authorship of these two fine citterns from the Paris and Ashmolean collections is not known.

The condition of the Paris instrument is very good, although the usual fretted rose is missing. The bridge, too, is positioned incorrectly, but has been resited in the right-hand side of the main drawing. Regrettably, the exceptional high-relief carving which covers the back of the 'solid' head, entwining a male and female satyr in a leafy bower from which grotesque masques emerge, cannot be seen from the front elevation of the main drawing.

The analysis of the instrument's design-geometry revealed a very careful use of commensurable proportions, particularly the ratio 2 : 3—simple proportions which not only governed the few outline radii, but also defined the fairly comprehensive body-outline grid. This grid is shown in Fig. 119, where the body outline is drawn within its containing rectangle, $MNOP$. $MNOP$ measures 340.5 mm (BD) × 227 mm (HH'), and therefore has a ratio of 340.5/227 = 1.5 or 3 : 2 (or alternatively 2 : 3).

The body is horizontally divided at the point of maximum width by line $H(C)H'$, so that $MNH'H$ is a square, $BC:BD$ also being 2 : 3. C, as we shall see later, is the centre of the 'lower-bout' semicircle, and is, in a sense, the 'mustard seed' of the design, from which much of the form is generated. If, for example, compasses are placed at C and opened to a radius of two-thirds distance CH' ($\frac{2}{3} \times 113.5$ mm = 75.66̇6 mm, i.e. one-third maximum width), a planning arc can be described as giving points G and G', the centres for the adjacent outline arcs, and point F, the centre of the rose ($BF:BC = 2:3$). The rose diameter is also decided by the grid of Fig. 119: rectangle $BNH'C(\sqrt{4}$ or 2 : 1) is divided vertically into quarters, the first of the dividing lines passing tangentially through the rose circumference, giving a rose radius of $\frac{1}{4} \times 113.5$ mm = 28.375 mm, or diameter 56.75 mm (56.5 mm as measured) and piercing the centre of the baluster terminal S'. Incidentally, a line drawn from the rose centre, F, through the left-hand baluster terminal, S, also pierces the eye of the volute which terminates the decorative figure in the left side of the lower finger-board.

The correct bridge position, E, was determined by simple calculation from the fixed frets of the finger-board. Having done so, however, no convincing mathematical reasoning would account for either the new string length, AE (444 mm), or, alternatively, the bridge position within the body axis, BD ($ED = 103$ mm).

The simple body outline, consisting of only three arcs per side, is drawn in Fig. 120. The lower part of the design, as we have seen, is a semicircle, centred at C. Dealing, as usual, with only half the outline, the arc of origin, centred at C, is quadrant arc DH', radius half the width, 113.5 mm. The remaining two arcs are both of the same radius. The centre for arc $H'I'$ is at G, on the other side of the model; it was arrived at by a process described above ($CG = \frac{2}{3}HC = \frac{2}{3} \times 113.5$ mm = 75.66̇6 mm) and gives $H'I'$ a radius of 189 mm (measured), or $(2 \times \frac{2}{3} \times 113.5$ mm$) + (\frac{1}{3} \times 113.5$ mm$)$ as calculated = 189.16̇6 mm.

The counter-curve of the shoulder arc, IK', centre J', was also measured as 189 mm, but here no mathematical justification for its centring could be found. The relationship of the two radius vectors of 113.5 mm (DH') and 189(.16̇6) mm ($H'I$ and $I'K'$) is another simple whole-number ratio: 189.16̇6 mm/113.5 mm = 1.66̇6 = 5 : 3 (or alternatively 3 : 5).

The complex side elevation of this cittern's head was judged unsuitable for geometrical analysis, as was the shallow, curved peg-box of the following Tielke cittern.

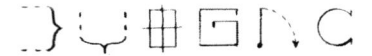

PLATE XXVIII

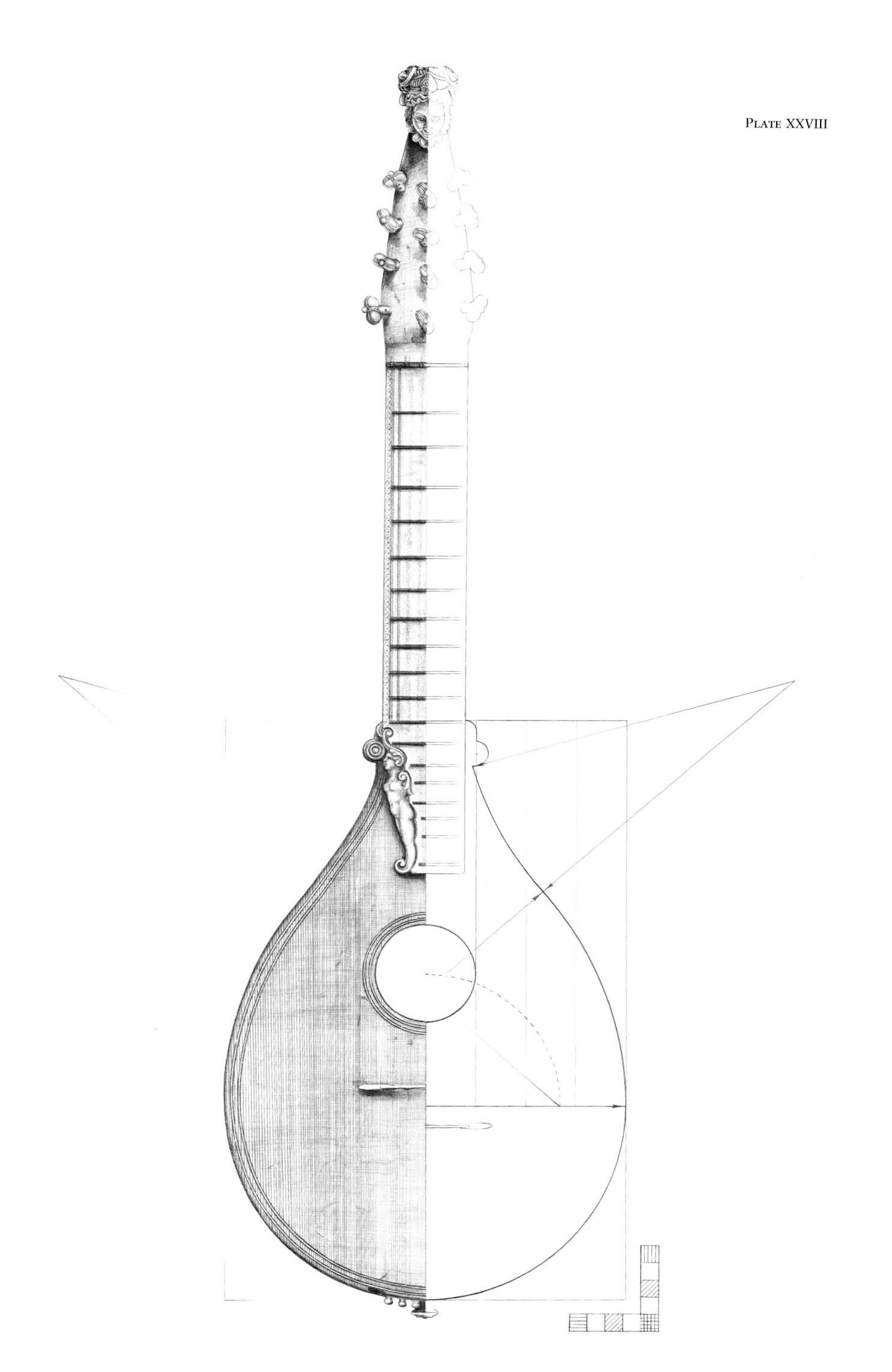

Ex. XXX
Figs. 121–123, Pl. XXIX

BELL CITTERN. GERMANY, HAMBURG, 1676
JOACHIM TIELKE
DONALDSON COLLECTION, ROYAL COLLEGE OF MUSIC, LONDON
Acc. No.: RCM 27

Known in Germany as the *Hamburger Cithrinchen* (little cittern of Hamburg), this late form of cittern was most probably the innovation of the great luthier Joachim Tielke, whose work this present example is. As this is the earliest Tielke cittern (1676)—it would seem that he made only the 'bell' type—then, by inference, it must also be the oldest surviving bell cittern. The instrument was made when Tielke was thirty-five years old, and compared with many of his later *œuvres*, with their familiar, extravagant intarsias of classical allegories, or sumptuous floral schemes, it is almost chaste and plain in appearance, despite its rich purfling, intricate roses, and fine carved head. Time and use, however, have not treated it kindly, adding to some careless asymmetry of manufacture the further distortion of damage. There also appears to be some alteration to the finger-board frets, and consequently the bridge position, this no doubt resulting from the difficult tuning problems inherent in the cittern.

The design-geometry of this cittern is a fairly complex blend of a seemingly irrational $\sqrt{3}$ variant ratio and simple commensurable proportions. Although, in this study, we have not dealt directly with $\sqrt{3}$ symmetry, it has, in fact, been tacitly encountered on numerous occasions in association with the vesica piscis. This last figure, so simply constructed, as we saw in Fig. 10, is shown once more in Fig. 121, where two circles, centred at U and at V, and of common radius UV, are in vesica piscis arrangement. The drawing has been made to show the rational commensurable affinities of the nevertheless irrational $\sqrt{3}$ proportion (1.732). The vesica piscis itself has a $\sqrt{3}$ ratio, i.e. $ST/UV = 1.732$. The $\sqrt{3}$ rectangle, in Fig. 121 *WXYZ*, possesses many other, rational, characteristics: it 'contains' two equilateral triangles, *SVU* and *UVT*, and its diagonal (*ZX*) is therefore twice its short side; its gnomon[89] is twice its own area, and its area, or ratio, is three times that of its reciprocal.[90] Thus, $\sqrt{3}$ symmetry is allied to the simple commensurable ratios of 1 : 2 and 1 : 3.

In the present example, the $\sqrt{3}$ variant ratio is 1.155; this is $\frac{2}{3} \times 1.732$, and is simply the ratio of the short half of a $\sqrt{3}$ rectangle—in Fig. 121 *WXVU* or *UVYZ*. This is the ratio of the rectangle surrounding, or containing, an equilateral triangle, or, indeed, a Gothic arch. It is used here to help plan the body area of the cittern, while the instrument's outline curves are determined by a related and sympathetic commensurable series.

No significant overall proportions of length concerning the nut position, string length, or head length could be discerned; nor could any rationale be determined for the assumed (and certainly not for the actual)[91] positioning of the main rose.[92] The proportional discussion therefore concentrates on the plan and outline of the body itself.

Rectangle *WXFE* (Fig. 122) is the overall body-containing rectangle of the cittern; it is a compound of 1.133 ratio (264 mm/233 mm), the main division being horizontal $U(Q)V$. Point Q is the longitudinal tip of a

---

[89] The figure which, added to a rectangle, will increase its size without alteration to its shape or ratio. See Hambidge, Part II, lesson 7.

[90] The reciprocal of a rectangle is a figure of similar shape, but smaller size; it is situated in the end of the major rectangle, whose short side forms the long side of the reciprocal. In this position, the diagonal of the major and that of the reciprocal intersect at right angles. See Hambidge, Part I, lesson 4.

[91] Amidst the distortions and asymmetry present in the instrument, the main rose was found to be 3 mm left of the centre line. Assuming this to be error in manufacture, the rose position has been corrected in the main drawing.

[92] These features—rose position, nut position, and neck/body relationship—differ considerably from the arrangement found in the V & A 'Tielke' bell cittern, an instrument which in outline design is very similar to the present (earlier) example.

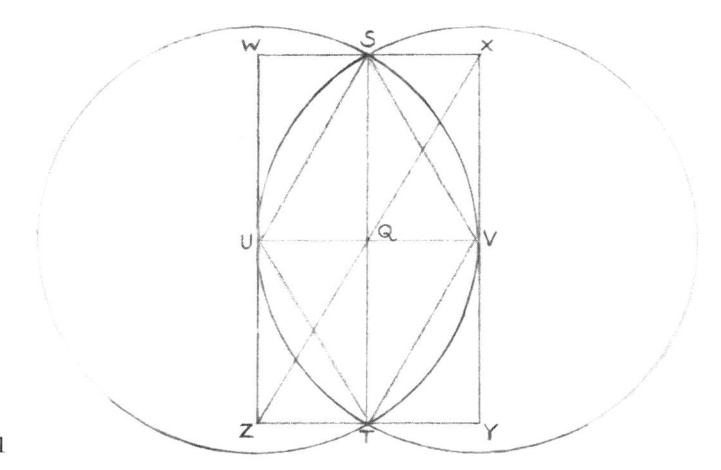

FIG. 121

constructional vesica, and rectangle WXVU (233 mm × 201.(7) mm) the short half (1.155) of the $\sqrt{3}$ vesica-containing rectangle. UV passes through the corners (U and V) of the instrument, and through the centres R and R' of the two small, lower roses. The remainder, rectangle UVFE (233 mm/62.3 mm = 3.73(9)), can be expressed as two squares and a $\sqrt{3}$ rectangle or, symmetrically, as two squares and two 1.155 rectangles. The body length, BD, can also be arrived at by calculation from the diagonal WV (or XU)—an important outline radius—and the ratio of its rectangle (WXVU):

$$\frac{306 \text{ mm}}{1.155} = 264(.935) \text{ mm}.$$

The body design is drawn in Fig. 123, contained within the important rectangles WXFE and WXVU, with outline reduced to component arcs and radii.

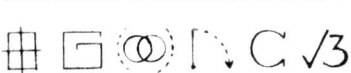

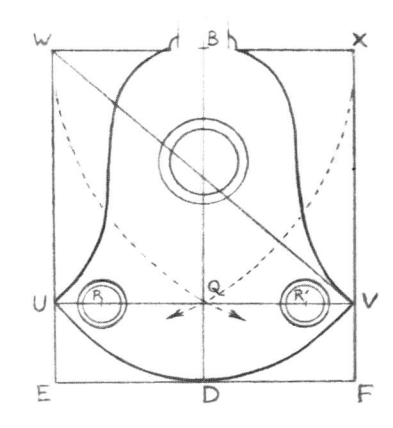

FIG. 122

The arc of origin, DH', is related to the major rectangle WXFE by their common centre at C, and by the arc's extreme radius, CH' (132 mm), which lies exactly on the important diagonal WF. All subsequent arcs relate (commensurably) by their radii to the diagonal of the minor rectangle WXVU which very beautifully forms the extreme radius of the next arc. This arc, H'V, whose centre lies at the opposite upper corner, W, of the containing rectangles, connects, by its inscribed segment, the two diagonals of WXFE and WXVU. Its radius, the diagonal WV of the latter, is 306 mm—which we have already encountered as the vector which, by calculation, was intermediary between the two 'containing' rectangles. These two arcs, DH' and H'V together, form the lower part of the outline.

The upper curvature begins at the corner V, with arc VI', centred at G', and of radius 102 mm; this is the first of the commensurable-radii relationships:

$$306 \text{ mm} : 102 \text{ mm} = 3 : 1.$$

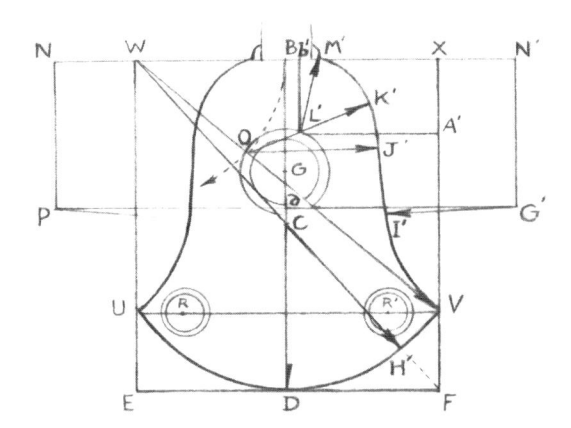

FIG. 123

Centre G' appears to be positioned by rectangle BN'G'C which, measuring 180 mm × 120 mm, has a 1.5, or 3 : 2, ratio. The outline continues with straight line I'J' connecting with arc J'K', centre O, on the opposite side of the model, and of radius 102 mm—echoing that of VI'. O lies on the diagonal WV, and is positioned by dropping an arc down from WB (116.5 mm). The final arc, K'M', is of radius 51 mm and is centred at L', rectangle b'XA'L' having a ratio of 1 : 2. The 51 mm radius yields commensurable ratios with the other radii of 1 : 2 (102 mm) and 1 : 6 (306 mm). Moreover, the radii of the roses, 13 mm and 26 mm, themselves in 1 : 2 ratio, also appear to conform, albeit not precisely, to this same commensurable scheme.

⌐ ⓪ ⌐ C √3

Plate XXIX

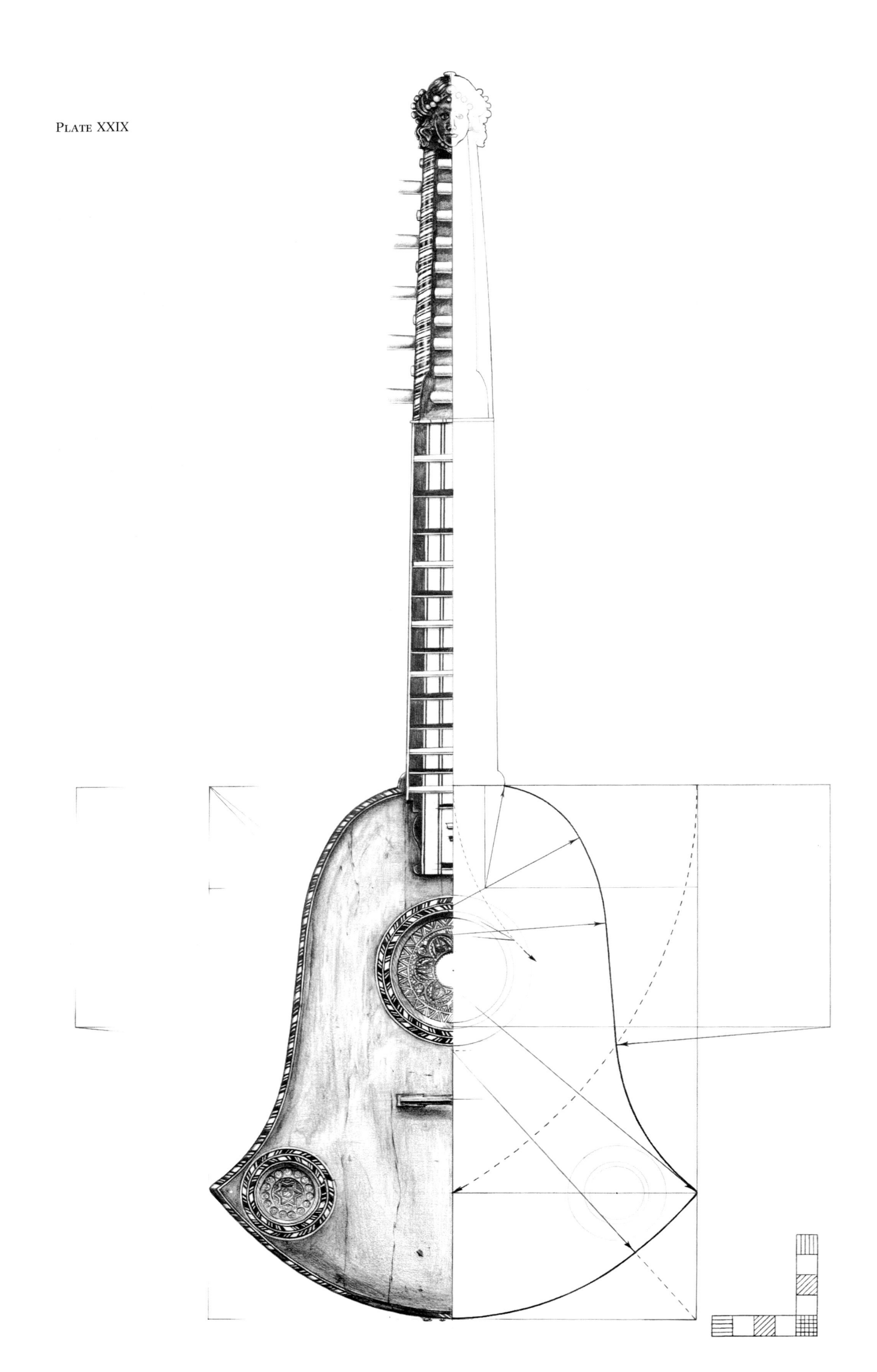

GUITARS

The origins and early history of the guitar, like those of so many instruments, lie in confusion and obscurity. Pitifully few early examples survive, no doubt partly owing to the instrument's extreme constructional fragility, and thus to confusion and obscurity is added the distortion of surviving evidence, arbitrarily selected by accident and the whim of fate. The Spanish vihuela (either *de mano* or *de péñola*), for example, is the first important guitar-type instrument, and was in its country as prestigious as the lute (of Arab origin) was elsewhere. Yet this instrument, for which exists a sizeable literature, is represented now by only one surviving example:[93] an artefact which could well owe its preservation to its own exceptional, rather than typical, features.

Two specimens of sixteenth-century guitars have come down to us, and both of them are exceptionally small (the vihuela, on the other hand, seems to have been a very large instrument). One of them, the instrument by Josef Dörfler,[94] is in the four-course state common at that time; the other, and the first instrument considered here, is by Belchior Diaz of Lisbon, and has five courses. The backs of both these intruments are of the vaulted type, which was perhaps the more usual early construction. The flat-back type is represented here by our second example—the ivory Cocho, one of the very earliest flat-backed guitars that are known. The magnificent chitarra battente by Mango Longo[95] has been selected as the third example.

Acoustically, the guitar evolved most rapidly during the nineteenth century, a period which lies outside the scope and purpose of this study. Apart from the change from five double courses to six single strings, the instrument then underwent major alteration, both to its outer shape, which broadened at lower and upper bouts and narrowed at the waist, and, most importantly, to its inner acoustic construction, where new linings and advanced barring innovations helped to create the rich sonorities which are so familiar to modern ears. It was in this period, too, that the old flush finger-board, with its movable tied frets, was replaced by an applied fixed-fretted one, and the elegant peg-board supplanted by the more convenient worm-geared machine heads—changes which, from an aesthetic viewpoint, can only be judged as retrograde. Before this design watershed, the body outline had changed very little in more than two centuries, remaining narrow, and only gently curved, its aspect demure to eyes accustomed to the hour-glass contours of the modern guitar.

[93] To be found at the Musée Jacquemart-André, Paris.

[94] *An Exhibition of European Musical Instruments* (Edinburgh, 1968).

[95] The chitarra battente state of this instrument is most likely a later alteration of function—see introduction to the Mango Longo, Ex. XXXIII.

Ex. XXXI

Figs. 124–126

GUITAR, SMALL FIVE-COURSE. PORTUGAL, LISBON, 1582
BELCHIOR DIAZ
DONALDSON COLLECTION, ROYAL COLLEGE OF MUSIC, LONDON
Acc. No.: 171

Regrettably, nothing is known about Belchior Diaz, the maker of this five-course guitar, perhaps his only surviving instrument. Four-course instruments (seven or eight strings) were seemingly the more popular in the sixteenth century, particularly in France, and it was for the four-course stringing that the earliest music was printed.[96] Diaz's guitar is beautifully made: the purfled design of the board is particularly handsome, with its interlaced, wave-like patterns—mysteriously coincident with the node and anti-node figuration made by a vibrating string, Fig. 124. The vaulted back consists of seven 'Doric'-fluted ribs of fruitwood, separated by ivory fillets. Damage, and subsequent restoration, however, as well as distorting the body outline, seem to have robbed the instrument of its original table, which for our purpose also means the loss of the vital original information of rose and bridge positions. It should be added that both these features, as restored, are in tolerably correct positions, although the rose is set slightly lower than an 'average' ratio, estimated from a dozen, albeit later (seventeenth-century), instruments. For this reason, that is, the replacement of the front, a full drawing and analysis of the guitar could not be made; its rarity, its provenance, and the quality of its discernible proportional scheme, however, justify its inclusion here, if only as the subject of an outline discussion.

Geometrically, the instrument is very beautiful, and has been carefully regulated by a proportional system based mainly on a single commensurable unit. The ratio of 5:2 governs the body-length to middle-bout proportion (see Fig. 125): $BD/TT' = 365$ mm$/146$ mm $= 2.5$, while the head, ZA (146 mm = middle bouts TT'), to neck, AB, to body length, BD, is $6:11:15$. For the rest of the instrument's planning, a unit, u, of $33.16\dot{6}$ mm, is the key, ruling both the containing grid of Fig. 125, and the component-arc radii of Fig. 126.

The body outline fits inside a 6:11 rectangle ($1.83\dot{3}$), in Fig. 125 $abcd$: $ad/dc = BD/JJ' = 365$ mm$/199$ mm $= 1.834$—the same ratio that was found in head:neck. Within this rectangle, $abcd$, two squares can be drawn: $efgh$, of side $165(.8)$ mm, or $5u$, which contains the upper bouts, and $mncd$, of side 199 mm ($198.99\dot{9}$ mm), or $6u$. The upper square is further divided equally into four by horizontal NN' and vertical BO, points N, N', and O all being centres of outline arcs. These small squares, $eBSN$, etc., are therefore of side $2\frac{1}{2}u$.

The outline (Fig. 126) commences with arc of origin DI', centre O, on the centre line (and at the division of the two major squares discussed above) and of radius 199 mm, $6u$, the lower-bout width. The curve is continued by a vesica piscis arc (the construction is centred at G and G'), arc $I'J'$, centre G', and radius $2u$. The next arc, $J'K'$, is centred at G, the opposite vesica centre, and therefore of radius $4u$. We have met this arrangement before in two Brescian instruments, the lira da braccio of Gasparo, Ex. VIII, and the Maggini viola, Ex. XIV. When produced, arc

FIG. 124. Small guitar by Belchior Diaz, Lisbon, 1582. (Royal College of Music)

[96] Found within a collection of vihuela music, made by Alonso Mudarra, printed in 1546 as *Tres Libros de Musica*.

FIG. 125

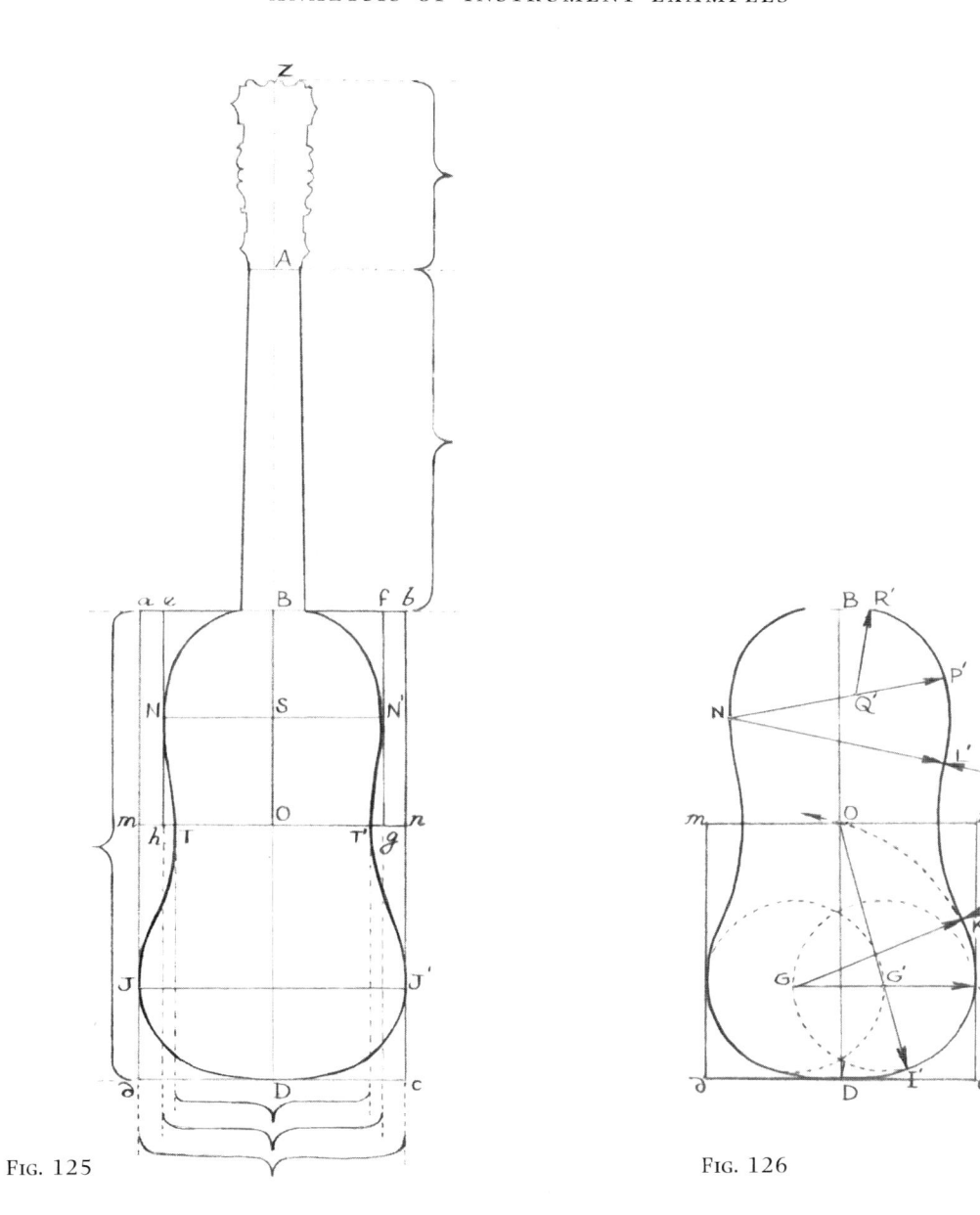

FIG. 126

J'K' crosses the centre line at point O, the centre of the arc of origin. The curve of the waist is provided by arc K'L', centre M', radius again 199 mm, or 6u.

The upper bout arc, L'P', is centred at grid point N, on the opposite edge of the instrument, its radius, the width of the upper bouts, being 165(.8) mm, or 5u. The outline is concluded by arc P'R', centre Q', radius 66(.33̇) mm, or 2u—the same as the vesica arcs of the lower bouts.

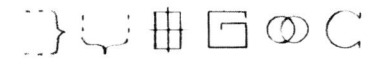

}⌣ ⌗ ⌐ ⊚ ⊂

Ex. XXXII

Figs. 127–129, Pl. XXX

GUITAR. ITALY, VENICE, 1602
CHRISTOPHO COCHO
CONSERVATOIRE DE MUSIQUE, PARIS
Acc. No.: E.2090

The flat back and the sides of this elegant early guitar, like the sound-box of the little mandore previously examined (Ex. XXVI), are composed of ribs or strips of ivory, separated by fillets of ebony–ivory–ebony stringing, producing a beautiful and impressive effect. The treatment of the rose and table decoration of the two instruments is also similar: the alliance of richness with restraint no doubt carefully calculated by the makers to appeal to the wealthy aesthete and amateur as a meritorious addition to his own personal Parnassus.

At least three other instruments of Christopho Cocho (also Choco, Cocco, Cocko, Cocks, and Choc) survive: a lute in the Germanisches Nationalmuseum in Nuremberg, a theorbo in the Victoria and Albert Museum, and another theorbo, together with this guitar, in the Paris Conservatoire collection.

Cocho worked in the first half of the seventeenth century in Venice, 'all'insegna dell'aquila d'oro'. A pyrographic stamp of an eagle is just discernible in the upper part of the table of this guitar, which, as we have mentioned in the introduction, is one of the earliest surviving guitars (1602) to have adopted the now familiar flat, unvaulted, back.

Alas, ivory, with all its beauty, is not the most stable of materials, and whilst its movements due to atmospheric changes are minimized by the engineering principles of strength and stability at work in a lute vault, they are, unfortunately, only weakly harnessed in the flat back and rib design found in the Cocho guitar. In fact, both left- and right-side edges of the top were warped and distorted in various places beyond the purfling; it was, however, possible to ascertain the original outline by generating the undistorted parts of both sides, using the unaltered, inner outline of the table itself as a guide. It is this supposed 'original' outline which is shown in the main drawing.

Geometrically, the instrument follows the majority of the other instruments here analysed, with a design once more defined by commensurable methods.

Fig. 127 gives the overall vertical and horizontal proportions found in the instrument. Two overall containing rectangles are employed: first *efcd*, which encloses the body from D to E, the extension of the table into the finger-board, and the proportional boundary of the table observed in the lutes; and, secondly, rectangle *abcd*, which encloses the sound-box alone, from D to B—the system used in the Neapolitan mandoline, Ex. XXVIII. The first rectangle, *efcd*, is a double square, or $\sqrt{4}$ rectangle, measuring 478 mm by 239 mm. Proportionally, it can also be expressed (apart from the ratio 2 : 1) either as the ratio 6 : 3, the width *JJ'* being divided by a vesica arrangement of radius 79.666 mm, the unit governing the lower arc radii with the arc of origin, centred, as we shall see, in the centre, C, of this major rectangle—or, alternatively, *efcd* can be expressed by the ratio 10 : 5, the smaller unit (47.8 mm) being common to both *efcd* and *abcd*. *ea* is one such 47.8 mm unit, leaving *abcd* as a rectangle of 9 : 5

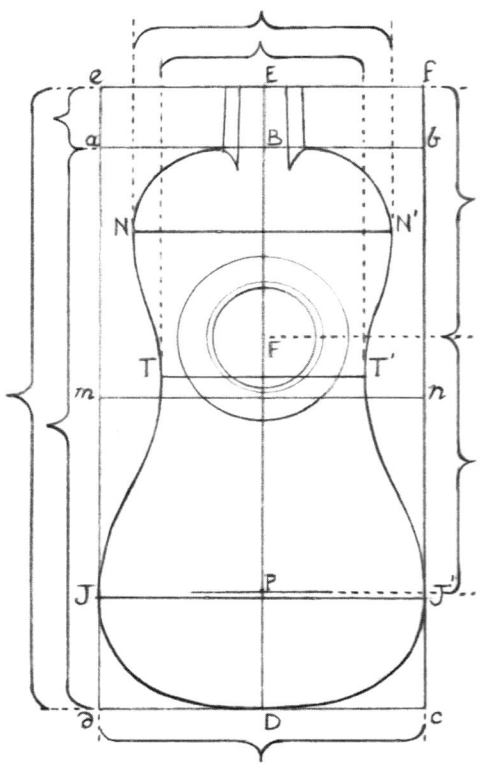

FIG. 127

ratio (430 mm/239 mm = 1.799, or 1.8). The position of the sound-hole, or rose centre, F, is also related to the upper horizontal, that is, to eEf, in that $EF = FP = 195$ mm; in other words, the rose is centred half-way between the bridge, P, and table boundary, E.

Rather unexpectedly, the upper-bout configuration, again a vesica-piscis based solution, does not directly relate proportionally to its lower-bout counterpart, which in turn means that overall widths of lower and upper bouts are not commensurable with each other. There does, however, appear to be such a relationship between the upper-bout width and the waist, or middle-bout width, that is, $NN' : TT'$:

$$\frac{NN'}{TT'} = \frac{188 \text{ mm}}{150.5 \text{ mm}} = 1.249 \text{ (or } 1.25, \text{ i.e. } 5:4).$$

The outline breakdown to component arcs and radii is drawn in Fig. 128. The square $m(C)ncd$, which is the lower half of $\sqrt{4}$ rectangle $efcd$ (see Fig. 127), encloses or 'contains' the lower-bout construction—an exact counterpart to the lower-bout design of the Belchior Diaz guitar. Here, however, the centre of the arc of origin, C, also coincides with the centre of the main rectangle, i.e. $EC = CD$, which suggests the possibility of a great-circle geometry, although in practice the middle-bout arc centres, M' and M, fall just 2 or 3 mm inside the circle's circumference. The radius (CH') of the arc of origin (DH'), which is equal to the lower-bout width, measures 239 mm, or $3U$ (where $U = 79.666$ mm). The vesica piscis arc $H'J'$, centred at G', continues the outline, its radius measured as 79.5 mm, but calculated as $79.66\dot{6}$ mm, or U. The curve then shallows with arc $J'K'$, centred at G—the opposite vesica centre—thus giving a radius of $2U$, or $159.33\dot{3}$ mm, and completing the lower-bout curvature; $J'K'$, when produced, crosses the centre line at C, centre of the model and of the arc of origin. One arc forms the curve of the waist, and it connects with the lower bouts by short straight line $K'O'$. This is arc $O'L'$, centred at M' (as previously stated, just short of the great circle) and of radius 159.5 mm, or $2U$ ($159.33\dot{3}$ mm).

The upper bouts, as we have said, do not correspond to this U-based, commensurable scheme, but instead follow an independent course, based on the unrelated radius, u ($62.66\dot{6}$ mm), of the upper vesica piscis arrangement. This is correspondingly centred at Q and Q', and gives (on the right-hand side) the arc $R'N'$ (radius $62.66\dot{6}$ mm, or u). The other upper-bout arc is centred not in the opposite vesica centre, as in the lower-bout arrangement, but on the opposite edge, so giving a radius equivalent to the maximum upper width of the instrument, and therefore three times the vesica radius; thus $N'L'$, centre N, has a radius of 188 mm, or $3u$. When produced, this arc meets the outer border of the rose, centre F, a border whose radius, 62.5 mm, could therefore also be said to be schematically related to the minor, u-based, commensurable scheme. This, then, completes the discussion of the body outline.

Following the drawing policy outlined in the discussion of the Neapolitan mandoline, Ex. XXVIII, the head of this guitar has been drawn in the same plane as the neck and body. Whilst no proportional significance could be found in the ratios governing the neck length to either head or body length, the head itself, measuring 66 mm in width and 176 mm in length, fits exactly into a rectangle (in Fig. 129, $WXYZ$) of $3:8$ ratio, the highest common factor, 22 mm, not relating to the rest of the scheme.

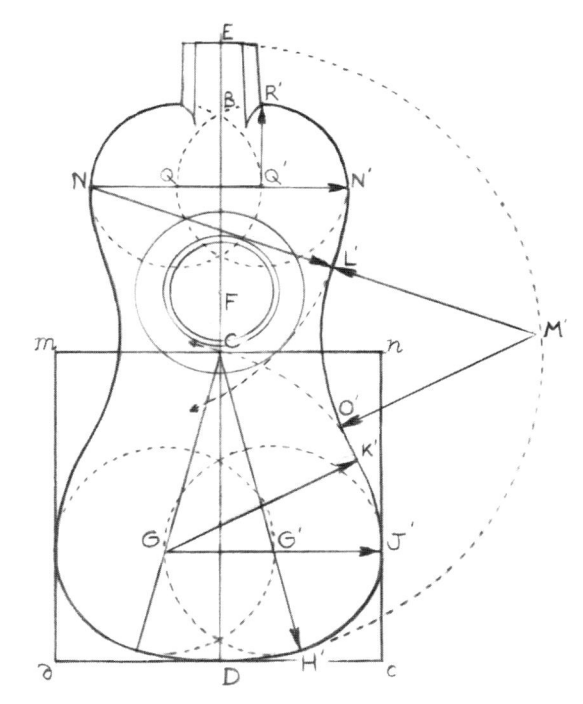

FIG. 128

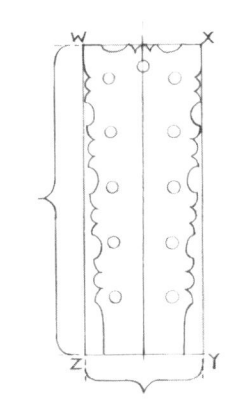

FIG. 129

Plate XXX

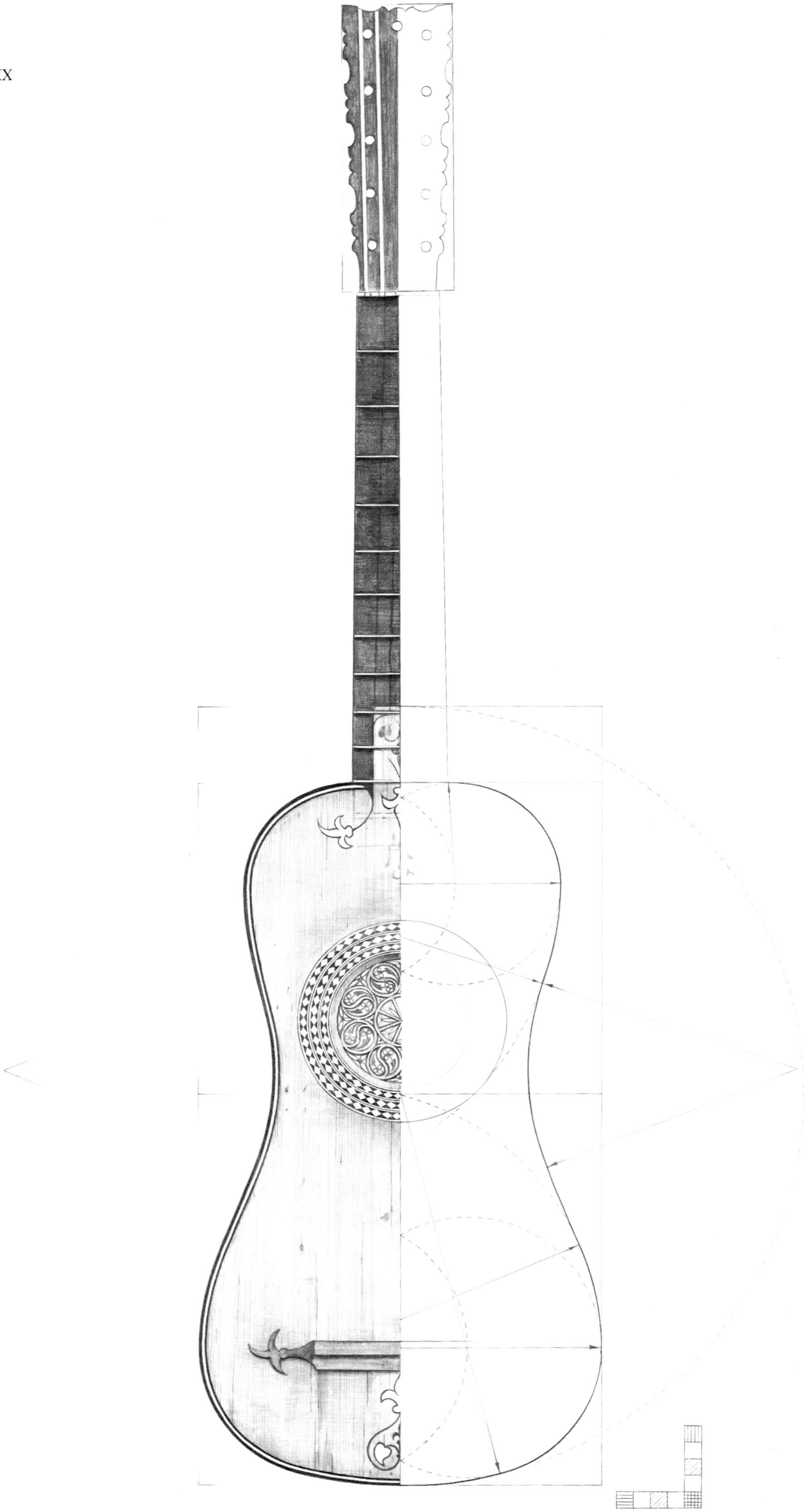

Ex. XXXIII
Figs. 130–131, Pl. XXXI

CHITARRA BATTENTE/GUITAR. ITALY, NAPLES, 1624
MANGO LONGO
CASTELLO SFORZESCO, MILAN
Acc. No.: 277

Perhaps the most richly inlaid and ornamented instrument to have been examined for this study, this magnificent instrument by Mango Longo was originally selected as an example of chitarra battente. Closer scrutiny, on measurement and drawing, however, suggests that its present battente state is not original, but a later conversion from a standard guitar. For our main purpose, though, there seems to be no practical difference whatsoever between guitar and chitarra battente, the body outlines having no generic characteristics peculiar to one or other type. The main difference is one of stringing, and its related acoustic and structural principles, namely: the guitar is gut-strung, with its strings tied to a bridge glued to a flat belly, while the chitarra battente (*battere* = 'to strike') is wire-strung, its more stable strings passing over a bridge (often only held in place by their pressure), this resting on the table, or sound-board, which has been given a rake or backward crease, in order to help resist the increased string pressure. String anchorage is by means of buttons fixed through the base into the bottom block of the instrument.

Conversions, usually of vault-backed guitars to chitarre battenti, were not uncommon, and many fine, signed guitars have undergone surgery, in some cases very crude surgery, in order to be used in this way. The work on this example has been done rather carefully. The 'crease' in the table was made at a one-quarter division of the body length, BD, probably at the old bridge-line (the present bridge is unlikely to be original). The flat table would have been scored, or grooved, underneath at this point and then slightly bent back below the bridge-line, the ribs and bottom block having been suitably lowered to accommodate the alteration. The fact that this was not an original feature also accounts for the slight distortion to the lower-bout 'corner' curves, which have an 'extra' inorganic bulge where the two, then marginally differing, contours of ribs and table have been forced together.

The neck, which does not have the inlaid fixed frets of bone or metal ordinarily found in an 'original' battente, has been shortened by a specific amount (three frets, from the nut), an amount common to one or two other such conversions, leaving eight fret divisions to the neck itself. The shortening of the neck has also meant the loss of an engraved ivory plaque, which would have appeared as the second of four episodes in an Arcadian sequence decorating the neck and head. The first scene, now at the top of the neck, depicts Orpheus charming the beasts (represented by the front quarter of a supine deer), whilst in plaques three and four, found in the head, a pair of hounds are in eternal pursuit of a hare. The remaining plaque, at the top of the head, is engraved:

M. MANGO

LONGO FECIT

IN NAPOLI

while the other large plaque in the neck bears an engraved crest, surmounted by a crown, with a cartouche bearing the numbers '7:4:9'—unfortunately, not some key design ratios, but apparently a method of writing the date in the eighteenth century (*idem quod* 1749), this presumably being the date of its possession (and possibly even of its battente conversion) by some noble owner. The inlaid design, incorporating two intertwined squares constituting a star octagon which borders the rose, is especially handsome, while the many-tiered and -layered rose itself is a whirlpool of dazzling intricacy, its Gothic traceries inhabited by singing, nesting birds, apparently modelled from glass!

The geometry of the Longo guitar, perhaps not surprisingly, combines aspects of both the design-geometries of the two earlier guitars previously analysed.

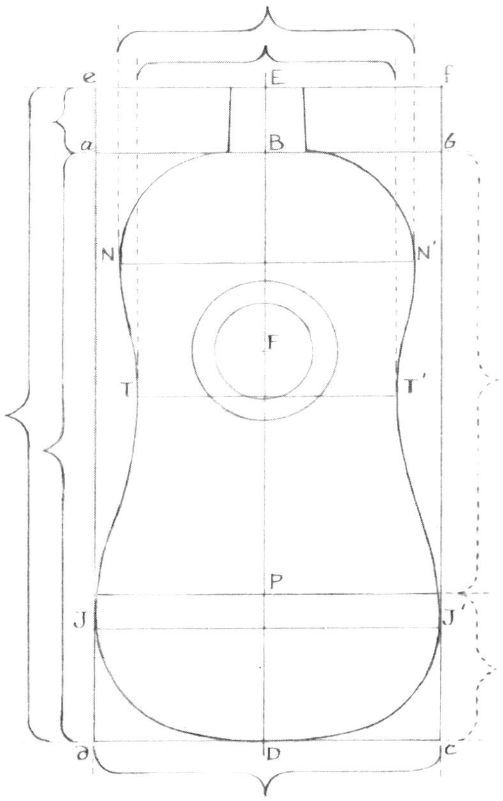

The overall vertical and horizontal proportions are shown bracketed in Fig. 130. Again, as in the Cocho guitar, two containing rectangles are employed: *efcd*, enclosing the body, BD, plus the extension of the table, EB (i.e. ED), and *abcd*, which encloses the sound-box, BD, alone. Their proportions are precisely the same as those found in the previous guitar, namely:

$$efcd, 509.5 \text{ mm} : 255 \text{ mm} = 1.998$$

or, allowing an error of 0.5 mm, 2 : 1, so that *efcd* is a double square, or $\sqrt{4}$ rectangle. Likewise,

$$abcd, 459 \text{ mm} : 255 \text{ mm} = 1.8 = 9 : 5.$$

The middle and upper bouts, once more, are unrelated in width to the lower bouts, although having a separate proportional relationship of their own:

$$NN' : TT'$$
$$216 \text{ mm} : 192 \text{ mm}$$
$$= 1.125$$
$$\text{or} \quad 9 : 8.$$

The present bridge position, also the level of the battente crease, crosses the centre line at P; this, as we have said, is most likely to be the original bridge position, and lies at a one-quarter division of body length BD ($BD/PD = 459 \text{ mm}/115 \text{ mm} = 3.991$ (or 4)). No proportional significance was found in the placing of the rose, centre F; if, however, it had been positioned 3.5 mm higher on the centre line, it would have had a 3 : 5 ratio with major body length ED, and a 2 : 3 ratio with sound-board length BD.

Although there is certainly some consistency shown in the length of the component-arc radii (see Fig. 131), an overall unit-based system of commensurability is not applicable to all the radii of the body outline. The geometric construction of the lower bouts also differs from the two preceding examples, which each employed a containing square, with the maximum width being equal to the arc-of-origin radius, and thus to the square side (see Figs. 126 and 128). Here the arc of origin, DH', is centred at F, the centre of the rose, and has a radius of 302 mm, which, whilst not directly divisible by the most commonly used unit (85 mm, being the vesica radius of the lower bouts), appears to be the sum of this unit and the upper-bout width and arc radius NN' (216 mm)—accepting, of course, the 1 mm difference as error. This means that the next arc, $H'J'$, can be centred by two methods, the familiar vesica piscis device, centred at G and G', and the implied arc of 216 mm (the upper-bout width) centred at F. The lower-bout arc following $H'J'$ (radius 85 mm) is arc $J'K'$, centre J, on

FIG. 130

the opposite edge; this has a radius of 255 mm, that is, three vesica radii of 85 mm, or the maximum lower-bout width. A short straight line, $K'O'$ (see also Cocho guitar), connects the lower-bout curves with the counter-curve arc, $O'L'$, of the middle bouts. Centred at M', this arc also has a radius of 255 mm.

The upper bouts follow approximately the pattern of those of the Diaz guitar, but in common with the Cocho, the upper-bout width also forms a radius for the curve, arc $L'N'$, leading from the middle bouts, here of radius 216 mm. The final curve of the outline, $N'R'$, centre Q', like the example by Diaz, echoes, in radius, the lower-bout vesica curve, in this case 85 mm.

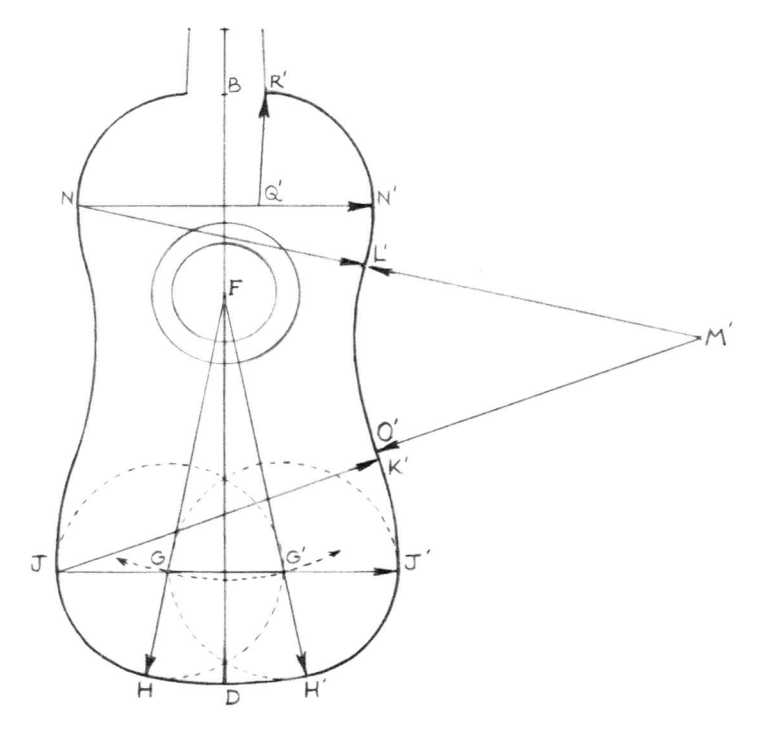

FIG. 131

The head of the guitar, with its pastoral scenes, has suffered damage and alteration to the lower parts of the engraved ivory borders; two alternative reconstructions of the original outline are given in the right-hand side of the main drawing, in dotted and dashed lines. In its present condition the head measures 161 mm × 65 mm, a rectangle of 2.476 proportion—1.5 mm short of 2.5, or a 5 : 2 ratio. It is curious that 65 mm seems to be almost a standard width for Italian guitar heads in the seventeenth and eighteenth centuries, and was the usual head width adopted by the makers of Neapolitan mandolines both in Italy and in the northern centres. In itself, of course, this is another example of the process of a design tradition, and thereby an aesthetic code, being established almost involuntarily by the natural conservatism of individual makers working within a guild master/apprentice structure.

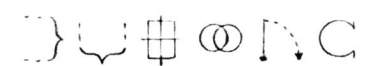

Plate XXXI

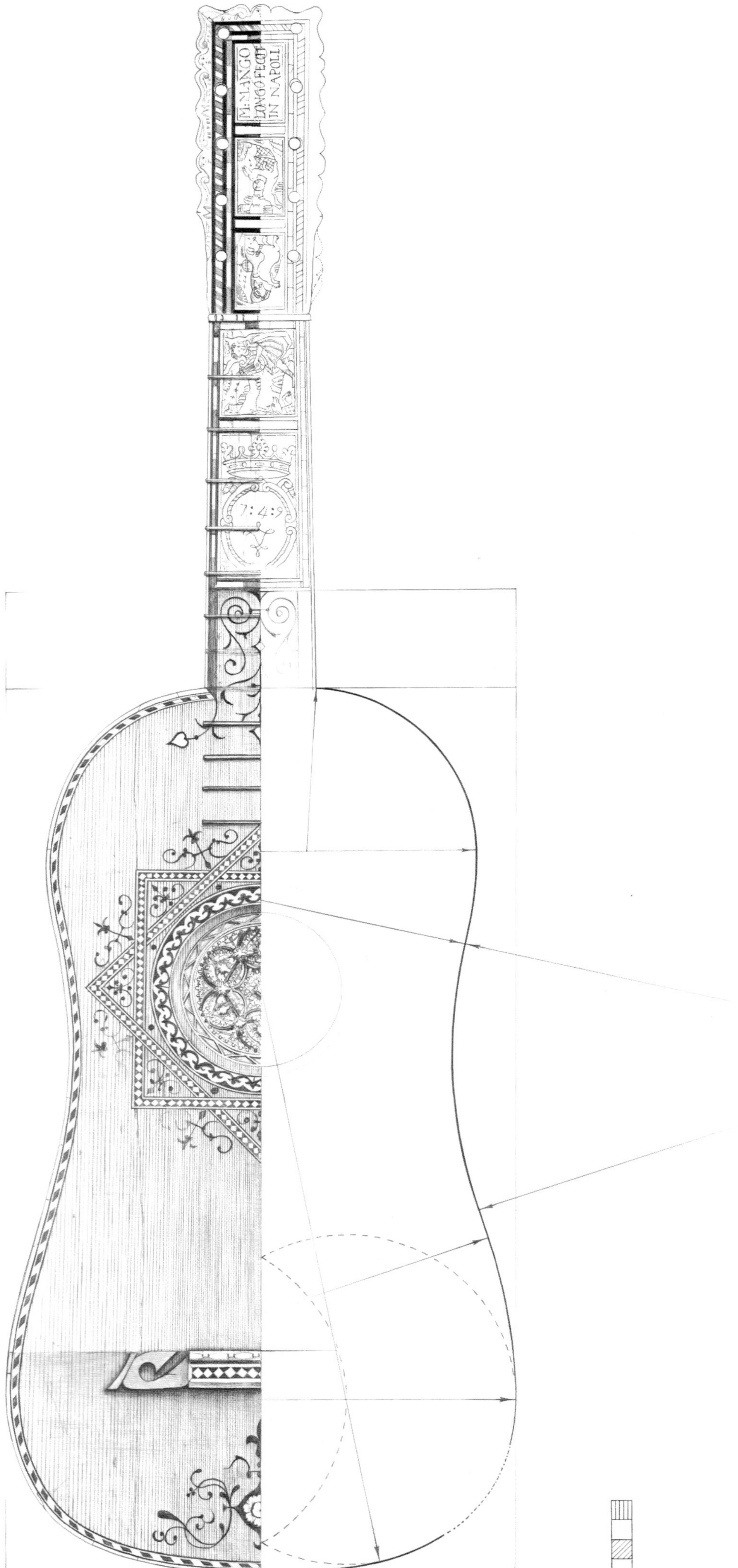

7 Summary of analyses

The analysis of thirty-three instrument designs, as even the most patient reader must by now admit, represents a fairly formidable task of fact-digestion. Of course, each analysis (with the exception of Ex. XXIV) is in itself an individual testimony supporting the thesis that geometry and numerical proportion were customary considerations of the early luthier, but by combining the results of these analyses in one common scheme— a 'summary chart'—additional information may become apparent. One reservation must be voiced, however, and that is that, while thirty-three instruments treated in this way require rather committed reading (writing and compilation aside), in the context of three centuries' diversity of stringed-instrument design, such a selection (necessarily restricted by the criteria outlined in Chapter 5, 'Selection of Examples') could, perhaps, be regarded as a minimal sample from which to draw firm general conclusions. With this proviso in mind, the few trends which do appear to emerge from this collation are discussed, following the chart itself.

The chart is simply a visual summary (with all the usual drawbacks of any summary) of the information put forward in the individual instrument-example texts. There are three major vertical divisions: the left-hand column (half-spaced) gives a simple drawing of the instrument outline and rose/sound-hole disposition; then follows the section consisting of five columns which repeat the information found at the head of each example analysis—that is, example number, instrument type and size, country and centre of origin, date, maker's name, and present whereabouts; finally, the last ten columns display, in symbol form (explained in Chapter 5, 'The Analyses'), the specific analysed information found in each example; this is the same sequence of symbols found at the end of each individual instrument text. It should be added that the decision to assign a symbol was not always a straightforward one—just as the award of a medal for gallantry cannot signify, or describe, the manner or even the true extent of gallantry operating, neither can the allocation of a particular symbol truly describe the extent, or quality, of the scheme it denotes. In the same way, it should not be thought that instruments displaying a larger number of symbols have more complete, or more interesting, schemes than those of few symbols; indeed, the contrary may well apply, on the grounds of purity and economy of means.

The order of instruments in the summary is the same as that observed in the preceding text.

Our discussion of the chart itself must perforce be statistical, and as every politician knows, statistics are really a question of viewpoint, often taken, to quote Andrew Lang, 'as a drunken man uses lamp-posts—for support rather than illumination'.

Considering, then, the number of variables present, and consequent points of view, the evaluation of any specific design trait must depend on establishing certain controls, to enable comparisons to be made. As we have already stressed, great caution must be observed before drawing

SUMMARY CHART I

Instrument Type (& Size)	Country and Centre of Making	Date of Manufacture	Maker	Collection	Vertical Linear Ratio	Horizontal Linear Ratio	Significant Containing Rectangle	Grid or Planning Rectangle	Great Circle	Vesica Piscis	Planning Arcs	Rational Proportion	Irrational Proportion	Spiral Geometry of Head
Ex. I VIOL BASS	ITALY BRESCIA	1550	PELEGRINO DI ZANETTO	BRUSSELS CONSERVATOIRE Acc. No.	}	⌣						C		ෆ
Ex. II VIOL TREBLE	ITALY VENICE	c1575	GIOVANNI MARIA DA BRESCIA	ASHMOLEAN MUS. OXFORD Acc. No. 1	}	⌣			⊕	∞			√5	ෆ
Ex. III VIOL BASS	ITALY VENICE	c1590	BATTISTA CICILIANO	BRUSSELS CONSERVATOIRE Acc. No. 1426						∞		C	∅	ෆ
Ex. IV VIOL TENOR	ENGLAND LONDON	1667	HENRY JAYE	VICTORIA and ALBERT MUS. Acc. No. 173-1882	}	⌣			⊕				∅	⬡
Ex. V VIOL BASS	GERMANY HAMBURG	c1700	JOACHIM TIELKE	VICTORIA and ALBERT MUS. Acc. No. 168-1882	}	⌣	#	G					√5	
Ex. VI VIOL PARDESSUS	FRANCE PARIS	1759	LOUIS GUERSAN	DONALDSON R.C.M. MUS. Acc. No. 149	}	⌣							√5	
Ex. VII LIRA DA BRACCIO	ITALY VENICE	c1575	GIOVANNI MARIA DA BRESCIA	ASHMOLEAN MUS. OXFORD Acc. No. 8	}	⌣	#		⊕			C		
Ex. VIII LIRA DA BRACCIO	ITALY BRESCIA	c1585	GASPARO DA SALO	ASHMOLEAN MUS. OXFORD Acc. No. 9						∞		C		
Ex. IX LIRA DA BRACCIO	ITALY BRESCIA	c1570	Maker Unknown	BRUSSELS CONSERVATOIRE Acc. No. 1415								C		
Ex. X VIOLIN (Small Model)	ITALY CREMONA	1564	ANDREA AMATI	ASHMOLEAN MUS. OXFORD Acc. No. 10					⊕	∞	⌐	C	∅	ෆ
Ex. XI VIOLIN	ITALY CREMONA	c1670	NICOLA AMATI	PRIVATE COLLECTION LONDON	}						⌐	C	∅	ෆ
Ex. XII VIOLIN	ITALY CREMONA	1666	ANTONIO STRADIVARI	PRIVATE COLLECTION LONDON	}						⌐	C	∅	ෆ
Ex. XIII VIOLIN	ITALY CREMONA	1703	ANTONIO STRADIVARI (Emiliani)	PRIVATE COLLECTION LONDON	}							C	∅	ෆ
Ex. XIV VIOLA	ITALY BRESCIA	c1610	GIOVANNI PAOLO MAGGINI	PRIVATE COLLECTION LONDON	}	⌣	#		⊕	∞		C		ෆ
Ex. XV VIOLONCELLO	ENGLAND LONDON	1718	BARAK NORMAN	PRIVATE COLLECTION LONDON	}	⌣		G				C	∅	ෆ
Ex. XVI VIOLA D'AMORE	BOHEMIA	c1750	Maker Unknown	PRIVATE COLLECTION LONDON	}	⌣	#	G	⊕	∞		C		
Ex. XVII VIOLA D'AMORE (English Violet)	GERMANY MUNICH	1724	PAULUS ALLETSEE	GEMEENTEMUSEUM THE HAGUE Ex Boomkamp. 8	}	⌣	#	G		∞	⌐		∅	
Ex. XVIII POCHETTE	BELGIUM BRUSSELS	1686	GASPAR BORBON	BRUSSELS CONSERVATOIRE Acc. No. 2764					⊕	∞		C		
Ex. XIX POCHETTE D'AMORE	ITALY TURIN	c1760	BATTISTA GENOVA	DONALDSON R.C.M. MUS. Acc. No. 38		⌣						C		
Ex. XX LUTE (DRAWING)	HOLLAND	c1460	HENRICUS ARNAULT of ZWOLLE	BIBLIOTHÈQUE NATIONALE PARIS Acc. No. 7295						∞		C		
Ex. XXI LUTE TENOR	ITALY BOLOGNA	c1550	HANS FREI	WARWICK COUNTY MUS. Acc. No. 67/1965	}	⌣	#			∞	⌐	C	∅	
Ex. XXII LUTE ALTO	ITALY VENICE	c1580	GIOVANNI HIEBER	BRUSSELS CONSERVATOIRE Acc. No. 1561	}					∞		C		
Ex. XXIII LUTE CHITTARONE	ITALY ROME	1614	MATTEO BUECHENBERG	VICTORIA and ALBERT MUS. Acc. No. 218-1882				G		∞		C		
Ex. XXIV LUTE THEORBO	GERMANY HAMBURG	1734	JACOBUS HENRICUS GOLDT	VICTORIA and ALBERT MUS. Acc. No. 4274-1856										
Ex. XXV LUTE THEORBO	ENGLAND LONDON	1762	MICHAEL RAUCHE	VICTORIA and ALBERT MUS. Acc. No. 9-1871	}			G		∞	⌐	C		
Ex. XXVI MANDORE	ITALY VENICE?	c1640	Maker Unknown	PARIS CONSERVATOIRE Acc. No. E.222 C.236	}	⌣	#			∞	⌐	C		ෆ
Ex. XXVII MANDOLINE MILANESE	ITALY CREMONA	c1710	ANTONIO STRADIVARI (Attrib.)	PRIVATE COLLECTION LONDON	}	⌣				∞		C		
Ex. XXVIII MANDOLINE NEAPOLITAN	ITALY NAPLES	1753	JOHANNES VINACCIA	PRIVATE COLLECTION LONDON	}	⌣	#	G		∞	⌐	C		
Ex. XXIX CITTERN	ITALY BRESCIA?	c1650	Maker Unknown	PARIS CONSERVATOIRE Acc. No. E.1271 C.1053	}	⌣	#	G			⌐	C		
Ex. XXX BELL CITTERN	GERMANY HAMBURG	1676	JOACHIM TIELKE	DONALDSON R.C.M. MUS. Acc. No. 27			#	G		∞	⌐	C	√3	
Ex. XXXI GUITAR	PORTUGAL LISBON	1582	BELCHIOR DIAZ	DONALDSON R.C.M. MUS. Acc. No. 171	}	⌣		G		∞		C		
Ex. XXXII GUITAR	ITALY VENICE	1602	CHRISTOPHO COCHO	PARIS CONSERVATOIRE Acc. No. E.2090	}	⌣	#	G		∞	⌐	C		
Ex. XXXIII GUITAR	ITALY NAPLES	1624	MANGO LONGO	MILAN CA. SFORZESCO Acc. No. 277	}	⌣	#			∞	⌐	C		

too-rigid conclusions, given such a cross-section of information. For example, a particular type of geometry might conceivably occur only in a certain type of instrument, the examples of which may belong to a common country of origin—is then the geometry unique to the type, or typical of the country? Of course, an acceptable answer to such a question could only be arrived at by further specific investigation and comparison.

Given these conditions, and the Summary Chart as raw material, however, information may be collated for comparison within three main structures which suggest themselves:

(a) instrument type, that is, a comparison of approach in the two *main* design categories of bowed and plucked instruments;
(b) country of origin, a comparison of the design make-up of instruments from Italy, where so many forms originated, with instruments from the other centres of Europe;
(c) chronology, a reordering of analysis results into date sequence.

In addition to these categories, which we will be examining shortly, certain other design idiosyncrasies became apparent during the course of the analyses and the compilation of the main Summary Chart. One of the most crucial parts of any of the preceding instrument outlines, for instance, was the exact disposition of the primary lower-bout arcs—the arc of origin and the adjacent 'corner' arcs. It is interesting that in many cases the same formula has been used with a vesica piscis device forming the 'corner' arcs, linked by the arc of origin. This arrangement was used in Exx. II, III, VIII, XIV, XVII, XVIII, XXI, XXII, XXIII, XXV, XXVIII, XXXI, XXXII, and XXXIII, with six of these schemes also employing the vesica in other situations. This is the prime use for the vesica piscis in the design of body outlines (although it does also occur in Exx. VIII, X, XVI, XX, XXVI, XXVII, and XXX in a 'planning' capacity). By linking, in this way, the two symmetrical halves of the design from the arc of origin, the outline is given a familiar rhythm (almost every instrument type has an example exhibiting this lower-bout pattern), and a harmonious foundation for radius-linked proportion. Perhaps the most beautiful and sustained corner-arc use of the vesica was found in the Buechenberg chitarrone (Ex. XXIII), where the same vesica arcs, their radii a basis of the numerical scheme, were used in front plan, longitudinal profile, and horizontal cross-section.

In fact, the vesica piscis occurred in the vast majority of plucked instruments, as did the commensurable approach to proportioning.

The 'great circle', like the vesica, has a classic aesthetic appeal, and it is not surprising that these two perfect figures are often found together. The great circle itself was only ever found in bowed instruments, never in plucked. This may well be due to the different method of reconciling neck and body in the two categories. In bowed instruments the body outline and neck with raised finger-board are considerably less design-integrated than the types of body and flush finger-board generally found in plucked instruments of the period. When required, this allows the arcs of upper- and lower-bout origin of bowed instruments to meet the arc of a great circle in a 'tangential' relationship at both extremes.

As might be expected, where grid-planning has been used more often than not a significant containing rectangle is found, although, of course, these also occur independently. It was interesting, too, to note that the instrument group most consistent in the ingredients of its design make-up was that of the guitars.

But to return to the main categories of summary: Chart 2 makes a specific comparison between bowed and plucked instruments. The left-hand column denotes, by symbol, the type of geometry or proportion. Vertical and horizontal linear proportion are grouped together, but counted separately, and the incommensurable symbols are also given a corporate grouping opposite the symbol of commensurability with a cross drawn through (⊠). The next two columns give the number of incidences of those symbols among bowed and plucked instruments respectively.

SUMMARY CHART 2

Geometry	Bowed	Plucked
⎬ ⎴	24	19
⊞	5	8
⌐┘	4	7
⊕	7	—
⌀⌀	8	12
⌐↘	4	8
C	14	13
⊠	11	2
(∅)	(8)	(1)
(√5)	(3)	(—)
(√3)	(—)	(1)

The conclusions drawn from this comparison, allowing for the 19 : 14 (1.357) ratio of bowed to plucked examples, can be listed thus:

⎬ ⎴ proportionally *fewer bowed* than *plucked* instruments exhibit *linear ratios*;

⊞ proportionally *fewer bowed* than *plucked* instruments exhibit a *significant containing rectangle*;

⌐┘ proportionally *fewer bowed* than *plucked* instruments exhibit *grid-planning*;

⊕ proportionally *more bowed* than *plucked* instruments exhibit *great-circle geometry*;

⌀⌀ proportionally *fewer bowed* than *plucked* instruments exhibit a *vesica piscis*;

⌐↘ proportionally *fewer bowed* than *plucked* instruments exhibit *planning arcs*;

C proportionally *fewer bowed* than *plucked* instruments exhibit *commensurable proportions*;

⊠ proportionally *more bowed* than *plucked* instruments exhibit *incommensurable proportions* (such as ϕ, $\sqrt{5}$, $\sqrt{3}$),

according to the instruments in the survey.

Similarly, Summary Chart 3 makes a specific comparison between Italian and non-Italian instruments. Again, the left-hand column denotes the type of geometry while the others give the breakdown of the Italian and non-Italian examples:

SUMMARY CHART 3

Geometry	Italian	Non-Italian
} ⌣	29	14
⊞	8	5
⌐┘	4	7
⊕	4	3
⊙⊙	13	7
⌐↘	9	3
C	20	7
⋈	7	6
(∅)	6	3
(√5)	1	2
(√3)	—	1

The conclusions drawn from this comparison, allowing for a 21:12 (1.75) ratio, can be listed as follows:

- } ⌣   proportionally *more Italian* than *non-Italian* instruments exhibit *linear ratios*;
- ⊞   proportionally *fewer Italian* than *non-Italian* instruments exhibit a *significant containing rectangle*;
- ⌐┘   proportionally *fewer Italian* than *non-Italian* instruments exhibit *grid-planning*;
- ⊕   proportionally *fewer Italian* than *non-Italian* instruments exhibit *great-circle geometry*;
- ⊙⊙   proportionally *more Italian* than *non-Italian* instruments exhibit a *vesica piscis*;
- ⌐↘   proportionally *more Italian* than *non-Italian* instruments exhibit *planning arcs*;
- C   proportionally *more Italian* than *non-Italian* instruments exhibit *commensurable proportions*;
- ⋈   proportionally *fewer Italian* than *non-Italian* instruments exhibit *incommensurable proportions* (such as ϕ, $\sqrt{5}$, $\sqrt{3}$),

according to the instruments analysed in the survey.

Summary Chart 4 is, in effect, a reordering of the main Summary Chart 1 according to chronology. It is interesting that no major patterns are immediately apparent; this suggests (if the selection of instruments is

SUMMARY CHART 4

Instrument Type (& Size)	Country and Centre of Making	Date of Manufacture	Maker	Collection	Vertical Linear Ratio	Horizontal Linear Ratio	Containing Rectangle	Grid or Planning Rectangle	Great Circle	Vesica Piscis	Planning Arcs	Rational Proportion	Irrational Proportion	Spiral Geometry of Head
Ex XX Lute (drawing)	Holland	c1460	Henricus Arnault de Zwolle	Bibliotheque Nationale Paris Acc. No 7295						⊙⊙		C		
Ex I Viol Bass	Italy Brescia	1550	Pellegrino di Zanetto	Brussels Conservatoire Acc. No.	}	⌣						C		⊙⊙
Ex XXI Lute Tenor	Italy Bologna	c1550	Hans Frei	Warwick County Mus Acc No 671966	}	⌣	‖‖			⊙⊙	⌐	C	∅	
Ex X Violin (Small Model)	Italy Cremona	1564	Andrea Amati	Ashmolean Mus Oxford Acc No 10					⊕	⊙⊙	⌐	C	∅	⊙⊙
Ex IX Lira da Braccio	Italy Brescia	c1570	Maker Unknown	Brussels Conservatoire Acc No 1415								C		
Ex II Viol Treble	Italy Venice	c1575	Giovanni Maria da Brescia	Ashmolean Mus Oxford Acc No 1	}	⌣			⊕	⊙⊙		√5	⊙⊙	
Ex VII Lira da Braccio	Italy Venice	c1575	Giovanni Maria da Brescia	Ashmolean Mus Oxford Acc No 8	}	⌣	‖‖		⊕			C		
Ex XXII Lute Alto	Italy Venice	c1580	Giovanni Hieber	Brussels Conservatoire Acc No 1561	}					⊙⊙		C		
Ex XXXI Guitar	Portugal Lisbon	1582	Belchior Diaz	Donaldson RCM Mus Acc No 171	}	⌣	‖‖	⌐		⊙⊙		C		
Ex VIII Lira da Braccio	Italy Brescia	c1585	Gasparo da Salo	Ashmolean Mus Oxford Acc No 9						⊙⊙		C		
Ex III Viol Bass	Italy Venice	c1590	Battista Ciciliano	Brussels Conservatoire Acc No 1426	}					⊙⊙		C	∅	⊙⊙
Ex XXXII Guitar	Italy Venice	1602	Christopho Cocho	Paris Conservatoire Acc No E2090	}	⌣	‖‖	⌐		⊙⊙	⌐	C		
Ex XIV Viola	Italy Brescia	c1610	Giovanni Paolo Maggini	Private Collection London	}	⌣	‖‖		⊕	⊙⊙		C		⊙⊙
Ex XXIII Lute Chittarone	Italy Rome	1614	Matteo Buechenberg	Victoria and Albert Mus Acc No 218 1882	}			⌐		⊙⊙		C		
Ex XXXIII Guitar	Italy Naples	1624	Mango Longo	Milan Ca Sforzesco Acc No 277	}	⌣	‖‖			⊙⊙	⌐	C		
Ex XXVI Mandore	Italy Venice?	c1640	Maker Unknown	Paris Conservatoire Acc No E7720735	}	⌣	‖‖			⊙⊙	⌐	C		⊙⊙
Ex XXIX Cittern	Italy Brescia?	c1650	Maker Unknown	Paris Conservatoire Acc No E1271C1053	}	⌣	‖‖	⌐			⌐	C		
Ex XII Violin	Italy Cremona	1666	Antonio Stradivari	Private Collection London	}						⌐	C	∅	⊙⊙
Ex IV Viol Tenor	England London	1667	Henry Jaye	Victoria and Albert Mus Acc No 1731882	}				⊕				∅	⬡
Ex XI Violin	Italy Cremona	c1670	Nicola Amati	Private Collection London	}						⌐	C	∅	⊙⊙
Ex XXX Bell Cittern	Germany Hamburg	1676	Joachim Tielke	Donaldson RCM Mus Acc No 27			‖‖	⌐		⊙⊙	⌐	C	√3	
Ex XVIII Pochette	Belgium Brussels	1686	Gaspar Borbon	Brussels Conservatoire Acc No 2764					⊕	⊙⊙		C		
Ex V Viol Bass	Germany Hamburg	c1700	Joachim Tielke	Victoria and Albert Mus Acc No 168 1882	}	⌣	‖‖	⌐					√5	
Ex XIII Violin	Italy Cremona	1703	Antonio Stradivari (Emiliani)	Private Collection London	}							C	∅	⊙⊙
Ex XXVII Mandoline Milanese	Italy Cremona	c1710	Antonio Stradivari (Attrib)	Private Collection London	}	⌣				⊙⊙		C		
Ex XV Violoncello	England London	1718	Barak Norman	Private Collection London	}	⌣		⌐				C	∅	⊙⊙
Ex XVII Viola d'Amore (English Violet)	Germany Munich	1724	Paulus Alletsee	Gemeentemuseum The Hague Ex Boomkamp 5	}	⌣	‖‖	⌐		⊙⊙	⌐		∅	
Ex XXIV Lute Theorbo	Germany Hamburg	1734	Jacobus Henricus Goldt	Victoria and Albert Mus Acc No 4274 1856										
Ex XVI Viola d'Amore	Bohemia	c1750	Maker Unknown	Private Collection London	}	⌣	‖‖	⌐	⊕	⊙⊙		C		
Ex XXVIII Mandoline Neapolitan	Italy Naples	1753	Johannes Vinaccia	Private Collection London	}	⌣	‖‖	⌐		⊙⊙	⌐	C		
Ex VI Viol Pardessus	France Paris	1759	Louis Guersan	Donaldson RCM Mus Acc No 149	}	⌣							√5	
Ex XIX Pochette d'Amore	Italy Turin	c1760	Battista Genova	Donaldson RCM Mus Acc No 38		⌣						C		
Ex XXV Lute Theorbo	England London	1762	Michael Rauche	Victoria and Albert Mus Acc No 9-1871	}			⌐		⊙⊙	⌐	C		

representative) that the various design practices belong to a long-established, fairly immutable tradition. Within this rather static picture, however, it is possible to make a few tentative observations, and to hope that by giving voice to them they are not given undue emphasis. Commensurable proportions, for example, appear consistently, as do the incommensurable schemes, and yet, bearing in mind the generally less significant use of incommensurable proportioning in the earlier schemes, it may be inferred that there is a slightly increased tendency for incommensurably planned instruments to appear later on in the chart.

The vesica piscis and the use of planning arcs are likewise well spread throughout, and yet both appear to 'bunch' slightly—the vesica from the third quarter of the sixteenth century to the second half of the seventeenth, and the planning arcs in the second and third quarters of the seventeenth century. The same effect is seen with the use of planning grids, which appear to have been employed more extensively among the later examples: indeed, what are perhaps the most interesting grid schemes both occur in eighteenth-century instruments (the Alletsee English Violet, 1724, Ex. XVII, and Vinaccia mandoline, 1753, Ex. XXVIII). It should, however, be remembered that both these examples were quite new types of instrument at their dates of manufacture, and their consequent nearness to their archetypes could also account for the greater consciousness of their grid-planning.

Ultimately, it is of course for the reader himself to draw what conclusions he will from the preceding charts and summaries. The numerous varying factors make it a complex knot to unravel, and there is no certainty that, were it possible to have a different thirty-three instruments which would satisfy the necessary conditions, they might not perhaps display differing trends.

Whatever the details might be, however, the body of facts drawn from these instruments presents irrefutable evidence and undeniable proof that geometry and numerical proportioning were constant, conscious considerations of the luthier throughout the period examined, providing a common design foundation, linking his work to that of others from whom he may have been separated by time, place, or speciality, but with whom he was united by a vital working tradition.

8 Observations

Earlier in this study we discussed the high degree of symmetry evident in the design of musical instruments, and remarked that this was most probably a design analogy with man's own symmetry. In fact, anthropomorphism in musical-instrument design goes further than merely mimicking man's symmetry. The whole form of a stringed instrument is quasi-human; the undulating contours of the guitar, for instance, are as archetypally Woman as those of any palaeolithic Venus; the drawing in Fig. 132 has all the refulgent poise of a Picasso nude, and yet it was drawn as a teaching aid in Lucas Ruiz de Ribayaz's *Luz y Norte Musical*, a manual for guitar and harp published in Madrid in 1677. This 'identification' is also apparent in the terminology we apply to the parts of stringed instruments—they can have a head, neck, body, back, belly, ribs; the scrolls have ears, and finger-boards can sometimes even have beards. To be French is to understand these things more fully: the sound-post, that vital transmitter of vibrations, lodged deep within the recesses of the body, is by them called *l'âme*, the 'soul' of the instrument. Of course, other artefacts, such as ceramics and furniture, are also described in such terms; after all, to return to the Platonism of our geometries, 'Man is the measure of all things.'[97] This crucial phrase once more brings to mind the Vitruvian figure encountered in Fig. 5. Purely as an expression of this universal concept of measure and proportion, but of no specific significance for the instrument concerned, it is nevertheless an interesting exercise (Fig. 133) to superimpose upon Leonardo's man-in-circle-and-square drawing the great-circle geometry of one of the early analyses (Figs. 31 and 32). In essence, it could be an illustration to Pacioli's remarks:

... from the human body derive all measures and their denominations, and in it is to be found all and every ratio and proportion by which God reveals the innermost secrets of nature.

In many cases the desire to humanize, or give expression to the animation which these instruments are felt to possess, is extended to their endowment with a human face carved into their own head or peg-box. This an anthropologist might well regard as a vestigial form of totemism; it is certainly a measure of the sense of mystery and magic with which music, and musical instruments, have been endowed by the mind of man, as is reflected in ancient myth and later literature. It is almost as though the idea of an instrument, whose voice, intangible, fugitive, a vehicle for human thought and emotion within the abstraction of music, having no familiar, *human* source, was a deeply disturbing one, needing a visual focus, the carved head, as a psychological release.

The typical shapes of stringed instruments have resulted in each case from an alliance of three considerations:

(i) acoustics—which dictate string length, bridge position, and a certain volume of air almost totally enclosed by a sound-box, one side of which forms the sound-board;

FIG. 132. Fret chart from *Luz y Norte Musical* by Lucas Ruiz de Ribayaz, Madrid 1677. (By courtesy of the Biblioteca Nacional, Madrid)

[97] Protagoras (c.485–451 BC) quoted by Plato in *Theaetetus*.

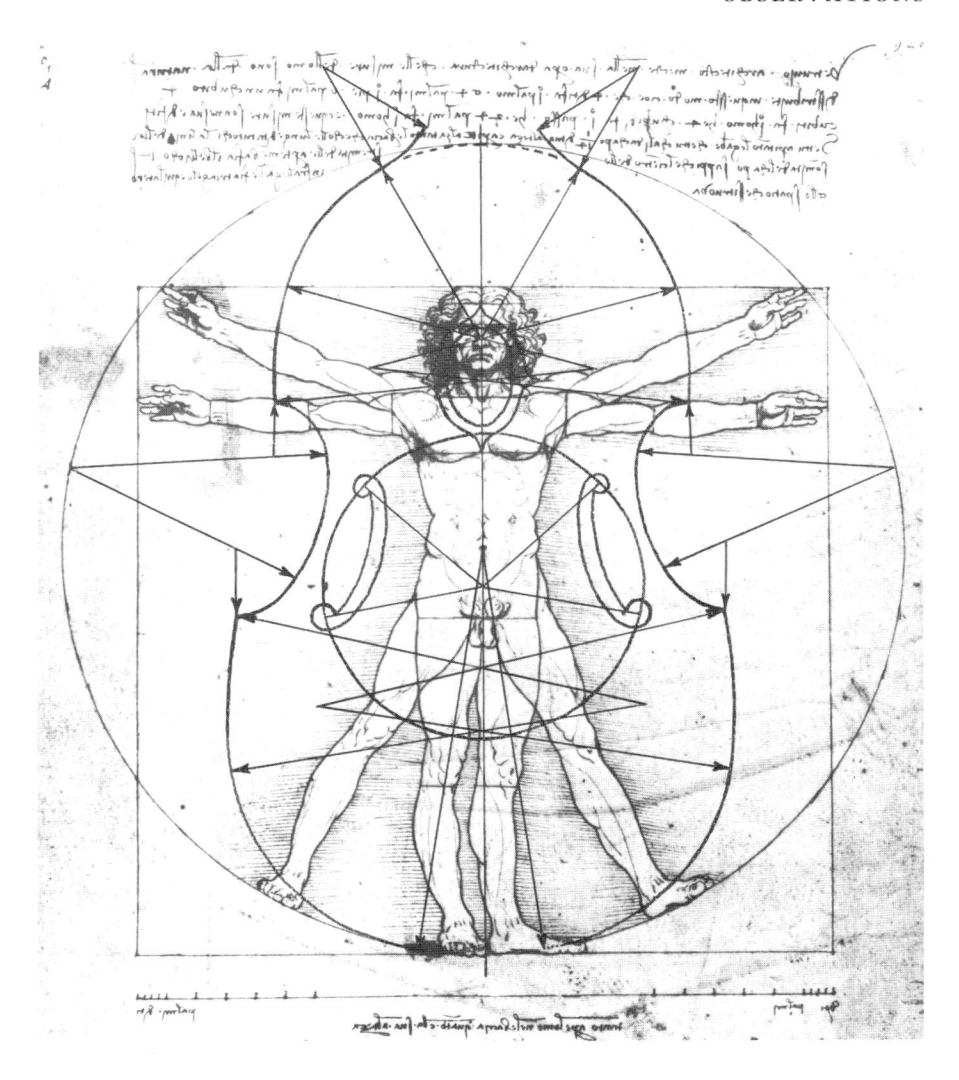

Fig. 133

(ii) ergonomics—which relate all the foregoing to playing function (this explains why, for example, bowed instruments[98] have incurved middle bouts which allow a bow to traverse all the strings);

(iii) aesthetics, perhaps the most difficult category to analyse; among numerous factors it also embraces considerations of tradition, covering details which may originally have served an acoustic or ergonomic purpose, but have survived only as 'characteristic' features. Primarily, however, aesthetics is a category which harmonizes (and humanizes) the requirements of the other two, a process, as we have seen, which is expressed in the grammar and syntax of geometry and proportion.

If we examine the use of geometry in instrument-design, we find, not surprisingly, a rather different approach from that found in the geometries of architecture or of painting. Painting begins with the predeterminate ratio of its canvas rectangle within, and often by, which the work is harmonized; but unlike architecture or musical instruments, painting, in the period we are examining, is not usually dealing with hard, geometrically defined borders and edges alone (although there are always those of the frame itself), but with emotional directions of force guiding the action, or containing the repose, of the subject-matter. Architecture, in a sense, also begins with a containing ratio or ratios, that is, of elevation (its façade), of its section, and of its plan. The complexity arises when these

---

[98] Guitars also have incurved middle bouts. This is thought to be due to their evolution as vihuela de pena from the vihuela de arco, a bowed form. Ergonomically, of course, the waist is still extremely convenient for positioning the instrument across the thigh.

breed to form volumes, which can be regarded as the products of ratios. But if there is complexity in architectural proportioning (which no doubt has been part of its fascination for theorists and practitioners alike), there is also the satisfying purity of the transparency of the scheme. By this I mean that in architecture something of the geometrizing of the designer is usually apparent to a receptive observer, owing to the usual retention of the rectilinear forms of the original geometry. This is less so, and needfully less so, in painting, where, as observers, we should be aware solely of the subject-matter set suitably harmoniously, or suitably tortuously, by the invisible agency of the planning geometry. And, of course, when we view stringed instruments, as with other decorative art forms, we do so to evoke similar *aesthetic* responses as we may with either painting or architecture. We enjoy the form and, as we move the instrument, the changing contour, the colour and mutability of wood and varnish in the play of light, the treatment of fine detail, and its balance and 'feel' as a handled object. So, as with painting, we may be excited and aware of beauty and harmony, but totally unaware of such conscious proportional planning as we perceive in architecture, save perhaps the suspicion that such integrity of form was not just the result of arbitrary whim or feeling.

This is because the design geometrizing of instruments, like that of painting, is an invisible one, and it is a method of arriving at a harmony of form within the prime consideration of economy of means.

It is an invisible process and, practically without exception in the cases examined, not regenerative. The one clear exception is, of course, the simple form of the Arnault lute drawing (Ex. XX, *c.*1460), which, if only by virtue of its being an instruction for the construction of an instrument, had to be generateable from a point. Geometrical planning most probably started with simple forms, such as the fifteenth-century Arnault lute, but the complexity and sophistication of sixteenth-century designs, and their later developments, very soon precludes any possibility of their outlines being reconstructed by a list of verbal or written instructions or formulae. There would be no purpose to their being so, and indeed, positive reason why they should not be thus conveyable and repeatable. Perhaps the nearest any later example approaches generation from a point is in Ex. XXIX, an Italian cittern, but even this body outline could not be completed by a sequence of instructions. This clearly is no more a part of the function of musical-instrument geometry than it is the function of the planning geometry of a painting.

This brings to mind a condition peculiar to the geometrical schemes of musical instruments, namely, that unlike almost every other artefact that could conceivably be so planned, they have no true 'up' or 'down', no certain relationship with gravity or the plane of the earth. When we display instruments in collections or in books, the tendency is to give them the upright, vertical axis of symmetry which we ourselves have (like the drawings and figures given here), but in use they are almost never seen in such a formal verticality, not even those instruments used in the 'downwards' gamba position.

9 Conclusions

Thus far, our studies have introduced us to the mathematical outlook of previous periods of our culture, where we have encountered its perennial preoccupation with the Platonic number cosmology. We have examined ancient methods of geometrizing, and modes of proportion, which we later observed, noted, and expounded from the the designs of thirty-three historic musical instruments. The resulting individual discussions were then collated and examined as a whole, and certain observations, intuitions, and such tentative conclusions as could safely be drawn, were voiced. In this way, the original thesis, that geometry and proportional systems were used by the luthiers of the sixteenth, seventeenth, and eighteenth centuries, has been established, but this answer to an initial enquiry now prompts two further inevitable questions: since it is not apparent to a casual observer that geometry or numerical proportion have been applied to stringed instruments, *why* then did luthiers use such systems in their designs, and, secondly, *why* has no written reference or record of their proportional considerations ever come to light?

Of course, in the absence of historical documentation, neither question can be given a conclusive answer; instead, explanation will have to be given by reason and deduction, rather than answer by scientific proof.

A reply to the first question—why systems of proportion and geometry were used by the early luthier—will have to be compounded from three main considerations, the *practical*, the *aesthetic*, and, for want of more suitable terminology, the *metaphysical*.

There are many *practical* reasons for employing such a design process. The stringed instruments we have been examining, with the acknowledged exception of the more elaborately festooned models, are all practically definitive examples of the old, perhaps overworked, design aesthetic of 'form following function'; their economy of form and parts, and limitations of decoration, are all ensured by the main acoustical consideration of lightness and freedom of vibration. Therefore, their function, and consequently much of their beauty, depends not on elaboration or decorative distraction, but on a perfect, fully considered, initial conception of pure linear form—a design method which demands adherence to some very rigid prerequisites. The understanding of some of these design factors, in the pure abstract terms of geometry, can therefore only be an enormous practical asset to the luthier. Occasionally instruments survive which were obviously made with little or no understanding of this knowledge, possibly as 'amateur' or at any rate as *non conoscente* instruments. Some have found reprieve, either by accident of fate, for their curiosity value, or for the possible reason that they might even have sounded well! Just such an ill-formed example is grudgingly granted an appearance here in Fig. 134.

It must also be appreciated that an understanding of these geometrical and proportional principles lends assurance and a sense of conviction to the designer in that most difficult area—decision-making. As Jay

Fig. 134. Violin, naïve design

Hambidge suggests in the preface to his *Elements of Dynamic Symmetry*,

> Knowledge of a basic law gives a feeling of sureness which enables the artist to put into realization dreams which otherwise would have been dissipated in uncertainty.

Thus, geometry and proportion, as principles of design, must have been an invaluable shorthand system to the early luthier. The known interrelationship of parts of a design allows it to be adapted to different pitch sizes of constant proportion—a characteristic of great importance to the instruments of the Renaissance, where the many differing pitch members of an instrument family required constancy of timbre, as well as the more obvious visual unity.

The *aesthetic* resources of geometry and numerical proportion have already been alluded to, and, indeed, observed at work in many of the analyses examined earlier. Their use in a design archetype, by an adept, produced a restrained simplicity, a 'rightness' of repose, which is usually called beauty, a beauty born of the unifying limitations of order, selected from the infinite possibilities of mathematics. This restrictive process, unlike the unfettered chaos of random 'intuitive' design, had *method*, and having method, was communicable at a certain level of understanding to other practitioners, thus establishing a design code which would guarantee a universal harmonic approach to shape and, in turn, emphasize a universal criterion in beauty of form.

Finally, in a *metaphysical* sense, the use of geometry in the formulation of a musical-instrument design is the natural development of a single idea, and a single root; for both music and geometry, two of the four Platonic arts, are united by number. In embracing geometry and mathematical proportion in his creation, the luthier also embraced an ancient and sacred tradition, a canon of measure, which in a sense was a consecration of both artist and work. If for Blake 'Mathematical form is eternal existence', so, too, for the initiates of this canon, form generated from mathematics was likewise eternal perfection, and, as such, the only worthy exemplar for the spiritual structure of an instrument of music.

> I do not, however, think the attempt to tell mankind of these matters a good thing, except in the case of some few who are capable of discovering the truth for themselves with a little guidance. In the case of the rest to do so would excite in some an unjustified contempt in a thoroughly offensive fashion, in others certain lofty and vain hopes, as if they had acquired some awesome lore.

Plato's words (*Letters*, vii) give a beautifully distilled answer to our remaining question, that of why no written reference of the luthier's use of this knowledge has ever appeared. For here we must be dealing with a conscious pact of secrecy—a secrecy which has almost always accompanied both the study of mathematics and the pursuit of any specialized art or craft.

This study has examined many instruments, a sizeable proportion of which can be regarded as being near to their archetypes—that is, the design originals which have emerged regularly, upon social or musicological demand, throughout the three hundred years of musical history covered by the chosen examples. And yet, despite this prolonged tradition of design, no sketches or working constructions, which reveal the vital design processes, would appear to have survived. Even the Stradivari archives in Cremona, which house the master's remaining moulds and paper patterns, offer no direct clues. These patterns indicate an interior 'rib plan' outline, and not the final outline of edge, which has been proved to be proportionally planned; neither can any *outline* arc constructional compass marks be found on the ones I was able to examine closely. I can therefore only conclude that these are working patterns, one stage removed from the original 'constructed' design outline, which one suspects may have been destroyed once suitable templates had been made from the 'master' drawing. (For a fuller discussion of the Stradivari violin moulds, see Appendix B, p. 172.)

One, I think, unique original drawing which does survive, although from an earlier epoch, is, of course, the lute drawing by Henricus Arnault (discussed here as Ex. XX) which, as we have already said, was of form simple enough to be repeated by a list of written instructions; nevertheless, nowhere in his discourse does the chatty Henricus mention the fact that his design is enthroned within a containing vesica piscis. Was this, then, so commonplace a figure that it was not worthy of mention? Was he unaware of it? Or was it simply not 'a good thing' to mention such phenomena?

A glance at Appendix A will demonstrate not only the contemporary preoccupation with 'mathematical matters', but also the extent to which painters, architects, and music theorists were willing openly to discuss geometry and proportion. Here is the basic dichotomy: for on the one hand we have articulate, humanist theorists and scholars opening wide their hearts and minds to this ancient number-cosmology, while on the other we have an equally ancient crafts tradition, whose secrets were zealously guarded, communicated only with the utmost trust and gravity by master to pupil initiated to the same tradition, and thus bound by its conditions. While in a practical sense Neoplatonic number dilettantism could be indulged in—albeit superficially—by a wealthy patron or amateur of architecture *au courant* with the latest treatises, no such design dabbling was possible in the secret arts of lutherie (even when it was sufficiently respectable) and any uninitiated amateur activity would naturally be restricted to the 'innocent' copying of profoundly considered forms.

What, then, was the nature of the craft societies which were able to reserve the secrets of this tradition? These were the guilds or, as they were sometimes, and here perhaps more aptly, known, the 'misteries'. The guild system was a vital part of society, regulating every aspect of business, maintaining standards of excellence, protecting the livelihoods of citizens, and controlling trade and industry. Within a complex hierarchical structure of guilds of *Arti Maggiori* (which, in Renaissance Florence, was led by *L'Arte de Giudici e Notai*—the Guild of Judges and Notaries), *Arti Mediane*, and *Arti Minori*, many of the artisans would belong to a mercers' or merchants' guild—on the same principle that value added tax is levied today, in that the craftsmen *bought* raw material(s) and *sold* a manufactured commodity. This explains why numerous researches have failed to uncover evidence of a specific 'luthiers' guild'. At a more prestigious time in its history (when it was still in technological advance of many contemporary skills, and not yet regarded as a reproductive, mechanical craft), the art of lutherie might well have been incorporated in the guild of painters, as were the harpsichord-makers, Ruckers included, of the Low Countries, in the famous Guild of St Luke (although in such a case there was also a practical reason of trade protection to consider, Flemish harpsichords being finished and decorated by paintwork).

We know from labels such as that of the early Stradivari violin of 1666 (Ex. XII) that a pupil or apprentice was regarded as *alumnus* or 'foster-son' of his *maestro*, in whose house and at whose table he would probably live, until he achieved his own *capo maestro*. At such a time when the apprentice's skills were proven, and judged worthy by both master and guild council, then would he be admitted into the guild on payment of the necessary fees, or tokens of work. Most likely, it would be at this stage, his sensibilities prepared, that he would have been initiated, *almost certainly verbally*, into the geometrical mysteries of his art, and sworn to a secrecy, which after all, would be in his own interests. Thus he became an independent master, able, if he had the innovative understanding of an original creator, to prepare his own patterns and designs according to the sacred principles which had been entrusted to him, or if not, he simply remained as the propagator of the models inherited from his master. Either way, the tradition both regenerated and protected itself. Its great strength, and paradoxically much of its weakness, lay in the conservatism of this tacit process, which thus built up universal aesthetic standards, and, by the apprentice's indoctrination and acceptance of its principles, conditional to his own mastership and obligatory guild membership, quietly and inexorably established a monopolism of design philosophy.

Here, then, is the final mystery of the lost tradition of design, which I have sought by this study to unveil. The decline of this tradition, as a living doctrine understood by its practitioners, inevitably accompanied the dissolution of the social structure of the guilds, which had fostered and maintained it. Their fate or transformation during the desolate struggles of the industrial revolution marked the end, as we have seen, not just of five or six centuries of guild patriarchy, but of a spiritual philosophy of work which had linked and harnessed the nobler thoughts of generations of creative minds.

Thanks to the enlightened genius of a few individual artists, however, these forms do survive in remaining instruments as the inspiration and model of later generations of copyists. But no matter how illustrious the talents of its present-day practitioners, the art of lutherie will never again achieve the same grace of enlightenment, of genuine creativity, unless it can return to its true centre, an understanding of the lost principles that nourished the genius we now mindlessly, or rather, soullessly, seek to replicate.

*

> Geometry . . . tends to draw the soul to truth,
> and be productive of a philosophical
> attitude of mind, directing up-
> ward the faculties that now
> wrongly are turned
> earthward.[99]

[99] Plato, *Republic* vii.

Appendix A Some early sources of geometrical and proportional information

GENERAL WORKS

FRA LUCA PACIOLI
de Divina Proportione, Venice 1509
Summa de Arithmetica, Geometria, Proportioni e Proportionalità
Euclid, vernacular edition, 1494 (lost)
　　Latin edition, 1509

FRANCESCO GIORGI
de Harmonia Mundi, Venice 1525

GIANGIORGIO TRISSINO
L'Italia liberata dai Goti, 1547

SILVIO BELLI
Della Proportione, et Proportionalità, 1573
Quattro libri geometrici, Venice 1595

PETRUS BUNGUS
Numerorum Mysteria, 1585

JOHANNES KEPLER
Mysterium Cosmographicum, 1596
Harmonia Mundi, 1619

ARCHITECTURE

LEON BATTISTA ALBERTI
de re aedificatoria [c.1450], 1485, 1550

ANTONIO FILARETE
Trattato di architettura [c.1462]

FRANCESCO DI GIORGIO MARTINI
Trattato di architettura civile e militare [after 1482]

PIETRO CATANEO
I quattro primi libri di architettura, Venice 1554

GIACOMO BAROZZI DA VIGNOLA
Regole delle cinque ordini, 1562

PHILIBERT DE L'ORME
Le premier tome de l'architecture, 1567

ANDREA PALLADIO
Quattro libri dell'architettura, Venice 1570

MARTINO BASSI
Dispareri in materia d'architettura, et perspettiva, Brescia 1572

SEBASTIANO MONTECCHIO
De Inventario haeredis, Venice 1574

VINCENZO SCAMOZZI
Idea dell'architettura universale, 1615

EDITIONS OF VITRUVIUS

CESARE CESARIANO
de architectura libri decem, Como 1521

DANIELE BARBARO
M. Vitruvii Pollionis de architectura libri decem, Latin edition, Venice 1567
　　Italian edition, Venice 1556

PAINTING AND SCULPTURE

LEON BATTISTA ALBERTI
della Pittura [1435]

PIERO DELLA FRANCESCA
de Prospettiva Pingendi [1470-90]

POMPONIUS GAURICUS
de Sculptura [1503]

ALBRECHT DÜRER
Underweysung der Messung mit dem Zyrkel und Rychtscheyd [1525]
Vier Buecher von Menschlicher Proportion, Nuremberg 1528
　　Latin edition, Nuremberg 1528
　　French edition, Paris 1557
　　Italian edition, Venice 1591
　　Portuguese edition, 1599
　　Dutch edition, Arnheim 1622

GIOVANNI PAOLO LOMAZZO
Trattato dell'Arte della Pittura, Scultura, ed Architettura [1584]
Idea de Tempio della Pittura [1590]

MUSIC

ANICIUS MANLIUS SEVERINUS BOETHIUS (c.AD 475-524)
de Musica, Venice 1492

FRANCHINO GAFURIO
Theorica Musice, 1492
Practica Musicae, 1496
Angelicum ac Divinum Opus Musice, 1508
de Harmonia Musicorum Instrumentorum, 1518

SEBASTIAN VIRDUNG
Musica Getuscht, Basle 1511

MARTIN AGRICOLA
Musica Instrumentalis Deudsch, Wittemberg 1528

GIOSEFFO ZARLINO
Istitutioni Harmoniche, 1558
Soppliменti Musicali, Venice 1558
Dimostrationi Harmoniche, 1571

MICHAEL PRAETORIUS
Syntagma Musicum, 1619

MARIN MERSENNE
Harmonie Universelle, 1636

Appendix B The violin moulds of Antonio Stradivari with reference to Exx. XII and XIII

The painstaking care taken by Stradivari in filing and annotating the hundreds of patterns in paper and wood which were amassed during a lifetime of ceaseless experimentation, together with the reputation that his achievements brought him, ensured that much of his workshop material has survived. Unfortunately, in passing through the practical hands of later luthiers, it has in part meant a working survival, and consequently some of the usable original moulds and patterns, for example those of the violoncellos, have been separated from the collection and since lost. The remaining body of material, which constitutes a unique record of a master luthier's workshop-practice, has now been catalogued, and is preserved in the Museo Civico in Cremona.

Among the instrument examples dealt with here are two violins by Stradivari (Ex. XII and Ex. XIII) and a mandoline (Ex. XXVII) attributed to him, and whose authorship was further confirmed by its correspondence to a paper pattern (no. 420) in the archive. Matching the violin outlines to their generating moulds was less straightforward, there being eleven surviving full-size violin moulds in the collection.

These moulds, or forms, which all appear to be made of walnut-wood, are the internal structures on which the instrument, here the violin, was assembled. Being an internal form, its outline accordingly corresponds to the inside of the ribs, that is to say about 3 or 4 mm inboard of the final outline which we see in the completed instrument. Fig. 135, a line drawing of a violin mould, shows this outline. The six breaks in the otherwise familiar form, one at the top, a, one at the bottom, b, and four, c, d, e, f, where the corners should be, are the gaps where blocks of wood forming the top, bottom, and four corner-blocks, which serve, as it were, as foundation work for the subsequent construction, would be located. These blocks would be temporarily glued in position and their outer, rib-butting, surfaces shaped to complete the outline following six small prepared patterns (indicated here by the dotted lines). The ten holes drilled through the mould are used in the gluing of the shaped ribs to the blocks providing, with a suitable dowel, binding string, and outer-shaped mould, a means of exerting pressure between the rib and the block under adhesion.

There are a number of markings to be found on the moulds. They are all inscribed with an identifying letter or letters doubling as descriptive shorthand, for example 'SL' is *secunda lunga*, 'PG' is *prima grande*, 'B' *buona*, etc., and some also bear a written date. On the central inscribed axial line there customarily appear also the marks, made with dividers, which by their opening give two measurements—the heights to which top and bottom blocks are to be made, the difference in height (usually 2 mm) between these blocks giving the scarcely noticeable taper to the rib-height line. The remaining markings are the two pairs of horizontal parallel lines, indicated in Fig. 135 between cd and ef. These are something of a mystery. They may be drawn in this way merely to ensure the precise and symmetrical cutting in the mould of the rib-block locating niches, for they coincide with their upper and lower extremities. They then also become the simplest means of locating the small corner patterns during use. The two outer lines, the extreme upper and extreme lower of the four, indicate the outer ends of the corner-blocks and also coincide with the point on the

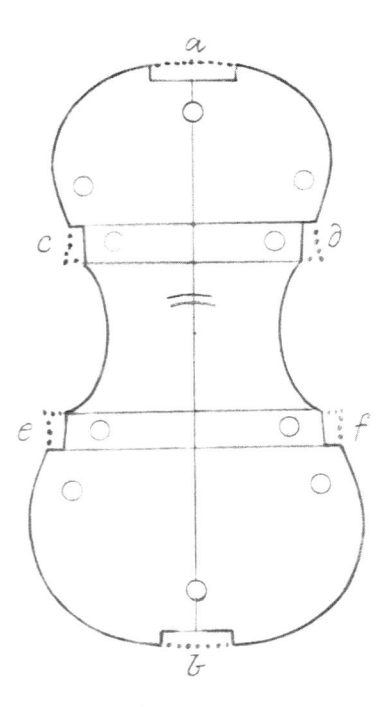

FIG. 135

mould where the main curves of the ribs change direction into the counter-curves of the corners, these corners coming to the points of the mould-plan corners at their intersection with the two inner inscribed lines produced. These sets of parallel lines did not appear to have any consistent relationship to the geometry of the outline, or between themselves. It has been thought that the distances between the two pairs of lines gave the radii of the small arcs of the corners. This I did not find to be consistently so in either the violin moulds or the patterns for the larger instruments. It would also be difficult to understand why, if this were the case, this information should be carried forward on to the mould when the curves for the cutting of the blocks are most conveniently obtained from the small patterns mentioned above, and made by Stradivari for use with the form. The mould, it should be remembered, is after all a tool, a practical device for constructing the instrument, itself at least a generation's remove from the geometrical construction, on paper, of the outline design.

The inner, mould outline, and the outer, seen, edge-line, are of course concentric, the arcs sharing the same centres, but the radii of the inner outline being, in the case of the convex-curve arcs, reduced, whilst the radii of the concave-curve arcs, conversely, are increased in length. The one instance of deviation from this rule of concentricity between mould- and edge-outline in Stradivari's work with violins occurs in the small-radius curves of the upper corner of the middle bouts where, particularly in the later patterns, there is a tendency of the rib outline to 'crease' inwards and not to flow through the component arcs with the same single line of curve that is given the overall edge outline.

Nevertheless, in studying the mould outlines, it was hoped that, thus effectively offered a new set of parameters within the same scheme, some further information might emerge regarding either the proportional scheme or the geometrical construction procedure. Lengthy analysing and cross-referencing of the many mould outlines, however, failed to reveal a convincing construction procedure, that is, one which could proceed from a point. In fact, given the constant variation in dimensions between parts and the subtle changes in proportions throughout the patterns examined, it is seemingly impossible even to imagine a system which could at once offer the necessary flexibility and yet retain the structural integrity of a guiding principle. Moreover, by the time Stradivari came to work his particular miracles of sophistication, the form of the violin—its broad layout, so to speak—had long been established and, indeed, had long travelled the path of evolution from its design archetype, a route undoubtedly originally charted by constructive proportional thought, but one increasingly guided by a more expressive, intuitive impulse.

The attempt to match the outlines of the two Stradivari violins, the 1666 (Ex. XII) and the 'Emiliani' of 1703 (Ex. XIII), with their design patterns was an interesting piece of historical detection-work. The earlier instrument presented little difficulty, the mould outline and edge-line fitting together as snugly as the successive layers of a Russian doll. The mould in question was that marked by the maker with the letters 'MB'—*modello buono*—and, not surprisingly, is thought to be the earliest of the surviving moulds.

The relationship between mould- and edge-outline, and their 'shared' geometry, can be seen here in Fig. 136, a drawing of the 'MB' form and the analysis of the 1666 instrument combined. No significant addition to the geometrical scheme was uncovered by the cross-referencing, but, apart from the expected schematic resonances, one or two new facts did emerge. One such was that the circle, centre C (the centre of the model, $BC = CD$), which intersects the four counter-curve arc centres ($a, a', b,$ and b'), was of radius measured 115.5 mm, that is, one-third mould length mh. This radius was in turn approximately five times the length of the radii of the mould-outline counter-curve arcs. Another circle, also centred at C, but of *diameter* 114 mm (115.5 mm?), that is, radius 57 mm, touches the *outline* curve of the middle bouts and two of

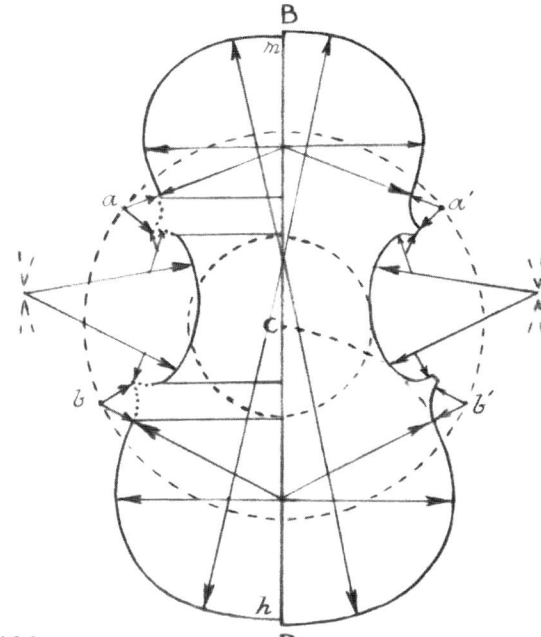

Fig. 136

the four points of intersection produced by the horizontal mould lines with the vertical line of axis. It must be stressed that the above relationships, all of minor significance, arose from the 'MB' mould alone, and did not apply to the other violin moulds examined.

The search for the mould of the 'Emiliani' was less rewarding, the outline failing to correspond entirely to any one mould. The three major divisions of upper, middle, and lower bouts found resonances in various patterns, including those marked 'PB' and 'S' (of 1703), but were not consistent with one alone. It is therefore to be deduced that the 'Emiliani's' mother-mould has regrettably since been lost.

Appendix C Body-outline chart of summary for development of four Cremonese violins

The following is a chart, for direct cross-reference, giving the comparative values of the component-arc radii of the violins' body outlines, together with an indication of their proportional status. A complete analysis of the individual body- and head-schemes, with a proportional exposition, is, of course, included in the relevant sections of the text.

The diagram, Fig. 137, indicates the constituent arcs common to the four examples, which are then listed in the extreme left-hand vertical column of the chart. The amounts are given in millimetre values, followed by a schematic qualification or interpretation expressed thus:

        ( ) primary scheme
        [ ] secondary or tertiary scheme
        — no proportional significance.

Radius of arc	Andrea Amati 1564 small model	Nicola Amati c.1670	Antonio Stradivari 1666	Antonio Stradivari 1703
BG	171.5 (ϕ_6)	135.5 (ϕ_1)	136 (ϕ_1)	135.5 (ϕ_1)
GM	65.5 (ϕ_4)	68 ($\frac{1}{2}\phi_1$)	68 ($\frac{1}{2}\phi_1$)	68 ($\frac{1}{2}\phi_1$) (C)
MN	79 —	84 (ϕ)	83.5 ($\simeq \phi$ (84))	83.5 (ϕ)
NS	21 —	30 [$1\frac{1}{4}$ Br. in.]	18 [$\frac{3}{4}$ Br. in.]	17 (C)
SX	9.5 (ϕ)	12 [$\frac{1}{2}$ Br. in.]	10 —	10 —
XY	25 (ϕ_2)	30 [$1\frac{1}{4}$ Br. in.]	24 [1 Br. in.]	24 —
YZ	70.7 [C]	68 ($\frac{1}{2}\phi_1$)	92.5 —	85 (C)
ZT	15.4 (ϕ_1)	18 [$\frac{3}{4}$ Br. in.]	18 [$\frac{3}{4}$ Br. in.]	17 (C)
TR	29 —	18 [$\frac{3}{4}$ Br. in.]	18 [$\frac{3}{4}$ Br. in.]	17 (C)
RP	70.7 [C]	104 —	103.5 —	102(.25) (C)
PH		71.5 [3 Br. in.] [C]	71.5 [3 Br. in.] [C]	71 [C]
HD	171.5 (ϕ_6)	219.5 (ϕ_2)	220 (ϕ_2)	219 (ϕ_2) [C]

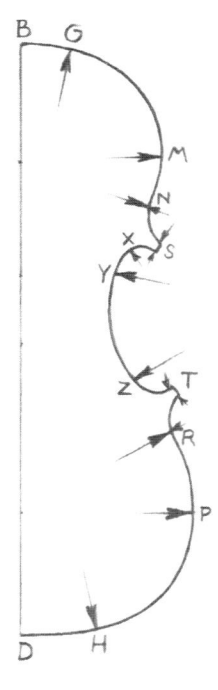

Fig. 137

Bibliography

ALBERTI, LEON BATTISTA, (De re aedificatoria, 1485 (tr. James Leoni, 1755)

BACHER, JOSEPH, *Die Viola da Gamba*, Bärenreiter, Kassel, 1932

BAINES, ANTHONY, *European and American Musical Instruments*, London 1966

——*Catalogue of Musical Instruments of Victoria and Albert Museum*, vol. ii (*Non-Keyboard Instruments*), London 1968

BLAIR, LAWRENCE, *Rhythms of Vision*, Paladin, 1976

BONANNI, FILIPPO, *Gabinetto Armonico*, Rome 1722

BONE, PHILIP J., *The Guitar and Mandolin*, London, 1972 edn.

BOULEAU, CHARLES, *The Painter's Secret Geometry*, Thames & Hudson, 1963

BOYDEN, DAVID D., *The Hill Collection*, OUP, 1970

BURCKHARDT, JACOB, *Civilisation of the Renaissance*, Oxford and London, Phaidon Press Ltd., 2nd edn. 1945

BURCKHARDT, TITUS, *Sacred Art in East and West*, London 1967

COATES, KEVIN, 'The Mandoline: an Unsung Serenader', *Early Music*, vol. 5, no. 1, January 1977

CORNFORD, CHRISTOPHER, *In Defence of a Preoccupation*, RCA, G.S. Paper No. 1

CORNFORD, F. M., *Plato's Cosmology*, London 1952

DANKS, HARRY, *The Viola D'Amore*, Bois de Boulogne 1976

DOLMETSCH, NATHALIE, *The Viola da Gamba*, London 1962

GALLINI, NATALE e FRANCO, *Catalogo del Museo degli Strumenti Musicali, Castello Sforzesco*, Comune di Milano, 1963

GALPIN, FRANCIS WILLIAM, *Textbook of European Musical Instruments*, London 1937

GWILT, JOSEPH, *Encyclopedia of Architecture*, London 1894

HADAWAY, ROBERT, 'The Cittern', *Early Music*, vol. 1, no. 2, April 1973

HAJDECKI, ALEXANDER, *Die Italienische Lira da Braccio*, Mostar, Hercegovina 1892

HAMBIDGE, JAY, *The Elements of Dynamic Symmetry*, Yale University Press, 1948

——*Practical Applications of Dynamic Symmetry*, Yale University Press, 1949

HAYES, GERALD, *Viols and Other Bowed Instruments* (*Musical Instruments and their Music, 1500–1750*, vol. 2), 1930

HELLWIG, F., 'Lute-Making in the Late 15th and 16th Century', *Lute Society Journal*, xvi, 1974

HERSEY, G. L., *Pythagorean Palaces*, Cornell University Press, London 1976

HILL, WILLIAM, ARTHUR, and ALFRED, *Antonio Stradivari, His Life and Work*, London 1902

HIPKINS, A. J., and GIBB, W., *Musical Instruments, Historic, Rare, and Unique*, Edinburgh 1888

HOLT, MICHAEL, *Mathematics in Art*, Studio Vista, London; Van Nostrand Reinhold Company, New York, 1971

JALOVEC, K., *Italian Violin Makers*, Orbis, Prague 1952

KLINE, MORRIS, *Mathematics in Western Culture*, Pelican, 1972

LEEUWEN BOOMKAMP, C. VAN, and MEER, J. H. VAN DER, *Descriptive Catalogue of the Carel van Leeuwen Boomkamp Collection of Musical Instruments*, Amsterdam 1971

LUND, FREDERICK MACODY, *Ad Quadratum, A Study of the Geometrical Bases of Architecture*, London 1921

MACE, THOMAS, *Musick's Monument*, 1676 (facsimile edn., Paris 1966)

MAHILLON, V. C., *Catalogue descriptif et analytique du Musée instrumental du Conservatoire Royal de Musique*, Brussels 1912

MARCUSE, S., *Musical Instruments: a Comprehensive Dictionary*, New York 1964

MERSENNE, MARIN, *Harmonie Universelle*, 1636 (R. E. Chapman, The Hague 1957)

MICHELL, JOHN, *City of Revelation*, Abacus, London 1973

——*The View Over Atlantis*, Abacus, London 1975

MILLIOT, SYLVETTE, *Documents inédits sur les luthiers parisiens du XVIIIème siècle*, Heugel et Cie, Paris 1970

MORGAN, MORRIS, *Vitruvius, 'The Ten Books on Architecture'*, Dover (NY) 1960

MORROW, GLEN, *Proclus's Commentary on the First Book of Euclid's Elements*, Princeton 1970

MUNROW, DAVID, *Instruments of the Middle Ages and Renaissance*, OUP, 1976

PACIOLI, LUCA DELLA, *de Divina Proportione*, 1509 (ed. by Constantin Winterberg 1889, reprinted 1974 in *Quellenschriften für Kunstgeschichte und Kunsttechnik des Mittelalters und der Neuzeit*, Georg Olms Verlag, Hildesheim)

PALLADIO, ANDREA, *Four Books of Architecture*, Dover (NY), 1965 reprint of 1737 English edn.

PAUL, E. M. W., Unpublished research notes from the Venetian guild archives, 1963

PEDOE, DAN, *Geometry and the Liberal Arts*, Penguin, 1976

PLATO, *Timaeus*, tr. H. D. P. Lee, Penguin, 1965

——*The Last Days of Socrates*, tr. Hugh Tredennick, Penguin, 1967

——*Collected Dialogues*, ed. Edith Hamilton and Huntington Cairns, New York 1961

POHLMANN, E., *Laute, Theorbe, Chitarrone*, Bremen 1968

PRAETORIUS, MICHAEL, *Syntagma Musicum*, 1619 (ed. W. Gurlitt, Bärenreiter, 1958)

ROBB, NESCA, *Neoplatonism of the Italian Renaissance*, London 1935

SACCONI, SIMONE F., *I 'Segreti' di Stradivari*, Cremona 1972

SACHS, CURT, *Real-Lexicon der Musikinstrumente* (J. Bard, Berlin, 1913)

SASSE, KONRAD, *Katalog zu den Sammlungen des Händel-Hauses in Halle, 6 Teil, Musikinstrumentensammlung Streich- und Supfinstrumente*, Halle an der Saale 1972

SPENCER, ROBERT, 'Chitarrone, Theorbo and Archlute', *Early Music*, vol. 4, no. 4, October 1976

STAINER, C., *A Dictionary of Violin Makers*, Novello, reprint of 1896 edn.

STALEY, E., *The Guilds of Florence*, New York, 1967 edn.

STIRLING, WILLIAM (ed.), *The Canon*, Garnstone Press, 1974

TURNBULL, H., *The Guitar, from the Renaissance to the Present Day*, Batsford 1974

VANNES, RENÉ, *Dictionnaire universel des luthiers*, 2nd edn., Brussels 1951

VASARI, GIORGIO, *The Lives of the Artists*, Penguin edn., 1978

VIRDUNG, SEBASTIAN, *Musica Getuscht*, 1511 (Kassel, 1931)

VOROBYOV, N. N., *The Fibonacci Numbers*, Boston 1966

WILSON, MICHAEL, *Musical Instruments, A List of Books and Articles in The National Art Library*, Victoria and Albert Museum, 1973 and 1976

WINTERNITZ, EMANUEL, *Musical Instruments of the Western World*, Thames & Hudson, 1966

—— *Musical Instruments and their Symbolism in Western Art*, Faber, 1967

—— 'Lira da Braccio', *Die Musik in Geschichte und Gegenwart*, viii, Kassel, 1960

WITTEN, LAURENCE, C., II, 'Apollo, Orpheus, and David', *Journal of the American Musical Instrument Society*, vol. i, 1975

WITTKOWER, RUDOLF, *Architectural Principles in the Age of Humanism*, London 1952

—— *Architects' Year Book*, v, London 1953

Index

Academy, 7
Al Kindi, 12, 13
Alard, 141
Alard violin, 73
Alberti, 14
Alexander, 9
Alexandria (University of), 7, 9, 10
alla gobba, 31, 107
Alletsee, Paulus, 17, 95 ff, 158, 162, 163
Amati, Andrea, 66 ff, 71, 72, 73, 76, 83, 158, 162, 174
Amati, Hieronymous and Antonius, 71
Amati, Nicola, 66, 71 ff, 75, 76, 77, 158, 162, 174
Andrea, Giovanni d', 55
anthropomorphism, 164 (see also p. 75 n. 49)
Apollo, 62
Archimedes, 9, 10
Aristotle, 5, 12
Arnault, Henricus, 107 ff, 110, 111, 112, 115, 119, 138, 158, 162, 166, 169
Ashmolean Museum, 35, 55, 56, 59, 66, 67, 141, 142, 158, 162
Athelhard of Bath, 12
Augustus, 10

Baines, Anthony, 48, 55, 59
Barbaro, Daniele, 11, 13
baryton, 27, 90
battente, 136, 154
Beauty, 1, 15
Betts violin, 79
Bibliothèque Nationale, Paris, 107, 158, 162
Bisiach, Leandro, 35
Blake, W., 168
Bohemia, 91, 158, 162
Bologna, 106, 110, 118, 158, 162
Bonanni, Filippo, 90
Borbon, Gaspar, 100 ff, 158, 162
Boyden, David, 35, 55, 59, 60
Brescia, 31, 35, 55, 62, 63, 82, 141
Brescian School, 21, 67, 148
Brunswick inch, 22, 39 ff, 42, 71, 72, 73, 76, 79, 92, 98
Buechenberg, Matteo, 107, 118 ff, 125, 128, 139, 158, 159, 162
Burwell, Mary, 110

Caesar, 10
Castello Sforzesco, 35, 147, 158, 162
Cawse, John, 48
Celoniati, Gian Francesco, 103
Chanot, F., 66
Charles IX, 66, 67
Chartres, 13
chitarra battente, 136, 147, 153
chitarroni, 118

Ciciliano, Battista, 39, 40, 41, 44, 107, 112, 158, 162
Cocho, Christopho, 147, 150, 154, 155, 158, 162
colascione, 27
Conservatoire de Musique, Paris, 128, 141, 142, 150, 158, 162
Conservatoire Royal de Musique, Brussels, 31, 39, 62, 100, 114, 158, 162
Copernicus, 8, 14
Cremona, 71, 75, 79, 100, 132, 168, 172
Cremonese inch, 77, 84
Cremonese School, 37, 65, 66, 71, 75, 80, 82, 83, 153, 174
Cupid, 90, 103
Cuypers, Johann Theodorus, 87

Danks, Harry, 95
del Gesu (Guarnerius), 82
diaposon, 5, 41
Diaz, Belchior, 147, 148, 151, 155, 158, 162
Donaldson Collection (R.C.M.), 52, 55, 100, 144, 158, 162
Dörfler, Josef, 147
double-bass, 27
Dürer, Albrecht, 14, 19

Eisel, 90
Emiliani violin, 66, 79, 132, 158, 162, 173
English Violet, 17, 91, 95, 158, 162, 163
Euclid, 8, 9, 12, 13, 14
Eudoxus of Cnidus, 9
Evelyn, John, 110

Fibonacci, 16, 17, 18
fiedel, 31, 35
Fludd, Robert, 6, 7
Frei, Hans, 107, 110 ff, 114, 115, 118, 119, 122, 158, 162

Gafurio, Franchino, 5, 6
Galileo, 14
Ganassi, Silvestro, 39, 40
Gasparo da Salò, 59 ff, 63, 82, 148, 158, 162
Gaultier, Jacques, 106
Gemeentemuseum (The Hague), 87, 95, 158, 162
Genova, Battista, 103 ff, 158, 162
Gherard of Cremona, 13
Ghiberti, 13
Guilds, 169, 170
Giorgio, Francesco di, 10, 12
gnomon, 144

Golden Section (ϕ), 16, 17, 26, 35, 41, 45, 46, 67, 68, 71, 73, 76, 80, 87, 96, 98, 110, 112, 118, 158, 162, 174
Goldt, Jacobus Henricus, 122, 158, 162
Greek Lyre, 141
Grosset, Paul Francois, 52
Guersan, Louis, 52 ff, 87, 91, 158, 162
Gwilt, Joseph, 21

Hajdecki, Major, 55
Halfpenny, Eric, 110
Hambidge, Jay, 18, 144, 168
Hamburg, 48, 122, 144, 158, 162
Hamburger Citrinchen, 141
Hardanger fiddle, 90
harp, 27
Hayes, Gerald, 31
Hellwig, Günther, 48
Herodotus, 5
Hieber, Giovanni, 107, 114 ff, 119, 158, 162
Hipkins, A. J. and Gibb, W., 141
Hoffmann, 122
hurdy-gurdy, 27, 52
Huygens, Constantin, 106

Ionic, 21, 26, 32, 37, 42, 60, 69, 73, 77, 80, 130, 158, 162

Jauck, 122
Jaye, Henry, 21, 44 ff, 52, 53, 67, 87, 91, 101, 158, 162
Johnson, Samuel, 106

Kepler, J., 14, 17
Khowarizmi, al, 12
Kinsky, G., 95
Kithara, 141
Kline, Morris, 4

Lambda, 8
Leeuwen Boomkamp, Carel van (Collection), 87, 95, 158, 162
Leonardo, 8, 10, 11, 13, 14, 24, 55, 164
Longo, Mango, 147, 153 ff, 158, 162

Mace, Thomas, 44, 65, 110
Maggini, Paolo, 21, 56, 67, 82 ff, 148, 158, 162
Majer, Joseph, 90
Maler, Lucas, 106
mandala, 19
mandolino, 127
Mandolino Coristo, 132
mandolas, 136
mandolones, 136
Maria, Giovanni, 35 ff, 42, 44, 45, 52, 55 ff, 67, 82, 83, 101, 158, 162
Mattheson, 90
Medici, Catherine de, 66

Mersenne, Marin, 65, 127
Michell, John, 19
'misteries' (see guilds)
Mozart, Leopold, 95
Muses, 3, 16
'music of the spheres', 6

Neoplatonist, 141, 169
Norman, Barak, 86 ff, 158, 162
North, Roger, 65

orpharion, 27
Orpheus, 1, 48, 153

Pacioli, Fra, 16, 17, 164
Padua, 118
Palladio, Andrea, 1, 15
'pearl-mould', 110
ϕ (phi), see 'Golden Section'
Philolaos, 6
phyllotaxis, 18
π, 9, 16
Piero della Francesca, 17
Pierray, Claude, 52
Pirkheimer, Wilibald, 14
Plato, 4, 7, 8, 9, 16, 164, 168, 170
Praetorius, Michael, 106, 118, 141
Proclus, 8
Protagoras, 164
Ptolemy I, 9
Pythagoras, 4, 5, 6, 7, 8, 13, 15, 39

quadrivium, 4

Raphael, 62
Rauche, Michael, 122, 125, 158, 162
rebec, 100
reciprocal, 144
Ribayaz, Lucas Ruiz de, 164
Roman theorbo, 118
Ruckers, 169

Sacconi, Simone, 132
Sanctus Seraphim, 21
Savart, F., 66
Schelle, S., 122
Sconvel(t), Nicholas, 106, 110
scordatura, 90
Sesostris, 5
sesquialtera, 5, 40
sesquioctava, 40
sesquitertia, 5, 40, 41
Settala, Manfredo, 31
Sforza, Ludovico, 55
Simpson, Christopher, 40
sordine, 100
Stainer, C., 44, 86
Staufer, J., 66
Stradivarius, Antonio, 66, 75 ff, 79 ff, 86, 100, 132 ff, 141, 158, 162, 168, 169, 170, 172, 173, 174

Tieffenbrucker, Gaspar, 55
Tielke, Joachim, 48 ff, 52, 91, 103, 142, 144 ff, 158, 162

Vasari, Giorgio, 55
Venice, 1, 14, 35, 39, 40, 55, 114, 118, 128, 150, 158, 162
'Venetian head', 37
Venus Aphrodite, 90, 164
Vesica Piscis, 18, 19, 36, 41, 60, 63, 68, 83, 84, 93, 96, 101, 109, 111, 112, 115, 116, 118, 119, 120, 122, 124, 125, 139, 144, 145, 148, 149, 150, 151, 154, 155, 158, 159, 160, 161, 162, 163, 169
Victoria and Albert Museum, 44, 48, 118, 122, 158, 162
vihuela, 27, 147, 148, 165
Vinaccia, Antonio, 137
Vinaccia family, 127, 136
Vinaccia, Johannes, 136 ff, 158, 162, 163
violetta, 95
violino piccolo, 65
violoncello piccolo, 65
violoncino, 86
violone, 27
Virchis, Girolamo di, 141
Vitruvius, 1, 10, 11, 21, 164
Voigt, Martin, 48
Vuillaume, Jean Baptiste, 141

Warwick County Museum, 110, 158, 162
Wittkower, Rudolf, 2, 13, 14, 17

Zanetto, Pelegrino di, 31 ff, 36, 37, 44, 80, 158, 162